Computer Concepts and Assembler Programming: 360/370 Systems

Computer Concepts and Assembler Programming: 360/370 Systems

RICHARD H. STARK
DONALD W. DEARHOLT

New Mexico State University

A C A D E M I C   P R E S S   New York   San Francisco   London

A Subsidiary of Harcourt Brace Jovanovich, Publishers

ACADEMIC PRESS, INC.
111 Fifth Avenue, New York, New York 10003

United Kingdom Edition published by
ACADEMIC PRESS, INC. (LONDON) LTD.
24/28 Oval Road, London NW1

Library of Congress Cataloging in Publication Data

Stark, Richard H
    Computer concepts and assembler programming.

    Bibliography: p.
    Includes index.
        1.   IBM 360 (Computer)–Programming.   2.   IBM 370
(Computer)–Programming.   3.   Assembler language (Com-
puter program language)   I.   Dearholt, Donald W
II.   Title.
QA76.8.I12S72   001.6'42   74-17972
ISBN 0–12–664550–7

Contents

Preface ix

Chapter 1 **The Evolution of Computers**

1.1 Why Study Digital Computers? 1
1.2 Automation of Digital Information Processing 4
1.3 The AXXION Computing Laboratory 5
1.4 Evaluating and Extending the AXXION Computer 10
1.5 Instruction Modification 15
1.6 Dishing Out the Credits 19
1.7 Organizing for Computerization 20
1.8 Digital Representation of Information 23
1.9 Pressures Influencing Evolution 28
1.10 Precursors of Change 29
     Problems 32

Chapter 2   Binary Arithmetic and Its Machine Implementation

2.1 An Analogy Using Coins 35
2.2 Binary Representation of Fractions 40
2.3 Computer Representations of Numbers 43
     Problems 51

Chapter 3   An Evolutionary Introduction to Computer Structure

3.1 A Rationale 55
3.2 The Components of BAREBONZ and Their Interrelations 57
3.3 The Instruction Set for BAREBONZ 64
3.4 Functional Analysis of Instructions 71
3.5 Linking Program Sequences 85
3.6 BAREBONZ II 93
     Problems 99

Chapter 4   Machine Translation of Symbolic Instructions

4.1 The Case for Machine Translation 107
4.2 A Standard Form for Symbolic Representation of Instructions 109
4.3 Some Essential Pseudoinstructions 112
4.4 A Scheme for Translation 117
4.5 The Prevention, Detection, and Elimination of Errors 124
4.6 Extensions to the Assembler Concept 140
4.7 Summary 155
     Problems 158

Chapter 5   Segmentation of Programs

5.1 Conventions for Invoking Subprograms 165
5.2 Linking with FORTRAN 171
5.3 Object Modules 175
5.4 Control Sections and Program Segmentation 177
5.5 The External Symbol and Relocation Dictionaries 183
5.6 Checkout Considerations for Segmented Programs 190
5.7 The Care and Feeding of Base Registers 193
5.8 Introduction to Macros 195
5.9 Assembler Building Project 200
     Problems 212

Chapter 6   Character and Bit Manipulation

6.1 Introduction 219
6.2 Symbolism for String Handling 222

6.3   Character String Instruction Formats 222
6.4   The Compare Instructions 230
6.5   Textual Records and Files 232
6.6   Operations of Logic with Bit Strings 246
6.7   Background of Conversion Methods 251
6.8   The TRanslate and TRanslate and Test Instructions 256
6.9   The MoVe Character Long and Compare Logical Character Long
      Instructions of the IBM 370 265
      Problems 273

Chapter 7   **Instruction Execution Times and Factors Affecting Them**

7.1   Introduction 285
7.2   Computer Characteristics Influencing Instruction Times 289
7.3   Some Alternative Sequences of Instructions 297
7.4   Summary 300
      Problems 301

Chapter 8   **Specialized Arithmetic**

8.1   Introduction 307
8.2   Decimal Arithmetic 308
8.3   Floating-Point Arithmetic 320
      Problems 330

Appendix A   **Extended Binary-Coded Decimal Interchange Code (EBCDIC)** 337

Appendix B   **List of Instructions by Set and Feature for the IBM 360/370 Systems** 341

Appendix C   **Description of BAREBONZ Instructions** 347

Appendix D   **Analysis of a System Dump** 351

Appendix E   **FORTRAN Input and Output Subprograms** 367

Appendix F   **Instruction Times for System/370 Model 158** 369

Appendix G   **Chopping, Rounding, and Truncation Error** 383

Index 387

Preface

Having taught assembler language programming for a complex computer over the past several years, we have evolved a body of material to be taught and a way of presenting that material which differs substantially from that in any text we have seen. Our text is intended for students previously exposed to some introductory concepts in computing. Flowcharting is assumed to be a familiar subject, and discussion of flowcharting is limited to some comments on structured programming. Experience in programming in a high-level language is helpful, especially in appreciating the role of subprograms. The only explicit dependence on such a language is the rudimentary use of FORTRAN input/output facilities in Chapter 5 and in a few of the exercises at the end of that chapter. All the necessary FORTRAN is covered in Appendix E. Thus a course based on this text could be taught as early as the latter part of the freshman year, or in the sophomore or junior years. At New Mexico State University, the course is taught at the sophomore level. This book provides sufficient preparation for a course in assembler and compiler design, or introductory systems programming.

Here are some principles on which our text is written and organized.

1. It is of utmost importance that the student become confident with computer characteristics as they appear without intermediate software. To that end, we begin with numeric coding and gain, through judicious selection of instructions, an early exposure to machine performance.

2. Machines have evolved since 1950 from logically simple to extremely complex devices. The clearest understanding will be gained by experiencing this evolution in one's own learning process, especially if the forces which provoked the major changes are well understood. Our first chapter considers evolution from desk calculators to stored-program computers, an aspect often neglected. The machine known as BAREBONZ, which is our starting point for the IBM 360/370, has about the complexity of von Neumann's IAS computer. We build from that toward the full internal logic of the 360/370 systems, extending assembler language features in parallel with concepts of structure. This pedagogical approach has the advantage of providing both historical motivation and perspective.

3. Today's assemblers, just as today's machines, are too sophisticated to permit ready understanding, and yet the programmer needs a detailed knowledge of the assembly process to use an assembler with confidence. Therefore, we rely on manual assembly in Chapter 3 and devote a major part of Chapter 4 to explaining a simplified assembler. In Chapter 5, we present a set of exercises (these can be distributed among groups of students to lessen the work and give team experiences) which culminate in a limited assembler.

4. While one has a much better vocabulary for explaining the program testing process at the end of a course, a debugging philosophy and logical debugging practices are needed early. We provide a substantial discussion in Chapter 4, after the assembly process is better understood.

5. We consider that programming of large problems is sensible only when the program is segmented into subprograms which can be independently tested. For that reason, we have devoted Chapter 5 to the major considerations involved in linking separately assembled, relocatable programs to form a load module. A student who works his way through this chapter should have a reasonable appreciation for external symbol and relocation dictionaries, and no qualms about linking assembler programs with object modules from another language. It is at this stage that we have committed ourselves to FORTRAN facilities for input and output. Students who have been trained in one higher level language to the extent that they can write closed subprograms in the language can, with the help of Appendix E, quickly gain all the FORTRAN we require. FORTRAN is our

choice because it is more universally available than any other language and because it has so many library facilities, and not because it is the best language. Using it has the advantage (over macros) of suggesting the eminently practical viewpoint that large programs should be written principally in an algorithmic language, with assembler language resorted to only when it provides superior power or economy.

6. In selecting among topics to conform to a one-semester offering, we have considered it more important to introduce instructions with built-in looping than instructions which combine several aspects of looping control into one instruction. The latter, including BCT, BXLE, and BXH, are important, but they really can save only a small percentage of computer time and a little memory, and these savings are evident only after detailed analysis. Instead, our preference has been to examine the string-handling instructions which have their own built-in looping controls; these do offer major time savings and, in some cases, easier programming.

7. Since one of the great pressures in the evolution of computers is the saving of execution time, we consider the ability to compare the execution times of alternative instruction sequences well worth developing. Chapter 7 is devoted to that purpose, and Appendix F provides additional times. Such comparisons are not easy to make when the architecture spans so many hardware implementations. Yet there is no better way to develop the skill of investing one's efforts at the right spots in a program and choosing appropriate implementations in those spots.

8. We have chosen to present the student with examples which are in structured form at the flowchart level. Of course the implementations in assembler language will contain branches and so they may not appear at first glance to be structured.

It would be entirely feasible to begin a course in assembler language programming with Chapter 3, leaving Chapter 1 for casual reading and Chapter 2 as remedial for those who have no exposure to binary arithmetic. Nevertheless, we feel that some class consideration of Chapter 1 to stimulate thinking about broader issues is a good investment.

Some instructors will prefer to cover character-handling instructions very early; this can be done by starting with Chapter 3, then venturing briefly into Chapter 4 to pick up some essential pseudo-instructions before proceeding to Chapter 6. The material on decimal and floating-point arithmetic in Chapter 8 also depends on some pseudo-instructions in Chapter 4, but otherwise can be taken up any time. Chapter 7 (on instruction execution times) is most meaningful after one has a large enough repertoire of instructions to develop alternative sequences of instructions for the same task. While considering other possible orders for presentation, we wish to reaffirm our belief in the importance of the material on linking separately compiled programs found in Chapter 5.

Using this text, an instructor can proceed from our initial models of a simple machine and assembler at whatever pace he wishes. Programming in numeric with a simple machine and building from there helps the student to distinguish between hardware facilities and the software surrounding him in its use. Another benefit of our simple-machine-first philosophy is the relatively easy transfer from our simpler models to some of the myriad small computers for which applications are often implemented in assembler language.

Our ordering of subject matter provides what we consider to be a very meaningful source of exercises, namely to accomplish the tasks of conversion, string manipulation, scaling, and table-lookup without the complete repertoire of a character-oriented machine. Except in Chapter 8 (where a few exercises are interspersed with text as an instructional device), all exercises for a chapter are grouped at its end. Exercises follow the ordering of the material which they illustrate.

**Computer Concepts and
Assembler Programming:
360/370 Systems**

Chapter 1

The Evolution of Computers

1.1 WHY STUDY DIGITAL COMPUTERS?

It is a matter of human experience that, given a finite set of symbols, including an alphabet, a set of digits, some punctuation, and a few more symbols of special nature, man can record a fantastic amount of the world's information. He may feel handicapped at not having graphs, pictures, paintings, sound, special mathematical symbols, or indicators such as speedometers, but by using combinations of symbols for special meanings he can get along. Just how well he can do is attested by the fact that television pictures are just arrays of colored dots on the surface of a screen. Dot positions can be serially numbered, and at each position a digit representing the color can be specified. Thus a television picture can be described by a set of number pairs, the first element of the pair being a position number, the second being a color and/or intensity code. In principle then, we should be able to consider television pictures as information we hope to "read" or generate for display.

1

Representation of information in terms of a finite number of symbols (we will call them the *character set*) is called *digital* representation. *Digital computers* are devices which process digital information; the information to be processed must be in *machine-recognizable* form. Let the array of symbols available to the process before it begins be called the *input*. Let the process operate on these symbols to produce another array of symbols recognizable to the observer and available to him as *output* when the process terminates. Then the device performing that process may be called a *digital computer*.

By this vague definition, there are myriad computers. Among them we could include automatic typesetters, optical scanners, bank tellers, and cryptographers. In fact, a person might serve at one time as a teller and at another time as a cryptographer, thus qualifying as an adaptable computer. We will be interested in general-purpose computers (the human being is an example) for which the observer can specify the input *and* the process to be applied. We are most interested in computers which give reproducible results (persons seldom do) so that, if the same process is applied twice to the same input, the same output will result.

It seems important that we explore further the concept of a general-purpose computer, for its influence promises to go far beyond the usurpation of individual routine tasks. We should ask whether or not our civilization will be completely transformed by new processes possible only with computers. If so, will we find the end result beneficial? One way to confront such questions is to look back a few decades to determine why they came about and what shaped the way they have developed. This may give a perspective for considering present uses and for groping into the future. While this is not a book dedicated to social implications, we would deem ourselves irresponsible to ignore two key facts: (1) The devices with which we are concerned have already influenced everyday living in dramatic ways. (2) They are available to be used by individuals or groups whether the user is well intentioned or not. The existence of this text is evidence that, in the judgment of the authors, there is great social benefit to be derived from computers. At the same time, they are deeply concerned about loss of rights and curtailment of individual reasoning and choice through ill-advised dependence on digital computers.

For the present, it will be sufficient for us to think of digital computers as devices which can represent and analyze sequences of symbols which may be digits representing a number, letters spelling a word, or letters, digits, and punctuation intermingled to constitute a novel, a telephone book, or the records of a company. They can perform arithmetic on symbol sequences which represent numbers, editing on sequences representing text, or searches on sequences constituting libraries. Human beings can also do these things, but computers contribute speed, accuracy, consistency, and endurance completely beyond the capabilities of humans. Just as the printing press caused books to become commonplace, computers cause monumental arithmetic and clerical undertakings to become more or less trivial. Is there more to the printing press analogy?

The printing press is itself impartial. It can record masterpieces of literature, scurrilous diatribes, or even pornography with equal ease. Its products can stir racial hatred or promote brotherhood. It has been destructive of our forests (as is the computer), for without paper it is worthless. Yet hardly anyone would condemn the printing press. Rather, he would agree it is the foundation of an enduring culture.

A short-sighted view might be that the printing press deprived a great many monks of their purpose in life, but in fact there are far more opportunities for work today resulting from the existence of books than there ever would have been for monks copying text.

Not every invention has such well-accepted results. Automobiles have provided an exciting era, but they may have distorted our way of life into a form which cannot be sustained. Television has great possibilities for distributing information and for mass education, but it may turn us into a civilization of tube watchers, unable to carry on conversations or to enjoy the company of others without outside stimuli. Even medicine has its detractors, for both overpopulation and a decrease of genetic quality are surely accelerated by it. We ask ourselves now what we can foresee regarding the use of computers: Are there uses everyone would applaud? Are there uses we would condemn? Is it possible that computers may distort civilization into practices which lead to its destruction?

The start of modern computers has a sinister ring. They were sponsored by military organizations for military purposes. These include trajectories for missiles and development of atomic weapons. With their assistance, weapons of almost incomprehensible destructive power have been developed. The first countries to acquire computers may consider this a good usage. Eventually, when everyone has them the benefit is not so clear.

There are applications of computers which are far less controversial. They can be used to analyze personal histories of patients to determine life patterns which favor a disease; to analyze accident reports to pinpoint unsafe vehicles; to schedule work in a job shop so as to increase throughput; to provide mass analysis of electrocardiograms to forestall heart attacks.

On a more massive scale, problems of the interaction of man with man and with his environment can be studied by simulation with a thoroughness not feasible in any other way. The development of new sources of energy to replace fossil fuels (fusion is one possibility) would be drastically more difficult without computers. Handling the information explosion of modern society seems beyond us, even with computers providing vast storage and retrieval systems. Without them, we would be lost.

We, the authors, are not overly optimistic about the eventual effect computers may have. Applications like those of the previous paragraph are our justification for believing computers should be developed further. But there are disturbing issues as well. We have in our society a trend toward massive files of information on individuals and temptations on the part of people in power to use such files for manipulation of lives. There are ominous signs in our government and in corporations as well of misuse of questionable information in cruel and unethical ways.

We have another concern. Faced with complex decisions which have no completely satisfactory answer, we may tend to "leave the decisions to the computer, which has all the information." The tendency is completely counter to our original purpose in developing computers. In the ultimate, it could lead to having weapons which automatically respond to sensor information and people whose entire careers are laid out by machine analyses of their characteristics. There are going to be attempts to use computers in self-serving ways. He who promotes the use of computers should, it seems to us, commit himself to supporting the development of legislation and of professional standards to protect society from detrimental uses.

Having raised these issues, we plan to concentrate on understanding digital computers with the expectation that such understanding will be helpful both in constructive uses and in intelligent consideration of the merits of various applications for society.

1.2   AUTOMATION OF DIGITAL INFORMATION PROCESSING

"Automation" is a word of fairly recent origin (not in Webster's Second), and it means "the establishment of ways to accomplish tasks without human intervention." At one time, the word "mechanization" would have done as well, for the devices employed then were assemblies of gears, wheels, levers, and the like. Some aspects of the automation of clerical tasks are mechanical, but the greatest success came when gears and relays were replaced by vacuum tubes, magnetic cores, transistors, and other semiconductors. Automation can be accomplished with devices which are partly mechanical, partly electrical, and partly electronic. Digital computers are constructed in this fashion.

A typical digital computer will include electromechanical devices such as card readers, printers, plotters, tape transports, magnetic disks, and magnetic drums involved in reading, storing, and transmitting information. It will also include a high-speed processor and a memory, each of which is almost entirely solid-state electronics. To exclude from our consideration the automation of such tasks as food packaging, car assemblies, and road building, we use *computerization* to signify a special kind of automation, that of digital information processing; we must also realize that, in a broader context, computerization would include computers which deal with continuously varying quantities (analog or hybrid computers) as well as the ones we shall study.

It is worth considering how computerization comes about. We should gain some insight into sources of ideas for replacing persons in a computation, the hazards of adhering too closely to previous patterns, the necessity of evolutionary development, and even the persistence of ideas far past their justified lifetime.

When a process to be automated is one previously accomplished another way (almost always true), then one thing to consider is to make the automated process a "carbon copy" of the previous one. In fact, the first step will likely be to automate the most troublesome processes (tedious, error-prone, time-consuming, costly, or even dangerous) and to use the resultant devices as building blocks for a semiautomatic process. In the next sections, we hope to develop some insight into the evolution of a process from manual or mental execution by persons to execution without human participation. To do so, we shall hypothesize a computing laboratory as it might have been in the period 1920–1940 before computers were available, and study its problems. Our goal is to see whether the ideas of modern computers might not have been forced on us, step by step, by the pressures of the tasks at hand.

1.3   THE AXXION COMPUTING LABORATORY

1.3.1   The Early Days

AXXION is a company developing a product in which the experimental approach of "cut and try" is inordinately expensive. Furthermore, the experimental cycle (the time from initial conception of the experiment to measuring results) is a period of years. Some of the important aspects of the experiment are extremely difficult to measure, and their not being known may cause destruction of the experiment. Anything that can be done to guide design and experiment by computation based on physical laws is likely to pay handsome dividends.

If one doubts that such an environment existed in the period 1920–1940, he has only to consider the development of aircraft. Whether the objective was military or commercial, the premium for being first and right was tremendous. It was not long before the people who understood the laws of physics governing flight and stresses in materials found they were spending 10 percent of their time formulating the numerical computations to be done, and 90 percent generating numerical answers. They turned to the earliest known form of "automation," hiring people to do the "clerical" tasks of carrying out the computations they had formulated. This particular company chose to add a component to its organization called the Computing Laboratory. At the stage where we get our first look, it had 100 persons sitting at desks in a large room, each with large data forms on his desk, a trusty slide rule, and a few tables of important functions on a nearby shelf. These persons were available for assignment individually or in groups to compute for the scientific staff.

If one had taken a poll of the users of this laboratory, he would surely have found frustration. Slide rules are great for short sequences of computation, but their inherent lack of precision (three decimal digits at best) is not usually sufficient to preserve meaning through long sequences of fifty or more arithmetic steps. On the other hand, when laboratory technicians undertake six or more digits of accuracy by hand, they are slow, error prone, and subject to fatigue. Manual arithmetic had to be replaced. We should not find it surprising that desk calculators, which were mechanical assemblies of wheels, levers, and gears and had essentially no capability except to add, subtract, multiply, and divide, found their way onto every desk.

Desk calculators of that era have largely been replaced by more powerful devices, but they have modern counterparts in electronic calculators, some of which are pocket size. Input to the old desk calculators was accomplished by a keyboard having ten keys for each of 8 to 10 digit positions. The digits of an operand could be set on the keyboard by depressing the one key in each column which corresponded to the digit in its position of the operand. Since arithmetic operations involve two operands, there had to be a register to which an operand could be transferred from the keyboard and held while a second operand could be set in the keyboard. In fact, there were two registers.

One register called the *accumulator* held the first operand for addition, subtraction, or division. Its name came from the fact that it represented the digits of its number in a form to which addition from the keyboard was feasible. Each digit in the accumulator was shown as the position of a wheel (as in the odometer of a car). A digit d in a keyboard position could be added to the corresponding position of the accumulator by rotation of the wheel with which it was aligned by d places, with a carry inserted as the wheel reached 0. A several-digit number could be added by performing such addition in each keyboard position.

The other register had to hold the multiplier and receive the quotient on division. It was natural to call it the *multiplier–quotient* (MQ) register. While the MQ matched the keyboard in number of positions, the accumulator (A) register had twice as many positions so as to be able to store all digits generated in a multiplication.

When both operands were in place, the desired operation (one of add, subtract, multiply, and divide) could be activated by depressing a lever, turning a crank, or pressing a button. Both the A and MQ registers displayed their contents so that the result could be copied onto a data sheet for future reference. There was the alternative of transferring the accumulator contents to the MQ by actuation of the appropriate lever, thus making it unnecessary to record a number to be used as a multiplier in the next operation.

There was great happiness at AXXION for some time after acquisition of desk calculators. Arithmetic accuracy was now easy, elapsed time for a computation was less, and employees enjoyed their new toys. Design engineers found that more complex computations were now within reach, and so more were planned. But soon another trouble spot came to light. Each step in a computation consisted of "copying" one or two operands from a data sheet, initiating the desired operation, and copying the result onto the data sheet. This transfer of numbers from calculator to data sheet and back seemed to be the major occupation of the laboratory technicians. The copying was tedious, it was susceptible to transposing or misreading of digits, and practitioners got bored. One of the complaints was that, after an operator had painstakingly copied all these numbers down, no one wanted to see them anyway unless he was trying to pinpoint an operator mistake.

1.3.2 Exit Manual Recording

When confronted with the manual recording problem the planning committee at AXXION solicited proposals for ways to improve the situation. All of them seemed to be variations on two ideas:

1. Since people cannot record and read back data properly, mechanize

this aspect of computation by letting the machine record on paper in a way that it can recognize later. The existence of 80-column punched cards was used as evidence of the feasibility of this approach.

2. Since recording on paper has only transitory usefulness, avoid it whenever possible. The MQ register already serves as a device for holding a previous result until it needs to be used. Maybe a few more registers could decrease recording problems until they are no longer serious.

After experiencing such a short period of satisfaction with desk calculators, the planning committee decided to ask for proposals on each approach. They were called the *paper approach* and the *register approach*.

In the paper approach, there would be a different machine for each arithmetic operation. A machine would read two operands from a card, and then perform its particular arithmetic operation to get a result which would then be punched in an unused portion of the same card. When a card became too full to accept another result, a portion of its contents would be copied onto an unmarked card, just enough to identify the card and to provide operands for future steps. The machines would have adapters called *control panels* enabling them to read from and punch in the correct card columns. No longer would a person have to copy numbers from result register to paper or from paper to keyboard. But someone would have to collect cards from one machine and feed them to another, choosing machine and control panel to fit the computation.

The engineers who looked into a register machine became so enthusiastic about their plan that they prepared explanatory material as summarized in Figures 1.3.1 and 1.3.2. As we can see, they adhered rather closely to the desk calculator concept. The arithmetic facilities were the same. Paths for transfer of data were limited for economy and simplicity. The keyboard was counted as one of ten registers and given its own register number. To provide access to the most significant half of the accumulator, some replacement for the positioning of summands and dividends by operators and saving the "best" ten digits from multiplication had to be found. The shift instructions provided a compromise solution.

1.3.3   A Choice Is Made

It is an interesting aspect of the register computer that there is an intimate involvement of a person with the computation. Each step requires the selection of an operation and a register. Yet for a given computation, this sequence could be specified and written well ahead of time. A member of the paper committee suggested an improvement: Why not use a numeric operation code? Then instruction sequences could be punched on cards to be read sequentially, with the execution of an instruction preceding reading of the next.

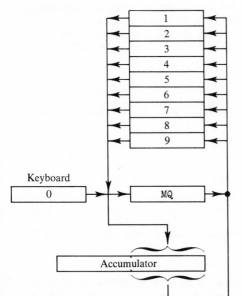

Registers 1–9, MQ, and keyboard each has 10 digit positions and a sign position.

The accumulator has 20 digit positions and a sign position.

Data paths are as shown by arrows in the schematic, namely:

There is a two-way path between the MQ and each of registers 1–9.

There is a two-way path between the low-order 10 digits of the accumulator and each of registers 1–9.

There is a one-way path from the keyboard to the MQ register and also to the low-order 10 digits of the A register.

Contents of all registers are visible.

Figure 1.3.1 Schematic of AXXION registers and data flow. The AXXION Computer (register approach) provides auxiliary registers which can be used to store parameters or intermediate results. There is a control keyboard not shown in the schematic. A computation is caused by a program which is a sequence of steps, each specified by an instruction providing a positive index (usually a register number) and an operation. There are operations for arithmetic, for loading and storing the MQ and A registers, and for shifting accumulator contents, all described in the table of instructions (Figure 1.3.2).

What choice would you make? Each plan had merits. In fact, the paper system was in practical use in record-keeping applications already. It surely was a more direct semiautomation of current practice than the register machine. But AXXION engineers saw more opportunity for continued development in the register machine and decided to back that approach.

Some clever engineers at AXXION collected the parts, wired them together, and in six weeks had a prototype operating. They made a rather arbitrary choice of numeric code for the operations, but since they were just starting something new, they did take the precaution of leaving room for expansion and used two decimal digits as shown in Figure 1.3.3. It was not long before a realistic test of the merits of this system could be made.

Notation: An instruction is an (operation, index) pair [e.g., (LA, 3)] where the operations are symbolic and the use of the index depends on the operation. In the table below, n represents the index in the instruction with the given symbolic operation; $c(X)$ is the signed number represented by the digits of X; $c(A_{i:r})$ is the number formed with the sign of the accumulator and digits numbered i through r, where $c(A) = c(A_{0:19})$; $sign(u) = 1$ if $u > 0$, 0 if $u = 0$, and -1 if $u < 0$. Alignment is as if all numbers were integers.

Operation mnemonic	Affected component	New contents † based on readings prior to execution
LMQ	MQ	$c(n)$
LA	A	$c(n)$
STMQ	n	$c(MQ)$
STA	n	$c(A_{10:19})$
A	A	$c(A) + c(n)$
S	A	$c(A) - c(n)$
M	A	$c(MQ) \cdot c(n)$
D	A,MQ	R,Q where $c(A) = c(n) \cdot Q + R$ and $sign(R) = sign(c(A))$ and $|R| < |c(n)|$
SHIL	A	$10^n \cdot c(A_{n:19})$
SHIR	A	$10^{-n} \cdot c(A_{0:19-n})$

Figure 1.3.2   AXXION Computer instruction table. The instruction set for the AXXION Computer allows data transfer, the four fundamental arithmetic operations, and shifting.

	Units digit			
Tens digit	0	1	2	3
0	LMQ	STMQ	LA	STA
1	A	S	M	D
2	SHIL	SHIR	—	—
3	—	—	—	—

Figure 1.3.3   Numeric codes for the operations of the AXXION Computer.

1.4   EVALUATING AND EXTENDING THE AXXION COMPUTER

The AXXION Computer was designed primarily for arithmetic and should be judged in that light. As described here, its reliance on keyboard

† If ever a negative sign is attached to a zero number, the sign is changed to positive. Note: If $n = 0$ and the operation is not a shift, there is a pause for keyboard input prior to execution.

for input and on manual recording for output was a severe handicap. We find those limitations susceptible to improvement, so the primary concern is the effectiveness of the rest of the design.

1.4.1   A Programming Example

In Figure 1.4.1, we show a sequence of coding to evaluate a quadratic expression $Ax^2 + Bx + C$. On the assumption that we shall want to evaluate this polynomial for integer values of x from 0 to 20, we store A, B, C, and the initial value of x.

	Card no.	Operation code	Index	Input	Explanation
Initialize	1	00	00	A	
	2	01	01		
	3	00	00	B	
	4	01	02		
	5	00	00	C	
	6	01	03		
	7	00	00	x	
	8	01	04		
	9	00	00	1	
	10	01	05		
Repeat	1	00	04		
	2	12	01		Ax
	3	10	02		$Ax + B$
	4	03	06		
	5	12	06		$(Ax + B)x$
	6	10	03		$(Ax + B)x + C$
	7	03	06		
	8	02	04		
	9	10	05		
	10	03	04		NEW x = OLD x + 1

Figure 1.4.1 This sequence of instructions has two parts: an initial data portion and a repeat portion. The repeat portion can be recirculated again and again through the card reader to get evaluation for new x values, but before this is done the result in register 6 must be copied down as a result to be saved. Computation stops after the last instruction card is executed. It can be resumed by insertion of more instruction cards.

The conditions hypothesized for the AXXION Company were not idle dreaming. Both the paper plan and the register plan were widely used prior to the existence of computers as known today. The paper plan was well adapted to doing the same operation in parallel for many cases (a characteristic of much data processing). The register plan was better suited to scientific processing and a machine called the Card Programmed Electronic Calculator based on an aircraft company's in-house development of just such a computer facility was marketed and heavily used starting in 1948.†

1.4.2 Decisions Required during Execution

In spite of these observations it does not take much ingenuity to conceive a kind of problem very difficult for the AXXION Computer. We need only consider the quadratic equation $Ax^2 + Bx + C = 0$ and ask for two values of x which satisfy it. The quadratic formula tells us to calculate (we assume $A \neq 0$)

$$D = B^2 - 4AC$$

and then to take a choice of three alternatives as follows:

If $D = 0$, then

$$x_1 = x_2 = -B/2A$$

If $D > 0$, then

$$x_1 = (-B + \sqrt{D})/2A \qquad \text{and} \qquad x_2 = (-B - \sqrt{D})/2A$$

If $D < 0$, then the roots are complex numbers

$$x_1 = (-B/2A, \sqrt{-D}/2A) \qquad \text{and} \qquad x_2 = (-B/2A, -\sqrt{-D}/2A)$$

The choice of instruction sequence to be followed once D has been calculated thus depends on the value of D. The AXXION Computer has no facility for making such "decisions."

To use the AXXION Computer as it exists, one would have to put into the card feed only enough instruction cards to deposit D in a register for observation. The operator would then read the value of D and—depending on its sign—select the next sequence of instructions. This next sequence could be just long enough to lead to the next "decision" as to instruction path.

Such cooperation between man and machine is not an impossibility. Splendid computations have been accomplished by such cumbersome

---

† G. S. Fenn, "Programming and Using the Type 603-405 Combination Machine in the Solution of Differential Equations," Scientific Computation Forum Proceedings, IBM Corp., 1948.

means. But surely one can see opportunities for errors in incorrectly reading the register, selecting the wrong deck, or spilling the cards. And even if none of these happens, the rate of computations is limited by dependence on human intervention.

The obvious way to decrease dependence on human intervention is to provide for the selection of instruction sequences by the computer from among all the ones that may be needed. They must be in machine-readable form and must be available without human intervention. In trying to extend the AXXION Computer, one might imagine an array of input devices among which the computer might select on the basis of a computed number. We might imagine each input device to be a paper or magnetic tape loop with many instruction sequences on it, and a computer able to spin its tape to the beginning of the correct sequence. But the real dreamer would note that instructions look just like numbers, and if there were enough registers, the instructions themselves could all be kept in memory along with data. Stored instructions might solve the problem of too much human intervention. Clearly, such a solution would require an immense "memory." Suppose there were one, and that instruction sequences were distributed in it. How would the computer find its way among them?

1.4.3   The Control Function

When instructions are executed as they are read, it is no problem for the computer to find the next instruction. It is the next one in the reader. But when the instructions of a problem solution are all in memory, the computer needs a marker to keep its place, like a person reading a novel. This is called a *pointer,* and for the AXXION Computer it is an address held in still another special register, which we call the *instruction pointer* register (IP). The address of the first instruction can be placed in that register manually if necessary, but once execution begins the computer itself must keep it current. When the time comes to begin another (possibly the first) instruction execution, that instruction can be copied into a decoding component for immediate use, and this permits the instruction pointer to be advanced to point to the next instruction. A reasonable convention is that, in the absence of other guidance, instructions are executed in the same sequence in which their registers are numbered; this requires that 1 be added to the instruction pointer in the IP.

Eventually a result will be calculated on which a choice of paths through the instructions in memory has to be made based on the value of some computed result. That means the instruction pointer may have to be changed, depending on the value of that result. No instruction in our repertoire will do it. But an instruction which might be called "load instruction pointer register if accumulator register holds a negative quantity" would cause such a change, the idea being to continue in the usual sequence if the accumulator register quantity is zero or positive. This is exactly what happens, but the mnemonics are different. The register examined is the accumulator; the replacement pointer is the integer in the address portion of the instruction; and the mnemonic operation is something like "branch on minus." While this one instruction is sufficient to control the most intricate computation, it is usual to include "branch on zero" and "branch on plus" defined similarly. The mnemonic and numeric operation codes we will use to demonstrate the idea are BZE(30), BMI(31), and BPL(32), respectively. We complete this aspect of automating computation with BR(33) for the instruction which loads its address portion into the instruction pointer register without test, and STOP(23) which only stops the execution. For convenient reference, we will christen as AXXICOMP the extension of the AXXION Computer to include 1000 registers, and control instructions and hardware to permit execution of a stored program. See Figure 1.4.2.

	Units digit			
Tens digit	0	1	2	3
0	LMQ	STMQ	LA	STA
1	A	S	M	D
2	SHIL	SHIR	—	STOP
3	BZE	BMI	BPL	BR

Figure 1.4.2   Numeric codes for the operations of the AXXICOMP Digital Computer, a direct descendent of the AXXION Computer but with memory sufficient to store both instructions and data.

With these minor additions to the instruction repertoire, the concepts in the AXXION Computer have been transformed just enough to provide true computerization. Of course these concepts are completely dependent on the feasibility of a large-capacity (1000 registers or more) memory. This *stored program* computer can perform arithmetic, it can reuse intermediate results without human intervention, and it can select its way through alternate instruction sequences on the basis of computed results. It can even modify instructions and store them where they will be executed. The significance of this last assertion needs to be explored, for, although it is now considered bad practice, computation of instructions and storing them in the execution sequence was a crucial step in attaining versatile programs which could execute on attainable machines.

1.5 INSTRUCTION MODIFICATION

As an exercise in programming a stored program computer, we utilize the AXXICOMP capabilities as defined in Section 1.4 and assume a grocery taking inventory and wanting to determine the value of its stock. This grocery has N distinct items numbered 1 to N, and for each item the quantity on hand is Q, and the value per item is V cents. The problem is to calculate

$$W = Q_1V_1 + Q_2V_2 + \cdots + Q_NV_N = \text{total value in cents}$$

Suppose that it is agreed to store Q_i in register $700 + i$ and V_i in $800 + i$ $(i = 1, 2, \ldots, N)$ and to accumulate the result in register 700. A sequence of instructions to accomplish this could be written as in Program 1.5.1. One may note the following:

1. This computation requires 399 instructions for $N = 100$.

2. There is a monotonous regularity to the sequence. One can compute one sequence of four instructions from the previous four by adding 1 to each of two indexes.

Symbolic operation	Numeric operation	Index
LMQ	00	701
M	12	801
STA	03	700
LMQ	00	702
M	12	802
A	10	700
STA	03	700
LMQ	00	703
M	12	803
.	.	.
.	.	.
.	.	.

Program 1.5.1 A program on AXXICOMP to compute total inventory value requires substantial memory for both instructions and data.

Such regularity suggests use of the computer to calculate the instructions and store them where they should be when execution takes place. But this possibility prompts another idea: Why not compute the instructions for adding one product and then execute them before computing any more? As soon as they are executed we can put the next set of four instructions right back in their place. This notion is somewhat analogous to the execution of instructions as they are read from cards in the original AXXION Computer. In that case, no instructions had to be stored in registers.

What is involved here is a blending of two kinds of computations: We calculate a set of instructions, then use these computed instructions to perform arithmetic of the problem. Once they are executed, we test for completion and, if more instructions of the same kind are to be used, we calculate them and then use them. For an easily read flowchart (see Figure 1.5.1), we can profit from a little more notation. Recalling that

$$W = Q_1 V_1 + Q_2 V_2 + \cdots + Q_N V_N$$

then

$$W_1 = Q_1 V_1, \qquad W_2 = Q_1 V_1 + Q_2 V_2,$$

and

$$W_I = Q_1 V_1 + Q_2 V_2 + \cdots + Q_I V_I$$

If we manage to establish a way to calculate W_I for each I and then stop when $I = N$, we will have calculated W. A flowchart for this is shown in Figure 1.5.1. Our first concern will be to consider the kind of work to be done in box 3 of this flowchart.

If interpreted as an instruction, the constant

$$\begin{array}{cc} 00000 & 00700 \\ \text{not used} & \text{op address} \end{array}$$

would load the MQ with the contents of register 700. We can form from this constant an instruction to load the MQ register with the contents of register $700 + I$ just by adding the value of I to the constant. Similarly, if interpreted as an instruction, the constant

$$\begin{array}{cc} 00000 & 12800 \\ \text{not used} & \text{op address} \end{array}$$

would multiply the number in the MQ register by the number in location 800. From this constant we can form an instruction to multiply the contents of the MQ register by the contents of register $800 + I$ just by adding the value of I to the constant.

It is a convenience to note that there is no need to save W_{I-1} after W_I is computed, so we reserve only two registers, one numbered 699 to hold I and one numbered 700 to hold the W_I determined by the I in register 699.

Constants needed during the computation include zero and one and the constants

$$\begin{array}{ccccc} 00000 & 00700 & \text{and} & 00000 & 12800 \end{array}$$

to which I is to be added to form instructions. We assume these are stored

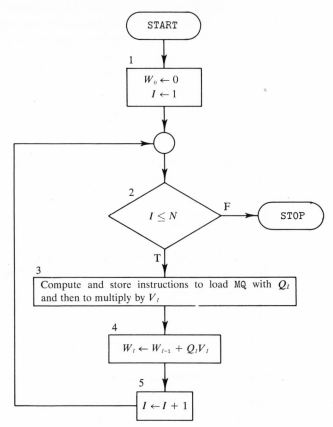

Figure 1.5.1 This flowchart specifies a step-by-step process for calculating $W = Q_1V_1 + \cdots + Q_NV_N$ and includes as well the computation of selected instructions to permit reuse of an instruction sequence.

in locations 694–697 and that N, the number of items in the inventory, is stored in 698. We summarize the totality of data items for our program in Table 1.5.1.

A stored program has to have a place in the registers, just as data. Where it is placed is somewhat arbitrary as long as the IP register can be set to hold the location of the first instruction. We shall assume that the first instruction is in register 0100 and write the coding implied by Figure 1.5.1 using register assignments from Table 1.5.1.

The instruction sequence in Program 1.5.2 is clearly a compromise because it commits a great number of instruction executions to the overhead

Register	Contents
694	00000
695	00001
696	00700
697	12800
698	N
699	I
700	W_I
700 + I	Quantity of Ith item, $1 \leq I \leq N$
800 + I	Value of Ith item, $1 \leq I \leq N$

Table 1.5.1 This table provides register locations for all data items of the flowchart of Figure 1.5.1, even those data which are used only in calculation of instructions.

Initialize	100 00000 02694	A ← 0
	101 00000 03700	W ← 0
	102 00000 02695	A ← 1
	103 00000 03699	I ← 1
Test for	104 00000 11698	A ← c(I) − c(N)
completion	105 00000 32120	SKIP TO 120 IF c(A)>0
	106 00000 02696	A ← LMQ 700
	107 00000 10699	A ← LMQ 700+c(I)
Calculate	108 00000 03112	STORE FOR EXECUTION
instructions	109 00000 02697	A ← M 800
	110 00000 10699	A ← M 800+c(I)
	111 00000 03113	STORE FOR EXECUTION
	112 00000 00700 + I	MQ ← Q_I
Arithmetic	113 00000 12800 + I	A ← $Q_I V_I$
of problem	114 00000 10700	A ← $W_{I-1} + Q_I V_I$
	115 00000 03700	STORE W_I
Increment	116 00000 02699	A ← c(I)
counter	117 00000 10695	A ← c(I)+1
	118 00000 03699	STORE NEW VALUE IN I
Return to test	119 00000 33104	GO TO TEST FOR COMPLETION
for completion	120 00000 23000	STOP

Program 1.5.2 A complete program for computing the inventory value requires only 21 instructions if the instructions themselves are modified. With this approach, the program length is *not* proportional to the number of items in the inventory.

of instruction modification and control. But there are some tremendous gains.

1. In the straightline coding of Program 1.5.1, the number of instructions depended on N and therefore instructions had to be added if N increased or deleted if N decreased. By contrast, N was a data item for Program 1.5.2 and thus had no effect on the program structure.

2. The number of registers occupied by instructions can be vastly reduced when instruction calculation is permitted. In this comparison, 399 instructions were required for the sequence in Program 1.5.1 with $N = 100$. By contrast, the sequence in Program 1.5.2 accomplishes identical results using 21 registers for instructions and 6 for data devoted to instruction calculation.

3. The tedium of writing, recording, and checking long sequences of instructions is reduced because there are fewer instructions and because the sequences created are more likely to be reusable (because they are independent of some problem parameters).

1.6   DISHING OUT THE CREDITS

In our semihistoric presentation of the development of computers, we have attempted to show that there is a logical, evolutionary way to arrive at the stored-program computer. Given the electronic technology to support large memories, it would surely have happened without being conceived in a flash by a genius. The extraordinary credits must go, it seems to us, to those men who first appreciated fully the overriding importance of a large memory so that instructions could be stored there, and then pushed aside all impediments to its availability. Several men deserve special mention in this regard.

Foremost among these was John von Neumann, a great mathematician prior to his interest in computers. Acting as a consultant to the US War Department, he authored a report entitled "First Draft of a Report on the EDVAC" (Univ. of Pennsylvania, Philadelphia, 1945), and detailed the logical design for a binary stored-program computer. Individual credits for ideas presented in this report are hard to assign, for there was a sharing of ideas among brilliant men behind the EDVAC (Electronic Discrete Variable Calculator). Two of the most influential were J. Presper Eckert and John W. Mauchly. This report had an inspirational effect on all who were concerned with the automation of computing. Not only did it specify a machine, it also justified the design.

In later papers, von Neumann and H. H. Goldstine went into great detail concerning "Planning and Coding Problems for an Electronic Computing Instrument." These papers are contained in the fifth volume of von Neumann's collected works (Pergamon, New York, 1963). It is interesting to note that design decisions made then (for example, to use binary complement arithmetic) have persisted and won out over competing designs. Further, the flowchart concepts von Neumann introduced in 1947 and 1948 have been sources of new developments (proving correctness of programs) over 20 years later.

Some of the attempts to automate computation which served as a basis for previous sections are documented in "Proceedings/Scientific Computation Forum 1948," edited by H. R. J. Grosch and published in 1950 by International Business Machines Corporation. Particular attention might be given to papers by Fenn and Polachek in that reference, not for the problems but for the computing devices they were using.

There are some fascinating references on historical development of computation, among which we recommend three.† Many more are sure to be written, at which time it may be possible to assign credits more accurately. Meantime, our task is to proceed with the device.

1.7   ORGANIZING FOR COMPUTERIZATION

1.7.1   The Objects of Computer Processing

We have taken a particular problem as an example to illustrate how methods of carrying out its solution may evolve as the processes being carried out are better understood and the pressures such as tedium, cost, and elapsed time force considerations of improvement. It is fitting that the example was concerned with a physical situation in which the ingredients were known, the physical principles were well understood, and the entire study could be done numerically. We say this not because these are the most appropriate uses of computers, but rather because understanding a process is essential to automating it. Some of the most ordinary things we do are not well understood. Determining whether or not two sentences in the same language convey the same message is an example. We shall not limit our thoughts on computerization to physical problems, but we shall assume a measure of understanding of the ingredients and of the process applied to them. Our examples in the next paragraphs will be taken from the development of the AXXICOMP computer, but in other parts of this text we will emphasize text material as might occur in a book, a mathematical formula, or a computer program. There, our concern will be with characters and strings of characters about which we will be more precise in the next section.

---

† Goldstine, H. H., "The Computer from Pascal to von Neumann," Princeton University Press, Princeton, New Jersey, 1972.

Fleck, G., ed., "A Computer Perspective," Harvard University Press, Cambridge, Massachusetts, 1973.

Rosen, S., "A Quarter Century View," Association for Computing Machinery, New York, 1971.

1.7.2   Operations on Objects

We shall assume a set of objects and certain elementary operations on
ordered pairs of these objects, each of which selects an object called the
result. In the AXXICOMP computer, the objects were ordered pairs of
real numbers and the original operations were add, subtract, multiply,
and divide. In each case, the operation applied to any ordered pair of
real numbers (excepting division by zero) and the result was a real number. As the model developed, another operation became important for
conditional branching. Using functional notation, we call this operation
nonneg(x). It is applied to a real number and the resulting object is not
a real number but one of the symbols (*true, false*), the value *true* being
selected for the number x if $x \geq 0$ and otherwise the value *false*.

We can expect that an operation will be defined only for a certain subset
of the objects under consideration. The subset for which it is defined is
called its *domain*. As an example, we would not expect the addition we
apply to real numbers to accept *true* or *false* as operands. The set of
objects obtained as results of an operation is called its *range*.

How does one select the set of operations he will use? For the AXXICOMP
computer, we more or less arbitrarily chose add, subtract, multiply, and
divide as fundamental for arithmetic of real numbers in the sense that we
did not define one in terms of the other. While arithmetic of real numbers
is convenient, we are free to limit our domain for arithmetic to integers
since any real number can be approximated to a prescribed tolerance as
a quotient of integers. Among arithmetic operations, addition is surely not
necessary, since any addition can be replaced by a pair of subtractions

$$A + B = A - (0 - B)$$

Multiplication and division for positive integer operands can be reduced
to successive additions or subtractions with counting. Clearly, there are
different choices for sets of arithmetic operations.

By considerations such as these, we can conclude that the necessities
for numerical computation are only subtraction of integers and being able
to base the sequence of operations to be performed on the sign of computed results. Any set of operations including these two will be sufficient.
The choice can then be decided on the bases of programming convenience,
execution time, equipment cost, and the like.

1.7.3   Primitives and Procedures

Those operations taken as fundamental in the sense that each can be
invoked without reference to any other is called a *primitive*. A primitive,

as we have defined it, can be pictured as a "black box." It should have (1) reading facilities for accepting operands, and (2) recording facilities for passing on a result. While we have usually had an ordered pair as input, some primitives may have a single object as input, some may have two, and some may have even more. The input objects could themselves be numbers, sequences, arrays, or more complex objects. The output can have the same kind of generality.

There is a tremendous gap between the primitives of our model and the massive computations we aspire to. One can ask how to organize his planning of computation. A natural progression leads to machines with more powerful primitives to suit the problem at hand. One might at a very low level, for example, introduce a square-root operation, a negation operation, or, as we shall see in Chapter 8, floating-point arithmetic. At a higher level, we could have a root finder or simultaneous equation solver. Such primitives can be implemented as "black boxes," thus specializing the machine to the functions they serve. They can alternatively be implemented in terms of other primitives, in which case we call them pseudoprimitives. A machine together with an appropriate set of pseudoprimitives constitutes an imaginary (virtual) machine for which we can write programs. A progression of such machines can then lead in an orderly manner to the solution of large problems.

We shall be concerned with sequences of instructions called *procedures* created to perform a specific function in much the same way as pseudoprimitives. They too have inputs and outputs, but in some cases they behave more like boxes with windows, for the activities inside them can affect data not identified as output. In any case, the purpose is the same: to bridge the gap between problem formulation and computer instructions.

Early astronomers would not have been at a loss to specify desired pseudoprimitives. They needed values of trigonometric functions at every turn. It matters little to the user whether these are made available from tables or from direct evaluation. A pseudoprimitive for trigonometric functions could be implemented either way. The choice would be based on machine characteristics.

In our mention of pseudoprimitives and procedures, we have refrained from implying that they perform correctly for every selection of operands. For some inputs, the result may be meaningless. It is even possible that execution might continue repetitiously until there was outside intervention like that to free a needle on a broken phonograph record. We would call this an *infinite loop*. The only important consideration to us now is that procedures (including pseudoprimitives) serve the purpose—when judiciously planned—to narrow the gap between the problem to be done and the computing device for doing it.

1.7.4 The Objects of Operations

There was more generality in the preceding portion of this section than will be exploited in this text. Our concern is going to be with numbers (integer or real) and with characters and strings of characters. The need for character-handling capability was not originally seen to be such an urgent problem as it has become, for the original motivation was completely numeric. With the advent of symbolic means for specifying computation and compilers to translate the commands into machine instructions, every type of machine use demands substantial character-string capabilities. For that reason, we now spend some effort to consider the representation of information.

1.8 DIGITAL REPRESENTATION OF INFORMATION

1.8.1 Introductory Concepts

Let the representation for 1 be a single vertical stroke, and, given the representation for a natural number, let the representation for its successor always be obtained by appending another vertical stroke. Then we have, as sample representations,

$$
\begin{array}{ll}
1 & | \\
5 & | | | | | \\
11 & | | | | | | | | | | |
\end{array}
$$

It is difficult to represent zero in this notation, but we could do so by letting the single stroke represent 0. Then the representations are

$$
\begin{array}{ll}
0 & | \\
1 & | | \\
5 & | | | | | | \\
11 & | | | | | | | | | | | |
\end{array}
$$

Sequences of numbers would still be difficult, because the blank is not easily represented and may not be recognized. But we could mark the separation of sequences of vertical strokes by a zero and represent the sequence 592 as

It does not require much ingenuity but it does take a lot of space to extend this idea to representing words. All we need do is to agree that some number of vertical strokes represents A and that, given the representation of a letter, we form the representation for its successor by appending another vertical stroke. Then if | | | | | | | | | | | represents A we could interpret the sequence

$$0\,|\,|\,|\,|\,|\,|\,|\,|\,|\,|\,|\,0\,|\,|\,|\,|\,|\,|\,|\,|\,|\,|\,|\,|\,0\,|\,|\,|\,|\,|\,|\,|\,|\,|\,|\,|\,|\,|\,|\,0$$

as the sequence of letters

B   A   D

Unfortunately, we have no way to decide whether or not it was intended to write a sequence of integers whose decimal representations are 11   10   13 instead. Problems of this sort must be solved, and not all of them are trivial. But the bulkiness of the representation is in fact so awkward that a more sophisticated approach is required anyway.

Our principal objective here has been to discover that whatever is encodable with many symbols can also be encoded with only two. Therefore we can choose our number of symbols to suit other needs like reliability, economy, and speed.

1.8.2   Some Pragmatics of Information Representation

In digital computers, we consider reading, processing, and recording information represented as finite linear sequences called *strings* of elements from a set of "building blocks" called *characters*. The set of elements recognized as characters will vary from one situation to another. It will almost always include the letters of the alphabet of some natural language. If the subject at hand is translation from one natural language to another, it may include two such alphabets. It may include both upper- and lower-case representations of those letters. It will surely include a set of digits, some punctuation, and some arithmetic operators, since the information to be processed includes items as diverse as the mathematical formulation of a space ship trajectory to the text of a computer-typeset newspaper.

What may be less obvious is that in computers we deal with several representations of the same character and with character sets which are not even in one-to-one correspondence. The most obvious characters are those which are marks on the printed page. The number of these is likely limited by the number of distinct characters on a print chain, on a typewriter typeball, or the number of acceptable marks in an electronic visual representation. In fact, if there are several printing devices, we can expect each to have its own *printable character set*.

While there are optical scanners which read printed output, it is more usual that, to be machine readable, characters are represented as:

1. Patterns of punched holes in a single column of a card.

2. Patterns of punched holes in a row across the width of a paper tape.

3. Patterns of magnetized spots in a row across the width of a magnetic tape.

Each of these representations may have its own character set, but whatever it is we should expect that every character which can be recorded on a medium should be readable from the same medium. Clearly, when it is read and its internal representation again recorded, the same external representation should result.

Computation is carried out with an *internal character set*. For each machine-readable character set, there must be a one-to-one correspondence between its elements and a subset of internal characters. Since computers are almost universally composites of binary elements (as is to some extent justified in Chapter 2), it is usual to decide on p-place representations of binary integers as internal characters where:

1. The machine-readable character set in the system has no more than 2^p elements.

2. Word length is divisible by p.

3. Words are segmented into storage segments of length p, called *bytes* in 360/370 terminology.†

The correspondences between printable and internal characters and between machine-readable and internal characters are somewhat arbitrary but are influenced by the operations which we wish to perform on characters. It will pay to look at one representation which was prevalent in the 1950s and then to consider string operations to understand how representations have evolved.

In the dominant computers of the decade 1954–1964, six bits were used to represent a character, yielding 64 distinct representations. Table 1.8.1 is taken from a typical encoding of this type, known as *binary coded decimal* (BCD).

---

† Note that we consider a byte to be a unit of storage beginning on a storage bit whose index is divisible by p. We do not accept the use of byte as synonymous with character.

	000	001	010	011	100	101	110	111
000	0	1	2	3	4	5	6	7
001	8	9						
010		A	B	C	D	E	F	G
011	H	I						
100		J	K	L	M	N	O	P
101	Q	R						
110			S	T	U	V	W	X
111	Y	Z						

Table 1.8.1 The bit pattern formed by appending the column pattern to the row pattern gives the BCD representation of the character in the selected row and column of the table.

It is much easier to understand the BCD coding of letters and digits if one realizes that card representations of these characters came first and were assigned without reference to binary numbers. The card representation of a digit used by Hollerith in the 1890 census and adopted by IBM for its punches, sorters, and printers used one card column to represent one character. The card, still current today, has twelve rows. On it, the representation of a character consists of one or more holes punched in selected rows of its column. If one numbers rows 12, 11, 0, 1, 2, . . . , 8, 9 starting from the top of the card, then the representation of a digit d is a single punch in row d of the card. Each representation of a letter has two punches, one in rows 12, 11, or 0 called the *zone punch* and one in rows 1–9 called the *digit punch*. The zone punches are the same for all letters A–I (a punch in row 12 only), for the letters J–R (a punch in row 11 only), and for the letters S–Z (a punch in row 0 only). Within a zone, the digit selects the letter. The rightmost four bits of the BCD internal code constitute a binary representation of the digit. The leftmost two bits in the BCD representation are fixed within a zone and therefore exclude hexadecimal A–F in the rightmost 4 bits as alphabetic character representations.

When special characters for arithmetic operators, parentheses, and punctuation are to be included, there is no choice but to place them in the gaps of Table 1.8.1. This seems natural enough, but there are complications. One principle concern with character handling is to place strings in dictionary order—as for telephone directories. In this case, the string consists of all information on a subscriber, but the ordering depends on only the name portion of the string—the *sort key*. At first thought, one might expect this ordering to depend only on alphabetic characters, but in scanning a directory we can find such items as

A-1	AIR–FLO
A A A	Phillips 66
AAA	Phil's
A L S	PIC-QUIK 7-11
A & W	MAC's

These force an ordering on the union of letters, digits, -, &, ', and blank. The nearer our correspondence between printed and internal characters preserves a textual ordering as an arithmetic ordering of internal representations, the more readily will compare instructions suffice to order character strings.

Another concern arises in translating a string of characters describing a computation. We may determine in scanning from left to right that a digit begins the representation of a number; for example,

$$+ \ 1XXXX$$

Our interest now is to find the first nondigit to the right of the initial digit, for it signifies either the end of the number or a break such as a decimal point in the sense of the representation. In looking for termination of a variable name (as in FORTRAN) our interest is to find the next non-alphanumeric character. We should hope that this testing is convenient, namely that determining membership of a character in a subset of the full character set is easy. While special instructions are helpful, it should be clear that having the members of each important subset (such as digits or letters) represented internally by consecutive integers would allow testing only on endpoints of the interval to determine membership. The BCD code does not allow this.

If one finds it desirable to represent the text of a book in digital form, then clearly 64 characters are not adequate. As of 1964, a rush to 8-bit representations of characters began. While there are many variations, there are two 8-bit character codes which dominate the field. One called Extended Binary-Coded Decimal Interchange Code (EBCDIC) was an outgrowth of BCD. The other, once known as USA Standard Code for Information Interchange (USASCII), is more recently called the ISO Code (International Standards Organization Code). EBCDIC is shown in Appendix A.

1.9 PRESSURES INFLUENCING EVOLUTION

Surely, there are few fields in which technology has made such dramatic strides as in computers. We assumed a 10,000-digit memory in the AXXION Computers, and that was fairly typical of early models. By contrast, the 360/370 logic permits addresses to access 2^{24} (roughly 16,000,000) bytes of memory. Memory access times have been cut by a factor of 100, arithmetic speeds are faster by a factor of 1000, error frequency in the central processor and memory cost have been cut by a factor of 1000 or more, power and environmental requirements are dramatically relaxed, and the price measured in any reasonable way is cut by a factor of 100.

In spite of these impressive developments, the proportion of income devoted to computers by industry, government, and universities has increased steadily. Clearly, more and more uses are being found for computers and dependence on them is thorough. The result of huge budget allotments to machines (and even more drastic allotments to development of programs for them) has produced extreme cost consciousness. Some of the costs associated with computers are easy to estimate and some are most difficult. The engineer, given a request to install a new machine instruction or a new machine component, can—on the basis of a market forecast—estimate its cost. Other costs, like the savings in programming time of having the new instruction or the new component, are extremely difficult to estimate. In the usual company decision, savings on computer components have received far more attention than savings in time for computer programmers and users.

There is a growing recognition that computer componentry has far outstripped our ability to use it effectively. One of the crying needs is development of hardware to improve the quality of programming and decrease the likelihood of undetected errors in execution. Such features will become available only as (1) programmers understand their problems well enough to know their needs, and (2) programmers and managers who make decisions realize enough of machine architecture to appreciate and pay for these hardware developments. Here is an excellent justification for the teaching of machine features as they are evidenced in programming at machine level, and for exploring a variety of architectures and their effects on problem solving.

Programming at machine level, while necessary to understanding, can be unbelievably tedious unless facilitated by symbolism. Assembler language is just a mnemonic form of representing machine instructions which is easily translated to numeric form by machine. A knowledge of the computer gained by programming at machine level with assembler support will enhance a programmer's understanding of what he is doing and what can be done. Thus, the end we are seeking is understanding of machine capabilities and their exploitation in problem solving. A necessary tool is a symbolic way of representing any conceivable numeric instruction in an understandable way; this representation is usually known as assembler language.

1.10 PRECURSORS OF CHANGE

1.10.1 Hardware Limitations

The evolution of computers has resulted in fast and reliable computation available to more people at less cost than ever before. Can this trend continue? And what are some of the limitations surrounding further development? One of the most obvious limitations is the fixed, finite velocity of light and electrical pulses at $3 \cdot 10^8$ m/sec. Electrical signals between the memory and the central processing unit require 1 nsec (10^{-9} sec) for each 0.3 m (approximately 1 ft) of physical separation. Although the nanosecond is an extremely small interval of time, many computers now on the market can perform simple operations such as adding or shifting in less than 100 nsec. Further improvement in this speed still seems likely, but clearly physical size is very important; the larger the physical dimensions of the wiring in the computer, the more time is "wasted" with electrical signals traveling between locations where operations are performed. Thus miniaturization is important in the quest for faster computation. One of the opposing forces in computer evolution is the need for increasing amounts of storage which is directly accessible to the central processor. For a particular application, these observations lead one to believe there is an optimum size–speed configuration for any given state of the art of miniaturization.

Virtual memory was a feature of the Burroughs B5000 long before its more recent availability on the B1700, B6700, B7700, IBM 370, and Hewlett-Packard's HP 3000. The notion is to let the program be developed as if there were an unlimited, directly accessible, high-speed memory available and to rely on special systems software to fit the program to the memory capacity of the machine. This is usually accomplished by swapping segments of subprograms or procedures from disk storage into main memory as they are needed. They are sent back to the disk when other segments must be brought into main memory and the least busy ones must give up their places to make room. This swapping is not always efficient—

it should not be forced upon every situation—but it does allow large programs with many subprograms to be processed by a machine with a main memory substantially smaller than would be required to store the entire program. The effect is to relieve somewhat the pressure toward larger main memory, while permitting the use of a large, slow, relatively inexpensive secondary memory like a disk with no increase in programming complexity. There may be a substantial reduction in machine efficiency, something to be expected whenever programs challenge the capacity of the computer on which they are executed.

1.10.2   Architectural Considerations

There are more subtle techniques for increasing computation speed than the brute-force method of increasing the speed of the internal electronic devices. One important technique is the processing of more than one computation at a time, which is known as *parallel computation* or *parallel processing*. Simultaneous operation of (1) the central processor on some computation and (2) an input or output operation such as reading a tape or cards or printing program output was introduced as early as 1958 on the IBM 709. This approach used a specialized processor dedicated to controlling the input or output operation, and represented a degree of decentralization of the overall computing power available in a machine. Central processors with multiple arithmetic units or systems with several equally powerful central processors have been developed since then.

In recent years, however, increased attention has been applied to recognizing segments of a computation which could be processed simultaneously, and machines (an example is ILLIAC IV) have been designed to take advantage of this independence. Getting a large number of processors to cooperate effectively in solutions of practical problems has taken (and still is taking) brilliance in design and a complete rethinking of programming language and practice. Programmers are discovering techniques which can be employed to make more optimal use of the internal hardware and software systems, primarily by making it easier to recognize which segments of computation are independent.

Although the use of multiple arithmetic units in ILLIAC IV represented a departure from previous computer design, other profound changes have also been introduced. In the early 1960s, Burroughs departed from usual concepts and designed its central processor around the concept of a last-in-first-out stack for storage in the processor. Hardware stacks are found in several more recent Burroughs computers, including the B1700, B6700, and B7700. Other designers have adopted stack architecture, one being Hewlett-Packard in its HP 3000 computer.

Stacks were originated as a concept useful in implementing compilers for well-structured languages. They were implemented in software on existing machines as data structures useful in evaluation and/or translation of arithmetic expressions, in managing subprogram calls, and in dynamic storage allocation. They have been conceptually powerful in models of devices for executing programs in nested declaration languages such as ALGOL and PL/1. Such models of computation provide a rich source of ideas for machine architects whose ultimate goal must be to provide the best machine to execute the programs conceived by users.

Another architectural development is the *distributed-function* computer. Decreasing hardware costs have provided substantial impetus for investigating this concept, although the possibility of increasing computer power and efficiency also contribute. Although "distributed-function computer" has not been formally defined, the concept includes elements of (1) resources working in concert to achieve a desired goal, (2) more than one activity occurring concurrently, for example, parallelism as discussed previously, and (3) significant delays in transferring information from one unit to another. Thus the processing of a program in such a computer might result in propagation of the machine representation of the program together with its developing record of execution through various hardware units at nearly the velocity of light. These units would each perform some of the computation required, one goal being that segments of computation recognized as independent would be done in parallel. Hopefully such a computer would be more apt to survive in the problem-solving environment than the dinosaur which possessed a small secondary brain at the base of the spinal cord. A good discussion of some of the features and problems of distributed-function architectures is found in the March 1974 issue of *Computer,* an IEEE Computer Society publication.

1.10.3   Minicomputers

One of the most far-reaching effects of continued miniaturization has been the development of powerful but simple computers which can easily fit on the top of a desk. Such minicomputers become cheaper, faster, more reliable, and more powerful from both hardware and software standpoints every year. They often contain amounts of main memory unavailable in the largest of the machines of the mid-1950s. In this way, substantial computing power has become available to more people than ever before. Except for the important concept of automatic coordination of effort, the abundance of minicomputers bears more than a little resemblance to the distributed-function concept.

The present generation of minicomputers are simpler machines than their big brothers like the IBM 360/370 systems. In fact, computers at their level of complexity provide a stepping stone for the student whose goal is to understand the more complex concepts associated with the "big" machines. The primary motivation for this book is, in fact, to simplify the concepts of the 360/370 systems by defining a "subset machine" faithful to the larger real-world system. Not accidentally, this subset machine (which we call BAREBONZ and present in Chapter 3) is also fairly faithful to both present minicomputers and the earliest stored-program computers.

PROBLEMS

1. List three applications for special-purpose computers (the operator can specify the input but not the process) with which you are personally familiar.

2. Do you feel that special-purpose or general-purpose computers are most likely to be misused? What differences in possible misuse between these two types of computers can you foresee?

3. List any misuses of computers with which you have direct personal knowledge. Were the computers involved special or general purpose?

4. How would a particular complex computation requiring many additions, subtractions, multiplications, and divisions be specified for solution on the paper-approach system? Do you believe the AXXION Company made the correct choice in selecting the register approach? Discuss your answer.

5. What features of the initial register-approach machine would soon be recognized as bottlenecks for computations performed on this machine?

6. For the program shown in Figure 1.4.1, why is there an initialization phase? For the programming example in Section 1.4, what value for x should the operator enter on the keyboard at the appropriate time during initialization? Could this task have been automated?

7. Assuming all instructions except Multiply and Divide require 1 sec each and these take 5 and 10 sec respectively, determine what percent of time in the loop in Program 1.5.2 is overhead of the stored program method of computation (the remainder of time in the loop will be effectively used for the desired computation).

8. The instructions of AXXICOMP use only half a word. One can try to get more out of each instruction by putting the addresses of two operands in one register along with an opcode. The result would still be left in the accumulator. To avoid having to store the accumulator in order to use its contents for a result, one can agree that an address of 0000 refers to the accumulator contents. The instruction format might then be

XXXX   YY   ZZZZ

address   op   address
of left   code   of right
operand   operand

Define enough such instructions to rewrite Program 1.5.2 in this manner, rewrite that program, and estimate the savings in instruction space and/or execution time.

9. Suppose you were responsible for enabling a computer to compose type for a book from one long character string. One problem would be to distinguish the syllables in each word to be hyphenated. See whether you can state the hyphenation primitive which would be required. Is hyphenation as you know it essential to the understanding of text, or is it a means of saving paper, or perhaps used just for aesthetic effect? Would hyphenation be a serious complication in mechanization of text editing?

10. Almost everyone has had the experience of receiving two or more mailings of the same flyer. Often this happens because of mailings from two distinct lists so that mailing labels may even be identical. Sometimes it happens that there are slight variations in name or address in two entries. Try devising a reasonable procedure for detecting the latter case when both entries are in the same file, remembering that complete solutions are difficult or they would have been used.

11. Decode the following octal string according to Table 1.8.1 with the additional code of 60 for the blank character. Then write the same message in EBCDIC as gleaned from Appendix A of this text.

2346444764632551626023214560222560646225266443

12. The telephone system has evolved in an environment which was highly influenced by cost of a set. Some of its characteristics resulting from this environment can be frustrating. For example, there is no easy way to trace a call. There is a great deal of effort expended trying to get a call through when traffic is heavy. If one were to take into account the time lost in ineffective dialing, he might press for features not currently available. If one were bothered by crank calls, he might set a high value on ability to trace calls quickly. Is there any reasonable way to influence evolution of such a system in a democratic society? Discuss.

Chapter 2

Binary Arithmetic and Its Machine Implementation

2.1 AN ANALOGY USING COINS

2.1.1 Economy of Representation

Ways to represent numerical information economically can be studied in a familiar setting if they are posed as problems of making change with coins. One may ask, for example, for a choice of coin values which will meet one of the following criteria:

1. Require as few distinct coin values as possible in making change for any purchase made with a ten-dollar bill, or

2. Require as few coins as possible to make change for any purchase made with a ten-dollar bill.

The answer to the first requirement is simple. We can get along with pennies only, but it will require 999 of them to make change for a one-cent purchase. The second requirement is more interesting. If we permit penny, dime, and dollar coins, with nine of each, we can make change for any permitted purchase. That requires 27 coins, which is an impressive drop from 999. Can we do any better? Let us experiment.

From our own experience, we are inclined to consider some in-between coins. We could replace five pennies by one nickel, five dimes by one 50-cent piece, and five dollars by a five-dollar coin. We would then be down to $27 - 12 = 15$ coins. It is worth noting that, to make change using as few coins as possible, we start with the most valuable coin no larger than the amount of change and take as many as do not exceed the amount of change; we then repeat this step with respect to the remaining change again and again until exact change is made.

Since smaller jumps in coin size seemed to be helpful, let us consider coins of value 1, 5, 25, 125, and 625 cents, respectively, in which case the representation has base 5 (coin values are powers of 5). To make change for an arbitrary purchase under ten dollars, one would need one 625-cent coin and four of each other denomination, a total of 17 coins in all. Intermediate coins having values of 2, 10, 50, and 250 cents would bring the number down to 13 coins required to make change for any purchase under ten dollars.

Consider the extreme case using powers of 2 for coin values of 1, 2, 4, 8, 16, 32, 64, 128, 256, and 512 cents. With this choice, one needs at most one coin of each value and, since there are only ten distinct values, the maximum number of coins required to make change for a purchase with a ten-dollar bill is ten.

2.1.2 Positional Notation

An excessive amount of writing is needed to record a way of making change if it is necessary to name the coin value and then the number of coins of that value which are to be used, as shown by the following example:

$1.18 =$ four quarters + one dime + one nickel + three cents

If the position in which a number of coins is written has attached to it a coin value, then we can write for each value only the number of coins used in its proper place. For example, the change described above could also be written

$$
\begin{array}{cccc}
25 & 10 & 5 & 1 \\
\hline
\$1.18 = \quad 4 & 1 & 1 & 3
\end{array}
$$

This is a type of positional notation, and for coins one could get used to interpreting a sequence of numbers separated by commas and without the labels in the same way, e.g., 4, 1, 1, 3. The commas separating numbers of coins are unfamiliar, but they do serve a purpose. For example,

$$0, 0, 0, 118$$
$$0, 0, 22, 8$$
$$0, 11, 1, 3$$
$$2, 5, 0, 18$$

are all acceptable ways of writing $1.18. Without commas, the meaning would be obscured by writing them as

$$000118$$
$$00228$$
$$01113$$
$$25018$$

Thus a second requirement of positional notation is that the number of coins of a particular value must be representable with just one character. Acceptable representations for $1.18 from quarters, dimes, nickels, and pennies would then include

$$4113$$
$$4033$$
$$4108$$
$$4028$$

and many other combinations with fewer quarters. Part of the versatility in this case comes from using the ten decimal digits as possible numbers of coins, even though the base is essentially 5. Limiting ourselves to fewer than five coins of a kind would eliminate some possibilities, and also cutting out dimes (which are convenient but unnecessary) would in fact permit only the 4033 solution.

2.1.3   Canonical Positional Notation

With pocket coins, it is desirable to be able to represent a number (an amount of change) in several different ways. For the number systems we wish to study, however, it is necessary to settle on a representation for a given number which is both standard and unique. This representation will be called *canonical,* and we will develop it within the context of the coin analogy, although its generality should be evident.

We must choose a *base* (also called a *radix*) for number representations. For the decimal system the base is 10, and for binary numbers the base is 2, but the base can be any integer other than 0 or ± 1. We will use only positive bases, and will denote the base by b. We will also assume there are sufficient distinct characters so that there is one to represent each nonnegative integer less than the base (including 0 and 1). For bases less than 10, it is natural to use those digits we need from the digits of the decimal system. For larger bases (16 is the key one for us), it is convenient to extend these digits with letters of the alphabet. The digits for a few important bases are listed below in ascending order:

Base	Digits
2	0, 1
5	0, 1, 2, 3, 4
8	0, 1, 2, 3, 4, 5, 6, 7
10	0, 1, 2, 3, 4, 5, 6, 7, 8, 9
16	0, 1, 2, 3, 4, 5, 6, 7, 8, 9, A, B, C, D, E, F

Now it should be clear that any nonnegative integer value less than b can be represented by a single digit. To go to values greater than b we introduce a coin of higher value worth b units. A single digit's worth of coins ($b-1$ coins) valued at b together with $b-1$ coins of value 1 can take us as high as b^2-1. To go higher in the same manner, we need a coin of value b^2. By such reasoning, we find it convenient to have positional values which are just the nonnegative integer powers of b, namely b^0, b^1, b^2, b^3, ... Since a single digit is used for the number of coins of any value, these digits may be written in succession without punctuation. It is standard to write them in decreasing order of coin value. Wherever the base is not clearly understood, we write the base as a subscript to the number. Table 2.1.1. illustrates several examples.

Canonical representation	Decimal equivalent		A noncanonical equivalent
1101_2	$1 \cdot 2^3 + 1 \cdot 2^2 + 0 \cdot 2^1 + 1 \cdot 2^0$	$= 13_{10}$	$0, 3, 0, 1_2$
3021_4	$3 \cdot 4^3 + 0 \cdot 4^2 + 2 \cdot 4^1 + 1 \cdot 4^0$	$= 201_{10}$	$3, 0, 0, 9_4$
354_8	$3 \cdot 8^2 + 5 \cdot 8^1 + 4 \cdot 8^0$	$= 236_{10}$	$3, 3, 20_8$
$A9F_{16}$	$10 \cdot 16^2 + 9 \cdot 16^1 + 15 \cdot 16^0$	$= 2719_{10}$	$9, 8, 287_{16}$

Table 2.1.1 Integers can be represented in canonical form for a given base, or as a sum of exponentials, or in a more awkward noncanonical form, as well as the most familiar decimal representation. The noncanonical equivalent integers invariably have a "digit" at least as large as the base.

2.1.4 Conversion to Canonical Notation

When adding or subtracting using unfamiliar bases, one is likely to be confused by the carrying or borrowing from one position to the next. It is sometimes helpful to work with positional notation which may not always be canonical, and then convert to canonical form as a separate operation when necessary. In this way we can learn to verify machine computation with small chance of error. As an example of this notion, we will perform a multiplication in decimal without carry during the multiplication phase.

$$
\begin{array}{rrrrr}
 & & 9 & 8 & 7 \\
 & \times\, 4 & 7 & 3 \\
\hline
 & & 27, & 24, & 21 \\
 & 63, & 56, & 49 \\
36, & 32, & 28 \\
\hline
36, & 95, & 111, & 73, & 21 \\
\end{array}
$$

This answer can be converted to canonical form in easy stages by successively replacing ten coins in one position by one coin in the next position to the left. We do this from the right in successive steps:

$$
\begin{array}{rrrrr}
36, & 95, & 111, & 75, & 1 \\
36, & 95, & 118, & 5, & 1 \\
36, & 106, & 8, & 5, & 1 \\
46, & 6, & 8, & 5, & 1 \\
4, & 6, & 6, & 8, & 5, 1 \\
\end{array}
$$

To perform the subtraction $1347 - 689$ one may choose to represent 1347 in noncanonical form so that each of its positions exceeds the corresponding one in the second operand:

$$1347 = 1, 3, 3, 17 = 1, 2, 13, 17 = 12, 13, 17$$

$$
\begin{array}{rrr}
 & 12, & 13, & 17 \\
- & 6, & 8, & 9 \\
\hline
 & 6, & 5, & 8 \\
\end{array}
$$

The general principle in conversion is that a coin in any position may be exchanged for b coins in the position to its right (if there is one), and b coins in any position may be replaced by one coin in the position to its left. Answers should be in canonical form (since that is what the computer uses) but intermediate values for hand computation may be more understandable in nonstandard representation.

2.1.5   Conversion of Integers between Decimal and Binary

While there are neat ways to consolidate conversion of a number to binary, we favor a method which one could reconstruct for himself as an outcast on a deserted island. To do this, one writes down the values of all coins he may use in the representation of an integer N, namely, all no larger in value than N. Then starting with the largest coin, he records a 1 for its position and reduces N by the position value if N exceeds the position value. If the position value exceeds N, he records a zero for the position and does not modify N. In either case, until there remain no coins of smaller value, he moves to the next position to the right and repeats the process. We will now illustrate the technique by converting 984_{10} to binary:

Remainders	984	472	216	88	24	24	8	0	0	0
Powers of 2	512	256	128	64	32	16	8	4	2	1
	472	216	88	24	—	8	0	—	—	—
	1	1	1	1	0	1	1	0	0	0

To convert from binary to decimal representation of an integer, one writes over each position its coin value and adds up all those position values for which the digit is 1.

These methods of conversion are adequate for all hand work. They need to be sharpened when one is writing a computer algorithm for conversion as might be suggested by some of the problems at the end of the chapter.

2.2   BINARY REPRESENTATION OF FRACTIONS

The analogy of coins is somewhat limited in that there is always a minimum-valued coin (the penny in our system) such that all prices and all amounts of change can be given as an integer number of these "pennies." There is no such minimum unit in physical measurements, for however small the unit there are measurements which cannot be represented satisfactorily as an integer number of these units. The situation is much better represented by the problem of weighing with a pan balance which we next consider.

A pan balance assumes a set of objects with known weights in such an assortment of sizes that, given an arbitrary object, one can find a combination of known weights to balance the object within a specified tolerance. The weight of the object is then approximated as the sum of the known weights in the pan. Of course, if exact balance is not achieved, one can still find the largest weight which is overbalanced by the unknown object and the smallest which is not. Actual weight is between the two values (perhaps equal to the larger).

Suppose that we have an object A whose weight we wish to compare to that of a standard weight W. We plan to choose an integer greater than one as base b and to take all standard weights to be of size $(b^p)W$, where p may be any integer (positive, zero, or negative) and W is a positive integer. For each p, we require b equal weights (we could get by with only $b-1$). A weighing procedure to come within a tolerance, TOL > 0, of the correct weight is given in Figure 2.2.1. Clearly the smallest unit of measure (in the coin analogy it was the penny) must be as small as the tolerance.

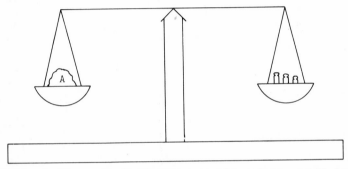

1. Place A, the object to be weighed (or the number to be converted), in the left pan.
2. Set p to zero; place weight of value $(b^p)W$ on the right pan, and allow the balance to stabilize.
3. If A is heavier (larger), do step 4; otherwise go to step 5.
4. Remove the weight in the pan; replace p by $p + 1$; place weight of value $(b^p)W$ on the right pan, and allow balance to stabilize; go to step 3.
5. If the pans balance exactly or if $(b^p)W \leq$ TOL, go to step 10; otherwise do steps 6–9.
6. Remove one weight of value $(b^p)W$, and replace p by $p - 1$.
7. If A is heavier, do step 8; otherwise go to step 9.
8. Place weight of value $(b^p)W$ on the right pan; go to step 7.
9. The weight of A is less than or equal to the sum S of weights on the right pan and greater than $S - (b^p)W$. Go to step 5.
10. If S is the sum of weights in the right pan, then $S -$ TOL $<$ weight of $A \leq S$; halt.

Figure 2.2.1 Here is a weighing procedure which always terminates, and will work for standard weights given in any units and with any base b. This weighing procedure is suitable for conversion of a number from one base to another base whether the number is an integer, a proper fraction, or has both integer and fraction parts. The weight in positional notation is a succession of digits, one for each p used in order on decreasing p. The radix point is inserted to the right of the $p = 0$ digit.

Example. Use the pan balance weighing algorithm to convert $A = 98_{10}$ to a base four representation. For conversion of integers, it is convenient to consider the standard weight W to be one, and the tolerance to be one as well. This choice of tolerance is adequate to give precise conversion for integers. Note that $S \geq 98 > S - 1$ and S is an integer; therefore $S = 98$.

Step number	p	256	64	16	4	1	Total weight (98 desired)
2	0					1	1
4	1				1		4
4	2			1			16
4	3		1				64
4	4	1					256
6	3						0
8	3		1				64
8	3		2				128
6	2		1				64
8	2		1	1			80
8	2		1	2			96
8	2		1	3			112
6	1		1	2			96
8	1		1	2	1		100
6	0		1	2	0		96
8	0		1	2	0	1	97
8	0		1	2	0	2	98
10	Halt						

The conversion technique we have just displayed requires arithmetic to be done to some base. It assumes that the standard weights and the number to be converted are expressed with respect to that base. This method is fine for conversion by a binary machine from binary to decimal, or for the human who works with decimal representations and performs decimal arithmetic. But it remains to display a procedure usable by a binary machine to convert a decimal *fraction* from decimal to binary. Since conversion of a decimal integer to a binary integer was discussed in the preceding section, we shall use some ideas presented there.

Let the proper fraction to be converted be

$$d_{-1} \cdot 10^{-1} + d_{-2} \cdot 10^{-2} + \cdots + d_{-n} \cdot 10^{-n}$$

We rewrite this expression as

$$((\cdots ((d_{-1} \cdot 10 + d_{-2}) \cdot 10 + d_{-3}) \cdot 10 + \cdots + d_{-n+1}) \cdot 10 + d_{-n})/10^n$$

to indicate the computation needed to perform the conversion. A binary arithmetic unit would use a binary representation for each d_{-k}, for 10, and for 10^n. This conversion will be accurate within 2^{-p}, where p is the number of bits in the quotient. The division by 10^n will not be exact; we use the quotient as the binary equivalent of the decimal fraction and discard the remainder.

2.3   COMPUTER REPRESENTATIONS OF NUMBERS

2.3.1   Number Base

One of the major decisions in computer architecture of the 1940s was whether the arithmetic operands should be decimal (so as to avoid conversions and to be easily intelligible to the user) or binary (to obtain the ultimate in compactness of storage and economy of arithmetic). This battle has been fought and won by computer manufacturers. The decision could have been predicted more easily than it was in accordance with a somewhat cynical but realistic principle:

> Buyers of equipment will allow small differences in easily evaluated costs to outweigh massive differences in costs which are not easily evaluated.

To apply the principle, note that engineers will have no trouble pricing a decimal machine versus a binary machine, but users have a terrible time estimating the cost in programmer and user time adjusting to the consequences of a binary computer.

The authors have no real concern that decimal should have been chosen, but we believe the principle above will help one to foresee the eventual outcome of other issues.

2.3.2   Word Length Considerations

Given that numbers are to be represented in binary, we may ask how many positions should be reserved for representing a single number. In fact, that question cannot be answered alone, for there are other items than numbers to be stored in a computer memory. It is necessary to establish a length in bits which is also economical for storing computer instructions and is an integral multiple of the length in bits of a character representation. That length chosen is called the *word length* of the computer, "word" being noncommittal regarding the contents to be stored. Some word lengths of well-known machines, past and present, are given in Table 2.3.1.

Machine	Word length in bits	Equivalent decimal digits
I. A. S.	40	12
IBM 701, ERA 1103, IBM 704	36	10
TRANSAC 2000, CDC 1604	48	14
Burroughs 5500, 6700, 7700	48	14
CDC 6400, 6600, 7600	60	19
IBM 360/370	32	9
UNIVAC 1108	36	10
CDC 3300 ˇ	24	7
HP 2100, 3000	16	4.8
PDP-8	12	3.6

Table 2.3.1 Word length varies greatly among computers, and the resulting precision attainable in arithmetic operations varies accordingly. Many of the computers using short words have the capability of double precision, in which two words are used to represent each number.

While some of these seem excessive in length, the longer words permit two instructions per word, or can be much more favorable to floating-point representation. Rather than argue for some supposedly optimum word length, we note only that most modern computers distinguish a word length; and for reasons of compatibility with major producers, word length is more and more an integral multiple of 8. Our machine's word length is 32 bits.

2.3.3   Assigning Meaning to Bits in a Word

To distinguish individual bits in a word, it is convenient to number them serially. This may be done from left to right or right to left, but on a given machine should always be done the same way. Positions in the 360/370 word are numbered from 0 through 31 starting from the left.

Although not absolutely necessary, it is convenient to have a fixed position for the sign in a number representation and of the binary point in the word. The universal choice for sign is to put it in the leftmost bit. It is usual to consider the binary point to be between bits 0 and 1 (in which case only proper fractions can be represented), or to the right of the rightmost bit (in which case only integers can be represented). The choice between these options for the 360/370 is made for us by the way multiplication and division are implemented (as explained in Chapter 3) and leads to placing the point to the extreme right. Thus, we find that the value associated with bit position p is 2^{31-p}, where $0 < p \leq 31$, position 0 being reserved for the sign bit.

2.3.4   Binary Representation of Integers

To avoid the tedious writing of long strings of zeros and ones, we establish the representation of integers as it would be in an eight-bit word. It will extend without complication to other word lengths.

It is universal practice to use 0 in bit position zero to indicate a positive number is stored in the word, and a one to indicate a negative number. The method of representing positive integers is also universal, namely, to assign a value of 2^{q-1} to the qth position from the right (not including the sign position) and place a 1 or 0 in a position according as its value is or is not to be added in forming the value of the integer. These universal practices coincide precisely with the way one would expect to form the binary representation of a nonnegative number in which the sign is taken by default to be positive. That is, we extend the representation to the left by *padding* with zeros to conform to the word length of the machine in question and record that bit string in the word. Thus, we encounter nothing new in interpreting 00000111, 00100100, and 01111111 as integer representations of 7, 36, and 127, respectively. Note that the last of these is easily calculated as $2^7 - 1$ since adding one to the number causes a carry into the sign position, leaving all other positions zero.

Historically, there have been several distinct ways to represent negative numbers. Clearly, one possible way to change the sign of a number is to leave all its bits intact except the sign and to reverse the sign bit. This representation would yield 10000111, 10100100, and 11111111 as representations of -7, -36, and -127, respectively. This absolute value with sign was used in the IBM 704-709-7090-7094 series and is practiced in floating-point representations on the 360/370. It has two interesting characteristics. If zero is represented by 00000000, then its negative is represented by 10000000, yielding two distinct representations of zero. The sign of an addition can actually depend on the ordering of the summands, sometimes being "positive zero" and sometimes "negative zero." Such characteristics lead to interesting games for programmers to play, but cause more confusion than is usually admitted. Conversion of a program from one language to another or one machine to another is obviously complicated by such possibilities.

Another characteristic of the absolute-value-with-sign representation is that addition and subtraction are distinct operations. One could ask for a representation of negative numbers such that adding a negative number is accomplished by the addition algorithm. Fortunately there are such representations, allowing computers to be built with no subtraction hardware. Suppose that b is positive and one seeks a representation for $-b$ such that using the representations for b and $-b$ in an addition operation yields zero. If a zero is recorded in every position for which b has a one, and a one is recorded in every position for which b has a zero (this is called forming the *one's complement*), then the sum of b and this one's complement is not zero but is a word filled with ones. If one is added in the rightmost position of this sum and the leftmost carry is ignored (it would not fit in an eight-bit register), then the "positive" zero results.

Example

$$
\begin{array}{rr}
b & 01011001 \\
\text{One's complement} & 10100110 \\
\hline
 & 11111111 \\
 & +\ 1 \\
\hline
 & 1|00000000
\end{array}
$$

We conclude that 1 added to the one's complement of b (called the *two's complement* of b) shows promise as a representation for $-b$.

Examples for an eight-bit register

b	Representation of b	One's complement of b	Two's complement of b
12	00001100	11110011	11110100
0	00000000	11111111	00000000
127	01111111	10000000	10000001

Note that if the same rule of conversion is applied from the right column to the left column the correct representation for b is regained. There is no complication with two representations of zero, and there seems to be no need for a subtraction operation distinct from addition. Subtraction instead becomes a matter of forming the two's complement and adding.

The original von Neumann design used two's complement arithmetic. Some machine designers avoided it, but IBM changed to that representation with the IBM 360. The one's complement representation is used on Control Data Corporation machines to good effect, even though having two representations for zero may complicate programming. We shall not even concern ourselves with proving the intuitive conclusion that two's complement arithmetic leads to no incorrect computations if proper attention is paid to carry into and out of the sign position to detect numbers out of range. The one exceptional case that must be kept in mind is that for an eight-bit word, 10000000 is a valid representation of a negative number but an attempt to find its two's complement returns the same value. Addition of 01111111 followed by addition of 00000001 shows the number to be larger in magnitude by 1 than the largest positive number the word can represent. Regardless of word size, there is always one negative number which is too large for its magnitude to be representable.

2.3.5 Octal and Hexadecimal Representation

Writing down the contents of a word of 16 or more bits is tedious in binary notation. Some shorthand is essential. It is customary to group the bits of a word by threes (octal) or by fours (hexadecimal) and then to represent each group as a single character. These characters were given in Section 2.1. Thus, our shorthand representation of the twelve-bit string

$$110110011011$$

would be 6633 in octal and D9B in hexadecimal shorthand. Observe that this grouping and naming actually converts from base 2 to base 8 and base 16 representations, so that these representations are really something more than shorthand. Since the 360/370 systems favor base 16 by having word length a multiple of four, we present the argument for hexadecimal and satisfy ourselves with examining only the nonnegative case.

Consider marking off groups of four bits starting from the right in the representation of a nonnegative integer and let

$$b_{4k+3}b_{4k+2}b_{4k+1}b_{4k}$$

be the kth such group, where counting starts with $k = 0$. Then the contribution of these bits to the binary integer is

$$b_{4k+3} \cdot 2^{4k+3} + b_{4k+2} \cdot 2^{4k+2} + b_{4k+1} \cdot 2^{4k+1} + b_{4k} \cdot 2^{4k}$$
$$= (b_{4k+3} \cdot 2^3 + b_{4k+2} \cdot 2^2 + b_{4k+1} \cdot 2^1 + b_{4k}) \cdot 16^k$$
$$= h_k \cdot 16^k$$

where h_k is the hexadecimal digit represented in parentheses. Since this argument holds for each k, the sum over all such groups will have the same value as the binary representation. We note that in the leftmost such set of 4, the leftmost bit is a sign bit so that $b_{4k+3} = 0$ in this formulation.

2.3.6 The Arithmetic of Integers in Hexadecimal

In Section 2.1, we established a pattern of performing arithmetic in such a way as to separate the carry operation from the addition or multi-

plication in a given position. Rather than memorize addition and multiplication tables, we advise the programmer to start with that method.

Example. Multiply $+9BF3$ by $+AC2D$.

We convert single digits to decimal equivalents and rewrite the problem
as

			9	11	15	3	
			×10	12	2	13	
			117	143	195	39	
		18	22	30	6		
	108	132	180	36			
90	110	150	30				
	90	218	300	349	209	201	39
6	14	20	22	13	12	2	carry
	104	238	322	362	221	203	39
6	8	E	2	A	D	B	7

Example. Add the numbers whose machine representations are
7ABC4E65 and FFF3A8D9.

One may be able to convert digit by digit to decimal and form a
decimal sum in each digit position. We assume that this is too error prone,
so we write the sum as

7	10	11	12	4	14	6	5
+15	15	15	3	10	8	13	9
22	25	26	15	14	22	19	14
1	1			1	1		
23	26	26	15	15	23	19	14
7	A	A	F	F	7	3	E

The carry from the leftmost addition is lost, but that is proper because
there was a carry both into and out of the sign bit.

Example. Add numbers with machine representations 80000000 and
FFFFFFFF.

The first of these operands represents the most negative representable
number and the second represents -1. Again, trouble should be expected.
It is detected as a carry out of the sign position without a carry into it.

These examples illustrate a rule which covers overflow situations, namely
that if the carry condition into the sign position differs from the carry

condition out of it, then overflow (loss of significant digits on the left) will take place.

We have not given any example of multiplication by complement representation. Multiplication is accomplished by multiplying magnitudes (forming two's complements as necessary) and then, if this positive result should be negated, the two's complement of the result is formed.

2.3.7   Division in Hexadecimal

As with multiplication, we may limit ourselves to nonnegative operands. Even so, just as division in the decimal system requires guessing the digits of the quotient one at a time, division in hexadecimal also requires guessing. The complicating factor is that the intuition for guessing in hexadecimal is not developed and also that multiplication in hexadecimal is more tedious than in decimal. In debugging, it is usually easiest and most accurate to verify division by adding the remainder to the product of the divisor and quotient and comparing the result to the dividend. It is this procedure we recommend rather than the more complex, brute-force division.

2.3.8   The Arithmetic Economy of Binary Representation

Logical as the binary representation may be, it would never have overwhelmed the reluctance of human beings to depart from the decimal system without a distinct advantage in computer design and manufacture. There are two aspects to consider: economy of storage and economy of arithmetic.

It takes four bits to represent a decimal digit and these in decimal serve to represent ten distinct numbers, although they are capable of representing 16 in binary. Suppose we consider a number representation in which a word holds nine decimal digits with sign. Each word would thus require 37 bits. With 30 bits, one can represent integers as large as $2^{30} - 1 > 10^9$. Therefore 31 bits are as effective in binary representation of integers as 37 bits are in decimal. This saving in every word of memory and every register of the processing unit has been a heavy burden for decimal enthusiasts to bear.

Another advantage of binary representation is in the simplicity of its arithmetic. Addition and multiplication by single digits have the simple tabular definition shown below:

+	0	1		×	0	1
0	0	1		0	0	0
1	1	10		1	0	1

Multiplication of many-bit operands requires initialization of a total to zero, writing the multiplier with units position coincident with that of the total, and then shifting the multiplicand so that its units position coincides with that of each 1 in the multiplier (shifting by zero the first time if the multiplier is odd) and, in that position, adding the shifted multiplicand to the total. An example is given below. Decimal multiplication of two integers by successive additions with a nine-digit multiplier could require 81 additions, each of some complexity. On the other hand, at most 30 binary additions would be required in binary multiplication of the same two integers.

Example

Multiplicand	10111001
Multiplier	10110101
Summand 5	10111001
Summand 4	10111001
Summand 3	10111001
Summand 2	10111001
Summand 1	10111001
Total	1000001011001101

2.3.9   Floating-Point Representation

Given any base b representation of a nonzero number, we can approximate it in the form

$$\pm 0 \cdot d_{-1} d_{-2} \cdots d_{-p} \cdot b^q$$

$$1 \leq d_{-1} < b \quad \text{and} \quad 0 \leq d_{-j} < b \quad \text{for} \quad 1 < j \leq p$$

Zero is a special case, and is represented by a word of zeros. Thus

$$123.19_{10} = 0.12319_{10} \cdot 10^{+3}$$
$$0.000A3FD_{16} = 0.A3FD_{16} \cdot 16^{-3}$$
$$-11111.011_2 = -0.11111011_2 \cdot 2^5$$

Our purpose is to pack the fraction to the right of the point (called the *mantissa*), its sign, the exponent of the base, and its sign all into one word in the sense that, given the binary representation, we can determine each. The advantage of doing so is a dramatic range of magnitudes of numbers which can be represented with suitable accuracy in one word.

The method is to dedicate a portion of the word to representing the mantissa, and another portion to the exponent which is applied to the base. For a particular computer, the base b is implicit in the hardware, and is not represented explicitly in the floating-point representation. Since all methods are similar but differ in detail, we shall specialize here to the representation used in the 360/370 systems.

Even though the 360/370 systems are basically binary machines, their floating-point representation base is hexadecimal. The use of bits is as follows:

Bit positions	Contents
0	Sign of the mantissa (0 means positive)
1–7	$64 + q$ in binary
8–31	6 hexadecimal digits for the mantissa

Some examples will facilitate reading such representations (Table 2.3.2).

Hexadecimal word	Binary $64 + q$	Decimal $64 + q$	q	Sign of mantissa	Number
43ABCDEF	1000011	67	3	+	$.ABCDEF \cdot 16^3$
8F194E2A	0001111	15	−49	−	$-.194E2A \cdot 16^{-49}$
41100000	1000001	65	1	+	$.100000 \cdot 16^1$
BC71A3CE	0111100	60	−4	−	$.71A3CE \cdot 16^{-4}$
7FFFFFFF	1111111	127	63	+	$.FFFFFF \cdot 16^{63}$
00100000	0000000	0	−64	+	$.100000 \cdot 16^{-64}$
00000000	Special case				$.000000$

Table 2.3.2 These examples illustrate the decoding of floating-point representation. The last three examples represent the largest number, the smallest nonzero number, and zero in this representation. Conversion to decimal still requires conversion of both the mantissa and the power of 16 by which it is multiplied.

PROBLEMS

1. Given the noncanonical numbers shown, find the canonical representation for each in the same base:

a. $5, 7, 0, 2, 4_3$ d. $17, 3, 6, 12, 19_{14}$

b. $7, 10, 5, 1, 2_4$ e. $8, 2, 5, 10, 3_2$

c. $1, 6, 8, 4, 11_9$ f. $25, 18, 7, 10, 19_{16}$

2. In a poker game with binary chips, the winner raked in 75 chips worth one cent, 48 worth two cents, 25 worth four cents, and three worth eight cents. What is the canonical binary representation of his take?

3. Perform the following arithmetic using noncanonical notation before finally converting the result to canonical representation in the same base:

a. 645_8
304_8
$+162_8$

b. $7AB9_{16}$
$\times 38D4_{16}$

c. 325014_6
-240535_6

4. Convert the following decimal integers to canonical binary representation:

a.	141	c.	512	e.	675
b.	78	d.	357	f.	91

5. Convert the following binary integers to canonical decimal representation.

a.	1110101101	c.	110111110100	e.	110011001100
b.	10110110111	d.	101010101010	f.	100110011111

6. While pan scales may be hard to manufacture in your study, it would be relatively easy to cut and mark a set of rods of lengths 1, 2, 4, 8, 16, 32, 64, . . . in. In this case the weight of the rod would be proportional to its value. Comment on the portability of a set of measuring sticks for base 2 versus a corresponding set for base 10 measurements where the maximum length to be measured is 999 in.

7. Use the weighing procedure in Figure 2.2.1 to convert 143_{10} to a base 5 representation.

8. Comment on the assertion that units of measure as evidenced by a tape measure are already partially binary. How would you mark a tape if it were to be read in binary? What about liquid measure? Is there any evidence of binary in the English system of units?

9. Assuming 12-bit word length and two's complement representation:

(a) Find the internal bit pattern for each of the following decimal integers:

$$+79 \qquad +1 \qquad -487$$
$$-79 \qquad -1 \qquad -1024$$

(b) What is the most positive integer representable using 12-bit word length? What is the most negative?

(c) Give the hexadecimal representation for each result in part (a).

10. There is an easy way to show that $\frac{1}{3}, \frac{1}{5}, \frac{1}{6}, \frac{1}{7}, \frac{1}{9}, \frac{1}{10}, \ldots$ all have non-terminating binary representations. Guess at a rule covering these observations and try to prove it. What relation might this situation have to binary banking?

11. Assuming 16-bit word length and two's complement representation, what decimal integers are represented by the following hexadecimal sequences:

a.	7F25	c.	FACE	e.	BADD
b.	D0A4	d.	47B5	f.	4522

12. Assuming 16-bit word length and two's complement representation, perform the indicated integer arithmetic:

a.	2BF7	b.	CE49	c.	09A4
	×95A2		+BEEF		+9BC3

Would any of these operations lead to invalid results on a machine with 16-bit registers? If so, why?

13. It is of value to devise easy decimal approximations to numbers which are powers of two. This facilitates checking for reasonable results. A key relation to remember for such cases is $2^{10} \simeq 1024$, where $\simeq$ means "approximately equals." For rough estimates, one can assume 1000 and 1024 are close. This estimate can also be written as $10^{0.3} \simeq 2$. Using these guides and the example

$$2^{15} \simeq (10^{0.3})^{15} = 10^{4.5} = (10)^{1/2} \cdot 10^4 \quad \text{or} \quad 2^{15} = 2^{10} \cdot 2^5 \simeq 32 \cdot 10^3$$

make estimates for the following values:

a. 2^{12} _____   c. 16^4 _____   e. 2^{20} _____

b. 2^{-7} _____   d. 2^{31} _____   f. 16^{-32} _____

14. Given the rules for representing floating-point numbers on the IBM 360/370 (see Section 2.3), how many hexadecimal strings of length eight should be recognized as representing zero? Which of these is preferred for arithmetic, and why?

15. Find internal floating-point representations for the following decimal numbers:

a. 5   b. $\frac{3}{8}$ c. -1.125 d. $\frac{3}{64}$

Chapter 3

An Evolutionary Introduction to Computer Structure

3.1 A RATIONALE

A prime objective in this text is to develop an understanding of the value of various machine features to the user. The technique is to start with a model (which we call BAREBONZ) possessing a small set of instructions and a minimal set of registers (A, B, C, and E), each of which is dedicated to a particular usage. We demonstrate a principal use of each instruction, covering enough examples to suggest that this model is capable of any aspect of binary integer arithmetic and has some facility in character manipulation. The value of being able to compute with such a stripped-down model is shown by considering the multiplicity of minicomputers already installed. In this regard, it seems particularly appropriate to recognize the existence of subprogram linkages which are simpler and more economical than the standard 360/370 linkage and still adequate for many tasks. We alleviate the complexities of looping through a sequence of instructions for a sequence of values of a parameter by introducing index registers in BAREBONZ II (in Section 3.6), their sole function being to modify addresses in tagged instructions. Once we have mastered this use of the registers, we will find—as programmers did historically—that registers adequate for indexing can be valuable in other ways as well.

Initially, instructions are written in numeric form. The tedium of numeric coding is relieved rather early by a symbolic format for coding which is then easily translated manually to numeric form for recording in machine-acceptable form. When machine translation is introduced, the format of symbolic instructions is kept consistent with 360/370 assembler language; but the symbolic format used is only as complex as needed for BAREBONZ II, thus yielding a translator which can be described adequately in a few pages. As new instructions demand it, we extend the notation for symbolic instruction representation.

As one might expect, this presentation of machine concepts is historical in spirit, starting from a model roughly equivalent to the first stored-program electronic calculator of von Neumann. It is intended to give the opportunity of actual computation almost immediately. It will also introduce frustration, for the machine features that early users desired but did not have will be missing on your model too. With a simple model and early computer experience as a foundation, we believe that more elaborate models will be appreciated for the convenient features they offer. These convenient features, of course, contribute substantially to the complexity of a modern computer, and are more easily understood once motivation is supplied. Similarly, starting with a simple translator model enables us to pinpoint those extensions of capability which complicate the assembler and to defer them until the need motivates acceptance.

There is no BAREBONZ computer. To get the effect of executing a BAREBONZ program, we utilize a portion of a host machine in an extremely limited way. BAREBONZ memory is a segment of the memory of the host machine. The address in the host machine of location zero in BAREBONZ memory is the base address from which all BARE-BONZ addresses are measured. Thus the BAREBONZ address is simply a displacement from the base address in the host machine. The control unit of the host machine acts in place of the control unit for BAREBONZ, so that the addresses it uses are those of the host machine. For memory references to get operands, the control unit combines the BAREBONZ address from an instruction with the base address held in register C to calculate the host-machine address. For instruction fetching, the control unit takes from its instruction location counter the host-machine address of its next instruction. These distinctions between BAREBONZ and host-machine addresses should be of little concern until subprogram linkages are studied in Section 3.5. At that point addressing will have been analyzed in more detail.

3.2 THE COMPONENTS OF BAREBONZ AND THEIR INTERRELATIONS

3.2.1   Justification of the BAREBONZ Model

Most of the essential concepts concerning even the most complex modern computer can be explained with respect to a very simple model. There is a distinct advantage in such an approach as long as the student finds that everything he learns about the model applies without change to his objective of mastering the programming of the electronic marvel in his immediate future. We take that marvel to be an IBM 360 or 370, and extract from this set of computers a model which has just enough features to qualify as a general-purpose stored-program computer. We call this model BAREBONZ. Programs written for BAREBONZ will execute on any 360/370.

It should not be surprising that BAREBONZ shows a considerable structural resemblance to some of the earlier machines. While our purpose is to keep the design simple for pedagogic purposes, early designers sought simplicity to conform to the electronic and systems technologies of the day. It is a tribute to their profound insights that modern computers employ the same fundamental concepts and differ mainly in speed, reliability, capacity, and special components to simplify oft-repeated tasks. Thus, one may consider the following overview of BAREBONZ to give a reasonable appreciation of von Neumann's Institute for Advanced Study (IAS) machine which is so thoroughly documented in "John von Neumann— Collected Works." †

3.2.2   The Major Components

We distinguish five components essential to the concepts in a stored-program computer. The first, called *memory,* is an information storage device. The next three components all are explained with respect to memory. The *reader* is a device which generates signals by the scanning of marks (symbols) recorded on an external medium. These signals are transmitted via a *channel* to memory where they cause an electromagnetic recording of equivalent marks in memory. The process of scanning, transmitting, and recording in memory is called *input.* The *writer* is a device which accepts signals, generated by the scanning of marks in memory and transmitted via channels to the writer, and converts these into equivalent marks on its external medium. The process of scanning memory, trans-

† A. W. Taub, ed., "John von Neumann—Collected Works," Vol. 5. Pergamon, New York, 1963.

mitting, and recording on an external medium is called *output*. The *processor* is a device which can copy information from memory into its own storage, operate on it to obtain new information (as one might use a scratch pad), and deposit the results in memory. The last component, called *control,* is there to cause each of the other four components to function when and as it should. In a stored-program computer, the key concept of control is that the control unit functions as directed by instructions which are found in memory together with the data on which the instructions operate. Stored in this way, instructions can themselves be modified or replaced during computation just as data can. These rudiments of structure are illustrated in the block diagram of Figure 3.2.1. A stored-program com-

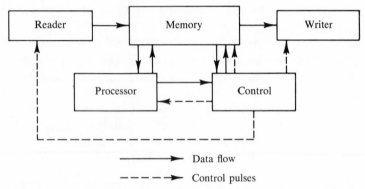

Figure 3.2.1   The initial BAREBONZ machine with data and control paths.

puter is put into execution by directing the control unit to a particular starting instruction in memory and impulsing it to execute. Execution is the repetition of a sequence of cycles each of which (except the last) has the following parts:

1. fetch and decode the instruction,
2. perform the indicated operation,
3. locate the next instruction.

Some instructions may call for input, some for processing, and some for output. Eventually, a halt instruction should be encountered which, of course, will have no next instruction. Our first job is to understand how numbers or instructions are found in memory, how instructions can be interpreted, and how the control unit sequences from one instruction to the next. We shall also be interested in a set of operations the processor can perform. These ideas are all independent of the input and output devices, so we shall concentrate first on memory, processor, instruction format, and control unit.

3.2.3   Memory

The memory of BAREBONZ may be thought of as a string of $2^{15} = 32,768$ bit positions, numbered 0 to 32,767 from left to right. However, it is much more economical and convenient to think of it as segmented into nonoverlapping substrings of bits which are a convenient length for representing numbers and instructions. These substrings are called *words*. In the 360/370 they are 32 bits in length. The BAREBONZ memory has 1024 of these, each beginning on a bit position divisible by 32.

Computers often represent a broad range of characters including letters, punctuation, digits, and mathematical symbols as well as numbers and instructions. The 360/370 use a generous eight bits to represent one character, and thus four such character representations can be packed into one word. Eight-bit strings of storage beginning at bit positions divisible by 8 are known as *bytes*. The bytes in memory are sequentially numbered from 0 to 4095. The number of a byte is called its *address*. It is equal to the position number of its leftmost bit divided by eight.

To designate a byte, we give its address. To designate a word, we give the address of its leftmost byte. There are times when a half word (a 16-bit substring beginning on a bit position divisible by 16) or a double word (a 64-bit substring beginning on a bit position divisible by 64) is the appropriate segment of memory to reference. In these cases as well, the address given is that of the leftmost byte. In BAREBONZ, almost every memory reference is to a word. These ideas and definitions are partly illustrated in Figure 3.2.2, in which it is to be understood that each byte consists of eight bit positions.

It can be very awkward to represent a segment of memory by one unbroken string of bits. Since they are considered somewhat independently, it is convenient to write successive instructions on successive lines of a

Figure 3.2.2   This graphical representation of the structure of the memory of the BAREBONZ machine illustrates addressing by byte address, and addressing of a word by using the address of its leftmost byte.

page and to understand that they appear as consecutive words in memory. This we will do.

3.2.4 The Processor

The processor unit on a modern computer must be capable of performing almost any computation imaginable, including character handling, logical operations, and many others. We purposefully restrict the BARE-BONZ model to a processor capable of integer arithmetic.

The BAREBONZ processor has two 32-bit registers named A and B which receive information from memory, provide operands to the processor, and receive results to be deposited in memory. The addition instruction, for example, names one of A or B as holding an operand to which is to be added the number in a memory word whose address the instruction also provides. The result is left in the register named in the addition instruction. The store instruction names a register whose contents are to replace those of a memory word whose address appears in the instruction. The rule for most of the BAREBONZ instructions is that an instruction provides an operation, a register, and a memory location.

Multiplication of two 31-bit numbers (the sign takes one bit) yields a result which may have as many as 62 nonzero bits. To hold such a result, the arithmetic unit forms one double-word register from A and B which we shall designate as AB. The coupling of A and B puts A on the left so that the 30 most significant bits of the result are in A and the 32 least significant bits are in B. For multiplication, the multiplier is understood to be in register B, the memory address of the instruction provides the multiplicand, and the register named in the instruction is A, signifying the high-order part of the result register. With these few observations about instruction components, we are in position to describe their arrangement in an instruction word.

3.2.5 Instruction Format

The 32-bit instruction is conveniently represented as a sequence of eight hexadecimal digits numbered 0 through 7 from the left. The instructions of BAREBONZ all conform to one of the two formats in Figure 3.2.3. Note that hexdigits 0 and 1 always constitute the operation code, hexdigit 2 with only one exception gives a register name, and hexdigit 3 (in BAREBONZ) is always zero.

When hexdigit 4 is nonzero, it names a register (we have chosen it to be C) which contains an address to be used in the same manner as a telephone area code. The address is the location in the host machine

Memory reference instructions

0 1	2	3	4	5 6 7
Operation code	Register name	0 †	Base register ‡	Memory location relative to base register contents

Instructions making no memory reference

0 1	2	3	4	5 6 7
Operation code	Register name	0 †	0	Instruction parameter

Figure 3.2.3   There are two formats for BAREBONZ instructions.

memory of the byte which has zero for its BAREBONZ address. This address is called a *base address* since the memory operand of the instruction is located by a displacement from it as given in hexdigit 5–7. The addressing scheme for the IBM 360/370 is discussed more fully in Section 3.4.5. When hexdigit 4 is zero, the parameter in hexdigits 5–7 has relevance without modification and in BAREBONZ represents a number of digit positions by which a binary operand is to be shifted.

3.2.6   Control

The BAREBONZ control unit makes use of three special registers. Their names and functions are as follows:

(1)   Instruction Address Counter (IAC)—on completion of one instruction, holds the address from which the next instruction is to be taken.

(2)   Current Instruction Register (CIR)—receives and decodes the next instruction to be executed.

(3)   Exit Register (E)—receives an address to which instruction sequencing can be returned.

We can now draw a more detailed block diagram of the BAREBONZ machine to include these features, as shown in Figure 3.2.4. It makes some very definite assignments of registers for particular functions, placing A

---

† Eventually, hexdigit 3 will be used in many instructions to designate another register which will play a part in the execution. One way in which this register may be used is shown in Section 3.6 where index registers are introduced.

‡ Although any general register may serve as base, we specialize for BAREBONZ instructions permitting only register C as base.

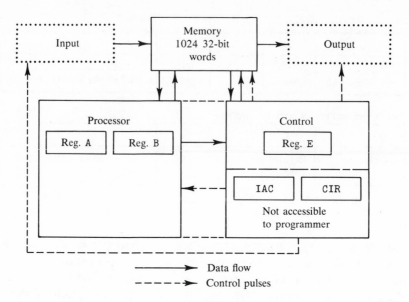

Figure 3.2.4 The expanded diagram of BAREBONZ shows the registers in the processor and control units. The IAC and the CIR are not directly accessible to the programmer.

and B in the processor, and placing IAC, CIR, and E in the control unit. Although these assignments are correct for BAREBONZ, we should anticipate that in the 360/370 all registers are equally accessible to the processor unit and the control unit. This intimate sharing of registers between these units is indicated by dashed lines joining these units. The input and output units are drawn with dotted lines because our primary goal in studying the BAREBONZ machine is to understand the interaction of the memory, processor, and control units. We will consider next how these registers we have just assigned to the control unit are used.

When an instruction has just been completed, the IAC address provides the address from which the next instruction is copied into the CIR. Then the IAC is incremented by 4 and the instruction in the CIR is decoded. We have seen above that hex digits 0 and 1 together constitute an operation code. This code determines how the rest of the instruction is to be interpreted and causes control impulses to effect execution. When an instruction (except a halt instruction) is completed, the control unit goes back to the IAC to obtain the address of the next instruction and the cycle repeats.

Among the instructions of any stored-program computer are some which break the pattern of finding the next instruction just after the current one in memory (thus branching to a secondary sequence located elsewhere in memory). They are called *branch* instructions and, to accomplish this branching, they replace the IAC address by one computed from the current instruction. Should it be desired to return later to an instruction following the branch, the address of that instruction, called the *return* address, is placed in register E before the branch occurs. When return is to be made, that address serves as an exit address from the secondary sequence. A schematic of these control actions is shown in Figure 3.2.5.

The person who is looking ahead may anticipate the need for special care in the use of register E. He may need to save one exit address (which he must have later) during temporary use of register E for such branching and return. This will be explored more fully when we study subprograms in Section 3.5.

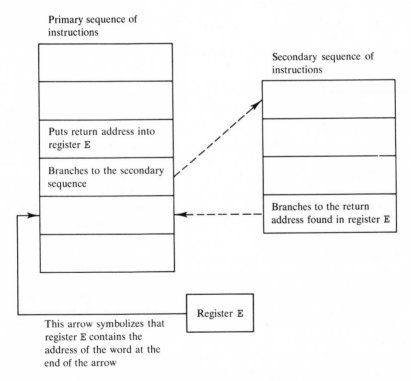

Figure 3.2.5 The schematic of branching to a secondary sequence of instructions shows that register E contains the address for the return to the primary sequence.

3.3 THE INSTRUCTION SET FOR BAREBONZ

3.3.1 A Complete Table of BAREBONZ Instructions

Every instruction in the repertoire of BAREBONZ is listed in Table 3.3.1, which also provides a symbolic description of the effect of the instruction on memory and register contents. The remainder of this section is devoted to explaining the notation in the table, and both symbolic and machine-recognizable representations of instructions. In the next section, the BAREBONZ instructions are classified as to their principal uses, and several examples are provided. The column headed "Type" in the table is not expected to have meaning until its CC entries are explained under Looping Control, and the RX or RS entries are distinguished in discussion of the shifting instructions. Meantime, the instructions can be used with confidence as long as the following temporary conventions are observed:

1. Hex digit 3 is 0 to signify no indexing.
2. Hex digit 4 is C for RX instructions.
3. Hex digit 4 is 0 for RS instructions.

3.3.2 Notation for Instruction Explanations

1. Use of m in Memory Reference and Shifts

We take the symbol m in the instruction explanations to symbolize the three-hex-digit number in hex positions 5–7 of the instruction being decoded. For RX instructions it is an address relative to the beginning of BAREBONZ memory. In the conversion and scaling instructions, m (which is still taken from hex positions 5–7 of the instruction) symbolizes an amount of shift, not a memory reference. This is our first example of an *immediate* operand, which is an operand carried in the instruction, using it rather than in a location designated by the instruction.

2. The Contents Operator, ( )

(a) Enclosing a register name in parentheses forms a symbol for denoting the *contents* of that register rather than the name of that register.

(b) Similarly, enclosing a memory address in parentheses forms a symbol for the *contents* of the four consecutive bytes beginning in that location.

3. The Bit-String Selector, i : j

A bit string is a sequence of 1's and 0's. We can denote a bit string in

Operation mnemonic	Operation code, hex	Register or mask	Type	Explanation
Integer arithmetic and data copying				
L	58	A	RX	$A \leftarrow (m)$
L	58	B	RX	$B \leftarrow (m)$
ST	50	A	RX	$m \leftarrow (A)$
ST	50	B	RX	$m \leftarrow (B)$
A	5A	A	RX,CC	$A \leftarrow (A) + (m)$
A	5A	B	RX,CC	$B \leftarrow (B) + (m)$
S	5B	A	RX,CC	$A \leftarrow (A) - (m)$
S	5B	B	RX,CC	$B \leftarrow (B) - (m)$
M	5C	A	RX	$AB \leftarrow (B)*(m)$
D	5D	A	RX	$B \leftarrow q; A \leftarrow r$ where $q*(m) + r = (AB)_{old}$, and $\|r\| < \|(m)\|$, sign $(r) =$ sign $(AB)_{old}$ if $r \neq 0$
Linking with subprograms				
L	58	E	RX	$E \leftarrow (m)$
ST	50	E	RX	$m \leftarrow (E)$
LA	41	E	RX	$E \leftarrow m + (C)$
BAL	45	E	RX	$E \leftarrow (IAC); IAC \leftarrow m + (C)$
STH	40	A	RX	$m_{0:15} \leftarrow (A)_{16:31}$
STH	40	B	RX	$m_{0:15} \leftarrow (B)_{16:31}$
Conversion and scaling				
SRDL	8C	A	RS	$AB_{m:63} \leftarrow (AB)_{0:63-m}; AB_i \leftarrow 0 \ (0 \leq i < m)$
SLDL	8D	A	RS	$AB_{0:63-m} \leftarrow (AB)_{m:63}; AB_i \leftarrow 0 \ (i > 63 - m)$
SRDA	8E	A	RS,CC	$AB_{m+1:63} \leftarrow (AB)_{1:63-m};$ $AB_i \leftarrow (AB)_0 \ (0 \leq i \leq m)$
SLDA	8F	A	RS,CC	$AB_{1:63-m} \leftarrow (AB)_{m+1:63}; AB_i \leftarrow 0 \ (i < 63 - m)$ $AB_0 \leftarrow (AB)_0$
Looping and decision making				
BC	47	M	RX	No effect if condition specified by M is not met; branch to address m if it is

Termination of program

The instruction to terminate—that is, to exit from the user program—is a variation on the BC instruction which needs to be used before the BC instruction has been analyzed. We choose to give the hexadecimal form of the termination instruction

$$47F0E000$$

and for the present to explain only that this instruction causes the address in register E to be substituted for that in the IAC. This causes the next instruction to be taken from the address provided to the user program in register E as a starting condition.

Table 3.3.1   The initial instruction set for BAREBONZ.

a register or in memory by using the contents operator; for example, (A) and (m) are bit strings of length 32 contained in register A and in word m of memory, respectively. To specify other strings we need a bit-string subscript.

(a) The leftmost bit in a string has index 0. Applying a bounds subscript of the form $i : j$ to any bit string of length greater than j forms a symbol for the substring beginning with the ith bit and ending with the jth bit, where $i \leq j$. A subscript of i is interpreted as $i : i$, and refers to the ith bit in the string. Note that (m) and $(m)_{0:31}$ have identical meanings.

(b) We have stated above that (m) stands for a bit string of length 32. So $(m)_{i:j}$ has not yet been defined for $j > 31$. If $j > 31$, then we define $(m)_{i:j}$ to be the bit string in memory beginning at the ith position beyond $(m)_0$ and ending at the jth.

(c) We also use these selectors to denote fields of a destination operand; for example, $A_{3:17}$ is used to denote the bit locations 3–17 of register A.

Examples. Assume the double-word register AB contains the hex number

$$0\ 1\ 2\ 3\ 4\ 5\ 6\ 7\ 8\ 9\ A\ B\ C\ D\ E\ F$$

and that bytes with addresses 102–109 have hex contents

$$0\ 8\ 1\ 9\ 2\ A\ 3\ B\ 4\ C\ 5\ D\ 6\ E\ 7\ F$$

Then

$$(A) = 0\ 1\ 2\ 3\ 4\ 5\ 6\ 7_{16}$$
$$(AB)_{30:34} = 11100_2$$
$$(AB)_{56:63} = (B)_{24:31} = 11101111_2$$
$$(103) = 192A3B4C_{16}$$
$$(102)_{27:35} = 110110100_2$$

4. The Assignment Operator, $\leftarrow$

The operator has two operands, P_l and P_v, and is written $P_l \leftarrow P_v$. P_l is a location (memory or register), and P_v is a value, so that the following forms might be used:

    $A \leftarrow (m)$ register A receives the contents of m
    $A \leftarrow 3$ register A receives the value 3
    $m \leftarrow (B)$ word m receives the contents of register B

In each case, the location receiving information is named on the left, and the value being copied is named on the right.

5. The Absolute-Value Operator $|$ $|$ and the Operator, sign(   )

For any numerical quantity X,

$$
\begin{array}{lll}
\text{if } X > 0, & \text{then } |X| = X & \text{and}\quad \text{sign}\,(X) = 1 \\
\text{if } X < 0, & \text{then } |X| = -X & \text{and}\quad \text{sign}\,(X) = -1 \\
\text{if } X = 0, & \text{then } |X| = 0 & \text{and}\quad \text{sign}\,(X) = 0
\end{array}
$$

Examples:

$$
\begin{array}{ll}
|3| = 3 & \text{sign}(3) = 1 \\
-2| = 2 & \text{sign}(-2) = -1 \\
|0| = 0 & \text{sign}(0) = 1
\end{array}
$$

6. Entries in the Type Column of Table 3.3.1

The condition-code register, denoted by CC, will be discussed in the section on control instructions where looping is introduced. The majority of instructions in BAREBONZ are RX instructions, and in BAREBONZ we always use these instructions to refer to memory, using register C to hold a base address. Thus we will use a zero in hex position 4 for shift instructions and a C in hex position 4 for RX instructions.

3.3.3   External Representation of Information

A BAREBONZ numeric program must be written so that each line of the program has a three-hex-digit address, and to its right an eight-hex-digit word to be placed in that address. The word may be an instruction or a data item. A conventional way to record this information in machine-readable form is to punch one card for each line of the program page, with standard columns for that line's address and for its corresponding word. The BAREBONZ system expects information in the format given below:

Columns	Contents
1–3	Hexadecimal address of location *l*
5–12	Hexadecimal word to be deposited in location *l*
14–80	Comments

The entire BAREBONZ memory is set to zero before any cards are read. As a card is read its word is deposited into memory in the location specified by the address in columns 1–3. If there are several cards with the same address in columns 1–3, the last one to be read will determine the final contents of the word.

The final card associated with your use of the computer should provide the BAREBONZ address of the first instruction to be executed. It is recognized as the first input data card which is blank in its first four columns. The starting address is punched in columns 10–12 of that card. Once registers C and E have been set appropriately, the program is put into execution.

The execution of a BAREBONZ program will yield an output page on which are printed the contents of the cards submitted, followed by a simple printout in hexadecimal (called a *hexadecimal dump*) of every location in BAREBONZ memory. These locations will be printed at eight words per line, except that any line having all eight words equal to zero is not printed.

Warning—an incorrect count in hexadecimal which leaves a word of zeros where an instruction was intended will cause trouble, for no valid instruction has 00 as its operation code.

The deck must be preceded by control cards which provide accounting information to the system and initiate BAREBONZ service. The particular nature of these varies from one installation to another and must be provided by the instructor.

3.3.4 Symbolic Representation of Instructions

When instruction sequences are written directly as numerical words to be interpreted by the machine, the programmer must mix his concern about the nature of a procedure with the "housekeeping" of assigning locations to instructions and data, and of remembering a table of operation codes. He can separate these concerns by first writing the program with instructions in symbolic form and then translating to numeric form in a separate step, a practice which appears in von Neumann's original papers. With judicious choice of mnemonic symbols, he can make his program far easier to understand in its symbolic form than in the numeric form derived from it.

Symbolic location names are assigned to the initial instruction of the program and to every instruction or data item named in the address portion of another instruction. It is good programming practice to assign a symbolic name to each line which places a data item (constant) in memory. We assume that words (whether instructions or data) which are written on consecutive lines of a programming page appear consecutively in memory. When instructions are written symbolically in this way, the assignment of a numeric address to one symbol determines all other addresses so that the translation to numeric form is trivial.

BAREBONZ numeric program		Symbolic location	Operation mnemonic	Register	Hex digit 3	Hex digit 4	Symbolic BAREBONZ address	Comments
000	58B0C010	BEGIN	L	B	0	C	RATE	
004	5CA0C014		M	A	0	C	HRS	
008	50B0C018		ST	B	0	C	PAY	Store PAY in its reserved location
00C	47F0E000	EXIT	DC				X'47F0E000'	Exit from program
010	00000002	RATE	DC				X'00000002'	Hourly rate = 2
014	00000028	HRS	DC				X'00000028'	Hours worked = 40
018	00000000	PAY	DC.				X'00000000'	Constant reserves location for PAY
000			END				BEGIN	

Program 3.3.1 For this program the symbolic instructions have been translated to numeric instructions, which appear on the left in the form of a BAREBONZ program. Symbolic representation of instructions is for explanatory purposes. It is printed on the output as punched but contributes nothing to program execution.

Program 3.3.1 is a brief program which illustrates the convenience of the symbolic representation of the numeric code. This program multiplies RATE and HRS to obtain PAY, and we assume the first instruction is stored in location 000. As can be seen from the BAREBONZ numeric program, the first three instructions have 0 in hex position 3 (no indexing), and C in hex position 4 (providing a base). These instructions (L, M, and ST) are listed in Table 3.3.1, and each requires a specific action from the computer. Program 3.3.1 has some unexplained features, however. The four lines preceding END are reserved for data, and the column headings are not directly applicable. For these lines, the operation mnemonic column has an entry DC, which means "define constant." This identifies the line as a *pseudoinstruction,* a line on a coding form which provides information used in translation but which does not ordinarily represent a machine instruction (our representation of the termination instruction by a pseudoinstruction is a temporary expedient). The pertinent facts for a data item are symbolic location, which appears in the column of that heading, and the item itself which is conventionally placed in the symbolic BAREBONZ address column. The constant is enclosed in single quote marks, and denoted as hexadecimal by the X which precedes it. The first of these DC's is the exit instruction; and, as is mentioned in Table 3.3.1, this instruction is temporarily being used in numeric form without explanation. Even though we have chosen to represent it as a hexadecimal data item, it will be interpreted as an instruction just because its address will appear in the IAC (when the ST operation is completed), at which time it causes control to return to BAREBONZ.

Another pseudoinstruction has the operation mnemonic END, and this is used to tell the translator (whether mechanical or human) that no more translation is needed. The symbolic BAREBONZ address for this pseudoinstruction must name the location of the first instruction to be executed (BEGIN in the example).

Program 3.3.1 can be executed on any IBM 360 or 370 which has installed the BAREBONZ system. For BAREBONZ, however, we must remember that the symbolic instructions are only aids to programming. The deck as submitted consists of the cards shown in Program 3.3.2 (and the control cards for your class). The output of the program consists of the hexadecimal record of the portion of memory used by the program.

```
000   58B0C010
004   5CA0C014
008   50B0C018
00C   47F0E000                        BAREBONZ card deck
010   00000002
014   00000028
018   00000000
      000
```

Hexadecimal record of memory used:

000 58B0C010 5CA0C014 50B0C018 47F0E000
00000002 00000028 00000050 00000000

Program 3.3.2   The printout of a BAREBONZ program consists of the instructions as submitted in the card deck, and the hexadecimal record of the portion of memory used as it appears after execution.

3.4   FUNCTIONAL ANALYSIS OF INSTRUCTIONS

3.4.1   Terminating Computation

The one aspect common to all programs one writes (except for those which function continuously, such as operating systems) is that there must be some way to stop. The word *stop* is used in a relative sense here for, even though the execution of a user's program is completed, it is usual that the processor should continue on other workload. What one should expect is that he relinquishes the processor to serve other purposes.

User programs are not in direct control of the machine but are put into execution by a supervisory program. When BAREBONZ programs are initiated, the supervisor first deposits a base address in register C and an exit address in register E. If the program does not destroy the address in register E, it will be there at termination time, and a branch to the address in register E will relinquish control to the supervisor. An appropriate exit instruction in hexadecimal is

47F0E000

This single instruction constitutes a complete do-nothing program, the shortest BAREBONZ program that one can write. Since one-instruction do-nothing programs are of little practical interest, it will be best to defer machine use until some arithmetic instructions are available.

If register E is subject to modification by a user program, then the exit address provided by the supervisor must be stored in memory before being replaced in E. Relinquishing the processor then requires restoring the exit address to register E before execution of the exit instruction, 47F0E000.

3.4.2   Integer Arithmetic

Each arithmetic operation requires just one instruction, but it is usual that one or more instructions are required to get an operand in place. It may be necessary to store the result in memory; if so, that will also require at least one instruction. Addition and subtraction are so similar that the two can be covered in one example. Multiplication and division have to be analyzed separately. In every case, we will make the assumption (which would demand careful consideration in a program) that the operands and the result are each representable as one-word binary integers; that is,

$$-2^{31} \leq \text{operands, result} < 2^{31}$$

Otherwise, special care must be taken not to lose the most significant part of the answer by overflow (losing bits by carry off the left end) or by getting a full answer in AB but failing to store the most significant part. Such matters are considered in Section 3.4.4.

Addition (or Subtraction)

The operation may be accomplished in register A or B. We explain in terms of a register R which can be either A or B. One operand must be in R when the instruction is initiated. The other operand is taken from memory, being selected by the memory address in the instruction. It is added to (or subtracted from) the number in R. The result is left in R, thus replacing the register operand. The memory operand remains intact. Program 3.4.1 illustrates these ideas, and the reader is urged to study the translation of the symbolic code to numeric code provided.

Note in Program 3.4.1 the necessity of reserving a location for the result, P, even though the constant placed there has no effect on the result. Initializing such locations to a standard value such as zero is good programming practice because the contents on termination are more likely to be helpful in checkout. Observe that we have introduced a new data type with type code F standing for "full-word integer." The item contained in quotes in the DC pseudoinstruction is a decimal representation of the desired integer. Whatever the length of the decimal integer, the binary representation stored internally is a full word. The translator (human or machine) is then responsible for conversion to hexadecimal.

Numeric location	Memory word	Symbolic location	Operation mnemonic	Reg-ister	Symbolic address	Comments
020	58A0C034	BEGIN	L	A	K	A ← (K)
024	5AA0C038		A	A	M	A ← (K) + (M)
028	5BA0C03C		S	A	N	A ← (K) + (M) − (N)
02C	50A0C040		ST	A	P	P ← (A)
030	47F0E000	EXIT	DC		X'47F0E000'	Exit from program
034	00000017	K	DC		F'23'	(K) = 23
038	00000031	M	DC		F'49'	(M) = 49
03C	0000002A	N	DC		F'42'	(N) = 42
040	00000000	P	DC		F'0'	Result destination
	00000020		END		BEGIN	No more instructions; the initial instruction of the program is at location named BEGIN

Program 3.4.1 This example illustrates addition, subtraction, and translation from symbolic to numeric form in the calculation of $P = K + M - N$ with test values $K = 23$, $M = 49$, and $N = 42$, and with starting address BEGIN $= 020_{16}$.

Multiplication

The multiplier operand must be in register B when the multiply instruction is initiated. The contents of register A prior to initiation have no effect on the result. The multiplicand operand is selected by the memory address in the multiply instruction. The result is placed in the double-word register AB. If the answer is representable in one word, as we have assumed, it will be entirely in register B and can be stored from there. Register A will then have the sign bit in every position in order to provide correct complement representation in the double-word register. In the example labeled Program 3.4.2, the reader is challenged to perform the translation to numeric code using starting location BEGIN $= 020_{16}$.

Numeric location	Memory word	Symbolic location	Operation mnemonic	Reg-ister	Symbolic address	Comments
		BEGIN	L	B	L	B ← (L)
			M	A	L	AB ← (L) · (L)
			M	A	M	AB ← (L) · (L) · (M)
			ST	B	V	V ← (B) = (AB)
		EXIT	DC		X'47F0E000'	Exit from program
		L	DC		F'28'	(L) = 28
		M	DC		F'45'	(M) = 45
		V	DC		F'0'	Result destination
			END		BEGIN	

Program 3.4.2 This example illustrates integer multiplication by the calculation of $V = L^2 \cdot M$ with test values $L = 28$ and $M = 45$.

Division

The dividend (that is, the numerator) must be in register AB when the division instruction is initiated. Since it has been assumed to be representable in one word, the dividend will fit into register B alone. However, register A must have the sign bit of the dividend in every bit position to conform to complement representation of a double-word operand. If it does not, an erroneous result will be obtained. If the dividend is known to be nonnegative, we need only load the dividend into B and zero into A. If the dividend has just been computed as the result of a multiplication, it will be properly represented in AB. This suggests a workable way to extend a one-word integer operand to a correct representation in AB, namely to multiply it by 1. This will work whether the dividend is positive or negative. We will see below that loading the dividend into A and then shifting AB right arithmetically by 32 positions yields the same result. In choosing between such equivalent sequences, we should be heavily influenced by a comparison of execution times (see Chapter 7). In any case, the divisor is selected from memory by the address in the divide instruction.

If the dividend is nonnegative and the divisor is positive, then the quotient is the largest integer to multiply the divisor and yield a result no larger than the dividend. The remainder is given by

$$(\text{remainder}) = (\text{dividend}) - (\text{quotient}) \cdot (\text{divisor})$$

When we assume nothing about the signs of dividend and divisor (we still must have a nonzero divisor), then the quotient and remainder have the magnitudes they would have if all negative signs were replaced by positives. The remainder has the sign of the dividend (or is zero) and the quotient is zero or else satisfies the relation

$$\text{sign}(\text{quotient}) \cdot \text{sign}(\text{divisor}) = \text{sign}(\text{dividend})$$

Division by zero is undefined for computer arithmetic just as it is in algebra. If division is initiated with a zero divisor, the processor recognizes an exceptional case it cannot handle. The division will be suppressed and execution will likely be terminated since there is every indication that some aspect of the computation has gone awry. Some sample results of integer division follow:

Dividend	Divisor	Quotient	Remainder
24	13	1	11
−16	7	−2	−2
12	−3	−4	0
−7	9	0	−7
−12	3	−4	0

Numeric location	Memory word	Symbolic location	Operation mnemonic	Reg-ister	Symbolic address	Comments
		BEGIN	L	A	K	A ← (K)
			A	A	L	A ← (K) + (L)
			ST	A	Q	Q ← (K) + (L)
			L	B	ONE	B ← 1
			M	A	J	AB ← (J)
			D	A	Q	(B) = (J) ÷ ((K) + (L))
			ST	B	Q	Q ← Quotient
			ST	A	R	R ← Remainder
		EXIT	DC		X'47F0E000'	Exit from program
		J	DC		F'-199'	(J) = -199
		K	DC		F'24'	(K) = 24
		L	DC		F'14'	(L) = 14
		Q	DC		F'0'	Quotient
		R	DC		F'0'	Remainder
		ONE	DC		F'1'	(ONE) = 1
			END		BEGIN	

Program 3.4.3 This example illustrates division and the attendant conversion between single-word and double-word representations by calculation of J ÷ (K + L) with test values J = −199, K = 24, and L = 14.

The divide instruction leaves the quotient in register B and the remainder in register A.

The example shown in Program 3.4.3 calculates J ÷ (K + L), storing the quotient as Q and the remainder as R. For an interesting exercise, the reader should translate this symbolic program to machine code in the space provided in Program 3.4.3 The test values used in this program are J = −199, K = 24, and L = 14.

3.4.3   Control Instructions

The property that really gives a stored-program computer tremendous power is its ability to execute a sequence of instructions again and again, each time with one or more addresses modified. To justify such a capability, which is informally called looping, we diagram the summation of integers which are stored in five consecutive words starting at the symbolic address GRADES, the answer being placed at the symbolic address SUM. The rectangular box numbered 3 in Figure 3.4.1 could clearly be executed by the following symbolic sequence:

Operation mnemonic	Register	Symbolic address
L	A	SUM
A	A	GRADES + i
ST	A	SUM

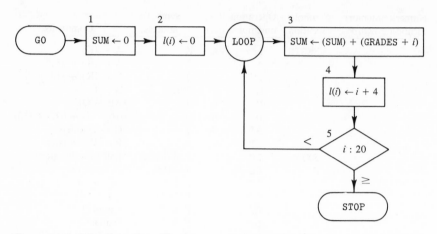

Figure 3.4.1 The flow chart illustrates a problem in which looping is highly desirable. Note that i represents an index value, the location of which is symbolized by $l(i)$.

But we must understand that GRADES + i represents five different addresses—depending on the value of i—and only one of these can be in the second instruction of the sequence written for box 3 at any one time. With the machine model we have, there is no alternative other than to include in the program a sequence which calculates the address GRADES + i each time box 3 is executed (except possibly the first or last) and stores the computed address in the instruction requiring it. One convenient way to proceed is to insert the address computation between the junction LOOP and box 3, and that is what we do.

There is a practice which may be even more convenient than working only with a variable address and that is to compute a variable instruction. The idea is to have the entire instruction which loads register A from GRADES available as a constant, add i to it, and store this new instruction as the second instruction of the sequence for box 3. In either case we achieve the same result, which is to vary the address portion of an instruction between successive uses in a program. This feat is made possible by having the program stored in memory. An example employing instruction computation to access consecutive locations appears in Program 3.4.4.

Box 5 in Figure 3.4.1, on the other hand, really requires capabilities not present in any arithmetic instructions. In this example, an instruction which could select between alternate paths according to the sign of i-20 would be suitable. The conditional branch instruction to be described next has this capability and more. Its action is based on a *condition code* which we explain first.

The control unit has a two-bit condition-code register denoted by CC for remembering the result of the most recent test made in a processor register. Some instructions cause such a test to be made on the result of their execution. Among these are Add (A) and Subtract (S), but not Multiply or Divide. Load (L) instructions do not cause a test. The "Type" column of Table 3.3.1 (the initial instruction set for BAREBONZ) has a CC for those instructions whose results are tested to set the condition-code register.

In all the BAREBONZ instructions which cause a test to be made, the condition code is set as follows:

Condition in result register	Condition code
Zero $(= 0)$	00
Negative (< 0)	01
Positive (> 0)	10
Invalid (e.g., overflow)	11

Hex digit 2 of the conditional branch instruction converts the condition code into a binary decision. Its value, called a *mask*, is the value of a four-position binary integer computed as follows:

$b_3 = 1$ if branching is to occur on zero; $b_3 = 0$ otherwise
$b_2 = 1$ if branching is to occur on negative; $b_2 = 0$ otherwise
$b_1 = 1$ if branching is to occur on positive; $b_1 = 0$ otherwise
$b_0 = 1$ if branching is to occur on invalid; $b_0 = 0$ otherwise.

The mask, M, is the sum $8 \cdot b_3 + 4 \cdot b_2 + 2 \cdot b_1 + b_0$. Its formation is summarized in Table 3.4.1. For example, the mask whose value is A (binary 1010) causes branching on ≥ 0. A mask of 6 (binary 0110) causes branching on > 0 or < 0. A mask of F (binary 1111) causes branching on any setting of the condition code, so it is called an *unconditional* branch. Our terminal instruction, 47F0E000, is an example of such an unconditional branch. In this case, it is a branch to the supervisory program.

	b_3	b_2	b_1	b_0
Binary digit of mask				
Positional value	8	4	2	1
Branch condition for which b_i has value 1	$= 0$	< 0	> 0	invalid
Condition code for which b_i has value 1	00	01	10	11

Table 3.4.1 This table shows how the mask is constructed from the value of the condition code on which branching is to occur.

We return to the conditional branch instruction. If the condition specified by the mask digit, M, in position 2 is not met, then the only effect of the instruction is an incrementing of the IAC by 4 so that the next instruction is taken from the next location so selected. However, if the condition is met, the IAC contents are replaced by the address determined by hex digits 5–7 of the conditional branch instruction. Since hex digit 4 is C, the IAC receives an address which is the sum of the BAREBONZ address and the base address in register C. All conditional branching is accomplished by variations on one instruction which has mnemonic BC (Branch on Condition). The address to which a branch may jump is in hex digits 5–7. The condition for branching is determined by the mask digit.

Operation mnemonic	Operation code, hex	Mask digit	Explanation
BC	47	M	Do nothing if condition specified by M is not met; branch to address specified by m if the condition is met

As this instruction is used in BAREBONZ, we require hex digit 3 to be 0 and hex digit 4 to be C.

An example which illustrates computation of instruction addresses and use of the condition code to control looping is given in Program 3.4.4. The program is an implementation of the procedure diagrammed in Figure 3.4.1.

To keep the input of data and the tedium of manual verification within reasonable bounds, we have limited the number of grades to five. While this program may seem long (we will find much more economical ways to accomplish the same thing) we should remember that no more instructions would be required to sum 100 or even 10,000 grades. In this sense, looping is far more economical of coding time and of memory consumed by instructions than *straight-line coding* (coding in which no branches of control occur). It is also more versatile, since to change the number of summands we need only change one data item.

We can observe that the initialization taking place in instructions 1–4 is unnecessary under the BAREBONZ system since it sets the entire BAREBONZ memory to zeros before initiating the user program. Since not every system initializes memory to zero, experienced programmers never rely on the supervisor to initialize a word, but choose to be sure by explicitly setting initial values from within their programs. Even so, we have

Symbolic location	Operation mnemonic	Register	Symbolic address	Comments
BEGIN	L	A	SUM	
	S	A	SUM	A ← 0
	ST	A	SUM	SUM ← 0
	ST	A	I	I ← 0
LOOP	L	A	SKELETON	Instruction constant
	A	A	I	
	ST	A	VARINSTR	Indexed instruction
	L	A	SUM	
VARINSTR	A	A	GRADES	Will be A A GRADES+I
	ST	A	SUM	
	L	A	I	
	A	A	FOUR	Increment index
	ST	A	I	Store new value for I
	S	A	TESTVAL	Subtract four times number of grades
	BC	4	LOOP	Reenter loop on negative
EXIT	DC		X'47F0E000'	Exit from program
I	DC		F'0'	
SKELETON	A	A	GRADES	
FOUR	DC		F'4'	
TESTVAL	DC		F'20'	Number of bytes for grades
SUM	DC		F'0'	
GRADES	DC		F'89'	
	DC		F'68'	
	DC		F'74'	
	DC		F'97'	
	DC		F'85'	
	END		BEGIN	

Program 3.4.4   This is a first example of a program with a loop, taken from the flow chart shown in Figure 3.4.1.

overdone initialization since we load SUM and I with zeros from cards. We consider this to be an example of overkill which is wholesome.

Exercise.   Substantial shortening of the looping example can be accomplished by

(1) using both A and B registers so that the traffic through A is not so intense;

(2) incrementing the variable instruction by 4 directly and testing it against its final value, thus avoiding separate storage of i.

Using these techniques and only the instructions in Table 3.3.1, try to rewrite Program 3.4.4 so that the number of instructions is minimal.

Now we can partially describe the instruction we have used for halting programs, which has been expressed as 47F0E000 in hexadecimal. The numeric operation code of 47 identifies this instruction as a Branch on Condition instruction, while the mask of F denotes an unconditional branch. The address to which the branch is made is the address in register E, which was placed there by the BAREBONZ system as discussed in Section 3.2. The computation of the address in this case utilizes register E rather than the base register C. The topic of addressing for the 360/370 is discussed in more detail in Section 3.4.5.

3.4.4 Conversion and Scaling

Instructions we have studied thus far are adequate for what one ordinarily describes as "scientific computation" except for two features:

1. The arithmetic instructions we have discussed have all required integers for operands. Although this requirement will be relaxed in Chapter 8, there is a technique to perform almost any practical numerical computation using only integer representation of numbers within the computer. This technique, called *scaling,* was essential to solving large problems on the earliest machines. Today, scaling is used mostly on the smaller digital machines for applications in which the superior speed of integer arithmetic is essential. Such applications include many data-acquisition and real-time problems. Scaling also turns out to be required in exploiting the decimal arithmetic feature of the 360/370 in accounting applications.

2. We may wish to present numerical information to the computer in a form more convenient for our external use than binary. Then we must have a program which can perform the conversion required from our external representation to binary. Of course, if we wish the computer to return results to us in a representation other than binary, then we must have a program to convert those results from binary to the desired representation. While for the moment we will concern ourselves principally with base 10 representations for external use, we should keep in mind that graphical displays are also convenient to the user and could be one convenient representation in our repertoire.

Programs which require scaling or which perform conversion are much easier to write and more economical with the aid of shift instructions. We will discuss scaling first, and thereby illustrate a useful application of arithmetic shifting. Then, as an example of conversion between binary and another form, we will discuss some of the problems of converting a base-10 integer from the EBCDIC character representation to its binary representation. This conversion will illustrate a useful application of logical shifting. By a proper combination of left and right logical shifts, one can isolate *any* substring of AB for further analysis.

It is a happy circumstance that shifting is inherent in the multiplication and division operations. Hence, it is easily made available in separate operations. There are two types of shift instructions:

1. Arithmetic shifting treats the sign bit in a special way (propagating it right to fill vacated positions on a right shift and holding it on left shifts while bits shifted from position 1 are lost) and serves principally for very high-speed multiplication or division by a power of 2. Vacated positions on the right are filled with zeros.

2. Logical shifting makes no distinctions about a sign bit; that is, it propagates no bit and it preserves no bit. Positions vacated on the left by a logical right shift are filled with zeros. On a nonzero logical left shift, the bit from position 1 moves into or through position 0. Bits shifted left from position 0 or right from position 63 are lost. Vacated positions on the right are filled with zeros.

It should be clear that, for any contents of the double-word register AB, an arithmetic shift of $m > 63$ places yields the same result as a shift of 63 places. Further, any logical shift of $m > 63$ places yields a zero result. Hence, it is reasonable to subtract the largest possible integer multiple of 64 (which leaves a positive integer ≤ 63) from the amount of shift. This amounts to using only the rightmost six bits of the address field of the shift instructions as the amount of shift and that is done. Bits 20–25 of the shift instructions have no effect.

Scaling

Suppose we wish to make a very precise calculation of the area of a rectangle as the product

$$p = xy$$

Moreover, suppose that from knowledge of the particular problem we know that values of x are restrained to the range 0.1–13.7, and values of y vary from 3.49 to 784. Also assume that we know that no rectangle has area greater than 250. To achieve maximum precision within the 31 bits allotted to represent each positive integer, we can profit by introducing new variables X, Y, and P. These variables are related to x, y, and p as shown in the following tabulation:

Relation	Justification
$X = 2^{27} \cdot x < 2^{31}$	$x < 2^4$
$Y = 2^{21} \cdot y < 2^{31}$	$y < 2^{10}$
$P = 2^{23} \cdot p < 2^{31}$	$p < 2^8$

The point of these observations is that carrying X and Y as integers is equivalent to carrying a great deal of precision in x and y. The fact that each of X and Y is less than 2^{31} in magnitude insures each is representable as a binary integer in one memory word.

Now

$$x = 2^{-27} \cdot X \qquad \text{and} \qquad y = 2^{-21} \cdot Y$$

so

$$p = 2^{-48} X \cdot Y$$

Similarly

$$p = 2^{-23} P$$

so that

$$2^{-23} P = 2^{-48} X \cdot Y$$

This yields the desired formula

$$P = 2^{-25} X \cdot Y$$

The product $X \cdot Y$ has a 62-bit representation in AB. Our formula for P now requires multiplication of $X \cdot Y$ by 2^{-25} before saving the result as P.

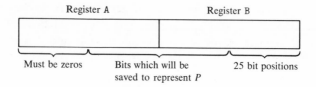

This can be accomplished by shifting all the bits in AB twenty-five positions to the right, proper consideration being given to handling of the sign in complement arithmetic.

Adjusting magnitudes by powers of 2 is extremely economical in a binary machine but difficult for the person attuned to decimal representation. Rather than print P, one might print $10^6 \cdot p = (10^6 / 2^{23})\ P$. Such a final adjustment requires multiplication and a final shift. Since far fewer numbers are printed than calculated, this is not expensive. Shifting to the left can be accomplished by multiplication and to the right by division (in the example, the divisor would be 2^{25}), but these operations are very time consuming compared to arithmetic shifting.

Conversion

The EBCDIC character string represented in hexadecimal as F3F4F1F9 stands for the decimal integer 3419, but it is not acceptable as an arith-

metic operand internal to the computer in EBCDIC form. What is needed
is the binary integer representation which is

$$1\ 1\ 0\ 1,\ 0\ 1\ 0\ 1,\ 1\ 0\ 1\ 1_2 = 0D5B_{16}$$

To obtain the binary integer representation from the EBCDIC representation, we need to strip off the left half of each byte and then to
calculate

$$((3 \cdot 10 + 4) \cdot 10 + 1) \cdot 10 + 9 = 3419$$

One way to isolate a single digit whose character representation is at
the left byte of a word is to load the word into register B, perform a
logical left shift of AB by four positions, and then set register A to zero.
Another logical left shift by 4 isolates the leftmost digit in A from which
it can be stored. This sequence is given for the example above, the character representation of 3419 being taken from a location named WORD.

Symbolic location	Operation mnemonic	Register	Symbolic address	Comments
L	B	WORD	B ← F3F4F1F9
SLDL	A	4	B ← 3F4F1F90
L	A	ZERO	A ← 0
SLDL	A	4	A ← 3; B ← F4F1F900
ST	A	DIGIT0	DIGIT0 ← 3

Note that what remains in B is in the form assumed for this instruction
sequence; that is, it leaves the character representation of the second
digit in the left byte of register B. Executing the second, third, and fourth
instruction again will isolate that digit in A, but of course the place in
which this digit is stored must be different from DIGIT0. Performing
the isolation of four digits in this way requires $5 + 3 \cdot 4 = 17$ instructions.
We defer more elaborate examples until we have simplified looping by
the enhancement of instructions with indexing. However, it is worth noting
that multiplication by 10 is repeatedly required once the digits have
been isolated and may actually be more economical when done by a combination of arithmetic shifts and additions than with a multiplication
operation. Further, building character representations from binary integers
to be able to print is just the inverse of the conversion we have indicated.
Thus, the shift instructions, both logical and arithmetic, play an important
role in translation of information from external to internal representation
and vice versa.

3.4.5 Addressing

In Section 3.2, the structure of the memory of BAREBONZ was discussed. There we found that the BAREBONZ address, consisting of the rightmost three hex digits of instructions referencing memory, is sufficient to address 1024 full words in memory. In the early days of computers, this was a memory of respectable and useful size. Since those days, however, larger memories have become practical to build. Furthermore, many applications of computer programming have progressed to the stage where larger memories are required. Thus it is not surprising that the IBM 360 really has a memory larger than the 1024 full words addressable by the three rightmost hex digits in an instruction. But if there is to be substantially more memory, then how can these additional words be addressed?

One way to address large amounts of memory would be to expand the general scheme used in the BAREBONZ address. That is, n bits in an instruction can be used to address 2^n bytes, or 2^{n-2} full words. Thus the use of 20 bits for addressing in this fashion would allow access to 2^{18} full words. The addressing scheme used by the IBM 360/370 is different, however; most of the precious bits in an instruction (usually 32) are dedicated to more important duties! The addressing scheme used in the IBM 360/370 allows addressing a large number of words in memory and yet uses only 16 bits in an instruction.

There is a simple way to extend the possible range of addressing beyond what is available within an instruction. It consists of having a reference address available in a register accessible to the control unit and letting the address in the instruction be added to that reference address to form the address actually used to retrieve information. The number of distinct addresses available in this way is determined by the size of the reference register and may be much larger than can be represented within the address portion of an instruction. This facility was available in machines as early as 1960, but the IBM 360 is the first widely used machine to make use of a reference register imperative.

When several forms of address are involved in each memory reference, it becomes convenient to have distinct names for each. These names may be peculiar to the machine in question. On the IBM 360/370, the reference register is called the *base register* and the number it holds is called the *base address*. The address in the instruction is relative to that base and is called a *displacement*. The address which actually locates the desired item in 360/370 memory is called the *effective address*. It always has a base component and a displacement component. As we shall see in Section 3.6, it may also have an index component.

If there were only one possible base register, it would not have to be named in the instruction, although one might want to disable its use on some instructions which make no memory reference (such as a shift instruction). But in fact, each memory reference in an instruction includes a base register name as well as a displacement. The base register name is a nonzero hex digit, selecting from among fifteen 32-bit registers (we have consistently used register C). Even though the base register has 32 bit positions, only the rightmost 24 bits are used as base address so that 2^{24} bytes or 2^{22} full words can conceivably be addressed. Of course, many computers today have less than 4 million words of memory, so these require correspondingly fewer bits than 24 for addressing.

For simple programs, the base register may be initially loaded with the address of the first instruction and left unchanged throughout the program. The different addresses required for a program are then achieved by varying the displacement, that is the rightmost 12 bits (hex positions 5, 6, and 7) of the RX and RS instructions we have seen. These positions are sufficient to allow us a "range" of 1024 full words. The effective address for a nonindexed memory reference is then found by adding the displacement to the base address. In this fashion, 16 bits in an instruction (and 24 bits in the base register) allow us to address as many as 2^{22} words.

In all BAREBONZ programs thus far, we have used a C in hex position 4 of every memory-reference instruction except the instruction to halt; this means we are using register C as base register. BAREBONZ was responsible for loading the address of the first instruction into register C, in order to establish the base address. The BAREBONZ programmer is then responsible for computing the displacement for each instruction. As the reader has probably concluded, what we have until now called the "BAREBONZ address" will from this point on be called a displacement, the displacement being measured from the base address.

In the sections which follow, we will need to understand very clearly the distinction between an effective address and the components of which it is the sum, namely the base address, displacement, and in some cases an index.

3.5   LINKING PROGRAM SEQUENCES

3.5.1   Subprograms

One can isolate certain processes that occur repeatedly in one program or are common to several different programs. Examples familiar to everyone include calculating a square root, finding the maximum or average of a set of numbers, arranging items alphabetically, and looking up entries from a table. Conversion from binary to decimal and from decimal to binary provide additional examples. It is a saving in programming time to write sequences of instructions called *subprograms* capable of performing these specialized tasks, and then to utilize them from within one's own program. The subprogram to be used would be loaded elsewhere in memory and activated (we use the verbs "invoke" and "call" to signify this) at the appropriate time with parameters provided for the computation and a return address to which exit will be made on completion.

The distinction in the previous paragraph of program and subprogram is artificial since subprograms are invoked as easily from other subprograms as from programs which are not themselves invoked. In fact, any user's program, whether it be one line or a program with a maze of subprograms, is treated by the supervisor as a parameterless subprogram. The distinction that is most important is between *calling* and *called* subprogram. We shall for convenience drop the prefix and speak only of calling and called programs.

The rules by which control and parameters are passed between calling program and called program are called *linkage conventions*. They vary widely among computer systems. Those of the 360/370 are quite complex, so we will consider simpler linkages first, although these will be consistent in spirit with the 360/370 linkage conventions.

Often, assembler language programs are called *routines* and subprograms are called *subroutines*. We consider these to be pairs of synonyms.

3.5.2 The Control Path

BAREBONZ already has distinguished register E as the exit register. It is natural to consider placing a return address in E before branching to another program and returning from it by a branch to that address in register E. As explained above, we must preserve the contents of register E before using it for linkage in that way. We will discuss conventions for saving such register contents after introducing two instructions which will place in register E the effective address of the location to which control should return.

Operation mnemonic	Operation code, hex	Register	Type	Explanation
LA	41	E	RX	$E \leftarrow m + (C)$
BAL	45	E	RX	$E \leftarrow (IAC); IAC \leftarrow m + (C)$

As these instructions are used in BAREBONZ, we require hex digit 3 to be 0 and hex digit 4 to be C.

The first of these, called the Load Address instruction, is simplicity itself. Its displacement is the BAREBONZ address of an instruction to which the called program should return control; this instruction adds this displacement to the base address to obtain the effective address for that return as is required by the control unit. This effective address is placed in the named register which we have taken to be E. Note that this RX instruction is unusual in that it refers to memory but requires no memory access. The address it places in register E is just the sum of components taken from register C and from the LA instruction itself.

For the purpose of discussing linkage in a program, we will assume there is an instruction at location M which is a branch to location N and that, when the sequence beginning at location N is completed, computation should be resumed at location $M + 4$. Control linkage through register E could be set up by the pair given in symbolic form as:

Symbolic location	Operation mnemonic	Register or mask	Symbolic address	Explanation
$M - 4$	LA	E	$M + 4$	Place effective address for return in E
M	BC	F	N	Branch to location N

The last instruction of the sequence beginning at location N should then have hex form 47F0E000.

The BAL (Branch After Linking) instruction replaces the instruction pair above by a single one: namely,

Symbolic location	Operation mnemonic	Register	Symbolic address
M	BAL	E	N

The advantage of the BAL instruction is not so overwhelming as it might seem, for when a return address is selected by the Load Address instruction, it need not be that of the next instruction in sequence as is required by the Branch After Linking instruction.

3.5.3   Saving Register Contents

There are two philosophies observable in the conventions established to save register contents:

1. The "I trust nobody" philosophy—what is in the registers when I call another program is important to me, the caller. I will save their contents in a place known only to me so that the called program cannot destroy them.

2. The "I trust everybody" philosophy—the program I call knows that the contents of the registers is important to me. I'll provide it a place to save register contents (its address will be a parameter) and depend on that program to do the saving for me. Clearly, no program I invoke will destroy my precious information inadvertently.

Either philosophy will work, since all components of a program must be correct before it can function properly. The first prevailed through a long sequence of machines and is still widely used; the second came about with the introduction of the IBM 360. It will be to our advantage to understand both philosophies.

Using the "I Trust Nobody" Philosophy

Consider any instruction sequence which is entered by a branch and from which return is made by a branch to the address in register E. Every user program is of that sort. But within user programs there may be many more instances of such sequences. Suppose that each such sequence reserves a set of words for the purpose of saving its own exit address and any other register contents not to be destroyed by a program it calls. Then just prior to such a call it can save these register contents by a series of store instructions and, after return, restore register contents as necessary. Register E is somewhat special in that saving the exit address at the beginning of the sequence and restoring it just before exit frees register E for other usage. To illustrate these ideas, we provide in Figure 3.5.1 a schematic for linkage in which contents of registers B and E must be saved before invocation of a parameterless program IN2 and restored on return, but only B must be saved before invocation of parameterless program IN3. The exit address of the calling sequence IN1 is saved and restored separately in order to make E available for other uses. Before considering the "I Trust Everybody" philosophy, we turn to the information-passing aspect of program calls.

3.5.4 Values as Parameters

Almost every called program needs data from the calling program to perform its function. Data items provided as part of the linkage are called *parameters* of the called program. The most straightforward way to provide one parameter to a called program is to place it in register A or register B prior to entry. If a single result is to be returned, it can be made available in like manner by placing it in register A or register B prior to return of control. In the exchange of information between programs, each program

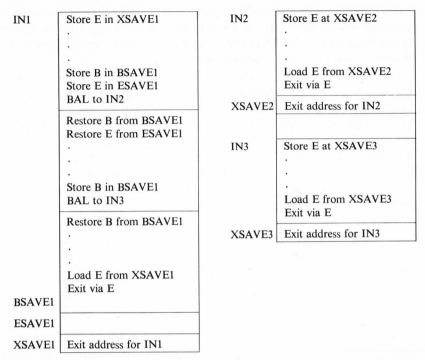

Figure 3.5.1   A schematic for program control linkage according to the "I Trust Nobody" philosophy shows each program saving and restoring its own exit address and separately preserving intermediate results during program call.

must take its information from the location to which that information was sent by the other. As will become clearer, there must also be consistency between programs as to *what* is being sent (integer, floating point number, address, character string, or flag) as well as where it is sent. Any well-documented program is very complete in spelling out these details.

3.5.5   Addresses as Parameters

It is easy to demonstrate the need for providing an address as a parameter to a program being called. A program to add *n* numbers from sequential locations beginning at a given location *l* is an example. In transmitting addresses, we need to be very careful. We have to distinguish precisely between

(1) the effective address used in getting data or an instruction from memory, and

(2) the address portion of an instruction which is relative to a base.

If an address is to be provided as a parameter to be inserted into a memory-reference instruction, then we should expect it to be an address relative to the beginning of BAREBONZ memory. We can easily accomplish the insertion using the STore Halfword instruction.

Among the data words of the calling program, we include one full word which qualifies as an instruction, has C for base register, and has the same relative address that is to be a parameter. To make the address available, we load this entire instruction into a processor register just prior to entering the called program. Within the called program, we apply the STore Halfword (STH) instruction to deposit the right half of this instruction parameter into any instruction of the called program which requires its address. Although the purpose of the STore Halfword instruction is to store a half word, note that this instruction is a full word in length. The STore Halfword description is:

Operation mnemonic	Operation code, hex	Register	Type	Explanation
STH	40	A	RX	$(m)_{0:15} \leftarrow (A)_{16:31}$
STH	40	B	RX	$(m)_{0:15} \leftarrow (B)_{16:31}$

As these instructions are used in BAREBONZ, we require hex digit 3 to be 0 and hex digit 4 to be C.

In Program 3.5.1 we provide an example of linkage between programs in which two parameters are values; one is an address, and the only register whose contents are to be saved is register E. We apply the first of the two kinds of register conventions, choosing to "trust nobody" for the present.

Using the "I Trust Everybody" Philosophy

Again we suppose that each program sequence reserves a set of consecutive words in memory for the purpose of saving register contents. But this time, the calling program relies on the called program to save its register contents in locations provided by the caller. Thus whenever information is saved it is done for the caller in his area by the called program.

The first requirement of such a plan is that the calling program must pass the effective address of a sequence of save locations to the called program. It does this by placing the save address in a register for the called program to use. We are going to assume a register devoted to this use, namely register D (that is just what 360/370 linkage uses), and apply the Load Address instruction to it as we did to E. If the beginning location

Symbolic location	Operation mnemonic	Register	Symbolic address	Comments
BEGIN	ST	E	EHOLD	Save exit address
	L	A	U	Load U as parameter
	L	B	VINST	Load address of V as parameter
	BAL	E	PLUS	Go to subprogram PLUS
	ST	A	W	Store results
	L	E	EHOLD	
EXIT	DC		X'47F0E000'	
U	DC		F'19'	U = 19
V	DC		F'186'	V = 186
W	DC		F'0'	
VINST	L	B	V	Provides address parameter
PLUS	STH	B	ADDV+2	Places address parameter
ADDV	A	A	000	Add V to U
EXITPLUS	DC		X'47F0E000'	Return
EHOLD	DC		F'0'	
	END		BEGIN	

Program 3.5.1 The three-line program beginning at PLUS receives the value of U in register A and the address of V in register B, and returns the value W = U + V in register A. The values are U = 19 and V = 186. The instruction at ADDV receives its address portion as a parameter. Note that the address of the half word receiving an address parameter exceeds by 2 the address of the instruction receiving it.

of the sequence of save locations (usually called a *save area*) is named SAVEREG, then the instruction

$$\text{LA D,SAVEREG †}$$

in the calling program puts its effective address into register D.

While we are lacking a symbolic representation for an instruction to store at a given numeric displacement from an effective address in D, we know very well how to write the numeric instruction. To store from register A into a location 10_{16} bytes beyond the address in D would be accomplished using 10_{16} as displacement and D as base register to yield 50A0D010 for the instruction. We defer the symbolic form to Section 3.6.

The called program must save the contents of the registers for the calling program just as they were on entry. Hence, it will store register contents in the save area immediately after entry, and will restore these values to the

---

† In this free symbolic form of an instruction, the comma separates register number on the left from memory operand on its right. A blank space separates operation mnemonic on its left from register number on its right. If there is a symbolic location, it is to the left of the operation code and separated from it by a blank space.

registers just before exit. Since it has no information from the calling program as to what registers must be saved, it must save all that it uses. A schematic for this kind of program linkage applied to the example in Figure 3.5.1 is given in Figure 3.5.2, in which we "trust everybody."

IN1

Store all registers except D in save area provided by the supervisor, the address of which is in D
Save register D contents within SVR1
Load Address of SVR1 into D
. . .
BAL to IN2
. . .
BAL to IN3
. . .
Restore register D contents as on entry from SVR1
Restore remaining registers from save area provided by the supervisor
Exit via E

SVR1

Accepts register D contents
Data storage for IN1

IN2

Store all registers except D in save area, the address of which is in D. It is SVR1
Save register D contents within SVR2
Load Address of SVR2 into D
. . .
Restore register D contents from SVR2
Restore remaining registers from SVR1
Exit via E

SVR2

Accepts register D contents
Data storage for IN2

IN3

Store all registers except D in save area, the address of which is in D. It is SVR1
Save register D contents within SVR3
Load address of SVR3 into D
. . .
Restore register D contents from SVR3
Restore remaining registers from SVR1
Exit via E

SVR3

Accepts register D contents
Data storage for IN3

Figure 3.5.2 A schematic for program control linkage according to the "I Trust Everybody" philosophy shows called program storing registers for calling program in workspace of the latter.

3.5.6   Summary

Each linking convention has its advantages. The first permits the programmer the opportunity to use a smaller save area where he knows saving certain registers is unnecessary. It has the disadvantage of requiring the saving and restoring sequences to be in the program on every call of a program. The second convention which we examined encourages saving all registers every time a call is made, but the saving and restoring sequences are in the program only at its entry and exit, respectively.

3.6   BAREBONZ II

Some aspects of computation with a computer as stripped as BARE-BONZ are really taxing. As we have seen in Section 3.4.3, looping can be accomplished by modifying instructions in memory, but it demands care and takes many housekeeping instructions. Scaling to maintain accuracy through a long sequence of calculations requires an intimate understanding of the origins of a problem. Conversion among number representations and more general symbol manipulations (as might be encountered in translating a FORTRAN program to machine language) are awkward if only shift and arithmetic instructions are used. Thus, it is no surprise that extensions to computer organization have eased each of these problems.

Among the features mentioned above, there are some which have become almost universally available, even in the low-cost computer at the neighborhood bank. Useful examples are index registers to simplify looping, and register-to-register instructions to simplify the use of the index registers. Indexing accomplishes looping with fewer instructions, but, even more importantly, it avoids modification of the program as was required in Section 3.4.3. Each of these characteristics helps minimize programming errors. Therefore, we take up indexing and instructions to facilitate it immediately.

On the other hand, processor instructions for floating-point arithmetic are unavailable on some of the less expensive machines, and may be an extra-cost option on otherwise-powerful computer systems. Therefore, every programmer should know something of scaling, which is the thinking-man's alternative to floating point. Similarly, instructions to facilitate conversion among number representations and special facilities for symbol manipulation are not universal. It happens also that these features have their greatest use in the writing of assemblers, compilers, and operating systems which we shall use but not develop. This explains our decision to defer some of these elegant features to Chapter 6.

3.6.1   Indexing in the Control Unit

We have seen the need for using arithmetic instructions to compute addresses in other instructions. The occasion arose in the process of looping through a program segment, and its use enabled us to make the effective address of the computed instruction depend on an index held in a memory location. Since the index is always applied by addition, it is reasonable to consider modifying the control unit so that it can add an index as a component of the effective address of any indexable instruction as it is being decoded. Of course, indexing should be done only if the instruction requests such modification.

Suppose there are one or more special registers, called *index* registers, available to the control unit, each identified by a nonzero binary integer. Let there be certain instructions called *indexable instructions* which have specific bit positions reserved for an index "tag" to be interpreted as follows:

> If the tag portion of an indexable instruction holds the number of an index register, then, during decoding of the instruction in the control unit, the integer in the designated index register is added to what would otherwise have been the effective address. If the tag portion is zero, the indexing capability is not used. The resultant address is the effective address applied in instruction execution.

With such an indexing capability in the control unit, the programmer's task is reduced to having the correct value of the index in an index register, and then putting the proper tag into the instruction to cause the index to be added. If there are instructions to load, increment, test, and store for index registers similar to those for processor registers, this indexing facility has several advantages beyond simplifying programming.

1. It permits programs to remain unmodified in memory.

2. It speeds execution since no instructions are devoted to instruction computations and since there is no need for a memory reference to obtain the index.

3. Finally, it makes setting and incrementing of the index more economical both in space occupied by instructions and in execution time.

BAREBONZ II has nine index registers, numbered 1–9. The index tag is hex digit 3 of indexable instructions. Indexable instructions are identified as such by their operation codes; essentially they are instructions which operate on contents of one processor register and one memory location which may be indexed. These are RX instructions (several are listed in Table 3.3.1), RX being a mnemonic for register-and-indexed-storage. Each index register has a 32-bit capacity. However, the computation of an effective address is as if it were made in a 24-bit register. This permits the leftmost eight bits to be used for program status information in the linking process, as discussed in Chapter 5.

Having a special register to hold an index is useful for indexing an instruction only if there are instructions to initialize the index, increment it, and compare to a test value. Storing its value is sometimes required. For $n = 1$–9, these capabilities for index arithmetic are available as follows:

Operation mnemonic	Register	Instruction type	Explanation
L	n	RX	Load register n from word m
A	n	RX,CC	Add to register n from word m
S	n	RX,CC	Subtract word m from register n
ST	n	RX	Store from register n into word m

As these instructions are used in BAREBONZ, we require hex digit 4 to be C.

While these instructions are themselves indexable, indexing should be considered initially where it is required to avoid explicit computation of instructions.

Example 1. The following symbolic program, Program 3.6.1, is a second symbolic implementation of the flowchart computation shown in Figure 3.4.1, and coded in Program 3.4.4.

Symbolic location	Operation mnemonic	Register	Index	Symbolic address	Comments
BEGIN	L	A	0	ZERO	Initialize sum register
	L	1	0	ZERO	$i \leftarrow 0$
LOOP	A	A	1	GRADES	Add one term
	S	1	0	TESTVAL	Test index
	BC	2	0	STOR	
	A	1	0	INCVAL	Restore and increment index
	BC	F	0	LOOP	Reenter loop
STOR	ST	A	0	SUM	Store result
EXIT	DC			X'47F0E000'	All done
ZERO	DC			F'0'	
TESTVAL	DC			F'16'	
INCVAL	DC			F'20'	Value to restore and increment index
SUM	DC			F'0'	
GRADES	DC			F'89'	
	DC			F'68'	
	DC			F'74'	
	DC			F'97'	
	DC			F'85'	
	END			BEGIN	

Program 3.6.1 This example demonstrates looping without instruction modification by use of an index register to modify the effective address.

From this example, we can observe that the use of indexing shortened the program noticeably. Can you list the reasons and the number of instructions saved because of each reason?

3.6.2   Register-to-Register Instructions

With an abundance of registers shared between the control unit and the processor, there are many instances when the desired operand locations are both in registers. This suggests instructions designed to name two registers. Here are some arguments for them.

1. Memory accesses are expensive in time compared to register accesses, so instructions which avoid them usually save execution time.

2. Since there are so few registers compared to memory locations, instructions with no memory reference can often be expressed in half as many bits, thus conserving memory.

3. Without register-to-register instructions, information would frequently need to be stored from one register into memory just to make it available to another register. The result would be longer programs and longer execution times.

Instructions with two register operands are known as RR (register-register) instructions, and occupy only a half word. The operation code occupies hex digits 0 and 1. Hex digit 2 names the first operand register and hex digit 3 names the second.

The IBM 360/370 has 16 general-purpose 32-bit registers which are shared by the processor and the control unit. The four-bit hex code used for register reference in an instruction is therefore just adequate to address each register individually, and the registers are numbered 0 to F in hex notation. In most instructions with two register operands, each register named may be any of 0 through F, and we will limit ourselves to a selection of these instructions for the present. With this understanding, the first operand register will be symbolized as R1 and the second as R2. Some instructions have RR format, but require hex digit 2 to be a mask. In that case, we take R1 to symbolize the mask. There is an elaborate repertoire of RR instructions. The first ones we mention are precise parallels of BAREBONZ RX instructions with a different way of accessing the second operand. See Table 3.6.1.

While it may seem unusual to set the condition code register when the sign of the result should be known (as for LPR and LNR) this does enable us to distinguish zero quantities from nonzero quantities. Further, it permits detection of overflow resulting from a Load Positive when $(R2) = -2^{31}$ (we have seen that 2^{31} does not have a one-word integer representation).

Operation mnemonic	Operation code, hex	Type	Explanation
LR	18	RR	R1 ← (R2)
AR	1A	RR,CC	R1 ← (R1) + (R2)
SR	1B	RR,CC	R1 ← (R1) − (R2)
BCR	07	RR	No effect if condition specified by R1 is not met; IAC ← (R2) if condition is met
BALR	05	RR	R1 ← (IAC); IAC ← (R2)

There is an easily explained set of variations on the LR instruction which we mention next.

LTR	12	RR,CC	R1 ← (R2)
LCR	13	RR,CC	R1 ← [−(R2)]
LPR	10	RR,CC	R1 ← |(R2)|
LNR	11	RR,CC	R1 ← [−|(R2)|]

Table 3.6.1 Several register-to-register instructions are available. These instructions are very efficient because no memory access is required to fetch an operand.

The explanation of the BALR instruction introduces a kind of generality which permeates the 360/370. We find that linking can be accomplished through a variety of registers, not just register E. While this fact is good to know and is occasionally useful, it is a fact that E is by convention the linking register, and we will continue to use only E for that purpose.

3.6.3 Some Consequences of Having Instructions of Different Lengths

Packing all the necessary information for one instruction into a half word conserves memory that is required for instructions. It may also speed execution, for (on some models of the 360/370) a memory access to bring the next instruction to the control unit may bring as many as four words. Thus fewer memory accesses for instructions may be required. We shall come to instructions which perform so many tasks that they occupy three half words. Here again, if one of these replaces several more-conventional instructions, there is likely to be a saving in memory used as well as in execution time. There may or may not be an improvement in programming ease and readability. There are, on the other hand, complications introduced by providing instructions of different lengths and we will discuss them now.

If instructions of different lengths are encountered, no longer can the IAC automatically increment by four to find the location of the next instruction. The increment must be determined from the operation code. One may say that he is not concerned how hard the control unit has to work, and that is a valid point. But there are other consequences resulting from the fact that full-word or three-half-word instructions may begin on half-word boundaries. Temporarily, until the transition from symbolic to numeric is handled by machine, we have the complication of incrementing the IAC from one instruction to the next by 2 or 4 or 6, depending on the instruction. We still record one instruction per line on the symbolic form. If an instruction is a half word in length, the numeric format requires putting its four hex digits in column 5–8 and leaving columns 9–12 blank.

The complications we have mentioned to this point are really book-keeping details and are surmounted with a little practice. A more profound result is that we can no longer reference a full-word instruction as a data word since the instruction may not begin on a full-word boundary. The alternatives are simple. The programmer works with half words and remembers to increment the address of a full-word instruction by two to obtain the address of its right half word. An added consideration is that data words, if packed immediately behind instructions, may themselves not begin on full-word boundaries. The person doing his own translation into symbolic code can take care to have data words begin on full-word boundaries. Among other things he can, if necessary, insert do-nothing RR instructions into his program as padding (the 360/370 logic abounds with them). On the other hand, when he relies on an assembler to translate for him—as is usual—he has to be aware of word boundaries and occasionally he has to force words, half words, or double words to begin on the appropriate boundaries. The response of the supervisor, when it detects a failure to observe boundaries properly, is to advise of a *specification* error.

3.6.4   How Many Processors?

We have restricted our view of computational capability in the registers to gain familiarity with the workings of one processor. There are more, at least in a logical sense. We have found that A and B form a register pair to cooperate in multiplication and division. In fact, it is reasonable to say that, regardless of electronic circuitry, it appears to the programmer that there are eight processors numbered 0–7, and that processor n has registers $2n$ and $2n + 1$ as its "A" and "B" registers, respectively. Thus, we have been working with processor number 5 which has registers A and B. We have seen that these processors can communicate with each other by means of RR instructions.

The two registers in a processor have distinct functions in multiplication and division, and in the related shifting operations. Historically the register which forms the left portion of the double-word register has been called the *accumulator* (usually it had more addition capabilities than the other register) and the right portion was called the *multiplier* register or the quotient register, or sometimes the *multiplier–quotient* register (MQ). It seems appropriate to retain such names as being more mnemonic than "even" and "odd." So we dignify registers $2n$ and $2n + 1$ of processor n as accumulator (ACC) and multiplier–quotient (MQ) of that processor.

Some of the processors (namely 0, 6, and 7) are very unlikely to be used to their full arithmetic capacity because of conventions for special uses. We have already seen examples of such conventions in BAREBONZ which pertained to registers C and E. The registers of processor 0 have not been assigned special functions in BAREBONZ, but the 360/370 software conventions utilize these in subprogram linkage. Most programmers will find it convenient to develop some of their own special patterns for using registers so as to avoid making decisions at every step.

3.6.5 Restatement of Instructions Using a Double-Word Register

The Multiply, Divide, and Double-Word Shifts all are defined with respect to the ACC and MQ registers of a processor and the double register AMQ formed from coupling these registers with the ACC register on the left. Hex digit 2 in instructions requiring register coupling always selects the ACC register of the processor. The descriptions of instructions given for processor 5 with registers A and B are valid for any processor if A and B are systematically replaced by $2n$ and $2n + 1$, where n is the number of the processor.

PROBLEMS

1. Demonstrate by placing nonzero numbers in the A registers just prior to the multiply/divide instruction that:

(a)   the result of multiplying two integers is *not* affected by the contents of register A prior to the multiplication;

(b)   the result of dividing an integer by another *is* affected by the contents of register A prior to division.

Choose numbers to avoid overflow, and explain in pencil on the output sheet the exact computation which was done.

2. Do an instruction-by-instruction analysis of the following BAREBONZ program, and determine the contents of the postexecution printout:

```
000   58A0C028
004   5AA0C02C
008   50A0C030
00C   58A0C004
```

```
010   5AA0C034
014   50A0C01C
018   58A0C03C
01C   00000000
020   50A0C040
024   47F0E000
028   00000035
02C   000000E4
030   00000000
034   0100000C
038   00000047
03C   000001A2
040   00000000
      000
```

3. Write a BAREBONZ program to approximate the average of five positive integers by integer division of the sum of the integers by five. Output should show both the quotient and remainder. If the integers are allowed to be negative (so that the sum can be negative) then what precautions must be taken in entering the dividend in the register pair AB?

4. Rewrite the program in the previous problem so that the average of five integers is calculated and stored to the nearest integer. That is, if the remainder divided by the divisor is less than 0.5, the integer quotient is the answer; otherwise, the integer quotient adjusted by one is the answer. You may assume that the sum of the integers is positive to simplify the rounding procedure, which should be applicable to divisors other than 5. Use only the integer instructions in Table 3.3.1.

5. Assume integers $M = 81$ and $N = 13$ (base 10) are stored in memory and write a program which will place in successive words starting at location 100_{16} the quantities

$$SUM = M + N$$
$$DIFF = M - N$$
$$PROD = M \cdot N$$
$$QUOT = M \div N \quad \text{(integer quotient)}$$
$$REM = M - N \cdot QUOT$$

To make the printout easily understood, record the symbolic instruction and comments starting in column 14. Your program should begin at 000, and can consist of as few as 14 executable instructions. Check results to be sure they are correct.

6. Write a BAREBONZ sequence with a loop whose only function is to fill the locations F60 through FD7 with EBCDIC blank characters, each of which is represented by hexadecimal 40. As we will see later, this problem is related to providing output. For this one program, you are to accomplish the task with a store instruction which is modified after each execution. Test the sequence by loading trash information into F5C-F63 and into FD4-FDB from cards and then applying your sequence. Note that the words beginning at F5C and FD8 should be undisturbed by your sequence, but the words beginning at F60 and FD4 should be replaced by blanks. In order to express this program completely in symbolic form, it is helpful to have a pseudoinstruction for resetting the location given to the next symbolic instruction. The interested reader should look up ORG in the assembler manual.

7. Given that a formula for translating degrees Fahrenheit F to degrees centigrade C is

$$C = (5F - 160)/9$$

write a program with a loop to determine the Centigrade temperatures corresponding to the Fahrenheit temperatures -127, -90, -40, 0, 32, 96, 150, 212, rounding off to the nearest integer. Use only the integer instructions in Table 3.3.1. See Appendix G for a discussion of rounding, and consider computing a rounded C directly by developing an expression for the rounded value before programming.

8. It is sometimes necessary to patch a program when one realizes he has omitted an essential instruction. If the program is punched in numeric form this can be a painful nuisance. A way out is to leave all existing cards just as they are and to override the one just prior to the omission by using a BC instruction to branch to a secondary sequence where the replaced and omitted instructions can be written. A branch back to the primary sequence completes the patch. One may prepare for trouble (as every programmer should) by saving register E contents as his first instruction and restoring them as his last. Then the patch can be made with a BAL instruction and the return can be made through register E. Demonstrate each method in a computation of $J = M^2 + N^2$ in which the instruction to store M^2 until N^2 is calculated was omitted.

9. Using only the single available test instruction in BAREBONZ, demonstrate how to realize a decision on each of the following relations:

		FORTRAN equivalent
a.	$M > N$	M.GT.N
b.	$M \geq N$	M.GE.N
c.	$M = N$	M.EQ.N
d.	$M \neq N$	M.NE.N
e.	$M \leq N$	M.LE.N
f.	$M < N$	M.LT.N

Execution should continue to the next instruction in sequence if the relation is false or if overflow is detected. There should be a branch to location A00 if the relation is true.

10. The flowchart just below resolves most of the questions that might occur in interpreting the FORTRAN segment on its right.

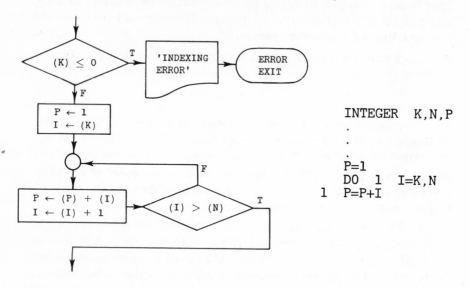

```
INTEGER   K,N,P
     .
     .
     .
     P=1
     DO  1   I=K,N
  1  P=P+I
```

Write a program segment using symbolic instructions which is faithful to the flowchart. Use only the instructions given in Table 3.3.1.

11. Consider arithmetic shifts to the right, which correspond in some sense to division by a power of two. To use them in this way, we must be careful to determine any differences between results obtained by shifting and results obtained by division. Give the precise result of a shift right arithmetic by 1 position for the cases

      a. $(AB) = 63$ c. $(AB) = -63$

      b. $(AB) = 2^{31} + 1$ d. $(AB) = -2^{63}$

and compare the results to those attainable from division by two. Explain any differences in results.

12. The number 2^{30} is represented in B as an integer and register A is set to zero. You perform a double left shift arithmetic by 1 position. What integer does B now represent? What integer does AB represent?

13. Frank the flea wishes to teeter-totter with Effluvius the elephant, but the dimensions of the teeter-totter need to be determined before it can be built. Frank and Effluvius decide to make the following assumptions:

    (a)   The teeter-totter is weightless.

    (b)   Frank will sit 80 million feet from the fulcrum.

The equation to be satisfied is

$$W_F D_F = W_E D_E$$

where W_F is Frank's weight ($= 0.0124$ ounce), D_F is Frank's distance from the fulcrum ($= 80$ million feet), W_E is Effluvius' weight ($= 6.18$ tons), and D_E is Effluvius' distance from the fulcrum. Using the scaling techniques discussed in Section 3.4, define new variables which are scaled by powers of 10 from those above, so that the resultant computation of D_E can be accomplished with a BAREBONZ program. Write the program and use it to compute D_E.

14. You are to devise a subprogram which receives in register B a non-negative binary integer to be converted to decimal, and in register A an address parameter for an array named DIGITS. The subprogram is to deposit the binary representation of the decimal coefficient of 10^p into DIGITS + $4p$. A straightforward approach is to perform 9 successive divisions of an integer quotient by 10, the initial quotient being the integer to be converted. Use register E for control linkage.

15. This problem is the inverse of Problem 14. A nonnegative integer of up to ten decimal digits has the coefficient of 10^p of its decimal representation stored as full-word binary integers in location DIGITS + $4p$ ($p = 0, \ldots, 9$). Calculate the binary representation of the decimal integer, assuming that the result is less than 2^{31}. Organize your instructions as a subprogram. The input parameter should be the address of DIGITS, and the result should be the value of the binary integer. Use register A for passing parameters and register E for control linkage.

16. Ten-digit nonnegative input numbers are punched one to a card in columns 3–12 of data cards. As a part of the conversion process, these numbers are to have the binary representations of their decimal digits stored in an array named DIGITS as specified in the previous problem. You are to write a subprogram to do this in which an address parameter for DIGITS is provided in register A when the subprogram is called. Note that use of this subprogram together with that of the previous problem will yield internal binary representations of unsigned decimal integer input.

17. Assume that information to be printed is to be stored in character form in locations F60–FD7. Your job is to print a decimal integer for which the full-word binary representation of the coefficient of 10^p is stored in DIGITS + $4p$ ($p = 0, \ldots, 9$). You should write a subprogram to deposit the character representations of these digits into F62–F6B properly ordered on p. Let an address parameter for DIGITS be provided in register A when the subprogram is called. Note that the use of this subprogram and that of Problem 14 together will give decimal output of binary integers.

18. Write a BAREBONZ program which has the simple purpose of determining the base address given to your program by the host machine. Then compute the effective address of each instruction in that program by hand, assuming no indexing and that the contents of registers C and E remain unchanged throughout the program. If you have real courage, modify the program so that it computes the effective address of every instruction in it. The end of program should be flagged.

19. Write a called program which has k as an input parameter, and on return to the calling program leaves the contents of the kth byte beyond location F00 in the rightmost byte of register A, the other bytes of register A being set to zero. Apply this subprogram to deposit the results for $k = 13, 26, 51$, and 72 into full words at locations 100, 104, 108, and 10C, respectively. Link to the subprogram using register E, being cautious to preserve the exit address to the supervisor.

20. Using the program control linkage according to (1) the "I trust nobody" philosophy, and then (2) the "I trust everybody" philosophy, write a calling program and a called program which accomplish the following:

(a) The calling program computes the area of a right triangle given the (integral) lengths of its perpendicular edges, and passes the area to the called program.

(b) The called program computes the least integer which, when squared, yields an area greater than or equal to the area of the triangle.

21. Rewrite the program requested in Problem 7 so that an index register is utilized to accomplish repetitive application of an instruction sequence to the elements of the temperature array.

22. Rewrite the program requested in Problem 10 so that an index register is used for the index of the loop. In your implementation, will the index be available from a location bearing the index name on exit from the loop?

23. Rewrite the program requested in Problem 3 to take maximum advantage of RR instructions. What special care must be taken with the addresses at which instructions (constants included) are stored?

Chapter 4

Machine Translation of Symbolic Instructions

4.1 THE CASE FOR MACHINE TRANSLATION

We have seen in Chapter 3 that the translation of symbolic representations of machine instructions into their numeric form is mechanical in nature. Any imagination applied to create an excellent program is expended in the planning and writing of the symbolic program prior to translation. This is a prime opportunity for the programmer to use the computer to take over some of the routine aspects of his programming job, so that his emphasis can be primarily on the algorithmic aspects of the problem rather than the clerical chores.

The word "translation" has very broad implications, being appropriate to any conversion of text from one language called a *source* language to another language called an *object* language. An example of natural language translation would be translating Russian to English, or vice versa; but translating a procedural source language (such as FORTRAN or

COBOL) to a machine language is easier to mechanize. The especially simple kind of translation we refer to here is done by a class of programs called *assemblers*. One may judge by the name that assemblers have functions other than translation, and some of these other functions will be studied later in this chapter. For now, our purpose is to utilize the translation capabilities of assemblers for the IBM 360/370.

It may seem strange that more than one assembler is needed to perform translations from a standard symbolic representation of instructions to machine code. Finding a standard representation is simple. The problem is that so many chores have been turned over to assemblers that those which do them all are relatively slow to use. Assemblers which are designed to do the most needed (but not all the possible) tasks, and which usually limit the size of program to which they are applicable, may be more efficient and convenient to use where they are adequate. The latter type is especially appropriate to give quick turnaround for simple programs in a student environment.

In discussing the assembly process, it is convenient to think of an instruction as being that symbolic representation occupying one line on the programming page. Instructions can then be subdivided into classes as follows:

Symbolic machine instruction.   A symbolic representation of a numeric machine instruction. A numeric machine instruction is a sequence of digits interpreted by the control unit as one instruction in the execution of the translated program. The BAREBONZ instructions in Chapter 3 are examples of numeric machine instructions.

Pseudoinstruction.   A symbolic instruction which does not translate into a numeric machine instruction in the translated program, but may call for action by the assembler or may provide machine-coded data in the translated program. The DC and END instructions discussed in Section 3.3.4 and used in Program 3.3.1 are the only pseudoinstructions we have seen thus far.

Macroinstruction.   A symbolic instruction which does not *directly* translate into a machine instruction but which may cause one or more words to be inserted into the translated program, some of which may be numeric machine instructions, and some data words.

To this point, we have encountered no macroinstructions. There are some which we will use later to facilitate both debugging and standardized "housekeeping" aspects of our programming. Learning to use an existing macro may be as simple as learning to use a machine instruction. Defining a macro, on the other hand, is a relatively complex programming task and we define only simple ones in this text. But for now, we wish to develop the definitions and ideas required to use an assembler, and to understand the assembly process.

The assembly process is illustrated in the block diagram in Figure 4.1.1. Our source language is assembler language, and the object language is machine code. Initially, we will be concerned with translating symbolic machine instructions to machine code.

Corresponding to the instruction set for BAREBONZ, we are going to describe a symbolic representation of machine instructions and pseudoinstructions which is adequate for any of the programs written in Chapter 3. Furthermore, these symbolic instructions and pseudoinstructions can be translated by any reasonable assembler for the IBM 360/370 into a correct machine program. As more elaborate features are required of the assembler, they will be described in succeeding chapters. The symbolic representation of instructions required by the IBM 360/370 assemblers is slightly different from what we have been using, so we now discuss a more standard format. This will complete our gradual transition from machine language to symbolic representation, and the new form will be more convenient for the programmer and more amenable to the mechanization we seek.

4.2   A STANDARD FORM FOR SYMBOLIC REPRESENTATION OF INSTRUCTIONS

1. We define a *symbolic name* to be a string of characters, each of

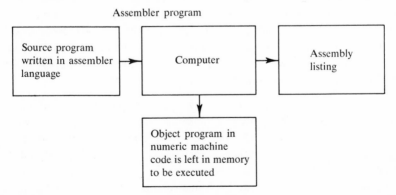

Figure 4.1.1   The source program is translated into machine code by the assembler, and an assembly listing of the translation is also provided. The assembler program regards the source program as data, and controls the computer so that an assembly listing and an object program are obtained.

which is numeric or alphabetic, and the first of which is alphabetic. Its length is the number of characters in the string, which must be at least one.

2. The *symbolic location* of an instruction is a symbolic name of length at most 8; this field may be blank.

3. The *operation mnemonic* of an instruction is a symbolic name. Except for macroinstructions, it is composed of alphabetic characters and has a length of five or less. These were introduced in Section 3.3.4, and were first used in Program 3.3.1.

4. To avoid confusion between symbolic names of length one and hexadecimal register numbers A, . . . , F, we henceforth agree to use a decimal integer to represent any number in an operand designation. This will include register numbers and immediate operands in the instruction such as a mask or an amount of shift.

5. We find it logically coherent to organize the remaining information according to its function in selecting operands. Almost all instructions have two operands, so we provide for *first operand* and *second operand* designations.

6. Whereas we were able to establish an arbitrary but reasonable maximum length for symbolic location and operation, the symbolic operands are so variable in length that we find it more convenient to pack the two operand representations into one string, separating them by a comma. We call the resulting string the *operand field*.

7. Normally the base register does not change from one instruction to the next. Therefore, it is convenient to avoid naming it in each symbolic instruction. To accomplish this, we introduce the USING pseudoinstruction to designate a base which will automatically be implied as hex digit 4 of each instruction which uses a base and does not supply its own explicitly. This is discussed in detail in the next section.

8. In this rudimentary assembler, we gain simplicity by (temporarily) limiting the variety of operand representations. For the present we will restrict ourselves to RR, RS, and RX instructions; thus we can assume that the first operand is either a register or a mask, represented by a decimal integer R1, where $0 \leq R1 \leq 15$. For the RR instructions given in Table 3.6.1 and the RS and RX instructions given in Table 3.3.1, we will (temporarily) restrict ourselves to the forms shown in Table 4.2.1 for the second operand.

Type	Second operand form	Explanation
RR	R2	R2 is a decimal integer representing a register number
RS	N	N is a decimal integer, and since shift instructions are the only RS instructions we have had, N denotes the amount of shift.
RX	SYM	SYM is a symbolic name as defined in number 1 above
RX	SYM + N	The displacement of SYM is incremented by the decimal integer N
RX	SYM(R2)	The symbolic name is tagged with the number of the index register

Table 4.2.1   If the second operand is limited to the forms in this table, it is adequate for all of the programs in Chapter 3, and the assembler algorithm (discussed in Section 4.4) can be simpler.

Some examples of these operands, and the machine instructions resulting from assembly, are shown to illustrate the precise meaning of the various operand forms in Table 4.2.2.

9. Since the symbolic representation of operands is so variable in length, the space for comments on a card varies also. We adopt a convention of permitting *no blanks within the operand field* so that the first blank encountered after the beginning of the operand field can be taken as the left boundary of the comments field.

Assume that register C is the base register, and that the symbolic name PAY is the address

$$PAY = (\text{Register C}) + 014_{16}$$

so that the displacement associated with PAY is 014_{16}.

Translated instruction	Symbolic instruction		Type
1A3B	AR	3,11	RR
8DA0001B	SLDL	10,27	RS
50D0C014	ST	13,PAY	RX
58A0C018	L	10,PAY+4	RX
5BA0C020	S	10,PAY+12	RX
5AB7C014	A	11,PAY(7)	RX
47E0C014	BC	14,PAY	RX

Table 4.2.2   When the second operand contains a symbolic name, the assembler inserts the number of the base register as hex digit 4 (at the request of the USING pseudoinstruction discussed in the next section).

10. We adopt card-column conventions as follows:

(a) The symbolic location is punched in consecutive columns beginning in column 1 and ending on or before column 8.

(b) The operation mnemonic must be punched in consecutive columns beginning at column 10.

(c) The symbolic operand field is normally punched in consecutive columns beginning in column 16, thus leaving at least one blank between the operation mnemonic and the operand field. For the rare cases that the operation mnemonic has length greater than five, the operand field begins two columns beyond the end of the operation mnemonic field, separated from it by an intervening blank column.

(d) The comments field begins two columns beyond the end of the operand field (there must be an intervening blank column) and ends on or before column 71.

(e) If one card (through column 71) is insufficient for the entire symbolic operand field, a continuation on the next card can be signified by a nonblank character in column 72. This character will not be interpreted as part of the operand field so it should not be part of the statement coding. The continuation begins in column 16 (the symbolic operand field) of the next card.

(f) Columns 73–80 are reserved for identification mnemonic and sequence numbers; such identification is essential for large programs, but may be ignored with short programs.

(g) An asterisk in column 1 causes the entire card to be treated as a comment.

4.3   SOME ESSENTIAL PSEUDOINSTRUCTIONS

4.3.1   Establishing a Base Address

The pseudoinstruction (mentioned in the seventh item in the list in Section 4.2) for specifying to the translator what register is to hold the base has USING for operation mnemonic. We shall apply a restricted version of this pseudoinstruction, permitting only two operands. The first is the symbolic name of the base address. The second is a decimal integer which names the base register. The pseudoinstruction below conforms to the examples of Chapter 3 by naming register C as base register and BEGIN as base address:

$$\text{USING} \qquad \text{BEGIN,12}$$

where BEGIN is the symbolic location of the first instruction which translates into numeric machine code and also marks the beginning of BAREBONZ memory. We shall continue to use the beginning of BARE-BONZ memory as the base address, but the two occurrences of BEGIN— one in the USING pseudoinstruction and one in the initial machine instruction—can be replaced by occurrences of any symbolic name of no more than eight characters.

Telling the translator (1) which register holds the base address, and (2) the name of the reference location, permits creation of correct instructions but it does not ensure that the correct address is actually in that register. Until now, we have relied on the BAREBONZ system to load register 12 with the base address. Conventions of the standard IBM 360/370 assembler established by the manufacturer (and therefore widely used) leave the effective address of the first machine instruction of the program in register 15. We can use this programming convention to establish a base register with the following instruction pair:

Symbolic location	Operation mnemonic	Operand field
BEGIN	LR	12,15
	USING	BEGIN,12

The LR instruction loads the address of the first machine instruction into register 12, and the USING instruction informs the assembler, so that displacements will be computed correctly. Thus we have established (1) register 12 as the base register, and (2) the base address as the location of the first instruction in memory of the program (to be used as the reference address). It may help understanding to be reminded that the USING pseudoinstruction is applied *only* during translation, and is neither available nor needed during program execution. On the other hand, the loading of register 12 from register 15 occurs during execution rather than during translation. Placing the USING pseudoinstruction after the instruction whose location is the reference point is done to simplify the task of one-scan assemblers, as will be discussed in Section 4.6.

4.3.2   Defining Constants

The way in which a constant is most conveniently defined depends to a large extent upon its use. As an example, we find it natural to use the external (decimal) representation to write an integer. But if a constant represents an instruction, the decimal integer which converts to a binary integer with the bit pattern that appears in the instruction would be most difficult to interpret. The natural representation for an instruction is a succession of hexadecimal digits. When distinct individual bits of a word have unrelated functions, it may be best to specify the binary digits (bits) of a constant directly. Thus, we can expect a variety of representations to be useful in defining constants.

It would divert us from major objectives to exhaust all of the various data representations possible with DC pseudoinstructions. We can get along well for the present with the ability to specify strings of like elements which may be bits, hexadecimal digits, or characters, and to specify integers in decimal representation.

In every DC pseudoinstruction, there is a single letter called the *type code*. We shall be concerned with type codes having the significance:

Type code	Data type
F	Full-word integer
H	Half-word integer
C	Character string
X	Hexadecimal digit string
B	Bit string

Among these, F and H clearly specify a length in bytes of the internal representation; on the other hand, strings are so variable that their length is determined otherwise. To avoid unnecessary detail, we will presently consider specifying as data only strings which begin and end on byte boundaries (hexadecimal strings will have an even number of elements and binary strings will have length divisible by 8). For these cases, the length is just the number of bytes in the string, which is determined implicitly by the assembler from the string itself.

It is assumed by the assembler that data items representing full-word or half-word integers will be accessed by instructions which require alignment of their second operands to full- or half-word boundaries, respectively. When a DC pseudoinstruction has type code F or H, the tentative address for its datum (as determined from the previous line of symbolic coding) is adjusted upward just enough to provide alignment, thus relieving the programmer of any such concern.

Strings of characters, hexadecimal digits, or binary bits are, by contrast, aligned only to the nearest byte boundary if aligned at all. Where alignment is necessary but not automatic (for example, when an integer is specified in hexadecimal) that alignment may have to be forced by insertion of a DC pseudoinstruction just ahead of it, one which does force alignment. We can get alignment on a full-word boundary by a DC pseudoinstruction with F for type code, and on a half-word boundary by a DC pseudoinstruction with H for type code.

The limited version of the DC operand field which we shall consider is as follows:

1. It begins with an integer called the *duplication factor,* which tells how many consecutive occurrences of the constant are to be placed in memory (default is to one occurrence if the duplication factor is missing, in which case the operand field begins with a letter). The duplication factor can be zero, in which case no constant is assembled, although indicated alignment will be done. If the symbolic location field contains a symbolic name, that name will be assigned the address of this constant relative to the beginning of allotted memory (the current translation address defined in Section 4.4.1).

2. The duplication factor is followed by a one-letter type code which specifies the type of representation of the constant in the pseudoinstruction and also its type in memory.

3. The type code is followed by the pseudoinstruction representation of the. constant enclosed by single quotes. This completes the operand field.

Some samples of DC instructions appear in Table 4.3.1 together with the hexadecimal representation which results. The duplication factor of zero, which appears as a type F example in Table 4.3.1, causes full-word alignment of the next constant, but no storage reservation.

The examples in Table 4.3.1 raise many questions about the possible variations of constant representations in the operand field. We do not intend to resolve them here. Our need for the present is only for a dupli-

Assembled constant (hex)	Operation mnemonic	Operand field
FFFFFFE5	DC	F'−27'
C2D6D5C2D6D5	DC	2C'BON'
FADE	DC	X'FADE'
F7	DC	B'11110111'
	DC	0F'123'
BC	DC	X'BC'
010F	DC	H'271'

The portion of memory set by this succession of DC's will contain:

FFFFFFE5C2D6D5C2D6D5FADEF7000000BC00010F

↑   ↑   ↑

Aligned to   Aligned to   Aligned to
  full-word   full-word   half-word
  boundary   boundary   boundary

Table 4.3.1   A segment of memory as set by a succession of DC pseudoinstructions displays the alignment properties of F and H type codes.

cation factor and for the convenience of defining full-word integers and some strings. We have defined the duplication factor. A positive integer is represented by its decimal digits, and a negative sign preceding the decimal digits results in the storage of the 2's complement. If positive, a full-word integer must have a magnitude less than 2^{31}; if it is negative, a magnitude of 2^{31} can be represented. The strings which we have permitted are largely self-explanatory, and are sufficient for the present.

4.3.3 Marking the End of Assembly

There is a pseudoinstruction with operation mnemonic END which serves to terminate assembly. Its operand field is the symbolic location of the initial instruction to be executed.

As an example of the symbolic representation of instructions discussed in Section 4.2 and the pseudoinstructions discussed in Section 4.3, we will rewrite Program 3.6.1. For all the programs in Chapter 3, the BAREBONZ system established the base register, but for each symbolic program the programmer must first establish a base register.

If the appropriate control cards are added, Program 4.3.1 will assemble and execute correctly on any IBM 360/370. As shown, however, there is

Symbolic location	Operation mnemonic	Symbolic operand field	Comments
BEGIN	LR	12,15	Load base address
	USING	BEGIN,12	Tell the assembler
	L	10,ZERO	Initialize sum register
	L	1,ZERO	$i \leftarrow 0$
LOOP	A	10,GRADES(1)	Add one term
	S	1,TESTVAL	Test index
	BC	2,STOR	Branch on positive
	A	1,INCVAL	Restore and increment index
	BC	15,LOOP	Reenter loop
STOR	ST	10,SUM	Store result
EXIT	BCR	15,14	All done
ZERO	DC	F'0'	
TESTVAL	DC	F'16'	
INCVAL	DC	F'20'	Value to restore and increment index
SUM	DC	F'0'	
GRADES	DC	F'89'	
	DC	F'68'	
	DC	F'74'	
	DC	F'97'	
	DC	F'85'	
	END	BEGIN	

Program 4.3.1 This program is a complete assembler language program, and should be correctly translated by any assembler for the IBM 360/370.

no provision for output—not even the hexadecimal record of memory content which was the only output available in Chapter 3! Although our present concern is the assembly process, we will learn how to request selective dumps in Section 4.5. In this way, we can view results computed by the program as we did in BAREBONZ programs.

4.4   A SCHEME FOR TRANSLATION

4.4.1   Building a Symbol Table

Translation to numeric code of an individual instruction is primarily dependent on the availability of numeric equivalents for all symbolic locations in its location and operand field. If these are measured relative to a single location at the beginning of the program—as is the BARE-BONZ practice—then it is an easy matter to determine these numeric addresses by one scan through the instructions to form a *symbol table* before any translation is attempted. On this scan we record all symbolic names which occur in the instruction location column together with a numeric address determined by the position in the program of that occurrence. Rules for the formation of the symbol table are given in the following procedure:

1. A Current Translation Address (CTA) is set to zero and a line count called LINECNT on the symbolic form is set to 1. The main purpose of the CTA is to hold the address relative to the beginning of the program of the instruction currently being analyzed.

2. The symbolic operation code on the current line is compared to 'END'; if it is 'END' this scan of the instructions is terminated. If it is not, we perform 3–5 below.

3. The symbolic operation code on the current line and the corresponding operand field if necessary are examined to determine whether or not alignment is required. If it is, the byte count in the CTA is adjusted upward only if its current address is not aligned and then by the smallest integer which will align it. Note that machine instructions must begin at half-word boundaries, while data have varying alignment requirements depending on the type code.

4. The symbolic location field on the current line is examined. If there is a symbolic name, that name is entered in the symbol table and its value for the table is taken directly from the CTA. This is said to *define* the symbolic name.

5. The CTA is incremented by the byte length of the item (instruction or data) determined by LINECNT, and then LINECNT is incremented by 1. Return to step 2.

The flowchart in Figure 4.4.1 illustrates this procedure for automatic generation of the symbol table during the first scan of instructions in more detail.

At this point it becomes necessary to mesh the terminology of this text with that of assemblers commonly available, for these will provide the titles on the assembler listings we are preparing to use. There are no great problems. We have consistently spoken of instructions, whether they be symbolic or numeric, machine, pseudo, or macro. Some authors consider a line of symbolic coding to be a *statement*. The assembler listing will probably label the symbolic representation of an instruction as a source statement and the instruction number as a statement number. With respect to their use in regard to symbolic programming, we take the words "instruction" and "statement" to be synonymous, each having symbolic and numeric form.

We have seen that the first scan (often called a *pass*) of an assembler over the instructions builds a symbol table; for each symbolic location, this table lists the corresponding numerical address relative to the first machine instruction of the program. This table may also hold a length for each symbol (the length in bytes of the information accessed by that symbol) and the number of the statement in which the value of the symbol is defined. This symbol table is the only result which needs to be retained from the first scan. It provides just enough information to permit complete translation on a second scan.

Program 4.4.1 illustrates the results of the first scan of Program 4.3.1 by a two-scan assembler. Ordinarily, the first scan gives no printed output, all printing being deferred until translation is complete. Then the printed output is arranged for convenience of the reader rather than in the order it was generated. In particular, the symbol table always follows the translation even though it was generated earlier. Note that the first scan has not generated object code; it has analyzed instructions only far enough to determine increments in the CTA from one line to the next. The printing of the symbolic program with statement numbers makes verification of symbol table entries convenient.

4.4.2 Translating Instructions

Given (1) a symbol table generated by the rules presented in the flowchart in Figure 4.4.1 (and illustrated in Program 4.4.1), (2) a base register, and (3) an agreement that the base register contains the effective address of the initial instruction of the program, the assembler (or the programmer) can easily construct the numeric equivalent of individual

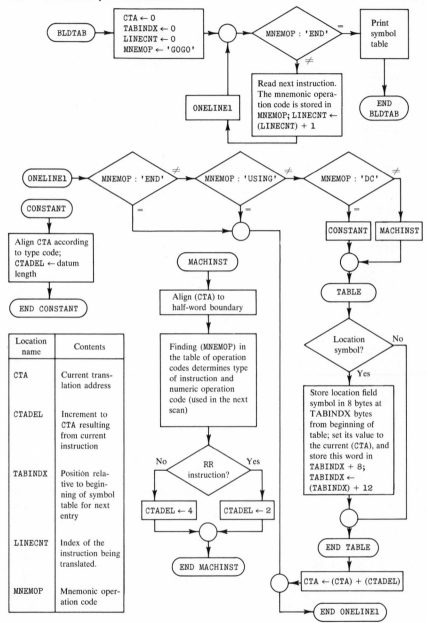

Figure 4.4.1 This flowchart shows many of the details involved in building the symbol table during the first scan through the symbolic instructions. It ignores some important possibilities for error detection such as finding if a name is defined more than once or is used in an operand and never defined.

LOC	STMT	SOURCE	STATEMENT	
000000	1	BEGIN	LR	12,15
000000	2		USING	BEGIN,12
000002	3		L	10,ZERO
000006	4		L	1,ZERO
00000A	5	LOOP	A	10,Grades(1)
00000E	6		S	1,TESTVAL
000012	7		BC	2,STOR
000016	8		A	1,INCVAL
00001A	9		BC	15,LOOP
00001E	10	STOR	ST	10,SUM
000022	11	EXIT	BCR	15,14
000024	12	ZERO	DC	F'0'
000028	13	TESTVAL	DC	F'16'
00002C	14	INCVAL	DC	F'20'
000030	15	SUM	DC	F'0'
000034	16	GRADES	DC	F'89'
000038	17		DC	F'68'
00003C	18		DC	F'74'
000040	19		DC	F'97'
000044	20		DC	F'85'
000000	21		END	BEGIN

SYMBOL	LENGTH	VALUE	DEFINITION
BEGIN	2	0	1
EXIT	2	22	11
GRADES	4	34	16
INCVAL	4	2C	14
LOOP	4	A	5
STOR	4	1E	10
SUM	4	30	15
TESTVAL	4	28	13
ZERO	4	24	12

Program 4.4.1 The first scan of Program 4.3.1 generates the information shown—a symbol table listing symbols and the corresponding numerical addresses. To do this, relative addresses are assigned by the CTA (these are listed in the column headed "LOC"). In addition, statements are numbered to provide a list of symbol definitions and references.

instructions in a second scan through them. Figures 4.4.2 and 4.4.3 show this second step in translating to machine code.

Although the flowcharts shown for the second scan are more complex than the flowchart for building the symbol table, the results of the second scan are easier to illustrate on a program. Program 4.4.2 shows the object code (numeric machine code) obtained from the second scan of the symbolic instructions of Program 4.4.1, thus finally completing the assembly process for this program.

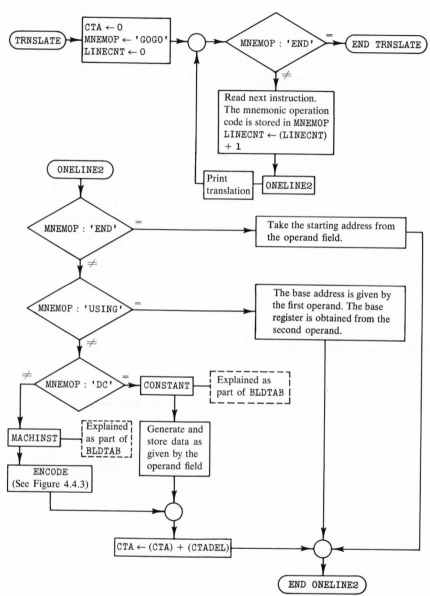

Figure 4.4.2 The second step in a two-scan assembler uses the symbol table to complete the address portion of instructions, and substitutes hexadecimal values for the operation mnemonic and the first operand. After the second scan is complete, the machine instruction or DC pseudoinstruction must have been completely translated into numeric form.

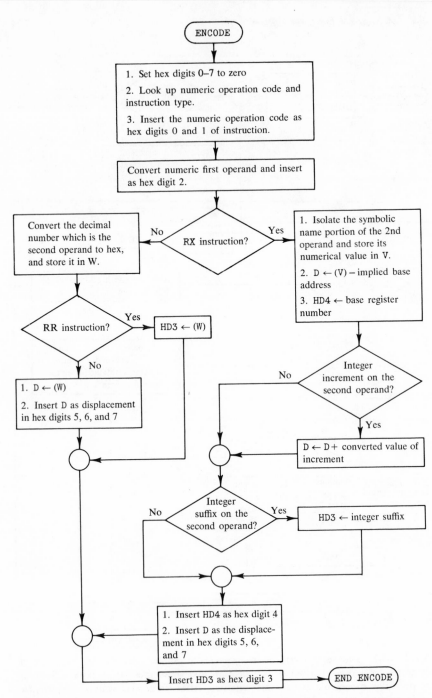

Figure 4.4.3 The purpose of ENCODE is to construct the numeric code for any individual machine instruction.

	OBJECT						
LOC	CODE	ADDR1	ADDR2	STMT	SOURCE		STATEMENT
000000	18CF			1	BEGIN	LR	12,15
000000				2		USING	BEGIN,12
000002	58A0 C024			3		L	10,ZERO
000006	5810 C024		00024	4		L	1,ZERO
00000A	5AA1 C034		00034	5	LOOP	A	10,GRADES(1)
00000E	5B10 C028		00028	6		S	1,TESTVAL
000012	4720 C01E		0001E	7		BC	2,STOR
000016	5A10 C02C		0002C	8		A	1,INCVAL
00001A	47F0 C00A		0000A	9		BC	15,LOOP
00001E	50A0 C030		00030	10	STOR	ST	10,SUM
000022	07FE			11	EXIT	BCR	15,14
000024	00000000			12	ZERO	DC	F'0'
000028	00000010			13	TESTVAL	DC	F'16'
00002C	00000014			14	INCVAL	DC	F'20'
000030	00000000			15	SUM	DC	F'0'
000034	00000059			16	GRADES	DC	F'89'
000038	00000044			17		DC	F'68'
00003C	0000004A			18		DC	F'74'
000040	00000061			19		DC	F'97'
000044	00000055			20		DC	F'85'
000000				21		END	BEGIN

Program 4.4.2   The second scan uses the symbol table, the base register, the first operand, and the numeric operation codes to complete the translation of machine instructions. The DC pseudoinstructions are also translated to the appropriate values, which are always listed in hexadecimal.

The numeric instruction resulting from translation of a symbolic machine instruction appears on the assembler listing on the same line under the heading "object code." Those instructions which refer to memory will contain one or two displacements from a base. To simplify checking for the programmer, the assembler prints addresses relative to the beginning of the program under the headings "address 1" or "address 2" for those operands of an instruction which refer to memory, using blank entries when the corresponding operand does not. These columns should be considered explanatory only.

After the second scan has been completed, the symbol table is printed with an additional column showing statement numbers of the instructions referencing a symbolic location. Since this information requires scanning operands for each instruction, it is not available until the second scan is complete. The resulting table is printed after the assembly process is completed. As an example, the symbol table for Program 4.4.2 is shown as a continuation of Program 4.4.2.

SYMBOL	LENGTH	VALUE	DEFINITION	REFERENCES	
BEGIN	00002	000000	00001	0002	0021
EXIT	00002	000022	00011		
GRADES	00004	000034	00016	0005	
INCVAL	00004	00002C	00014	0008	
LOOP	00004	00000A	00005	0009	
STOR	00004	00001E	00010	0007	
SUM	00004	000030	00015	0010	
TESTVAL	00004	000028	00013	0006	
ZERO	00004	000024	00012	0003	0004

Program 4.4.2 (Continued)   The completed symbol table contains the statement numbers of the instructions referencing each symbolic location, in addition to the information computed during the first scan.

4.5   THE PREVENTION, DETECTION, AND ELIMINATION OF ERRORS

There is opportunity for error in every aspect of program planning and implementation. A major aspect of a programmer's job is to expect them, detect them, and eliminate them. Some errors will be detected for him by the assembler. Some are not caught by the assembler but will make themselves known in an attempt to execute. The most insidious errors will execute innocently, but yield incorrect results; these will never be caught unless the programmer forces them to surface. It is of utmost importance to develop an understanding of effective teamwork between man and machine in eliminating program faults.

4.5.1   The Program Development Cycle

Programmer heaven admits only those whose programming is an implementation of an algorithm (effective procedure) which is well defined before programming begins in the form of a decision table, flowchart, or stepwise description. Thus we assume that the steps in solving a programming problem are:

(1) specify the algorithm,
(2) write the program,
(3) record the program in machine-acceptable form,
(4) eliminate clerical errors,
(5) eliminate syntax errors,
(6) make the program conform to the algorithm,
(7) correct the algorithm.

One should note a last-in, first-out nature of errors in this sequence of steps. Clerical errors are usually made in step 3 and are the first to be found. Errors in the algorithm—at the other extreme—are displayed only after a program has been generated which can perform its steps and in doing so gives unacceptable results. It is often ignored, but the prevention of faults in steps 1–3 and the insertion of error-detection devices in the algorithm and the program (in the expectation that faults will exist despite all precautions) are the keynotes of good programming.

Preventing Errors in the Algorithm

The most important step here is to have an algorithm defined in writing or in diagram or both (not just vague thoughts about one) and to try it on a few test cases. We must be certain that in trial execution which is faithful to the *definition* of the algorithm (rather than to the general principles on which it was based), it performs the steps expected and obtains valid results. The machine is of no help here.

Algorithms can be expressed in many ways. For clarity, one should constrain his algorithm to have a simple structure. The use of *structured* algorithms is helpful in keeping algorithms simple and elegant,† and we will find that a program which realizes a structured algorithm (called a *structured program*) has certain advantages during the inevitable debugging stage. A structured algorithm is built up from *actions* (also called segments) by concatenation of actions, selection among actions, or iteration of an action. There is no standardized definition for action, but the definitions that have been used agree that an action has exactly one entry and one exit. Figure 4.5.1 show the basic flowchart symbols, and the ways we will use to construct more complex actions from the basic flowchart symbols.

Henceforth, the structure we will use for drawing flowcharts of all algorithms consists of:

(1) begin,
(2) any number of actions,
(3) end.

---

† The concepts of structured programming are developed in E. W. Dijkstra, The structure of the "THE"—multiprogramming system, *Comm. ACM* May (1968). More recently, a paper by F. T. Baker entitled Chief programmer team management of production programming, *IBM Systems J.* **11** (1972) gives explicit concepts and evaluation. For a presentation in more depth, we recommend *Structured Programming* by Dahl, Dijkstra, and Hoare, Academic Press, 1972.

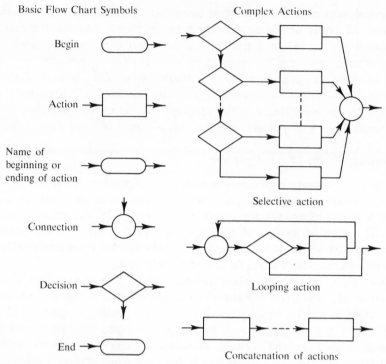

Figure 4.5.1 The basic flowchart symbols are shown on the left. In a structured program, we admit only those diagrams which are achievable from the symbol (except for begin, end, or name symbols)

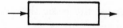

by repeated replacement of any action box by one of the complex actions shown on the right. Complex actions are formed from existing actions by the concatenation of actions, selection among actions, or by iterative application of an action. The result is a highly nested structure of which the basic building blocks are segments of code called actions, which have just one entry and one exit.

Note that neither the connection symbol nor the decision symbol forms actions, so that neither will be used alone in a flowchart. Moreover, the only way either symbol is used is in the selective action or in the looping action.

It may be convenient to assign a name to some of the actions in a program. An oval box

preceding an action assigns the name within the oval to that action. The
end of the action can be marked with another oval box containing **END**
followed by the name. This makes it easy to package a sequence of
actions into one, as illustrated by the action marked at entry by

in Figure 4.5.2. The end marker for the single action named **PEAR** is *not*
a name for the action which follows it; we include end markers for every
named action to remove all ambiguities as to the scope of a name.

The beginner (and some hard-core programming artists) will rebel at
the sense of confinement experienced in using only flowcharts constructed in this way. They will note that the branching instruction is
limited in scope; in fact, the only way to accomplish a branch is (1) as
part of a selective action, in which case all alternatives exit to a common
junction, or (2) as part of a loop. The loop is also restricted in nature,
having the test for completion before even one execution of the action it
controls. This is not the pattern of the **FORTRAN DO** statement, and
in fact a program diagrammed with these symbols could not make effective
use of the **FORTRAN DO** statement.

There is a growing tendency in programming to eliminate the unconditional branch (the **GO TO** of **FORTRAN**) or at least to restrict its
use drastically. That tendency should be noted here with respect to the
flowchart for structured programs, but we must recognize that, even when
a structured algorithm is implemented in machine language, the branch
is necessary. That does not keep the machine program from being structured; its branches will be only those required to select among actions,

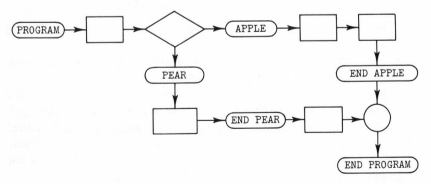

Figure 4.5.2 The entire algorithm is an action named PROGRAM; every action
name is matched by an end marker to delimit the action or sequence of actions.

to implement the iteration of an action, and (later on) to execute sequences at a remote location.

One may look upon the branch as an appendage from the early history of computers which was natural to programmers who had been weaned on machine instructions. Even some algorithms which were created well before computers were available have the branching concept in them—for example, an instruction to test the cake batter viscosity and, if it is too thin, return to step 13 of the cake-making procedure.

It is fair to ask why such limitations are recommended. The answer is that structured programming has been found more readable, more modular, and more susceptible to analysis. Although planning the algorithm may take longer, achieving a working, documented program is likely to be more economical in programming effort, elapsed time, and machine use. Some of the most successful programming projects have used structured programming exclusively, such as those described by Dijkstra and Baker in the articles referenced earlier in this section. Starting with Chapter 4, the algorithms in this book are structured algorithms and the programs are implementations of structured algorithms. Even though one is not required to work only from structured algorithms, he should as a matter of self-discipline know why he deviates when he does.

Preventing Errors in the Program

An assembler language program is a sequence of a great many instructions, usually considerably longer than the sequence of procedural language instructions needed for the corresponding procedural language program. Even so, if he is given a well-specified algorithm, the programmer can methodically convert to assembler language with few errors. The occasions in which error is to be expected are the following:

1. Use of an unfamiliar instruction without checking all details used in a reference manual.

2. Use of a programming convention (such as linkage between subroutines) without strict attention to its details.

3. Multipurpose use of registers or memory locations in which one risks seeking a parameter either before it is defined or after it is destroyed.

4. Use of complex instructions designed to accomplish several distinct tasks (e.g., the IBM 360/370 systems have instructions which increment an index, test its value, and then branch on the condition code, all in one instruction).

5. Deviating from conventional practices to save an instruction or a few microseconds by intricate programming.

6. Failure to have one's own conventional use of registers and of patterns of instructions for frequently repeated tasks.

There are occasions when the programmer should invest a great deal of effort in finding ingenious ways to eliminate an instruction, to short-circuit a convention, to save a memory location, or to avoid saving and restoring a register. The program should probably be written methodically in a first version and then improved upon as necessary after it works. These improvements should be made with eyes open and full expectation of error.

The rules according to which a sequence of instructions is accepted as a program by the assembler constitute its *syntax*. An assembler is quite meticulous in the way it requires individual instructions to be written. On the other hand, it will accept as a program almost any sequence of instructions which are individually consistent with syntax rules. Any error can be costly, but syntax errors are less costly than most because warnings of incorrect formatting of instructions and of other inconsistencies (such as undefined symbols in the operand field) are given by the assembler. Keeping an assembler manual in arm's reach to verify conjectures about permissible formats and using it when in doubt is a time-saving practice to be adopted from the beginning.

Preventing and Eliminating Clerical Errors

Clerical errors can usually be attributed to one of the following:

1. Poor handwriting, especially failure to distinguish distinct but similar characters.
2. Inept use of recording devices such as the keypunch.
3. Attempting to compose a program or a program modification at the keypunch.
4. Human error such as transposing digits when transcribing information.

The corrective action for prevention is clear: write clearly; punch carefully, since few of us are skilled at a keypunch; have a complete record of information to be punched before going to a keypunch; minimize transcriptions and do them carefully. There should be a careful proofreading of punched cards before they are submitted to machine processing. Further, it should be standard procedure that one's program prints its input data before they are used. This practice allows one to proofread data as they have gotten into memory, at the last possible checkpoint before use. It also displays input along with resultant output. The response of a program often seems capricious until a review shows that input was not what the programmer had expected it to be.

Eliminating Syntax Errors

The assembler expects instructions in a specific format. If they are not in that format, then it will yield a diagnostic. For example, an attempt to provide an operand from memory for an RR instruction will yield a diagnostic. So will an unlisted symbolic operation. An assembler can also check for some more devious errors. An operand name which is never defined by appearance in a location field, or an instruction requiring an implied base before one is assigned will yield a diagnostic. One can expect a good assembler to detect and print diagnostics for all such errors in the program in one attempt at assembly. If one is careful, he can resolve all these diagnosed errors and on the second run have a diagnostic-free program. It should be clear that this does not mean the program is error-free. The challenging part of fault elimination is still ahead. That consists of getting the program to execute the algorithm as documented.

Overall Checkout Practices

While intensive efforts are being made in universities and industrial laboratories to develop methods for proving program validity, there is essentially only one technique now being practiced for finding and eliminating discrepancies between program and algorithm. It consists of providing test data as input and insisting that the output obtained for those test data is correct. When the program yields correct results for suitably varied sets of input data, the program is declared operational. It may be used under close observation for months before it is declared valid. That depends on its complexity, and on the risks its users are willing to take. Usually, the inexperienced programmer underestimates time to program, time to test, and the number of undetected programming errors still in the program. We shall be concerned here with getting the program to function as the algorithm does for a particular input data set. Our principal tool is the selective snapshot. We relegate the trace, for example, to the class of desperation measures.

4.5.2 Use of the Selective Snapshot

By a *selective snapshot,* we mean a printed record of the information content of a set of registers and/or memory locations at a particular stage of computation. It is understood that taking a snapshot leaves all program information just as it was at initiation of the snapshot so that computation may be resumed after the snapshot if that is desired. It now becomes important to distinguish which key registers and memory locations to include in the snapshot, and for each set to determine:

1. What kinds of information should one expect to get?
2. How does one invoke the snapshot?
3. What are the appropriate times for such a snapshot?

Before considering these matters more generally, we examine a particular aspect of number 2, namely the distinction in character between *system-initiated* and *programmer-initiated* snapshots. The former come in response to a machine-detected exception (an unacceptable use of or result from an instruction), while the programmer-initiated snapshot is taken at a point in execution selected by the programmer.

System snapshots are an attempt, in ignorance of the nature of the program, to print enough so that the reader can find his way to the useful information. They can make few assumptions about the nature of the words being printed, for that depends on the program which has lost control. Consequently, system snapshots are likely to be in hexadecimal (perhaps character mode as well) and the reader must provide the proper interpretation for the particular problem. In this light, it is not unreasonable that the name *dump* has been attached to such snapshots. They try to make up in quantity for the fact that the system has no way to determine which are the key items of information to display the program flow. On the other hand, it is just those times when control has been lost that *any* information about the cause is treasured. An annotated system dump is presented in Appendix D.

In finding program faults, a major objective of the programmer is to reach the stage that the printout from an attempt at execution of his program yields snapshots which he initiated. Snapshots under programmer control can be specific in marking progress through the program, in selecting just those items which are of interest and labeling them in mnemonic fashion, and in printing each item in the appropriate mode for easy interpretation. Some compilers provide elegant facilities for the editing which yields a good snapshot. Assemblers will probably leave it to the programmer to compose his own edit for the case at hand. Such editing of snapshots takes effort and the choice may be a rather primitive editing to save programming time, but having a choice can be helpful.

Another choice in programmer-initiated snapshots is to intersperse snapshots at intermediate stages of execution. System snapshots are involuntary responses to serious trouble symptoms, and usually terminate the program. But the programmer who is concerned about a loop, for example, may print selected information each time through the loop. We will now discuss the possible ingredients of a snapshot.

The Program Status Word

Until now, we have spoken of a condition code register (CC) of two bits and an instruction address counter (IAC) of 24 bits as distinct items. In fact there is a double-word register (64 bits) called the *program status word* (PSW) which holds these items and several others as well. Bits 32-63 of the PSW will be helpful to us now (see Table 4.5.1), but more background is required to appreciate the left half of the PSW. As a program is being executed (after translation by the assembler), the numeric operation code of an instruction must be decoded by the CIR before the length of that instruction is known. Thus the instruction length code (ILC) in the PSW represents the length of the *last* instruction decoded by the CIR. The instruction address (which is stored in the IAC) contained in the PSW, however, is the address of the *next* instruction to be fetched from memory and then translated in the CIR. The mask bits explain the kinds of masking in effect. The essential reason for a printout of the PSW is to inform the programmer what instruction was in execution when an exception (violation of acceptable conditions for execution) occurred. The instruction address in the PSW fails to give this directly, for it points to the next instruction to be executed. However, if the instruction just completed or underway is not a branch, then subtracting the ILC from the instruction address will locate it in memory.

Knowing the location of the last instruction decoded may not be of substantial help. A user program may branch to any location in all of memory and attempt to execute the contents as an instruction. If the execution is successful, control will advance to the next "instruction" and

Bit positions in PSW	Contents
32–33	Instruction length code (ILC) in half words
34–35	Condition code
36†	Fixed-point overflow mask
37†	Decimal overflow mask
38†	Exponent underflow mask
39†	Significance mask
40–63	Instruction address

Table 4.5.1 The right half of the program status word contains information which can be very helpful in isolating errors.

† If the mask bit is one, an exception of the type which names the mask causes an interruption. If the mask bit is zero, the interruption is suppressed.

continue until an operation code is invalid, or an effective address for storing information is outside the user's available storage, or some other such inconsistency shows itself. When such a halt occurs, the user may know where control is but have no idea how control reached that point. There are no complete solutions to this problem which are economical. However, one observation worth considering is that a BAL or BALR instruction leaves in a general register the return location. Being consistent in using register 14 for linking and in preceding every other branch instruction with a BALR 15,0 should leave in one of these registers a location from which the last branch was made. A combination of PSW and general register contents will then usually allow one to find the offending branch. Such instructions inserted for checkout can be removed after the program is working.

The General Registers

Of the registers directly available to the programmer, none are more active than general registers 0–15. They are the site of all fixed-point arithmetic, all indexing, almost all control activity, and all standard linking activity except the return of a floating-point result as a function value. We will study floating-point arithmetic in Chapter 8. As we have seen, one of the general registers serves as a base register, and we will find that more than one base register can be useful in some programs.

We have seen that in case of a program interruption the PSW may enable us to find the instruction causing the exception. However, it will not usually enable us to reconstruct the effective address in an instruction which references memory, for the instruction must reference a base (in some cases two) and it may be indexed. Even a shift instruction may apply a base which influences the amount of shift. No matter what index register and/or base register an instruction applies, that register is one of the general registers 1–15 and will be printed by a snapshot of the general registers. Some control instructions put together several individual steps (incrementing, testing, and branching) and to do so may reference up to three different registers. In fact, we generalize to assert that as a class only RR instructions are completely specified without reference to a general register for an address, and that with the PSW and general register contents any instruction is completely specified.

Segments of Memory

Knowing the offending instruction may be of no help unless its operands are known, for they may be the cause of the exception. A division which gets its divisor from memory, for example, will succeed or fail depending on the magnitude of the divisor. Then a snapshot of a memory segment can be helpful. As another example, a programmer may have so firmly fixed in his mind what he expects to happen that he will not consider all alternatives until he sees a display of computed values in memory. A convenient way to specify a memory segment snapshot is to give symbolic names of full words which contain its endpoints. Since such a segment can contain instructions as well as a variety of data types, the external representation will likely be hexadecimal.

Save Areas

The linkage between programs is made via register contents. We have yet to detail the IBM 360/370 assembler conventions for program linkage, but we can generalize to assert that any reasonable linkage will save in a dedicated save area the ingredients of a snapshot of the general registers at the time of branching. In the IBM 360/370 conventions, program B's save area contains (1) a pointer to the save area of the program A which called B, and (2) a pointer to the save area of any program C which is currently activated by B. It is possible to cause the save areas of all programs currently in execution to be written by giving one command to print current save areas. One should do this at every indication of a fault in program linkage.

4.5.3   Invoking the SNAP Macroinstruction

There is a macroinstruction with operation mnemonic SNAP in the macro library which facilitates user initiation of snapshots. While there are simpler macros to understand, they are not nearly so specific to current needs; therefore, we start with a limited use of SNAP. First, we consider what we want of a snapshot macro and then how to ask for it.

In a user-invoked snapshot, we need the facility of specifying what information is to be printed. In any one use of SNAP, we are permitted to request printing of named areas by naming options as follows:

Area to be printed	Designation
Program status word	PSW
Contents of general registers	REGS
Save areas	SA
Storage from SYM1 to SYM2	SYM1, SYM2

The SNAP macro has *keyword* parameters; that is, the meaning of each parameter is specified by a keyword rather than implicitly by position in a parameter list. These keywords are part of the vocabulary of the macro.

Whenever a large number of choices among options is to be made, it is convenient to name the class of option with a keyword and then to give the assignments to that option in the form

keyword = (option list)

In case the option list can never exceed one word, the parentheses are dropped and we use the form

keyword = option

As an example, the first three items listed above under "area to be printed" are classified as program data for which the keyword is PDATA. If any program data are to be printed, then the keyword PDATA will be used. The list of options to be used is then assigned to PDATA. Thus

PDATA = (PSW,REGS)

calls for printing of the program status word and the general registers but not the save areas, while

PDATA = (PSW,SA)

calls for printing of the program status word and the save areas but not the registers. If just the PSW were to be printed, parentheses would still be used, yielding

PDATA = (PSW)

The keyword STORAGE is used if any segments of memory are to be printed by giving location names for the beginning and end of segment, respectively. If so, a list of name pairs is assigned to STORAGE. As an example,

STORAGE = (B1,E1,B2,E2,B3,E3)

would call for printout of three sequences of full words: one which includes B1 through E1, one which includes B2 through E2, and one which includes B3 through E3.

Until now, output data and the entire program have been automatically printed by BAREBONZ. The technique used for printing output of assembler language programs requires that the output data be gathered together in a special *file*. BAREBONZ did this "gathering together" for us, but it is now our responsibility. The idea is to have in one's program a block of data describing the file to be used for SNAP output and to store the data of the file on disk. The description of the file constitutes a data control block (DCB), the formation of which will be described just below. The data control block must have a name so that the SNAP macro can refer to it by the assignment

DCB = data control block name

If the DCB has name SNAPPER, then this assignment would read

DCB = SNAPPER

The assignments to DCB, PDATA, and STORAGE are listed with separating commas to form the operand field of the SNAP macro. Here is an example illustrating a call of the SNAP macro:

Operation mnemonic	Operand field
SNAP	DCB = SNAPPER,PDATA = (PSW),STORAGE = (B1,E1,B2,E2,B3,E3)

Creating a Data Control Block for SNAP

The SNAP macro is executable in that it causes machine action, but a different kind of macro is used to create the data control block. This macro, named DCB, provides data but no machine instructions. Because it cannot be executed, it should be thought of as a sequence of constants and placed in the program only where constants would be appropriate (never in the path of control).

Like SNAP, the DCB macro is a keyword macro. It has far too much flexibility for us to discuss in full. In one sense, we need know nothing about it since, for use with SNAP, the data control block can always be the same. As an alternative, we will describe the nature of the file informally, then tell one way to present this description in a DCB macro. The file which we are describing will be known as SNAPDUMP.

1. The file is named SNAPDUMP—this is signified by DDNAME = SNAPDUMP.

2. The file is sequential—that is, from a particular position in the file, one cannot access another position without passing over all positions between them. This is signified by DSORG = PS.

3. Record format is variable and blocked—data records vary in length, but they are packed into fixed-length blocks for physical transmission. This is signified by RECFM = VBA.

4. Block size is fixed—the fixed-length blocks occupy 882 bytes, signified by BLKSIZE = 882.

5. There is a maximum length for logical records—logical records can vary in length but cannot exceed the assigned maximum length. We use LRECL = 125.

6. The file is for output using the WRITE macro—there are various levels of system assistance in writing information. The WRITE macro provides less automatic help than the PUT macro. The snapshot is eventually provided by the supervisor which uses the WRITE macro to give it maximum control. This is signified by MACRF = (W).

The DCB macro for use with SNAP may be written

```
SNAPPER DCB DDNAME=SNAPDUMP,DSORG=PS,RECFM=VBA,        X
            BLKSIZE=882,LRECL=125,MACRF=(W)
```

Remaining Details for Using SNAP

Prior to any use of SNAP, its data control block must be initialized by use of an OPEN macro. For the case above, this macro would be written

Operation mnemonic	Operand field
OPEN	(SNAPPER,OUTPUT)

in which the operand field designates the name of the data control block and the intended use of the file. This macro is executable and so it must be in the path of control, and it must be executed before any execution of SNAP.

The machine and pseudoinstructions generated by a macro are normally printed in the assembler listing. In this case, these are so numerous that it is a blessing to suppress such printing. A pseudoinstruction

Operation mnemonic	Operand field
PRINT	NOGEN

suppresses the printing of instructions generated by macros. It should precede in the text any macro of which the printing of the expansion is to be suppressed. Finally, a job control card to establish SNAPDUMP as an output file directed to the printer is required. It may be placed immediately after the END card which marks the end of assembly. Its content shows as the last line in Program 4.5.1. A deck segment for a program which incorporates all the above aspects of using the SNAP macro can be as illustrated in Program 4.5.1. The SNAP macro can be called whenever a snapshot is desired, and more than one SNAP instruction can name the same data control block. To obtain the same information from storage as in the BAREBONZ programs of Chapter 3, we would place a SNAP instruction just before exit, with the keyword STORAGE having a designation as shown in Program 4.5.1. This will cause all of the instructions in the SNAP and DCB macros to be included in the snapshot, since they occupy words in memory between BEGIN and TERM. As an exercise, the reader should think of a method of omitting these instructions from the snapshot.

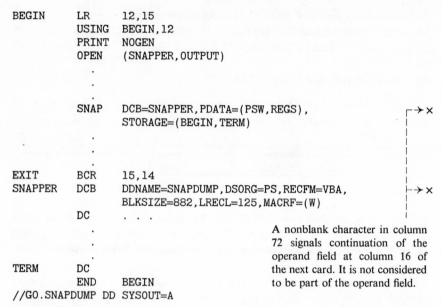

```
BEGIN     LR      12,15
          USING   BEGIN,12
          PRINT   NOGEN
          OPEN    (SNAPPER,OUTPUT)
                  .
                  .
                  .
          SNAP    DCB=SNAPPER,PDATA=(PSW,REGS),
                  STORAGE=(BEGIN,TERM)
                  .
                  .
                  .
EXIT      BCR     15,14
SNAPPER   DCB     DDNAME=SNAPDUMP,DSORG=PS,RECFM=VBA,
                  BLKSIZE=882,LRECL=125,MACRF=(W)
          DC      . . .
                  .
                  .
                  .
TERM      DC
          END     BEGIN
//GO.SNAPDUMP DD SYSOUT=A
```

A nonblank character in column 72 signals continuation of the operand field at column 16 of the next card. It is not considered to be part of the operand field.

Program 4.5.1   As shown, SNAP will print the PSW, the contents of the registers, and the contents of storage from BEGIN through TERM, at the time SNAP is executed.

Precautions to Be Taken with Macros

The description of machine instructions in the IBM manual "Principles of Operation" presumably advises the reader of every effect the execution of an instruction can have on his program. The corresponding IBM manual for macro instructions entitled "Supervisor and Data Management Macro Instructions" is not so explicit. It does name the "Supervisor and Data Management Services" manual as a required supplement, and the early pages of the latter are devoted to the conventions of program linkage and macro construction. These manuals provide the general principles according to which system-supplied macros are built, whereas absolutely anything can happen in a user-composed macro. When in doubt, one has little alternative to being conservative, studying the macro expansion (obtained by omitting the PRINT NOGEN card recommended in Program 4.5.1), and then possibly experimenting to see just what registers may be used by it to call other macros or the supervisor. For system-supplied macros, the expectations should be:

1. No word of the user's memory will be changed by the macro unless that change is implied in the description of its function. The only possible exception is that a macro would use the address in register 13 as if it

designates the beginning of a register save area. If it does, and if register 13 holds an address for program or other data, these items may be destroyed. The explanation of standard linkage conventions in the next chapter should be helpful in this regard. The "Supervisor and Data Management Services" manual recommends a standard practice under the heading "Saving Registers":

> If your program is going to use any system macro instruction (other than SAVE, RETURN, or the register forms of GETMAIN and FREEMAIN) . . . your program is going to be a calling program and must provide another save area.

We have found that the register save area is not strictly required for the use we have made of the SNAP macro. However, we shall demonstrate in the next chapter that it is good programming practice to establish a save area to be filled in the initial instructions of any called program. From then on, the ability to avoid establishing a save area becomes academic.

2. Registers 0, 1, 14, and 15 are subject to modification in some macros. It is a convention to leave registers 2–13 intact excepting as the macro description explicitly calls for their modification. As an example of the latter, the RETURN macro is specifically designed to restore general register contents from memory prior to exit from a subprogram, and so it may change them all.

3. There are system-supplied macros in which not all of 0, 1, 14, and 15 are modified, one example being the SAVE macro for saving register contents in an 18-word memory segment reserved by the calling program. The beginning address of that segment is supplied by the calling program in register 13. The SAVE macro changes no registers.

4. When it is important to the programmer that one of the registers 0, 1, 14, or 15 be preserved through the use of a macro, he should study the individual macro definition as well as the macro expansion. Then he should experiment with use of the macro, storing the key registers before and after call of the macro at distinct places for examination in a post-execution dump.

5. The programmer should note that on some macros, including SNAP, a code to indicate whether or not the use of the macro was successful is returned in register 15. If register 15 is filled with zeros, this usually signifies successful completion of the macro. Nonzero codes are explained in the descriptions of individual macros which use them. These codes can be most helpful in error diagnosis and should be tested or displayed whenever there is suspicion that the macro may not be functioning as expected.

4.6   EXTENSIONS TO THE ASSEMBLER CONCEPT

4.6.1   Some Limitations in Our Assembler

The assembler specified in this chapter resembles assemblers for some of the early machines. It has some obvious flaws beyond its failure to detect and document programming errors. Three areas for which we will provide some relief in this section are:

1. All the components (driver and subprograms) of a program must be assembled together even though the assembled version of a given subprogram in one program bears a close resemblance to the assembled version in any other. The concept of relocatability and its implementation solve this problem.

2. Constants enter programs in many ways, and—for easy understanding—require a variety of ways to specify them. We can extend the capabilities of the assembler for defining constants substantially without undue complication. For a complete picture, a reference manual will still be the only answer.

3. It is possible to improve the mnemonics of branching by defining a variety of pseudoinstructions each with its own distinct opcode and implementing all of these with a Branch on Condition for which the opcode selects the mask.

4.6.2   Operand Expressions

One may consider an operand to be given as an expression E which may or may not have a suffix T as a modifier written E(T). We may then specify what forms E and T will be permitted to have. Severe restrictions were placed on E and T in Section 4.2 to achieve simplicity in the assembly process. It should now be possible to remove some of these leaving their effect on the writing of assemblers to those who are paid for meticulous construction of complex assemblers.

Modern assemblers, except those for the smallest machines, generate *relocatable* code. This means that the object code resulting from assembly carries with it sufficient information to execute correctly, beginning at any location which satisfies all possible alignment requirements (a double-word boundary in the IBM 360/370 systems). The assembly is made assuming the beginning of the program to be at location zero. Let us now consider (1) what the assembler can do, and (2) what must be done as the program is deposited in memory so that execution can adjust for things the assembler cannot do. We will need to take a close look at operand expressions and the way the information in them transforms to numeric instruction components. In doing so, we limit ourselves to expressions in which all the components come from a single program. The concepts we develop here must be extended when object programs from separate assemblies are linked to form a composite program.

1. If the expression E is known at assembly time, then its value cannot depend on the position of the program in memory. Such expressions might be called *relocation invariant,* but a more common terminology is to say that they are *absolute.* Among absolute expressions, there are some which are nonnegative. When the nature of a machine instruction provides that an operand be absolute, nonnegative, and sufficiently small, then the instruction may be designed to include the expression value in the instruction. We classify constants provided in the instruction as *instruction constants* (see Section 4.6.4) since they require no reference to memory. They are also widely known as *immediate values.* On the IBM 360/370 systems, masks, register numbers, and displacements are provided as instruction constants. A negative absolute expression will be considered invalid for an instruction constant. For example, let A, B, and C be distinct locations in a program. Then 12, A − B, B − A, A − A + 4, and B − C + 7 are all known at assembly time since the spacing in bytes from B to A or B to C will not change with relocation. One of the expressions A − B or B − A is negative and therefore invalid. The operand expressions considered here would qualify as arithmetic expressions in a higher-level language such as FORTRAN. Yet they have a profoundly different meaning. The computations here are with *addresses* (relative values of which are known at assembly time) rather than with the *contents* of addresses.

2. If the expression E is not known at assembly time because its value changes when the program moves in memory (as with the name of a data location), then clearly its value cannot be inserted as an instruction constant at assembly time. It may be possible, however, to represent E as the sum of two terms

$$E = B + D$$

where the displacement D is an absolute expression and B is a reference address in the program which therefore changes with relocation by just the number of bytes that the program is moved. If E can be represented in this way, then the expression is not absolute but it is relocatable. Such expressions cannot be put directly into the instruction, but if D is nonnegative its value can be inserted as an immediate value, thus providing within the instruction the address determined by E relative to the address B. As an example, consider the address expression

$$B + C - D + 4$$

and group the elements into two terms

$$B + [C - D + 4]$$

Now if B, C, and D are names and locations in a single program which is moved about in memory, their addresses will change but the difference C − D will not. Thus C − D + 4 is absolute and, if it is also non-negative, its value can be carried in the instruction. Clearly, an expression which changes with relocation by the amount of relocation is to be interpreted as a memory address and is not meaningful as an amount of shift or as a mask or register number. The value for B is determined only when the program is deposited in memory for execution. Depending on machine structure, B either can be added to the displacement D to make a composite instruction constant equal to B + D when the program is being loaded into memory for execution, or it can be added to the displacement within the control unit as the instruction is being interpreted. The latter method is used in the IBM 360/370 systems as a part of the base-register mechanism.

Since some operand expressions are absolute and some must be adjusted for program position, there must be a way to include information in the object code from the assembly as to which addresses are to have a value for B added to them. One possibility is that the assembler generate a relocation tag for this purpose (external to the instruction itself) to be carried with the instruction for use by the loader. To make it possible to use the same B for every relocatable expression and still keep all absolute portions nonnegative, it would be convenient to take B as the beginning address of the program. Its value would be added to any displacement already in the instruction if its tag is 1 and not added if its tag is 0.

The IBM 360/370 systems, by contrast, rely on information within the instruction to manage the relocation adjustment of operand expressions. The rule is simple: If the base register digit is zero, then the displacement is the value of the operand expression. If the base register digit is nonzero, then the effective address determined by the operand expression and base combined, whether the expression is absolute or not, is the sum of the displacement and the base address.

To see that this simple rule is valid, we next consider some specific cases. If an operand expression is to change with relocation by the amount of relocation, then a base address must have previously been established by a USING instruction. The base address is an address within the program, and therefore it changes with relocation by the amount the program is moved. The nonzero base register number causes that base to be added to the displacement when the instruction is interpreted, yielding a sum which is the correct value for the relocatable expression. If, on the other hand, the operand expression is absolute, the base established by the

USING instruction is ignored. If no explicit base is provided in the suffix expression, the base register digit is set to zero and the displacement is correctly taken as the value of the operand expression. Finally, if the operand expression is absolute, a base register may be named explicitly in the suffix and, if its number is nonzero, the base will be added to the displacement as is specified by the symbolic instruction.

There is a significant difference in our use of the word "relocatable" from the use in some texts and manuals. We consider a program to be relocatable if and only if its effect is independent of choice of double-word boundary on which it begins. Every instruction in a relocatable program and every expression in such an instruction is also relocatable. Thus relocation-invariant expressions and instructions are relocatable. The Venn diagram below illustrates the terminology we endorse.

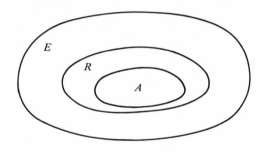

E is the set of all operand expressions.

R is the set of all relocatable expressions.

A is the set of all absolute expressions.

$A \subseteq R \subseteq E$.

$E - R$ is the set of invalid expressions.

We have yet to give a rule for establishing whether or not an expression is absolute, relocatable, or neither. An easy rule to apply for our single-program case is the following:

Given an operand expression, replace every occurrence of a location name X in the expression (including * to signify the location of the instruction being analyzed) by $(X + \lambda)$, and collect coefficients of λ in the resulting expression. If the resulting expression is not of the form $a\lambda + b$ with $a = 0$ or $a = 1$, it is invalid. If it is of the form $a\lambda + b$ with $a = 0$, the expression is absolute, but if $a = 0$ or $a = 1$ the expression is relocatable. As examples, consider the operands given in Table 4.6.1.

Not every relocatable expression is accepted by the assembler as valid. The rules are complex, but the programmer who strives for simplicity and clarity will have little trouble with them. Expressions are formed from elements which are constants or location symbols by use of binary integer arithmetic operations of $+$, $-$, $*$, $/$ (unary $+$ and $-$ are prohibited),

Let A, B, and C be location names, and * be the contents of the IAC

Operand E	Expansion	Classification
A + B	A + B + 2λ	Invalid
A + B − C	A + B − C + λ	Relocatable, not absolute
A − B	A − B	Absolute and relocatable
A − *	A − *	Absolute and relocatable
A + 4	A + 4 + λ	Relocatable, not absolute
A − B + 4	A − B + 4	Absolute and relocatable

Table 4.6.1 We can determine whether these operands are absolute, relocatable, or invalid by substituting A + λ for A, B + λ for B, and C + λ for C, expanding the expression to collect all λ's together, and then examining the coefficient of λ.

and by grouping with parentheses. It is deemed erroneous to involve a nonabsolute subexpression in a multiplication or division. Thus A − B + A − C would be legal but 2 * A − B − C would not.

The fuss we have made over operand expressions should be justified by at least one example in which reasonable use is made of arithmetic operations. For example, if a table is given in the form

```
TABL        DC      F'...'
            DC      F'...'
             .
             .
             .
            DC      F'...'
ENDTABL  DC         0F'0',
```

then ENDTABL–TABL is the length in bytes of the table. Insertion of additional entries in the table will not require any change in operand expressions which depend on table length if it is expressed in this way. The middle of the table would be at the location

$$TABL + (ENDTABL − TABL)/2$$

although to stay on full-word boundaries, one might choose to use

$$TABL + 4 * ((ENDTABL − TABL)/8)$$

as the entry typical of the middle.

Even more complex operand expressions are useful in macro definition, for they permit macros to be defined so that they can be made to fit into a wide variety of programs. That subject remains to be explored later.

4.6.3 Suffix Modifiers

An operand may consist of an operand expression E without a suffix, in which case the effective address has been defined above. There is also the possibility of a suffix modifier (T), in which case the operand is written E(T). T may be an absolute expression or a pair of absolute expressions separated by a comma. Usually, but not always, an empty absolute expression stands for zero. One can find the details in the IBM assembler language manual under the heading "Operand Fields and Subfields." The uses of these absolute expressions vary instruction format, so we now consider some specific cases.

First operand (RR, RS, RX instructions). The first operand expression must be absolute and have no modifier (T). Its value must be a register number.

Second operand (RR instructions). The second operand expression must be absolute and have no modifier (T). Its value must be a register number.

Second operand (RS instructions). If the second operand expression is absolute, then a modifier (T) is possible where T is a single absolute expression. Its value must be a register number which we will denote by B. The register selected by B is used as a base register in computation of the effective address. If the second operand expression is not absolute no modifier suffix is possible.

Second operand (RX instructions). If the second operand expression E is absolute, then no base is implied and a modifier (T) is possible. If E(T) = D(X,B) where D, X, and B are each absolute expressions then D is the displacement, the register selected by the value of X serves as an index register, and that selected by the value of B serves as a base register. If T is a single absolute expression, its value must be a register number, and (T) can appear as (X) or as (,B).

If the second operand expression is not absolute, then a base is implied; then, if there is a modifier T, it must be a single absolute expression X, its value being the number of a register used as an index. Examples of second operands with suffixes are shown in Table 4.6.2.

Third operand (RS instructions). In case there is a third operand (we have seen none yet), its operand expression must be absolute and its value must be a register number. There can be no suffix modifier.

Throughout Chapters 3 and 4, we found that with suitable restrictions on the assembler the symbolic name for a quantity was adequate for specifying an operand. Resolving this operand address into base and displacement quantities was a chore for the assembler. Yet in Table 4.6.2

U, V, and W are location names, D is the assembled displacement,
B and X are the assembled base and index registers, respectively.

| Second operand | | | Result of assembly | | |
E(T)	Type	Restriction	B	D	X
24(U − V)	RS	$0 \leq (U − V) \leq 15$	U − V	18_{16}	0
17 (U − V)	RX	$0 \leq (U − V) \leq 15$	0	11_{16}	U − V
50(5, 12)	RX	—	12	32_{16}	5
U(V − W)	RX	$0 \leq (V − W) \leq 15$	Implied because U is not absolute	U − B	
U(V − W, 5)	—	—	An error message results, because B is implied by U and also given explicitly as 5		

Table 4.6.2 These examples show some possible suffixes to operation expressions and conditions for their validity. The possibility of contradiction is also demonstrated.

and in this section we introduce the notion of explicitly naming the base and providing displacement in the symbolic instruction. It is pertinent to ask why the two methods of operand specification are necessary and how to choose between them in a given instruction.

As a general principle, one should avoid the explicit naming of base registers in order both to minimize numerical chores and errors, and maintain maximum mnemonic content in instructions. We list the following situations in which base displacement format may be required:

1. In discussing an instruction in isolation (as in a reference manual), in which case one cannot assume an established base.

2. In using an address in one program which is provided from another which is separately assembled. Such addresses (as we shall see in Section 5.2) are always provided in absolute form, and thus are natural for use as base addresses.

3. In providing facilities not in the instruction but essential to the computation. As a prime example we cite the inability to index storage addresses in the MVC (MoVe Character) instruction introduced in Chapter 6.

4.6.4 One-Scan (One-Pass) Assemblers

We have seen that the principal purpose of the first scan of a two-scan assembler is to form a symbol table in which one can look up the value assigned to any symbolic name when he encounters it in an operand field. One could ask whether it is possible to avoid two scans by using one or all of the following practices, the second of which is clearly limited in value:

1. Place the reservations for data storage textually ahead of the instructions which reference these data so that symbols will have been defined before their appearance in operand expressions.

2. Place instructions which are referenced from other instructions ahead of those which reference them, the objective being the same as in 1. Usually this is not possible, and sometimes when it is possible it is undesirable.

3. Where a symbol is referenced in an operand field before it has been defined by appearance in a location field, make a note that this operand field must be resolved after definition of its symbols. Complete the partial instruction when all symbols in its operand field have been defined.

It is easy to conform to the first suggestion. On the other hand, the second recommendation would prohibit branches to instructions which are farther along in the text, and so this strategy must be used with discretion. The "fixups" suggested in the third recommendation are not difficult, and as a result there are one-scan assemblers in common use. Every fixup makes the assembler listing more difficult to read, for the resolution of an operand expression is ordinarily printed in a table of fixups separate from the rest of the instruction to which it belongs. Therefore, one who uses a one-scan assembler should attempt to minimize the number of fixups. This explains the rather peculiar ordering of data and instructions in Program 4.6.1, in which a one-scan assembler has only one fixup to make. One should note the seemingly illogical placement of the exit sequence near the beginning of the program just to avoid a forward reference to an instruction and below the data location named SUM to avoid a forward reference to data.

Many instructions (including one in Program 4.6.1) cannot be completely assembled as they are encountered in one scan of the instructions, but require completion after a continuation of the scan to resolve all forward references. The forward references are easily detected in the program or in the symbol table; in either case the statement number of the symbol definition exceeds the statement number of a reference. The reader should study carefully the instruction sequence in Program 4.6.1, as it required careful ordering to achieve only one forward reference. He should also take care not to let such arranging destroy the readability of his own programs.

4.6.5   Defining Constants

There are two different destinations for constants of a program which must be distinguished:

1. Insertion into an instruction as a register number, mask, or displacement. Such insertion will also be useful in character-handling instructions

LOC	OBJECT CODE	ADDR1	ADDR2	STMT	SOURCE STATEMENT		
16D3A8	18CF			1	MYJOB	LR	12,15
16D3A8				2		USING	MYJOB,12
16D3AA	47F0....		......	3		BC	15,MYCODE
16D3B0	00000000			4	SUM	DC	F'0'
16D3B4	50A0C008		16D3B0	5	ALLDONE	ST	10,SUM
16D3B8	07FE			6		BCR	15,14
16D3BC	0000004F			7	GRADES	DC	F'79'
16D3C0	0000005D			8		DC	F'93'
16D3C4	00000037			9		DC	F'55'
16D3C8	00000052			10		DC	F'82'
16D3CC	00000045			11		DC	F'69'
16D3D0	00000010			12	SIXTEEN	DC	F'16'
16D3D4	00000014			13	TWENTY	DC	F'20'
16D3D8	1B33			14	MYCODE	SR	3,3
16D3DA	1BAA			15		SR	10,10
16D3DC	5AA3C014		16D3BC	16	LOOP	A	10,GRADES(3)
16D3E0	5B30C028		16D3D0	17		S	3,SIXTEEN
16D3E4	47A0C00C		16D3B4	18		BC	10,ALLDONE
16D3E8	5A30C02C		16D3D4	19		A	3,TWENTY
16D3EC	47F0C034		16D3DC	20		BC	15,LOOP
16D3A8				21		END	MYJOB

Fixups

LOC	RESOLUTIONS	ADDR1	ADDR2	STMT	SUBFIELD
16D3AA	....C030		16D3D8	3	S2

Symbol Table and Cross Reference

SYMBOL	VALUE	LENGTH	DEFINITION	REFERENCES	
ALLDONE	16D3B4	0004	5	18	
GRADES	16D3BC	0004	7	16	
LOOP	16D3DC	0004	16	20	
MYCODE	16D3D8	0002	14	3	
MYJOB	16D3A8	0002	1	2	21
SIXTEEN	16D3D0	0004	12	17	
SUM	16D3B0	0004	4	5	
TWENTY	16D3D4	0004	13	19	

Program 4.6.1   Output of a one-scan assembler.

(detailed in Chapter 6). We refer to these as *instruction constants*, also sometimes called *immediate constants* or *self-defining constants*.

2. Placement in memory for the purpose of being accessed by an instruction carrying the address of the constant. We will refer to these as *addressable constants*. They include both *defined constants* and *literals*.

Thus we shall name all constants used in specifying an instruction *instruction constants* or *immediate constants*, and all those which are reached through an address as *addressable constants*. Within each class there are subdivisions.

Instruction Constants

An instruction constant has a very specific destination which determines its length in bits. That destination also has no provision for sign bits in the constant. We will find that these observations reflect in the way the constant is specified. Instruction constants are given in one of the four types: decimal, hexadecimal, binary, or character, and the type of representation chosen is at the convenience of the user. All representations are right justified (even for character types as shown in Table 4.6.3) so that a representation shorter than the allotted space is automatically filled on the left with binary zeros. The components of an instruction constant representation are given as follows:

1. The leftmost character denotes type (X for hexadecimal, B for binary, C for character, and—by default—empty for decimal).

2. The constant representation immediately follows the type character and consists of a string of characters of that type enclosed in single quotes if the type is X, B, or C, but is not delimited by single quotes in the absence of a type character (for decimal). In any case, the bit string determined by the constant should not exceed in length (except for leading zeros on the left) the destination field in the instruction.

Constants of type C (character) are subject to a special rule based on multiple use of the single quote (') and ampersand (&). The rule is that an occurrence of one of these characters within the string being represented is replaced by two successive occurrences of the same character. Thus the character string ' '& would be defined by C' ' ' ' '&&' but would be decoded by the assembler as a three-character string. Some examples of instruction constants are illustrated and translated in Table 4.6.3.

Addressable Constants

Suppose that a program needs the constant three as an operand. We can name a location to hold the constant and also define the contents of that location by using the symbolic instruction

THREE DC F'3'

Use of the name THREE as an operand expression would bring the contents of its location to the processor for use. For example, one could add three to the contents of register 10 by the instruction

A   10,THREE

Symbolic instruction	Assembled instruction
BCR B'1010',X'E'	07AE
LA X'E',X'10'(3,X'C')	41E3C010

In the following instructions which insert the 8 bits specified by the second operand into a memory byte selected by the first operand, the bit pattern has no printable representation, so character mode is inappropriate. While all three forms below give the same result, we have a clear preference for one of the first two.

MVI 16(3),B'10000000'	92803010
MVI 16(3),X'80'	92803010
MVI 16(3),128	92803010

In order to demonstrate that, in contrast with the usual character-string practices, even character type instruction contants are justified to the right, we include three examples of character specification. One must indeed be careful in reading a listing such as these would generate in which a nonprintable internal code is selected by the multiple punching in a card column. Columns 9 of the operand field in the second example and 10 in the third example were punched 12-0-1-8-9 to give EBCDIC internal code of zero. The symbolic instruction printout is clearly not adequate to determine the assembled instruction completely.

MVI 16(3),C'A'	92C13010
MVI 16(3),C' A'	92C13010
MVI 16(3),C'A '	Will not assemble

Table 4.6.3 Instruction constants give a great deal of freedom in the way instructions are specified. That freedom carries with it a responsibility to use instruction constants so that they clarify purpose rather than confuse.

Note that it is unnecessary to be able to specify where in memory the number three is stored, only that it is available. We observe that a special symbol placed in the operand field of an instruction (to be decoded by the assembler) could be used to mean: "See that the number 3 is available as a constant in memory, provide a name for its location, and replace me (the symbol being decoded) by that name." This special operand would accomplish the same for the programmer as the use of a DC instruction, but would free him of making a storage reservation. Such a symbol is called a *literal,* and, for the case just described, a literal could be used directly in the addition instruction

$$A\ 10,=F'3'$$

In this literal, the representation of 3 is the same as in the DC instruction, namely F'3'. The signal that the assembler is to reserve a word of memory for that constant and replace =F'3' by the name of that location is given by the equal sign.

Usually, we think of constants as being numbers characteristic of a problem, but one may also consider addresses in a program as constants. These latter are surely not characteristic of a problem, for they usually depend on the location of the program in memory. It is helpful to partition addressable constants into address constants (which do represent addresses) and problem constants (which do not). All of these qualify as addressable constants, but in this chapter we will discuss only problem constants.

Clearly, the representation of a constant used in a literal should be quite similar to that used in a corresponding Define Constant instruction. The main differences are some additional freedoms in specifying certain modifiers for problem constants in the DC representation and two address-type constants not permissible in literals. We shall first consider the representation of those single (as distinguished from multiple) problem constants which can be handled by the current machine model (floating-point and internal decimal arithmetic constants will be described along with floating-point and decimal arithmetic instructions). Thus we defer consideration of modifiers, multiple constants, and multiple operands for they apply only to DC instructions. The remaining representations are alike in DC instructions and literals.

Problem Constants without Modifiers

Each constant definition consists of a character denoting type followed immediately by a representation of the constant enclosed in single quotes. For binary, character, and hexadecimal, the length in bytes of the representation is inferred by the assembler to be the minimum number of bytes which can hold the bit string represented by the quoted string. The rules in Table 4.6.4 use integer division to compute this number of bytes. In performing this computation for character strings, one must count the number of characters in the string being represented, rather than the number in the representation enclosed in quotes, for the number of single quote (') and ampersand (&) characters in the definition is twice the number in the string being represented. For integer constants, the length is implied by the character denoting type, thus justifying F for full-word integers and H for half-word integers.

Type code	Internal representation	Implied length in bytes (use integer part in quotients)	Maximum length
B	Binary	(Bit string length + 7)/8	256
C	Character	Character string length	256
F	Integer	4	4
H	Integer	2	2
X	Hexadecimal	(Hexadecimal string length + 1)/2	256

Table 4.6.4 Every problem constant representation has an implied length which is determined by a combination of the type code and the constant being represented.

In describing the relation between the quoted string in the external representation and the bit string obtained from it, we need to characterize precisely what we will mean by the phrases decimal number, shifted decimal number, and complement representation.

1. A decimal number is a succession of characters of which the leftmost may be + or − or . or a decimal digit and of which the remaining are either . or a decimal digit, there being at least one digit and at most one period. Examples are +.123, −349, 127., 0057, and −28.039.

2. A shifted decimal number is a decimal number followed immediately by En where n is a signed or unsigned succession of decimal digits. The suffix En signifies multiplication by 10^n. Examples are .127E−9, 3.04E0, −.0097E5, and 64.8E+7.

3. The two's complement representation of a positive binary integer (when not truncated on the left by a word boundary) is a binary number which when added to that positive integer gives a zero digit and a carry in every position, as discussed in Chapter 2.

The relation between the quoted string in the external representation and the bit string obtained from it is described in Table 4.6.5 for B, C, F, H, and X type constants.

For a problem constant of type B, X, or C which is no more than 256 bytes in length, the implied length is always sufficient to hold the bit string constructed from its external representation. There may be unfilled posi-

Type code	External representation	Resultant bit string
B	Binary string	Identical binary string
C	Character string	Catenation of the EBCDIC binary representations of characters in the represented string (after successive single quotes or successive ampersands are paired and replaced by single characters of the same type)
F or H	Decimal number or shifted decimal number	Binary representation of the integer part† (complement representation for negative numbers)
X	Hex digit string	Catenation of binary representations of hex digits in the string

Table 4.6.5   The external representation defines a resultant bit string which is independent of the implied length. This string in being inserted into storage reserved for it may be truncated or extended if it is not an exact fit.

† Modifiers may be used to permit a fractional part for the external representation.

tions for types B or X. Integer representations (recall that negative numbers are represented by their two's compliment) may be shorter or longer than the reserved byte sequence. For all but character mode (which in this case has the precisely correct length anyway) there is a uniform practice of forming the bit string from the external representation, justifying it to the right, and then (1) truncating on the left if it is too long, or (2) filling with zeros on the left if there are unfilled positions.

There are additional variations in Define Constant instructions and in literals, but these are described after appropriate background development in succeeding chapters. Similarly there are constant types which we have deferred. In particular, linkage between programs provides a strong motivation for addresses as constants, so this topic is presented in Chapter 5. More details about binary, hexadecimal, and character constants are presented as needed in Chapter 6, while floating-point and decimal constants are motivated and discussed in Chapter 8.

Any definition of an addressable constant may carry an explicit length of the constant in bytes which will override the implied length. It is specified in the form Lm immediately to the right of the type code, where m is either an unsigned integer or a parenthesized absolute integer expression. As examples, CL3'CAT' and C'CAT' represent the same constant, as do XL4'2A' and X'0000002A'. Note that when implicit and explicit length determinations are not the same, an adjustment to fit the constant to the explicit length must be made. For all types except character strings and floating-point constants, the constant is inserted into the reserved byte string justified to the right as far as possible. It is then chopped or extended by zeros on the left to fit the reserved byte-string. For character strings (floating-point constants) the constant is justified left and chopped or extended on the right by blanks (zeros) to fit the reserved byte-string. Explicit lengths are especially convenient for string constants. When they are used for other types, it is important to know that the usual alignment implicit in a data type is not carried out when length is explicitly given, an important consideration in one of the problems in Chapter 6.

4.6.6 Extended Mnemonic Codes

It has been evident throughout this chapter that the purpose of assemblers is to remove some of the numerical details from machine-level programming. This has been accomplished by using mnemonic operation codes and names for numeric locations, and by having the assembler translate operands from decimal to binary and compute binary representations for other constants, such as characters, positive or negative decimal integers, or hexadecimal numbers. Another way to remove some numerical detail is to extend the influence of the symbolic operation code on instructions. Traditionally, computers have had a whole array of branching operation codes, some of which might be verbalized as

branch on zero
branch on nonzero
branch on nonnegative
branch on positive

The 360/370 systems utilize the same operation code for all of these, but select among the branching criteria by specification of a mask. But there is no difficulty in asking the assembler to generate both the traditional operation code (BC or BCR) and the mask from a symbolic operation code which is sufficient to determine the mask. The advantage is purely one of improved mnemonics for those who frequently err in or are repulsed by mask computations. While one may still occasionally have to look up a more specialized operation code to know, for example, whether to use BN or BM (for branch on negative or branch on minus), the symbolic instruction is undoubtedly more easily read once it has been correctly formed. Symbolic operation codes which determine bits of an instruction other than 0–7 are called *extended mnemonic operation codes,* or *extended mnemonics.* Table 4.6.6 illustrates the extended mnemonics for branching on the arithmetic contents of a general register as well as for unconditional branches and for instructions which only advance the IAC. Extended mnemonics for branching in response to comparison instructions and to test under mask may be found in the assembler manual.

Extended Code		Meaning	Type	The extended code is assembled the same as the machine instruction	
B	D(X,B)	Branch unconditional	RX	BC	15,D(X,B)
BR	R	Branch unconditional	RR	BCR	15,R
NOP	D(X,B)	No operation	RX	BC	0,D(X,B)
NOPR	R	No operation	RR	BCR	0,R
BO	D(X,B)	Branch on overflow	RX	BC	1,D(X,B)
BP	D(X,B)	Branch on plus	RX	BC	2,D(X,B)
BM	D(X,B)	Branch on minus	RX	BC	4,D(X,B)
BZ	D(X,B)	Branch on zero	RX	BC	8,D(X,B)
BNP	D(X,B)	Branch on not plus	RX	BC	13,D(X,B)
BNM	D(X,B)	Branch on not minus	RX	BC	11,D(X,B)
BNZ	D(X,B)	Branch on not zero	RX	BC	7,D(X,B)

Table 4.6.6 The coding keys for these extended mnemonics are B for branch, R for register, NOP for no operation, O for overflow, P for plus, M for minus, N for not (rather than for negative), and Z for zero.

4.7 SUMMARY

It is time to remove ourselves for a moment from the mass of detail we are beginning to accumulate and ask ourselves a few questions of intent. Except for input and output, we have defined a reasonably powerful computer in Chapter 3; and in Chapter 4 we discussed an assembler which, though straightforward, accomplishes most of the translation we need. These tools are relatively simple, yet we keep finding new details to consider. Should it be necessary that devices designed to simplify our lives are so complex to learn? How much variety is necessary in our use of the computer, and what does this imply about the adequacy of our tools to date? We can get a reasonable estimate by looking at the nature of some diverse kinds of problems. The types we distinguish are

(1) numerical computation,
(2) character-oriented applications,
(3) systems programming.

The IBM 360/370 makes a valiant attempt to provide all the features any one of these programmers needs. Is it too much to try to satisfy these diverse users on one machine? From some viewpoints, perhaps it is, but the alternative can be undesirable, for it means programmers have to acquaint themselves with two or more unlike machines and develop overall software systems for all of them. Also, many firms will get only the one machine most suitable to their principal justification, but then use that machine in all three ways. For these firms, versatility in the software is very helpful.

4.7.1 Principal Additional Needs for Numerical Computation

The most urgent needs in numerical computation are data types and corresponding hardware to permit the writing of programs in a language suited to the problem (usually described as algorithmic or procedural) and also suited to mechanical translation into assembler language without catastrophic loss in computational power. The key answers are:

(1) floating-point data-types so that problems in scaling numbers at every arithmetic step to maintain accuracy can be avoided,

(2) hardware implementation of floating-point arthmetic to maintain speed,

(3) the data types and character-handling instructions to make translation from procedural to assembler language feasible.

The natural representation of arithmetic, logical, and relational operators along with delimiters and array elements places some rather major demands for extended character sets (e.g., $+$, $-$, $*$, $/$, $\vee$, $<$, $\leq$, $>$, $\geq$, $=$, $\neq$, $;$, $[$, $]$, $($, $)$, $:$) and character-handling instructions suited to analyzing statements in procedural language. While it is common to think of numerical computation as being the province of physical scientists tracking atomic particles or engineers designing turbines, we recall that statistical analyses are numerical computations and are the heart of political forecasting, marketing surveys, or agricultural experiment analysis. Modern business uses numerical computation to optimize use of resources, and highway engineers use it to determine how much to cut from the high spot to fill the low ones.

4.7.2 Principal Additional Needs for Character Processing Applications

Here we may be concerned with record keeping as practiced by the accountant, personnel ófficer, or parts departments of a repair shop. But the mathematician trying to simplify algebraic expressions by computer, the librarian attempting to retrieve titles pertinent to a given topic, the publishing house using automatic type setting, and the poet or musician attempting to analyze compositions are also interested in character string facilities. These users are concerned with masses of information which need to be filed away in memory, rearranged in various ways, perhaps updated or corrected from time to time, and edited for printing. There is little arithmetic. Binary arithmetic is a disadvantage here, for it forces conversions between base 2 and base 10 representations, and each conversion is subject to round-off error and costly in machine time. In such applications, base 10 arithmetic is much preferred, and character strings are the convenient operands. Some procedural languages pertinent to such applications are COBOL, SNOBOL, text editors, and symbol manipulation languages.

The data elements in data processing, often involving names or addresses, tend to be variable in length, so it is no accident that the addressable constants of character and decimal types have implied lengths determined by the individual data item rather than inherent in the type. A test one might apply to judge the adequacy of the DC instruction types we have studied is whether or not they would permit specifying a portion of memory as it might be at any point in the processing of a file. A simple flaw we can find is that, to put a short name such as RAY into an allotted space of 25 positions, we would need to extend the name with 22 blanks. Modifiers to accomplish this and other neat tricks are part of many modern assemblers (the length modifier is a simple example).

Special arithmetic hardware, in this case for decimal arithmetic, is a delight in character-oriented applications where relatively little numerical work is needed, just as floating-point arithmetic was the key to numerical computation. Finally, mechanical translation from the appropriate character-oriented procedural language to assembler language (hopefully, for the systems programmer, the same assembler language as used in numerical computation) is essential to simplify programming and documentation.

4.7.3 Principal Additional Needs for Systems Programming

The problems of the systems programmer are to provide superb computational facilities for the large variety of applications which in our simple analysis are typified as numerical and character-oriented applications. Interestingly enough, his data are the programs these applications programmers create, and his challenge is to funnel the needs of unlike users—who may hardly speak the same language with respect to their problems—into one processor without choking it.

Since his data are programs, one can expect an intensive interest on the part of the systems programmer in character-handling facilities. He will want the utmost flexibility in defining constants of the sort he finds as data (namely programs) or of the sort he creates as output (e.g., machine instructions or symbolic assembler language). An attempt to use the DC facilities we now have to splice together (concatenate) bit strings not conforming to byte boundaries will demonstrate a need for increased versatility. Perhaps the systems programmer's largest demand on the hardware is for massive amounts of memory for his operating system and massive backup storage for his and other libraries. He has a major interest in linking together existing programs saved in various forms to build larger programs.

But the overriding concern of the systems programmer is to have one assembler serving all users with standard data representations, standard linkage conventions among programs, standard references to files, and standard responses to errors. In order to accommodate a wide variety of users, he is willing to accept a large amount of detail. On occasion, he carries this to the extreme of forcing large amounts of such detail on users, as illustrated by the existence of the Job Control Language of the 360/370 systems.

In this brief summary, we find some aspects special to a particular kind of user. Among these are floating-point arithmetic for the scientific programmer and decimal arithmetic for the data processing programmer. What we find in common to the needs of all and therefore worthy of immediate attention are:

(1) standard linkages among programs,

(2) versatile character-handling instructions,

(3) standardization of often-repeated functions (e.g., input and output), the solution being a library of system-supplied macros.

PROBLEMS

1. The method we have used for setting a base is not the most widely used. All that is needed is for the assembler to be informed what register contains the base address and what its value will be, and then to have that base inserted at execution time. The instruction pair

$$\text{BALR} \qquad \text{REG,0}$$
$$\text{USING} \qquad *, \text{REG}$$

accomplishes just that for $1 \le \text{REG} \le 15$. We call it the standard method.

(a) While it is nonsense as a practice, it is instructive to think of one instruction to precede the pair

$$\text{BALR} \qquad 12, 10$$
$$\text{USING} \qquad *, 12$$

to yield the same result as the standard. Can you do it?

(b) How could you use the pair

$$\text{USING} \qquad ?, 12$$
$$\text{BALR} \qquad 12, ?$$

so as to accomplish the same result as the standard?

(c) Can you adjust only the first operand field of the USING instruction in the sequence

$$\text{USING} \qquad *, 12$$
$$\text{BALR} \qquad 12, 0$$

to yield a correct base register setting?

2. We have used a DC instruction with zero for duplication factor and F for type code as a means of aligning to a full-word boundary. We can also use a DC instruction with zero for duplication factor to assign a location name to the place an instruction is stored without putting the name on the same card as the instruction. In this case, alignment to a half-word boundary using H for the type code is appropriate. These practices make no use of the constant which follows the type code, although the type itself is quite important. There is an alternate pseudoinstruction with code DS (Define Storage) which performs the same functions as DC with respect to alignment and reservation of storage but requires no quoted data item. Clearly it will not initialize the reserved storage as the DC does. Where the initialization is not required, it is often preferred.

(a) Write a program with a loop which has no label on any executable instruction.

(b) Demonstrate in the same program that DC and DS can be used interchangeably for alignment purposes.

(c) Use your assembler language manual to find and demonstrate in that same program a way of aligning to a double-word boundary.

3. As mentioned in Problem 2, one may use the DC instruction to reserve storage and at the same time initialize it. He may reserve storage without initializing the reserved positions with the DS instruction. Even if a quoted strings such as 'ABC' is provided with a type code of C in a DS instruction the only effect of the string is to imply a length of 3 bytes. More generally, if an actual data constant is supplied with a DS instruction it is not assembled, although it implies a length in just the same way as for a DC instruction. For character and hexadecimal data, the maximum length is 2^{16} for DS instructions while it is 2^8 for DC instructions. Otherwise the storage reservation mechanisms are identical. Questions you are to answer are:

(a) What disadvantage can you see to initializing storage as it is reserved?

(b) What advantages can you see to initializing storage as it is reserved?

(c) Can you suggest any principle for selecting initial values in case the DC instruction is used and the initial value is not to be used as data?

Note: The following problems require output in some form. It may be best to defer them until use of the SNAP macro has been defined in Section 4.5.

4. The machine defined in Chapter 3 has only 23 operation codes. You should plan an op-code table which has for each symbolic operation code a corresponding byte which holds the numeric operation code, and a second byte which specifies the instruction type. Then write a subprogram which accepts as many as four letters of a symbolic operation code, checks for it in the table, and returns values as follows:

Register 9   Numeric operation code
Register 10   Instruction length in bytes
Register 11   Instruction type:

$$
\begin{array}{ccc}
0 & \text{for} & \text{RR} \\
1 & \text{for} & \text{RS} \\
2 & \text{for} & \text{RX}
\end{array}
$$

Register 15   0 if operation code is in the table

1 if operation code is not in the table

5. It is important to know what constitutes a blank location field to your assembler. Must the entire field be blank? Perhaps it is considered blank if it begins with a blank. Write a program to demonstrate the rules used to determine that a location field is blank. Then write a subprogram which, given an eight-byte location field, tests in the same way whether or not it is blank and, on the basis of this test:

(a)   if the field tests blank, returns to the calling program,

(b)   if the field is not blank, increments the number of elements in the symbol table, adds the new symbol to the end of the table, assigns it the current value of the CTA, and then returns to the calling program.

How error-prone is this way of constructing a symbol table?

6. There are several possibilities for decimal numbers in the operand field. Let us agree that each will be exactly two digits so that register 3 is written register 03 and the increment applied to the displacement does not exceed 99. Then it is convenient to have a conversion subroutine which will accept a two-byte character representation of a decimal number and convert this number to binary for insertion into the instruction or for addition. Create such a routine which accepts as input a two-character representation of a decimal number and gives for output the full-word binary equivalent of the two-digit decimal operand.

7. Without extending the instruction types or the nature of the operand field, we can make excellent use of four instructions not included in BAREBONZ II. Two of these provide ways of comparing quantities to set condition codes rather than forming and testing the difference of these quantities. The other two provide a means for loading and storing byte-sized quantities rather than half words or full words as has been the case until now. The mnemonics for the latter (Insert Character and STore Character) reflect the use of one byte to store one character.

Instruction mnemonic	Type	Explanation
CR	RR,CC	No change in general registers or memory
C	RX,CC	$CC \leftarrow \begin{cases} 0 \text{ if operands are equal} \\ 1 \text{ if first operand is low} \\ 2 \text{ if first operand is high} \end{cases}$
IC	RX	$R1_{24:31} \leftarrow (S2)_{0:7}$
STC	RX	$S2_{0:7} \leftarrow (R1)_{24:31}$

Develop a subprogram which receives in register 3 the absolute address of the beginning of a character string and returns in register 4 the index in that string of the first element which is ' ' or ' + ' or ' (' or ','. Let the string address in register 3 remain unchanged by using register 4 as an index register. Is it possible with this formulation to have a search go far beyond the intended string?

8. Given (1) that a name occupies bytes 0 through $n - 1$ ($1 \leq n \leq 8$) of a second-operand string starting at an effective address in register 3, and (2) that n is in register 4, develop a subprogram which leaves in the double-word register addressed as 10 an eight-character string which is identical to the original in bytes 0 through $n - 1$ and has blanks (not zeros) in byte k for $n \leq k < 8$. This eight-character string should appear in the symbol table. Follow structured programming concepts. Hint: Load the n bytes one at a time into register $11_{24:31}$ shifting left double logical eight bit positions just prior to each such load. If $n < 8$, complete the double word by loading a blank into this position $8 - n$ times, again shifting left double logical by 8 just prior to the load.

9. A simple assembler has a byte reserved for the number of the base register and a word reserved for the value to be used for the base in calculating displacements. Assume (1) that the first operand in a USING instruction is either an asterisk or a symbolic name already defined in the symbol table, and (2) that the second operand is a two-digit decimal integer greater than 0 and less than 16. Write a subprogram which, in response to the USING mnemonic, will properly store the appropriate address to be used as base in a full-word location named BASEADR and the number of the base register in a byte location named BASEREG. This is a time-consuming exercise and can make good use of previous subprogram exercises.

10. Construct a structured flowchart for the program requested in Problem 4. Does this flowchart represent a different algorithm than the one you originally used to solve Problem 4? If so, then write a program to realize the structured algorithm. In either case, use the selective snapshot within your programs for locating errors and providing output.

11. One can use any register except 0 as a base register. Had we used register 15 as base, we could have avoided the initial half-word instruction LR 12,15 in the examples of this chapter. What relation do these statements have to the use of the SNAP macro?

12. Determine for each of the expressions whether it is absolute, relocatable, or invalid, assuming A, B, and C are location names:

a. $*-A+4$ b. $A+16+B$

c. $2*(A-B)+C$ d. $2*A-B-C$

13. Although Program 4.4.2 does not utilize any of the suggestions made in Section 4.6.4 for improving the assembly process using one-scan assemblers, a one-scan assembler should translate this program correctly. If the source statements are as shown in Program 4.4.2, list (a) the object code and location assignments as determined by the first scan (before any fixups), and (b) the fixup table as computed by a one-scan assembler.

14. Conversion of data from external to internal representation for the general case is complex, and can be tedious. However, we can consider the conversion of full-word hexadecimal input, such as

$$DC \quad X'F0F3C5D7'$$

to be adequate for the simplest possible assembler. Within memory, the representation of these eight digits can be read as a string of 16 hexadecimal digits, C6F0C6F3C3F5C4F7 for the example given. Develop a closed subprogram to convert this internal representation to the binary word it represents.

15. Given an array named AGES, you are to write a program to count the number n of elements such that $21 \leq$ age < 65. Suppose the total number of elements in the array to be scanned is 10. In this program, use instruction constants as follows:

For register numbers	hexadecimal
For masks in conditionals	binary
For address increments	hexadecimal
For constants of the problem	decimal

Use decimal literals to establish bounds, and practice structured programming concepts.

16. It helps in understanding instructions to try to get the same effect from a sequence of other instructions. Consider doing so for SLA and SRA where these are shifts of a single register. Use double shifts and consider distinct cases when the named register is an odd- or an even-numbered register. Use an auxiliary register as needed. Remember that arithmetic shifts affect the condition code.

17. The Load Address instruction has been limited by our assembler to having a relocatable second operand expression. Yet it is used more frequently than almost any other instruction. Particular uses making no mention of a memory location are:

•   to set a register to a nonnegative constant,

- to increment a register by a positive constant,
- to form an address in a register which is the sum of quantities in one or two other registers and in fact to increment by a positive constant in the process.

Analyze the effect of the following versions of Load Address:

a. LA 10,0	b. LA 10,0(10)	c. LA 10,0(4)
d. LA 10,0(3,4)	e. LA 10,0(4,3)	f. LA 10,3(0)

by proposing for each case a sequence of other instructions which will have the same effect on the rightmost 24 bits.

Chapter 5

Segmentation of Programs

The material in this chapter is one solution (that chosen for 360/370 systems) to getting consistency in programming practices involved in interfacing separately compiled programs. This interfacing problem has to be solved for every general-purpose system. But the conventions adopted in one system may be radically different from those of another, as was suggested with respect to linkage conventions in Section 3.5. Even though this material is specific to one architecture, it should be studied and practiced until thoroughly familiar. A close acquaintance with one solution to intercommunication among programs will remove the tendency to attribute magical powers to an all-knowing operating supervisor. In so doing, it will not only sharpen a person's use of the 360/370 systems but also provide confidence and insights which will ease the transition to others.

5.1 CONVENTIONS FOR INVOKING SUBPROGRAMS

There is seldom a program proposed which is so different from all previous programs that development independent of existing program libraries is justified. Rather, for every application it is expedient to look for programs in existing libraries which will perform some of the needed functions well. As an example, we now have need to use IBM 360/370 input and output subprograms. To do so, we must know the interface between our program and the software which provides access to the card reader and printer.

In Chapter 3, we explored some techniques which could serve to provide communication between programs. But to obtain the greatest flexibility, designers of software systems have found it desirable to establish standard conventions (usually called *subprogram linkage conventions*) which will be used in every program when it communicates with other programs developed separately. These conventions permeate compilers, service programs, and operating systems, almost all of which are written or translated into assembler language. The conventions must be comprehensive enough to permit programs to cooperate effectively in all these applications. It should be no surprise that they make greater demands on memory, registers, and time than might be necessary for a particular application. Although we will eventually want to examine the roles played by tables called the *relocation dictionary* and the *external symbol dictionary* in supporting these conventions, we defer further mention of them until standards for subprogram invocation are established. These are built around the concept of a standard save area, which we discuss next.

5.1.1   The Standard Save Area for Programs

In Section 3.5, we mentioned the use of a sequence of memory words called a *save area,* which is used to preserve (for subsequent restoration) the information items subject to change by a called program. A principal concern is that the called program be able to restore, as it returns control, the contents of any of the 16 general registers it has modified. In fact, a set of 18 consecutive words in each program's data area is reserved for preserving pertinent data for the program, 16 for the registers we have mentioned and two for information used by the operating supervisor. The mapping of registers into the save area merits explanation.

As noted in Section 3.5, the IBM 360/370 calling program relies on the called program to save its register contents in a save area provided by the calling program. A pointer to the first word of that save area is provided to the called program as the contents of register 13. Since this pointer must be accessible when the stored register contents are to be retrieved, it must be saved separately. That is, we must not bury the treasure map with the treasure! The practice is that it be stored by the called program as word 2 of its own save area. Thus, while only fifteen of the general registers are preserved in the calling program's save area, the contents of general register 13 are preserved, but in the *called* program's save area.

For the fifteen registers stored in the calling program's save area, the correspondence (determined by the STore Multiple instruction to be discussed below) is

Register number	Save area word†
14	4
15	5
i	$i + 6$ $(i = 0, \ldots, 12)$

The pointers in word 2 of save areas constitute a chain enabling any program to find the save area of the program which called it. But the supervisor, in tracing activities of programs it initiates, requires a chaining in the opposite direction. Word 3 of the save area is dedicated to this chain. A called program is responsible to place in word 3 of the calling program's save area a pointer to its own save area. The supervisor can follow these from its own save area down through individual save areas to the lowest level save area of any subprogram in execution.

There has been no mention of the first word of the save areas. This word is not available to the programmer, but is reserved for systems purposes. Figure 5.1.1 illustrates the structure of save areas and the two-way linking of save area addresses.

5.1.2   Storing and Restoring Registers

The storing of 15 registers in consecutive memory words and the subsequent restoring of the same information (implicit in our save area descriptions) would be costly in time and instruction space if there were not instructions specifically designed for the purpose. These instructions, known as STM (STore Multiple) and LM Load Multiple), are of RS type, but unlike instructions we have seen thus far they refer to three registers. The two labeled as R1 and R3 denote the first and last of a sequence of general registers to be stored in or loaded from a corresponding sequence of memory words beginning at the location denoted by the base-displacement pair D2(B2). In case R3 < R1, the sequence takes 0 to be the

---

† For consistency with other documentation, we number the words of the save area from 1 to 18.

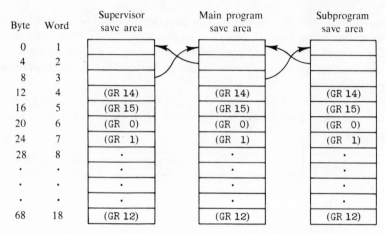

Figure 5.1.1   The save area conventions are illustrated for a supervisor program which calls a main program which in turn calls a subprogram. Each arrow points to the beginning of a save area.

successor to 15 so that R1,. . ., 15,0,. . ., R3 is signified. The assembler representations of these instructions are

Symbolic operation code	Operand field
STM	R1,R3,D2(B2)
LM	R1,R3,D2(B2)

5.1.3   Duties of the Calling Program and the Called Program

Within the following list, the parts with no vertical bar refer to duties of the calling program, and those portions with a vertical bar refer to duties of the called program under the linkage conventions.

1. Register 1 makes arguments available to the called program. It provides a pointer to a sequence of consecutive words in the calling program's data area, the *i*th word of the sequence providing an address for the *i*th argument. We call this sequence the *argument address list*. Note that access to an argument requires one instruction to obtain its address and another to obtain its value.

2. Register 15 is set by the calling program to the address in the called program to which control is passed. That address is inserted in the calling program at load time as a V-type literal or data constant (see Section 5.3).

3. Register 13 is set by the calling program to the beginning address of the save area of 18 words in the calling program's data area.

| Then, by convention, the called program can accomplish its first responsi-

bility, the saving of each general register that it may change. Usually it saves all except register 13 with the command

$$\text{STM}\quad 14,12,12(13)$$

so that registers 14 and 15 are copied into words 4 and 5 of the calling program's save area, and for $0 \leq i \leq 12$, register i is copied into word $6 + i$ of that area. This mapping of registers into the save area is used even though not all of the registers are saved in every case.

4. Register 14 receives the content of the low-order half of the PSW (program status word) as it stands at the time the exit to the called program is initiated. This places the return address in bits 8–31 of register 14; additionally, it saves the instruction length code, condition code, and program mask in bits 0–7 of register 14. The presence of these bits could be used on return to reestablish the environment as it was at the time the subprogram was called. Their presence may be of use in the called program, but there are times when forgetting these bits can confuse the programmer who expects zeros in bits 0–7 of register 14.

5. A sequence of instructions which will accomplish the proper setting of registers as prescribed in numbers 1–4 is

$$
\begin{array}{ll}
\text{L} & 1, = \text{A(ARGADLST)} \\
\text{LA} & 13,\text{SAVEAREA} \\
\text{L} & 15, = \text{V(SUBPROG)} \\
\text{BALR} & 14,15
\end{array}
$$

where the mnemonic names have significance as follows:

ARGADLST	Argument address list
SAVEAREA	Save area of 18 words in the calling program data area
SUBPROG	Name of subprogram being called

6. A called program must save the address it receives via register 13, for it must use that address to restore registers on exit. Clearly, it must provide its own location, since saving the address of a save area in that same save area would be useless. Each 18-word save area has its second word (bytes 4–7) dedicated to that purpose. Thus, if a called program also calls another, it will have its own save area and will save register 13 in its second word. If the called program does not call another, it needs no 18-word save area, but it must preserve register 13 throughout its execution either in a dedicated memory location or in a register.

7. In order to address a word in its own save area, the called program must first establish its own base address. Assuming the base is to be in register 12 this could be accomplished by the pair

```
BALR    12,0
USING   *,12
```

as discussed in Problem 1 of Chapter 4. Establishing a base register must follow the saving of that register's contents as discussed above.

8. The save area pointers are the responsibility of the called program, and can be set by the following instructions (which use register 10 as auxiliary):

```
LA      10,SAVEAREA
ST      13,4(10)
ST      10,8(13)
```

Once these pointers have been saved, it is customary in all but the lowest level programs to execute (given the above sequence of instructions)

```
LR      13,10
```

so that register 13 is already set for any call to a subprogram.

9. If we now make the same arbitrary choices of register 12 for base register and of register 10 to pass to the calling program a pointer to the called program's save area, we can standardize the opening sequence to be found in the usual called program to the following prologue:

```
STM     14,12,12(13)
BALR    12,0
USING   *,12
LA      10,SAVEAREA
ST      13,4(10)
ST      10,8(13)
LR      13,10
```

10. Exit from a called program is relatively simple. We merely restore register 13 to point to the calling program's save area, perform a Load Multiple to restore registers to their values on entry, and return via register 14. This works unless the called program returns additional information via registers. There are two opportunities for this to happen:

(a) Register 15 sometimes returns a code having to do with subprogram performance. For example, see Appendix C in the FORTRAN Programmer's Guide.†

(b) When the subprogram returns a value via function reference, that value is deposited in register 0.

---

† IBM System/360 Operating System: FORTRAN IV (G and H) Programmer's Guide Form C28–6817.

If neither of these happens, the exit sequence matching the prologue of number 9 would be the following epilogue:

```
L    13,SAVEAREA+4
LM   14,12,12(13)
BR   14
```

If registers 15 and 0 are returning results, the modification would be

```
L    13,SAVEAREA+4
L    14,12(13)
LM   1,12,24(13)
BR   14
```

Other variations are possible and are handled in similar fashion.

5.2 LINKING WITH FORTRAN

A key issue in getting the utmost in performance from a computing system is the capability of utilizing in cooperating subprograms the most appropriate features of two or more languages. This allows a programmer to use the most powerful features of each language, features which can in fact be unique to a particular language. Two such features in FOR-TRAN are its conciseness for expressing scientific procedures and its massive library of useful programs. The discussion of the standard IBM 360/370 linkage conventions in the previous section provides substantially all the information to allow us to link an assembler language program and a FORTRAN program. We will show how to provide such linkage in this section, and in the following sections we will explore in more detail the addressing problems which arise in assembling, linking, and loading a program which calls other programs. We will begin by writing an assembler language program which calls a FORTRAN program.

5.2.1 Linking with a FORTRAN Subprogram

Two of the reasons for linking with FORTRAN are (1) saving programming effort in complex arithmetic computations, and (2) providing a ready-made (though sometimes cumbersome) input and output. We will illustrate these features separately. First we present an assembler language program which calls a FORTRAN subprogram to perform a computation. The results of the computation are then returned to the calling program, where they can be used in any fashion desired.

Problem statement. As a simple example, suppose we wish to use a FORTRAN subprogram to calculate the average of three integers. We will return both the quotient and the remainder to the calling program, which could use these results in further computation. To display the results we employ a snap dump (within the assembler language program) as discussed in Section 4.5.

MAIN	CSECT		Opens a control section; discussed later
	STM	14,12,12(13)	PROLG—In this prologue, the first in-
	BALR	12,0	struction stores all registers except 13,
	USING	*,12	the next two instructions establish a
	LA	10,SAVE	base register, and the last four instruc-
	ST	13,4(10)	tions accomplish the linking between
	ST	10,8(13)	save areas as discussed in the previous
	LR	13,10	section
	PRINT	NOGEN	Suppresses printout of macro expansions
	OPEN	(SNAPPER,OUTPUT)	Establishes complete description in DCB file to accept snapshot information
	L	15,=V(IBCOM#)	Initialization of return coding and in-
	BAL	14,64(15)	terruption exceptions.†
	LA	1,ARGL	The address of the argument list is loaded
	L	15,ADAVG	into register 1 and the address of the
	BALR	14,15	subprogram is loaded into register 15 before branching to the subprogram; return address is saved in register 14
	SNAP	DCB=SNAPPER,STORAGE=(A,R)	Snapshot of pertinent storage.
	L	13,SAVE+4	EPILG—All registers are restored and con-
	LM	14,12,12(13)	trol is returned to the supervisor
	BR	14	
A	DC	F'7'	The three integers to be averaged in this
B	DC	F'12'	problem
C	DC	F'13'	

Program 5.2.1 (continued on next page)

†An important detail when an assembler language main program calls a FORTRAN subprogram is to call IBCOM# before the first FORTRAN subprogram call using the instructions

```
L   15,=V(IBCOM#)
BAL 14,64(15)
```

These instructions cause initialization of return coding and interruption exceptions. If they are not used and a FORTRAN subprogram terminates either with a STOP statement or because of an execution-time error, the cause of the termination cannot be predicted. Thus these instructions provide the benefit of any diagnostics generated during execution of a FORTRAN subprogram.

```
Q          DC    F'0'                The subprogram will place the quotient
R          DC    F'0'                   and remainder here

ARGL       DC    A(A)                The argument list is a list of addresses
           DC    A(B)                   of the arguments to be passed to the
           DC    A(C)                   subprogram; the A-type addresses will
           DC    A(Q)                   be discussed in more detail in the next
           DC    A(R)                   section

ADAVG      DC    V(AVRAG)            The entry address of the FORTRAN sub-
                                        program is defined
SAVE       DC    18F'0'              The save area of calling program
SNAPPER    DCB   DDNAME=SNAPDUMP,DSORG=PS,RECFM=VBA,                  ×
                 BLKSIZE=882,LRECL=125,MACRF=(W),
           END   MAIN

           SUBROUTINE AVRAG(I,J,K,Q,R)
           INTEGER I,J,K,Q,R,SUM
           SUM=I+J+K
           Q=SUM/3                       FORTRAN subprogram
           R=SUM-3*Q
           RETURN
           END
```

Program 5.2.1 The assembler-language calling program illustrates the linkage conventions described in the previous section. The FORTRAN program calculates the average of the integers labeled A, B, and C, returning the quotient and remainder to the calling program. The CSECT pseudoinstruction, and the A- and V-type DC's, will be discussed in the next two sections.

The linkage in the assembler program is always visible, but we must realize that high-level compilers (such as FORTRAN) for the IBM 360/370 machines which use the assembler language as an intermediate version must conform to these same linkage conventions we have been discussing. In the higher-level languages, however, the linkage is handled automatically, and the programmer is aware of only a few rules regarding the parameters in the calling statement pertaining to such items as order and the type of variable (integer or floating point).

Although the snap dump procedure is not difficult as a means of obtaining a crude form of output (primarily useful for debugging), FORTRAN can provide input and output in more convenient forms, with fewer details to remember. We will next illustrate a FORTRAN calling program to provide input and output, and an assembler language subprogram which performs a computation.

5.2.2 Linking FORTRAN with an Assembler Language Subprogram

To illustrate the use of a FORTRAN calling program and an assembler language subprogram (see Program 5.2.2), we will solve the same problem

```
      INTEGER I,J,K,Q,R
      READ(5,1) I,J,K
    1 FORMAT(3I3)
      CALL AVRAG(I,J,K,Q,R)
      WRITE(6,2) I,J,K,Q,R
    2 FORMAT('1','I=',I5,'J=',I5,'K=',I5,'Q=',I5,'R=',I5)
      RETURN
      END
```

AVRAG	CSECT		
	STM	14,12,12(13)	
	BALR	12,0	PROLG
	USING	*,12	
	LA	10,SAVE	
	ST	13,4(10)	
	ST	10,8(13)	
	LR	13,10	
	LM	3,7,0(1)	Load the addresses from the argument list into registers 3 through 7
	L	8,0(3)	Load I into register 8
	A	8,0(4)	Add J
	A	8,0(5)	Add K
	SRDA	8,32	Position numerator for division
	D	8,=F'3'	Divide by 3
	ST	8,0(7)	Store remainder and quotient in locations given
	ST	9,0(6)	in registers 7 and 6, placed there by the LM instruction
	L	13,SAVE+4	EPILG
	LM	14,12,12(13)	
	BR	14	
SAVE	DC	18F'0'	
	END		

Program 5.2.2 Since the FORTRAN program is the calling program, it accomplishes the linkage conventions required of the calling program. Although the assembler language program saves all registers, establishes a save area, establishes the links with the save area in the calling program, and loads register 13 with the address of its own save area, this area is used only to store the address of the FORTRAN save area (in the second word). If the assembler language subprogram were to call another subprogram, then it would be the responsibility of the latter to store the registers in the former program's save area.

illustrated in Program 5.2.1. Now, however, we can use the FORTRAN input capabilities to read in the three integers, and the FORTRAN output capabilities to write the results. Just for a comparison of the work involved, we will compute the sum of the three integers, and the quotient and remainder when the sum is divided by three, in the assembler language subprogram.

5.3   OBJECT MODULES

Now that we know the programming mechanism for linking with FORTRAN, it is important to look behind the linkage conventions the programmer uses to see what to expect of the software system. The output of most high-level compilers is an equivalent program in assembler-language coding, so that the assembler is used as (1) a second step in the translation of high-level languages, or (2) a first step in the translation of an assembler-language program.

The output from a standard assembly (as distinguished from that of Chapter 4) resembles machine code, but in fact it is not committed to a particular location in memory; consequently, some of the location names cannot be defined within the program. This output is called (in IBM 360/370 terminology) an *object module,* and its format is chosen to make the following feasible:

1. An object module is relocatable: The assembled version of a program P which in executable form will occupy L consecutive bytes of memory must be translatable by machine to execute correctly with its initial byte at any double-word boundary which leaves room for the L bytes beyond it.

2. A program may be synthesized from object modules: Large programs must be realizable as composites of separately assembled object modules. The breaking up of a large program into manageable sections (subprograms) is called *segmentation.* Combining subprograms is an act of synthesis called *linking.* This linking of object modules is accomplished prior to execution and distinct from (but related to) subprogram linkage conventions which are practiced during programming and are used during execution.

Relocation requires identification of those addresses which would be dependent upon the final location of the program in memory. This is accomplished in a *relocation dictionary* (RLD) which is described in Section 5.5. Linking requires that those symbols common to two or more programs be especially identified in each program. Each object module will carry these symbols and some information about them in an *external symbol dictionary* (ESD), also described in Section 5.5. The remaining key element (besides the RLD and ESD) of an object module is *text,* which is the translation of instructions as if the initial byte were at memory location zero—but there will usually be some incomplete translations where external symbols occur. It should be realized that some of the object modules to be combined are created in the current job by translation from assembler language while some reside in libraries as part of system resources for the programmer.

Relocation Revisited

In Section 4.6, we considered relocation from the standpoint of a single object module. We were implicitly assuming no use of separately assembled subprograms, but we must now generalize to the more complex situation. The conclusions drawn there about executable instructions remain valid, namely that no executable instruction is modified by relocation. In fact, there is a special pseudoinstruction, the address constant instruction, which can define addresses from other programs to be used either for getting data or for branching to another program. Communication of either addresses or a function result among programs is supported by:

(1) external symbol dictionaries, one per object module;

(2) relocation dictionaries, one per object module;

(3) conventions for invoking subprograms.

Address Constants (Limited to A and V Types)

An A- or V-type address constant location is a full word reserved in the data area of a program. It is dedicated to holding an address in absolute form (that is, with respect to location zero of memory) at execution time. The address occupies bytes 1–3 of the word. Byte 0 may have other uses, one of which is to flag the last item in a variable-length argument address list. The reservation of address constant locations is made with a pseudoinstruction which has DC for operation code and an operand field of the form

$$T(E_1, E_2, \ldots, E_m)$$

where T is a type that determines (1) which are acceptable expressions E, and (2) whether the instruction must be supplemented with other pseudoinstructions. The two types we will consider here are A and V with limitations as follows:

1. V-type constants permit a sequence of address constant expressions to be specified in one pseudoinstruction, each of which must be an

externally defined location name (which will be provided through the external symbol dictionary of another module). No modifying pseudo-instruction is required.

2. A-type constants also permit a sequence of address constant expressions to be specified in one pseudoinstruction. Each expression in the sequence must be either a relocatable operand expression with no external names, or the sum of an external name and an absolute operand expression with no external names. Every external name in an A-type address specification must be in an operand list of an EXTRN pseudoinstruction.

```
VSUBRT    DC    V(SUBRT)
RGADLIST  DC    A(X,Y+E-B,B+14,Z-10)
          EXTRN X,Y,Z
TABLE     DC    0F'0'
B         DC    F'-17'
E         DC    F'79'
```

Program Segment 5.3.1 The expressions in a V-type address constant must be external names. External names in an A-type address constant must also appear in the operand field of an EXTRN instruction.

It is a tradition at least partially supported by implementation that targets of branch instructions should be specified by V-type address constants, while data references should be specified by A-type address constants. However, there may be occasions when the tradition can be intelligently violated. The address as stored in memory is the same for either A- or V-type address constants. Note that in the example just above we managed to specify a whole list of argument addresses in one instruction, a very convenient facility for passing locations of parameters to a called subprogram.

5.4 CONTROL SECTIONS AND PROGRAM SEGMENTATION

Continuing with the primary objective of this chapter, which is to study the independent assembly of programs which cooperate during execution, we now propose a standardized, constrained form of the assembler instructions constituting the input to one assembly. Each program entity to be assembled independently is called a *control section*. Its first instruction has the name of the subprogram in its location field, CSECT for symbolic operation code, and a blank operand field. Its last instruction is the END pseudoinstruction. The operand field of the END instruction is blank unless this control section begins execution (it is then called the *driver program*). In the latter case, the name of the control section constitutes the operand field of the END instruction. Between the CSECT and END instructions, we presently permit no other CSECT pseudoinstructions.† The CSECT pseudoinstruction serves to force the name in its location field into the external symbol dictionary as the name of this program. We now consider ways for this individual program to do its part in communicating with other control sections.

5.4.1 Information Flow among Control Sections

There are two reasons for another subprogram to refer to a location within a program we create. It may need to branch to a location within our program, or it may need to use data we have. It can accomplish either if it has the appropriate address. In writing our program, we need only put the appropriate names in our external symbol dictionary and the Linkage Editor or Loader will accomplish the rest if the other subprogram is properly written.

The CSECT instruction causes the assembler to place the name for our beginning location in the external symbol dictionary. Every other name to be shared with other programs must appear in the operand field of an ENTRY instruction. The operand field of an ENTRY instruction is a list of location names, that is, a succession of location names with successive names separated by a comma. For example, the instruction

    ENTRY   NTREE1,NTREE2,NTREE3,DATA1,DATA2

would cause these five names to appear in the external symbol dictionary along with the name in the location field of the CSECT instruction. All six of these names would be classified as known in our external symbol dictionary, since the loading of our program determines them without reference to any other program. Clearly, they must each appear in the location field of an instruction of our program. It is the responsibility of other control sections to use these addresses properly.

If our program makes reference to data not within it, or branches to an entry point in another program, then we must inform the assembler that the respective location names are to be in our external symbol dictionary. External names used in the operand field of an A-type address constant instruction must appear in the name list operand field of an EXTRN instruction to be recognized as external. Any name in the operand field of a V-type address constant instruction is recognized as external

---

† We have ignored the START pseudoinstruction, the possibility of unnamed control sections, and the intermingling of different control sections as described in the assembler manual.

without further mention. V-type address constants are normally the target of a branch, while A-type constants are normally for accessing data. For example, the instructions

```
                EXTRN   ITEM1,ITEM2
ADRITEM1    DC      A(ITEM1)
ADRITEM2    DC      A(ITEM2)
PLACE       DC      V(WHERE)
```

would put ITEM1, ITEM2, and WHERE into the external symbol dictionary, all marked as unknown, and provide places for their addresses to be inserted when they are known. It is intended that WHERE is an entry point in another subprogram to which our program contemplates branching. The A- and V-type DC pseudoinstructions should each have a label since, at some time in our program, we expect to load the address constant into a register for use as an explicit base or as a branch destination. Names appearing in the operand field of an EXTRN instruction or in a V-type address constant will be classified as unknown in our ESD since they must be provided from another ESD.

We have just seen that there are two ways of placing external names (the names of external locations which appear in the operand field of address constant instructions) in the external symbol dictionary, one primarily for data and one primarily for locations to which we wish to branch. To find a location name we begin searching the external symbol dictionaries of all the control sections which constitute our program. But if the name is not defined in one of these, the system has to search the libraries it has available on the chance we are addressing a previously assembled control section stored there. Limiting use of V-type address constants to branch destinations and of A-type address constants to data references is recommended, although in some cases the roles can be interchanged.

While it is not explicitly stated above, the use of external addresses within a program is somewhat awkward. The addresses made available are absolute (relative to the origin of memory) and these do not fit into any instruction with an implied base. In fact, there are only a few reasonable instructions to accommodate an absolute address, and these are the DC pseudoinstructions. From the various address types of DC instructions, we will find that our present needs are satisfied with the A and V types. The absolute address provided by an address constant is useful only when it is loaded into a register and used either as an explicit base or for a branch destination.

5.4.2 Deck Assembly

When two or more object modules are to be linked together to form
a program, the key issue is that all object modules be available before
any attempt to link them is made. Because of the importance of FOR-
TRAN and its vast libraries, we will consider the following four sources
of object modules:

(1) from an assembly in a job step, saved on disk through the current
job;

(2) from a FORTRAN compilation, saved on disk through the current
job;

(3) from a punched card deck created on a prior assembly or compilation;

(4) from a library accessible during the linking process.

We consider a case in which all four types occur.

If there are m separate control sections to be assembled, then each
should have a job control card which causes assembly only (no linking
and no execution) placed ahead of it; these control sections can be stacked
in arbitrary order. We assume there is a *catalogued procedure* † which
retains these modules on a disk until the job ends.

As options, one may choose to print the ESD and the RLD for an
assembly-produced object module. This is accomplished by appending

$$,PARM = \text{'ESD,RLD'}$$

immediately after the catalogued procedure name on the execute (abbre-
viated EXEC) card.

If there are n FORTRAN programs, then these can be stacked in any
order, and one control card which causes compilation only should be
placed on top. These cards are then stacked with the m control sections
to be assembled. It does not matter which is first. Again, we assume there

---

† The casual user of a computer system which is controlled by an operating
supervisor is unprepared to write the sequences of job control cards required to
accomplish both assembly and execution, for example, in one machine use. To enable
him to function, systems programmers create catalogued procedures representing
control card sequences for the tasks he usually wants to accomplish and file them on a
disk. The programmer needs to provide only an execute control card which begins

$$// \text{ EXEC}$$

and name the catalogued procedure in the subsequent columns to gain the effect
of having in his deck the control cards represented by that catalogued procedure.

is a catalogued procedure which retains these *n* modules on a disk until the job ends.

The last catalogued procedure must:

1. Extract from appropriate libraries the remaining modules which go to make up the complete program.

2. Determine a memory map which shows the positions all these modules will have in memory, relative to the first module loaded.

3. Load these modules into memory for execution.

4. Resolve all address constants (this can not be done while the modules reside on the disk, as individual words are not addressable on the disk).

5. Initiate execution.

For this last catalogued procedure on 360 or 370 systems, one possibility is a "link-edit and go" procedure which (1) uses the Linkage Editor program to create a load module during the "link-edit" phase, and (2) loads that module using Program Fetch and initiates execution in the "go" phase. Another choice is to use a linking loader program called Loader which does not separate these steps, is somewhat less versatile, and therefore likely to be faster. For many purposes, however, the latter is entirely adequate.

This last catalogued procedure must be chosen to provide whatever library modules are required. If none are required, then any "link-edit and go" or any "loader" procedure should be suitable. In the latter case, two that would be suitable from the authors' shop are ASMGLG and FORTGLG, the last two letters in either case signifying Link-edit and Go. If there are library modules to be retrieved then, in a sense, these library modules select the catalogued procedure whose library contains them. Since FORTRAN libraries are very large compared to those of other languages, and since programmer-defined FORTRAN subprograms may themselves require additional modules from FORTRAN libraries, a FORTRAN "link-edit and go" procedure is often useful. The EXECute control card for this step should follow the assembler and FORTRAN source programs, and precede the object modules and the data description card announcing them as input. A printout of the memory map mentioned above can be useful in trouble shooting. It is obtained by appending ,PARM = 'MAP' to the name of the catalogued procedure for linking (or loading) on its EXECute card.

Of all the modules mentioned until now, one and only one must be the main (driver) program. If the driver is a FORTRAN program, it is recognized as one which does not begin with a SUBROUTINE or

FUNCTION statement. If the driver is an assembler language program, it is the only one with its CSECT name in the operand field of the END instruction.

To illustrate, in Figure 5.4.1 we detail the card arrangement for a deck as it would be arranged on one computer system. Changes to suit local system conventions may be required.

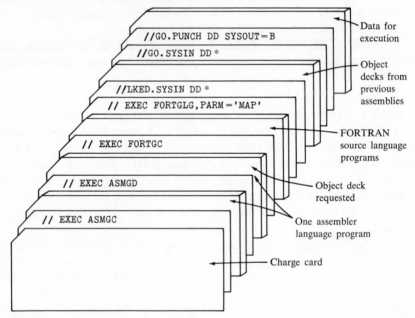

Control card functions:

ASMGC—A catalogued procedure which creates one object module from one assembler language control section and saves the module for later use until the end of the job. ASMGD additionally causes an object deck to be punched.

FORTGC—A catalogued procedure which creates one object module from each FORTRAN program which follows this card, and saves the modules for later use. FORTGD additionally causes an object deck to be punched.

FORTGLG—A catalogued procedure which links object modules from previous job steps, the input stream, or FORTRAN libraries to create a composite of these object modules which is loaded into memory for execution.

//LKED. SYSIN DD *—Indicates that object modules recorded on cards will follow.

//GO.SYSIN DD *—Indicates that data for the problem will follow.

//GO.PUNCH DD SYSOUT=B—Provides a file for recording object modules to be punched.

Figure 5.4.1 The deck structure shown is sufficient for almost all programs composed of FORTRAN and assembler segments.

For the special case in which no translation takes place, the catalogued procedure which corresponds to FORTGLG may have to be replaced by one which expects no object module from previous job steps. At the authors' installation, FORTGNLG serves this purpose. As an alternative, one may satisfy this hunger of FORTGLG with a dummy source program in assembler language which only invokes the main program.

5.5   THE EXTERNAL SYMBOL AND RELOCATION DICTIONARIES

Although our primary concern has been and will continue to be with object modules as produced by the assembler program, the *load module* is closely related. Produced by a program called the *linkage editor,* the load module contains much the same information content as the object modules, but has a different format. Studying load modules will help clarify some of the ideas involved with linking and relocating cooperating programs. We may think of a load module as the result of bringing together enough object modules so that, when linked into one composite program, the result is a module with no external references. Such a load module will have one *composite external symbol dictionary* (CESD), but it will have an updated relocation dictionary (perhaps an empty one) associated with the text of each of the component object modules. Each of these updated relocation dictionaries will have the same number of entries as before, but each entry will be altered so that its references by line number to symbols in the external symbol dictionary are adjusted to their new positions in the composite external symbol dictionary. In the relocation dictionary, each pointer to an occurrence in the text of an address constant instruction will be made relative to the beginning of the load module.

An ESD (see Figure 5.5.1) is a two-way street. There is a line reserved in it for every symbol having significance both in the text to which it is attached and in some other module. Some of these symbols have their values determined by the text and/or position in memory of another module. These are typed as *external references* (ER). On the other hand, other symbols (entries) in the ESD represent data locations or control entries in the attached text, and their values are determined without information about other modules. Their presence in the ESD makes their values accessible to other programs, and they are called *entry symbols.* In the external symbol dictionary, they are typed as *label definitions*

(LD). Names of control sections qualify as entry symbols in the sense we have mentioned, but are distinguished as *section definition* (SD) symbols since they carry with them an important item of information, the length of the control section. Neither entry symbols (label definitions) nor external references have a corresponding length, but each label definition symbol carries the line number (its heading in our ESD printout is "LD ID") in the ESD of the name of the control section containing the symbol as an entry point. Under the assumptions of Section 5.4, this line number can differ from one only in a composite external symbol dictionary, and is included in each object module's ESD for uniformity. The nonsense sequence of instructions in the "program" of Figure 5.5.1 yields on assembly the ESD in the same figure. Note that in this printout the section definition(s) (with restrictions stated in the next section, there will be one per object module), external references, and label definitions are listed in the order that instructions marked their symbols as external (that is, by appearance in the label field of a CSECT, in the operand

```
 LOC     OBJECT CODE  ADDR1 ADDR2 STMT        SOURCE STATEMENT
000000                              1 PROG1   CSECT
000000                              2 NTREE1  DC    OF'0'
000000 00000000                     3         DC    A(U)
000004 00000000                     4         DC    A(X)
000008 00000000                     5         DC    V(Y)
                                    6         EXTRN X
00000C 00000000                     7         DC    V(Z)
                                    8         ENTRY NTREE2,NTREE1
000010                              9 NTREE2  DC    OF'0'
                                   10         EXTRN U
                                   11         END

              EXTERNAL SYMBOL DICTIONARY
       SYMBOL TYPE ID  ADDR  LENGTH LD ID
       PROG1   SD  01 000000 000010
       Y       ER  02
       X       ER  03
       Z       ER  04
       NTREE2  LD     000010        01
       NTREE1  LD     000000        01
       U       ER  05
```

Figure 5.5.1 Assembly of the "program" at the top of this figure generates the ESD at the bottom. Note that the order of appearance in this table is determined by the order of occurrence of the instruction (or within the instruction) which marks the label as external.

field of an EXTRN or ENTRY or as a label in the operand field of a
V-type address constant instruction). The section definition(s) and external references are indexed sequentially in the column headed "ID".
The remaining item in an ESD line is the address of the symbol's occurrence as an instruction location name relative to the beginning of the
control section (not defined for external references). While still other
symbol types can be carried in the ESD, they are not essential now, and
will not be discussed in this section.

The value of an external symbol influences memory contents at execution time only in address constant locations. The address constant type (we
are considering only A- and V-types) is carried in the relocation dictionary and it determines the way the value is applied. A-type address
constant expressions need not include an external symbol, and if they do
not, they can be set for execution entirely from relocation information in
the object module. When an external symbol X does appear in an A-type
address constant expression, then we must be able to rewrite the expression in the form $X + E'$, where E' contains no external symbols and is
absolute. The following example shows two A-type expressions which
would be assembled properly, provided IN and OUT are not external
references.

```
          EXTRN   BEAN,CARROT
            .
            .
            .
          DC      A(BEAN+8,CARROT+IN-OUT)
```

With an A-type address constant, each external symbol must be forced
into the external symbol dictionary by its appearance in the operand field
of an EXTRN pseudoinstruction. Under these conditions, the value of E'
assigned to the address constant by the assembler is incremented by the
value of X (the external address) during the loading process. Each
operand expression of a V-type address constant must be a single external
name. The appearance of a symbol in the operand of a V-type address
constant assures its inclusion in the external symbol dictionary. Then the
value of the external symbol is inserted (not added) into bytes 1–3 of
the address constant location during the loading process. All symbols
appearing in the ESD because of their occurrence in an A-type or V-type
address constant operand field are tagged with the code ER (which stands
for external reference).

There is a line in the relocation dictionary of a module (either object or load) for each of its address constants. It contains four items of information, the first two being pointers to pertinent lines of the external symbol dictionary for the module. One, called the P (*position*) pointer, is the ID number in the external symbol dictionary of the name of the control section which determines the value of the address constant. For mnemonic purposes, we will also call this the *control section pointer*. The other, called the R (*relocation*) pointer, is the ID number in the external symbol dictionary of the one symbol whose value is used to set the address constant. Note that for an A-type address constant having no external symbol, this value is just the initial location of the control section so that the two pointers select the same line of the ESD.

The remaining items in a relocation dictionary line are (1) the type of its address constant (in a column headed "Flags" these are coded 0C for A-type and 1C for V-type, the two types of primary interest now) and (2) the address within the control section of the address constant.† There is an excellent tutorial paper on the linking and loading stages which we recommend. It includes a classification of loaders, analyzes the linking process and the various times it can occur, and concludes with a careful examination of their implementation in the IBM 360.‡

When two control sections are assembled separately, the ESD and RLD for each control section is made up independently from the other control section. Entries in the ESD are section definitions, entry points (label definitions), names declared external, and V-type address constants, and appearance of those items in the ESD is in the same order as in the instruction sequence of the control section. Entries in the RLD are address-type DC's, with the internal ones (A-type) appearing before the external ones (A-type declared external or V-type) in the table.

Resolution of all DC's takes place at loading time, for only then are the locations of control sections assigned. Internal DC's (A-type containing no external name) can be resolved by adding the address of the control section to the assembled value of the data constant. External DC's (V-type or A-type containing an external name) can be resolved only after the control section in which that external name is defined has also been loaded. Loading a control section determines the beginning

---

† For a more detailed discussion and some examples of how the linkage editor handles address constants, see "Relocation of Address Constants." in "IBM System/360 Operating System Linkage Editor (F)." Program Logic, Form GY28-6667.

‡ L. Presser, and J. R. White, Linkers and loaders, *ACM Computing Surveys,* September, 1972.

address of that control section, of course. The external name is type **LD** in that control section, so its address relative to the beginning of the control section is in the ESD. The sum of the control section address and this relative address gives an absolute address for the external name. This value is inserted into a V-type address constant with that external name; it is added to the assembled value of an A-type address constant expression containing that name as an external reference.

As an example of the external symbol and relocation dictionaries for cooperating object modules, Program 5.5.1 shows a main program A, which calls a subprogram B on two occasions. As shown, the program will have no output to determine if it executed properly, but our present interest is in the assembler-constructed dictionaries. Output at any point during execution can be obtained using SNAP as discussed in Section 4.5, or a FORTRAN subprogram as discussed in Section 5.4. The two control sections in this program illustrate a complex way of adding four integers; the pedagogical benefits of such a ridiculous approach to simple addition stem from the fact that, when a number is needed, it is accessed from the other control section. Thus the two cooperating control sections yield nontrivial ESD's and RLD's.

Address computation 1.   The first entry in the RLD for control section A has an assembled hexadecimal address of 000030, and has symbolic location ADRAIN1. The operand field is A(AIN1) and, since AIN1 has not been declared external, this DC can be resolved at loading time by (1) determining the beginning address from control section A, and (2) adding the assembled value for AIN1 which is 000034.

Address computation 2.   The fourth entry in the RLD for control section A has an assembled hexadecimal address of 00004C, and has symbolic location ADRN. The operand field A(M+4) and the EXTRN M,BIN1 statement appearing above indicate that M is a symbolic location in a different control section. Therefore this DC can be resolved at loading time by (1) determining the beginning address for control section B, (2) adding the assembled (relative) location of M in control section B, which happens to be 000030 in this case, and (3) adding the assembled value of the DC in control section A, which is 00000004 in this case.

Address computation 3.   The last entry in the RLD for control section A has an assembled hexadecimal address of 000050, and has symbolic location ADRBIN2. The operand field V(BIN2) indicates that this DC can

```
LOC      OBJECT CODE    ADDR1 ADDR2 STMT      SOURCE STATEMENT
000000                              1   A       CSECT
                                    2           ENTRY AIN1,AIN2,J,K
000000 90EC D00C              00000 3           STM   14,12,12(13)
000004 05C0                         4           BALR  12,0
000006                              5           USING *,12
000006 41A0 C062              00068 6           LA    10,SAVE
00000A 50DA 0004              00004 7           ST    13,4(10)
00000E 50AD 0008              00008 8           ST    10,8(13)
000012 18DA                         9           LR    13,10
000014 58A0 C022              00028 10          L     10,ADRM
000018 589A 0000              00000 11          L     9,0(10)
00001C 58E0 C02A              00030 12          L     14,ADRAIN1
000020 58F0 C026              0002C 13          L     15,ADRBIN1
000024 07FF                         14          BR    15
000026 0000
000028 00000000                     15  ADRM    DC    V(M)
00002C 00000000                     16  ADRBIN1 DC    A(BIN1)
000030 00000034                     17  ADRAIN1 DC    A(AIN1)
                                    18          EXTRN M,BIN1
000034 58A0 C046              0004C 19  AIN1    L     10,ADRN
000038 5A9A 0000              00000 20          A     9,0(10)
00003C 41D0 C062              00068 21          LA    13,SAVE
000040 58E0 C04E              00054 22          L     14,ADRAIN2
000044 58F0 C04A              00050 23          L     15,ADRBIN2
000048 07FF                         24          BR    15
00004A 0000
00004C 00000004                     25  ADRN    DC    A(M+4)
000050 00000000                     26  ADRBIN2 DC    V(BIN2)
000054 00000058                     27  ADRAIN2 DC    A(AIN2)
000058 5090 C0AA              000B0 28  AIN2    ST    9,ANSWER
00005C 58D0 C066              0006C 29          L     13,SAVE+4
000060 98EC D00C              0000C 30          LM    14,12,12(13)
000064 07FE                         31          BR    14
000066 0000
000068 0000000000000000             32  SAVE    DC    18F'0'
0000B0 00000000                     33  ANSWER  DC    F'0'
0000B4 FFFFFFCE                     34  J       DC    F'-50'
0000B8 00000007                     35  K       DC    F'7'
000000                              36          END   A
```

EXTERNAL SYMBOL DICTIONARY						RELOCATION DICTIONARY			
SYMBOL	TYPE	ID	ADDR	LENGTH	LD ID	POS.ID	REL.ID	FLAGS	ADDRESS
A	SD	01	000000	0000BC		01	01	0C	000030
AIN1	LD		000034		01	01	01	0C	000054
AIN2	LD		000058		01	01	02	1C	000028
J	LD		0000B4		01	01	02	0C	00004C
K	LD		0000B8		01	01	03	0C	00002C
M	ER	02				01	04	1C	000050
BIN1	ER	03							
BIN2	ER	04							

Program 5.5.1 Cooperating control sections A and B (next page) with their ESD's and RLD's.

```
  LOC    OBJECT CODE   ADDR1 ADDR2 STMT         SOURCE STATEMENT
000000                              1  B       CSECT
                                    2          ENTRY BIN1,BIN2,M,N
                                    3          EXTRN J
000000 90EC D00C          0000C     4  BIN1    STM   14,12,12(13)
000004 05C0                         5          BALR  12,0
000006                              6          USING *,12
000006 41A0 C062          00068     7          LA    10,SAVE
00000A 50DA 0004          00004     8          ST    13,4(10)
00000E 50AD 0008          00008     9          ST    10,8(13)
000012 18DA                        10          LR    13,10
000014 58A0 C026          0002C    11          L     10,ADRK
000018 5A9A 0000          00000    12          A     9,0(10)
00001C 58D0 C066          0006C    13          L     13,SAVE+4
000020 98E8 D00C          0000C    14          LM    14,8,12(13)
000024 98AC D03C          0003C    15          LM    10,12,60(13)
000028 07FE                        16          BR    14
00002A 0000
00002C 00000000                    17  ADRK    DC    V(K)
000030 00000015                    18  M       DC    F'21'
000034 00000013                    19  N       DC    F'19'
000038 90EC D00C          0000C    20  BIN2    STM   14,12,12(13)
00003C 05C0                        21          BALR  12,0
00003E                             22          USING *,12
00003E 41A0 C02A          00068    23          LA    10,SAVE
000042 50DA 0004          00004    24          ST    13,4(10)
000046 50AD 0008          00008    25          ST    10,8(13)
00004A 18DA                        26          LR    13,10
00004C 58A0 C026          00064    27          L     10,ADRJ
000050 5A9A 0000          00000    28          A     9,0(10)
000054 58D0 C02E          0006C    29          L     13,SAVE+4
000058 98E8 D00C          0000C    30          LM    14,8,12(13)
00005C 98AC D03C          0003C    31          LM    10,12,60(13)
000060 07FE                        32          BR    14
000062 0000
000064 00000000                    33  ADRJ    DC    A(J)
000068 0000000000000000            34  SAVE    DC    18F'0'
                                   35          END
```

EXTERNAL SYMBOL DICTIONARY						RELOCATION DICTIONARY			
SYMBOL	TYPE	ID	ADDR	LENGTH	LD ID		POS.ID	REL.ID	FLAGS	ADDRESS
B	SD	01	000000	0000B0			01	02	0C	000064
BIN1	LD		000000		01		01	03	1C	00002C
BIN2	LD		000038		01					
M	LD		000030		01					
N	LD		000034		01					
J	ER	02								
K	ER	03								

Program 5.5.1 (continued) Control section B.

be resolved at loading time by (1) determining the beginning address of control section B, (2) adding the assembled location of BIN2 in control section B, which in this case is 000038, and (3) inserting this sum as the address constant (since the only value which can be assembled for a V-type address constant is 00000000, adding would yield the same result).

5.6   CHECKOUT CONSIDERATIONS FOR SEGMENTED PROGRAMS

Ideally, one should expect that a major program can be resolved into subprograms so as to ease programming, facilitate debugging and validation, and yield a program flexible to change. Three specific objectives in this regard should be:

(1) that each subprogram can be conveniently tested by an easily constructed test program independently from each unvalidated subprogram and, for the most part, independent of the other subprograms;

(2) that the major program is clearly expressed in terms of these subprograms;

(3) that any one change necessary to the major program as its applications are extended can be accomplished by changes in only one or at the most very few subprograms.

This last objective is perhaps the most difficult aspect of program design and development. It is a proper subject of study which is independent of any particular implementation language, although it is also appropriate in courses which are strongly oriented toward a particular language. We consider this subject so problem oriented (versus machine oriented) that its study is better pursued in the study of a problem-oriented language or of algorithmic processes in general. Therefore we will assume that a sensible segmentation has been accomplished and that we are implementing the major program as a cooperating set of subprograms, one of which is the main (driver) subprogram.

Assuming a subprogram which can be easily tested independent of all others, we are still faced with simultaneous checkout of two error-prone programs, the one under test and the program which tests it. The first of the three objectives listed above was that the test program should be easily constructed with the hope that its checkout would be relatively simple. Nevertheless, it may well be desired to obtain snapshots from each of these in the same machine run and/or to have a snapshot in one show the contents of a data segment in the other. A few extensions of our snapshot instructions of Section 4.5 are required to make this feasible.

5.6.1 Snapshots from Distinct Assemblies

Opening a file for snapshot information (we have called ours SNAP-DUMP) creates a data set to receive snapshot information. If each of two cooperating programs has a control block for such a file and uses the same file name, then there is going to be an addressing problem; namely, there will be two data control blocks created, and one file to be controlled by them. Even if the file specifications in the data control blocks are consistent, the information on file status during execution will be incomplete in at least one of them. There are two ways to try to solve the problem.

One method is to create a distinct snapshot file for each program. If there were two cooperating programs, we might name their files SNAPDMP1 and SNAPDMP2, respectively. These files would collect information on the disk and, when the job terminates, one after the other would be printed. Since all printing from one file precedes all printing from the other, the ordering in time of snapshots from distinct assemblies would be lost.

A better method is to have a DCB macro for a SNAPDUMP file in one and only one control section and to refer to the data control block it creates from other control sections as necessary. To do this will require that the name of the DCB, say SNAPPER, appear in the operand list of an ENTRY instruction in the control section where it is defined and be made available in an address constant location as an external address as discussed in Section 5.5. Even then, the use of this address in other macros requires explanation.

Where we have until now expected a location name to appear as an address in a macro, we may place instead the parenthesized number of a register (one of 2–12†) which holds the absolute address for that name. For example,

$$DCB=(2),STORAGE=((3),(4))$$

in the operand field of the SNAP macro specifies use of a data control block of which the absolute address is in register 2 as well as the printout of a storage area bounded by absolute addresses which are in register 3 and register 4. In one use of a macro, there can be some addresses specified by symbolic name and some given in absolute form. Thus

$$STORAGE=(AN,BE,(2),(3))$$

† In Section 4.5, we urged the reader to expect registers 0, 1, 14, and 15 to be modified by a macro. While one might be tempted to use one of these registers in hopes that the macro would not destroy its contents before it is used, this is justified only if confirmed by study of its coding and thorough testing.

would be acceptable and would permit printing from two regions, the first of which is in the same control section as the SNAP, the second in some other control section which contains the storage segment whose bounds are the absolute addresses in registers 2 and 3.

The SNAPDUMP file must be opened before it is to be used, and there could be some situations where one would need to have an OPEN macro at the beginning of several control sections so that, no matter which one was entered first, the OPEN would have occurred in time. The macro manual† indicates that to open an open file is technically an error, but that it has no effect. This permits opening the file in several control sections as needed. The address of the data control block can be given in the OPEN instruction either by symbolic name (if the OPEN and DCB macros are in the same control section) or by parenthesized number of a register containing the absolute address of the data control block in other control sections. Thus,

$$\text{OPEN (SNAPPER,OUTPUT)}$$

might appear in the same control section as the DCB and

$$\text{OPEN ((2),OUTPUT)}$$

in another.

The use of absolute addresses to locate the data control block may make a heavy demand on registers. In this case, one can picture saving the general register contents prior to loading these absolute addresses for use in a SNAP instruction and then restoring the registers after the snapshot is completed.

5.6.2   The Ordering of Checkout

Subprograms which call on no others are candidates for early checkout, especially those which serve a utility function for several others. In this regard, input and output subprograms which (1) enable one to deposit test data in memory, (2) print not only the answers but all input data as read in, and (3) also print the intermediate status of computations, can be invaluable during checkout of other subprograms.

Subprograms which do call on others can still be checked well by substitution of dummy subprograms for those not yet validated. The dummy program may in some cases do no more than return fixed results independent of actual arguments and still serve adequately. Such techniques make possible one of the major advantages of segmentation, which is the opportunity to be testing several subprograms of the same problem in par-

---

† "IBM System/360 Operating System: Supervisor and Data Management Macro Instructions," Form C28–6647.

allel. Whether one programmer juggles several control sections or a team cooperates in a major development, it affords great flexibility.

As soon as a subprogram has stood up under substantial test, one should consider punching an object module for that deck so that (1) subsequent usage will not require further assemblies, and (2) the role of the source-language deck can be taken in future job requests by the much more compact object module. Since this object module does not need translating, it becomes input to the link editing or loading step of a job request. There should be a catalogued procedure for assembling (or compiling) a source deck and then punching an object deck at a usual 360/370 installation. One can also obtain the deck by exercising assembler options. In that case, one must provide a data description card for the output to the punch. At the authors' facility, the catalogued procedure for compiling and punching a deck is selected by the control card

> `// EXEC ASMGD`

The second alternative for getting a deck at this facility is

> `// EXEC ASMGC,PARM='DECK'`
>
> [assembler language program]
>
> `//SYSPUNCH DD SYSOUT=B`

One may be required also to supply a "limits card" to notify the operation that punched output is expected. Such a card specifies a maximum on cards to be punched and overrides a default option which could normally be zero.

5.7 THE CARE AND FEEDING OF BASE REGISTERS

To this point, we have assumed a program which never exceeds 4096 bytes in length, and which is entered only at its initial byte. These assumptions, inherent for BAREBONZ, were only temporary limitations put on base register use. There is little difficulty in generalizing to larger programs, since the USING instruction can name several base registers to be operative at once. The operand field can be of the form shown.

$$\text{USING} \quad E, r_1, r_2, \ldots, r_n$$

where

(1)   E is a relocatable, nonabsolute expression;

(2) $n \leq 15$;

(3) $1 \leq r_i \leq 15$;

(4) $r_i \neq r_j$ if $i \neq j$;

(5) $c(r_i)$ is taken to be the value $(E) + 4096(i-1)$ for $1 \leq i \leq n$.

In representing a given operand expression when several bases are operative, the assembler selects that one which yields the least nonnegative displacement.

The rule just given resolves another less obvious situation. One may choose to have two or more base registers current which differ in content by something other than 4096. A sequence to establish two bases differing by 1000 bytes is given as an example below, where we observe that the programmer is responsible for loading the base registers with the appropriate addresses, as before.

```
BEGIN LR     12,15
      LA     11,1000(12)
      USING  BEGIN,12
      USING  BEGIN+1000,11
```

In order to have displacements exactly equal to assembled addresses, we have consistently set the least base equal to the address of the initial byte of the program. This is not necessary and is relatively inflexible, especially in segmented programs. There is, in fact, an idiomatic sequence ordinarily used for specifying and setting the base, first presented in Problem 1 of Chapter 4. We use the instruction

$$\text{BALR REG,0} \quad 1 \leq \text{REG} \leq 15$$

to store in the named register the contents of the IAC. The fact that the second-named register is register 0 inhibits the branching normally expected with the BALR operation. To ensure that the assembler expects the same value as the BALR places in REG, we follow that instruction immediately with the pseudoinstruction

$$\text{USING } *, \text{REG}$$

The explanation in Section 4.3.1 that the first instruction of our idiomatic pair is applied only during execution and the second is applied only during assembly is still pertinent.

There are various clever sequences for establishing several registers as multiple bases and setting their contents appropriately; an example taken directly from the Assembler Language reference manual† is

```
         BALR  2,0
         USING HERE,2,3,4,5
HERE     LM    3,5,BASEADDR
         B     FIRST
BASEADDR DC    A(HERE+4096,HERE+8192,HERE+12288)
FIRST    ...
```

---

†"IBM System/360 Operating System: Assembler anguage," Number GC28–6514.

Observations about the USING instruction:

1. The expression E which begins the operand field of a USING in-struction has been implicitly a relocatable, nonabsolute expression. We shall always take it to be such. The reference manual asserts it can also be absolute, and that even register 0 can be named as a base. These are con-siderations for systems programmers, for they have to do with the nonrelo-catable program segments he may place in the lowest addresses of memory as part of the operating system. We will not consider this specialized ap-plication.

2. A USING assignment of a particular program address (as a base in a given register) is utilized within an assembly until it is overridden by an-other USING instruction for the same register or a DROP pseudoin-struction which includes its number in an operand list of registers. Drop-ping a register would be required if it were to be subject to modification by computation in the ensuing text. As with substitutions in a football (not baseball) game, the DROP applies only until the next USING.

3. There are hazards to be anticipated in any control section which es-tablishes a base near the beginning and one or more bases farther down in the text. The primary danger is that a reference to a location may be sepa-rated from that location by the establishment of a base. In that case, the displacement in the reference instruction is computed during assembly with respect to a different base than that used during execution.

5.8   INTRODUCTION TO MACROS

5.8.1   Open versus Closed Subprograms

To obtain the benefits of program segmentation, we have placed sub-stantial stress on distinguishing subprograms which could be assembled and tested separately. Among other things, we find it desirable to obtain object modules of validated subprograms and to use them in cooperation with assembler programs still being debugged to avoid unnecessary reas-sembly. While all the benefits we have claimed are real, it is important to recognize that there are subprograms for which the avoidance of repeated assembly is not important, but in which the substantial overhead of stand-ardized subprogram linkage may be of real concern. For these, it is often advantageous to maintain the subprogram in symbolic form—either on cards or in a system-accessible library—and to combine it with other sym-bolic programming at assembly time. We distinguish two ways to do this. If the subprogram resides in one segment of memory and is referenced from one or more places in the program, we call the subprogram *closed*. The subprograms used earlier in this chapter and in Chapter 3 were closed subprograms. If, prior to assembly, a symbolic version of the subprogram replaces each of its invocations, and if "exit" is always to the next instruction following the insertion, the subprogram is called an *open subprogram* or *macro*. Assembly occurs only after all macro invocations have been so replaced. There is a very substantial provision in IBM 360/370 assemblers for macros.

Before introducing the construction of macros, we would like to comment that the distinction between a macro and a closed subprogram is really, for the most part, one of programming detail and not one of computational organization. In each case, one is isolating a segment of a computation to be invoked with a minimal sequence of instructions which provides both parameters and a name for the segment. In each case, the normal continuation after completion of the segment is the coding following the invocation. Because macro-invoked code is generated for each textual invocation, it is possible to insert the names of actual arguments prior to assembly, thus avoiding the passing of parameters or their addresses which is inherent in each execution of a closed subprogram which has parameters. For the same reason, one may be able (by tests of symbolic arguments at assembly time) to tailor the macro to the specific use being made, thus avoiding execution of instructions which—in the particular situation—accomplish nothing. A macro, as distinguished from a closed subroutine, can be entered without a branch instruction. Hence, it can be utilized when no base address has been established. Thus a macro is applicable for short sequences in which a closed subprogram would not be. These advantages—there are surely others—are made at some cost in assembly time and possible additional memory requirements for repetitions of the segment.

As in the introduction of the machine itself, we avoid the elaborate details of macros to get launched with some simple ones first.

5.8.2   Substitution-Generated Macros

We consider in this section the class of macros which can be generated with the one operation of substituting actual arguments for dummy names in an instruction sequence. As an example, if &A and &B are dummy names in the sequence

```
        L   10,&B
        ST  10,&A
```

and if the corresponding actual arguments in a given instance of use are HAY and BARN, then the sequence generated is

```
L   10,HAY
ST  10,BARN
```

In this example, the two instructions containing the dummy arguments to be replaced constitute the *model*. We could at least imagine a macro instruction

```
HARVEST HAY,BARN
```

used to cause the generating of actual instructions and a substitution-defining line

```
HARVEST &B,&A
```

called a *prototype* instruction which, by its appearance in the macro definition, establishes that the first operand replaces &B throughout the model and the second replaces &A throughout. In this sense, the operation code of the macro plays the role of a subprogram name, and the prototype instruction plays the role of the SUBROUTINE or FUNCTION statement of FORTRAN. The prototype instruction is recognized as the first instruction following a so-called header. The header has MACRO for its symbolic operation code, and has empty label and operand fields. The end of the model is marked by an instruction which is blank except for its symbolic operation code which is MEND for Macro END. This instruction is called a *trailer*. Thus, our complete definition of the HARVEST macro would be

Macro definition		Instruction type
MACRO		Header
HARVEST	&B,&A	Prototype
L	10,&B ⎫	Model
ST	10,&A ⎭	
MEND		Trailer

User-defined macros may be stored on line in a macro-library, but we defer that option for the present and assume they are provided in the input stream along with the program which refers to them. In that case, all macro definitions should be together and precede any control section definitions of the assembly.

Having an example in mind, we look at a more precise formulation of concepts. We note first that the dummy arguments of a macro definition are distinct from the usual variable names. They are marked by having & as their first character, and are called *symbolic parameters*. A symbolic parameter (as defined in the IBM System/360 OS Assembler Language) is a string of from two through eight characters of which the first is "&", the second is alphabetic, and the remaining characters (there may not be any) are alphabetic or numeric. Any string beginning &SYS is reserved for the system and cannot be used.

One may ask why it is necessary that the dummy arguments in the macro definition have a distinguishing first character. For our particularly simple beginning, it is not necessary. The distinguished first character becomes a useful delimiter when the beginning of a dummy variable might otherwise be considered the continuation of another symbol (e.g., the dummy variable might provide a suffix to a symbolic operation code). An example of this use would be a macro to increment a storage location by 1 in which the purpose is to handle the half-word and full-word cases in the same macro. Table 5.8.1 shows the macro definition and two different macro instructions patterned after the prototype, with the resulting code for each.

```
MACRO
BUMP      &NAME,&TYPE
L&TYPE    10,&NAME
LA        10,1(10)
ST&TYPE   10,&NAME
MEND
```

Macro	BUMP A or BUMP A,		BUMP A,H	
Generated code	L	10,A	LH	10,A
	LA	10,1(10)	LA	10,1(10)
	ST	10,A	STH	10,A

Table 5.8.1 Here we show two versions of the same macro in which a substitution actually modifies a symbolic operation code.

The prototype instruction in a macro definition has the macro name for symbolic operation code, blank or a symbolic parameter in the label field, and blank or a succession of symbolic parameters separated by commas in the operand field. The symbolic parameter in the label field of the prototype is replaced throughout the model during macro generation by the label in the macro instruction. Ordinarily, this symbolic parameter will appear only in the label field of the prototype statement and of the first instruction of the model, its purpose being to permit the label on the macro instruction to be applied to the generated sequence. If the macro instruction lacks a label in the name field, then the generated statements will not be labeled.

The argument list of a macro instruction should be in one-to-one correspondence with the list of symbolic parameters (dummy arguments) of the macro prototype. This correspondence establishes the remaining substitutions to be made in instructions of the model to obtain the sequence which replaces the macro instruction. A blank operand field permits no substitutions except for that determined by the label field.

The instructions between the prototype and the trailer of a macro definition constitute the model. Symbolic parameters can be inserted freely with the understanding that each is in the operand list of the prototype and that the substitution of actual arguments always generates legal assembler instructions. Clearly, a macro definition can be valid for one invocation and invalid for another. For example, if a symbolic parameter representing a register number is replaced by an actual argument of 73, the resulting instruction will be invalid.

As another example of a macro, consider the macro definition shown in Table 5.8.2. This macro can be used for either addition or subtraction, since the dummy variable &OP in the prototype statement can be replaced in the macro instruction by a meaningful, valid operation code such as A or S. Similarly, &REG is a stand-in for the register in which the operation is to be performed, and &C, &D, and &E stand for memory location names for two operands and the result. Two possible "calls" of the macro (in the control section following the macro definition) are shown in Table 5.8.2, with the resulting code generated before assembly.

```
&NAME MACRO
&NAME ADSUB &OP,&REG,&C,&D,&E
&NAME L     &REG,&C
      &OP   &REG,&D
      ST    &REG,&E
      MEND
```

Macro	ADD1	ADSUB	A,10,X,Y,Z	SUBTRACT	ADSUB	S,8,P,Q,R
Generated code	ADD1	L	10,X	SUBTRACT	L	8,P
		A	10,Y		S	8,Q
		ST	10,Z		ST	8,R

Table 5.8.2   This macro illustrates that location names and operation codes can be specified in the name and operand fields, respectively, of the macro instruction.

Macros can serve an excellent purpose in facilitating the concepts of structured programming. A simple example of such use is provided in Problem 11 at the end of this chapter.

5.9 ASSEMBLER BUILDING PROJECT

It is entirely feasible at this stage for a class to construct as a team project a meaningful although woefully inadequate assembler for a language like BAREBONZ II. We have available the flow diagrams of Chapter 4 as a guide, but we will want to organize the task into subprograms which are separately assembled and tested according to principles developed in this chapter. The purpose is, of course, to become familiar with the process, not to become systems programmers overnight. This project represents an organized set of exercises illustrating many of the concepts of Chapters 4 and 5.

Because we still have not studied many aspects of the 360/370 systems, including string-oriented instructions and use of auxiliary storage, we will make some severely limiting, simplifying assumptions. If we design our assembler properly, these can be relaxed individually without a complete redesign.

To make the process reasonably straightforward and to permit excursions partway into the task without a commitment to go all the way, we have designed a set of exercises, each representing a small segment of the assembler. The first ones provide general utility subprograms and the later exercises build on earlier ones until the entire system is tied together. The planning of these exercises was surely not done in the order indicated by their appearance; on the contrary, it began, as all large tasks should, with a definition of major components, and progressed from there through levels introducing more and more detail.

This problem contains data items with widely varying sizes measured in bytes of storage required for their representation. It is convenient to use the word *cell* for a storage segment assigned to a data item. When many cells are treated similarly, it is convenient to establish a name for the set of cells. If there are rules for finding one cell from the location of another, then it is reasonable to speak of the set of cells along with these rules as a *data structure* with one name identifying the entire structure. Arrays as defined in FORTRAN or PL/1 or ALGOL are data structures with cell sizes ranging from 1 to 16 bytes, depending on data types. In assembler language, we have unusual freedom in assigning cell sizes, and we find this especially convenient for the structures in our assembler. A data structure is called *linear* if each cell except the last has a single successor and the initial byte of a successor cell immediately follows the last byte of its predecessor in memory. We will find linear data structures adequate for this project.

We assume the assembler and all related data are contained in processor memory. Therefore, three fundamental data structures will be in memory at all times: there will be one for source code, one for a symbol table, and one for generated code. We call them SOURCE, SYMTAB, and TARGET, respectively, and characterize them and related single-cell items in Table 5.9.1. Limitation of a source line to 40 storage bytes, as shown there, is a memory conservation practice consistent with the simplified operand fields we will allow. The main program which contains these data structures will evolve into a complete assembler and should be given the name ASSMBLR.

Although one might expect the first need to be for an input program, we wish to emphasize that a great deal of computation can be checked by judicious initializing of the major data structures of our assembler with test data. For example, SOURCE can be initialized with some representative symbolic instructions, SYMTAB with symbolic names and addresses, and TARGET with what looks like numeric code. It is not really necessary that these data be consistent, only that they provide reasonable input to programs which use them.

5.9.1 Utility Programs

1. Let SORCOUT be an assembler subprogram which is to print the meaningful contents of the SOURCE data structure as contained in memory. The printing of SOURCE should be done one cell per line until a cell is reached which has "ENDb" (the "b" represents a blank) in bytes 9–12 beyond its beginning or until the entire data structure has been printed. The argument list for SORCOUT should be

SOURCE,MAXLINZ

where MAXLINZ is the number of cells reserved for SOURCE and in ASSMBLR is initialized (for current testing) to 25. SORCOUT should in-

Name	Cell size	Number of cells	Align to	Cell contents
SOURCE	40	(MAXLINZ)	DW	Columns 1–40 of an instruction card
SYMTAB	12	(MAXLINZ)	FW	An eight-byte symbol and its address
TARGET	1	4(MAXLINZ)	FW	One byte of generated code
MAXLINZ	4	1	FW	Number of lines of source permitted
TABLNGT	4	1	FW	Number of bytes in SYMTAB
STARTADR	4	1	FW	Absolute address where execution begins

Table 5.9.1 Specification of its data structures is one of the first steps in designing the assembler, and serves as a base for more detailed planning to follow.

voke a FORTRAN subprogram named WR40CH to output a single line. Write and test this subprogram. It will be necessary to compute in SORCOUT the address of the initial byte of the source line to be printed and place it in the argument address list for WR40CH. SORCOUT can be checked by a single call from within ASSMBLR.

2. You are to prepare an assembler-language output program which will print the contents of SYMTAB. We call it PRINTAB and take its argument list to be

SYMTAB,TABLNGT

Recall that SYMTAB cells are 12 bytes in length, the first eight being characters, the last four being a binary address. When the address of the cell to be printed is properly set in an argument list, PRINTAB should invoke a FORTRAN subprogram named WRITAB to print one line of table information using A format for characters and Z format for hexadecimal addresses. To test PRINTAB, insert instructions into ASSMBLR to set TABLNGT, and then invoke PRINTAB. The result should be a printing of SYMTAB as initialized in ASSMBLR.

3. The TARGET array will hold hexadecimal instructions, some of which occupy two bytes and some of which occupy four. That distinction is not crucial for the present. When it is important, there will be a cell named GENLNGT (this was CTADEL in the Chapter 4 flowcharts) which contains the number of bytes in the target string which are filled with information as a result of translating the current source line. Let PRNTCODE be an assembler program which has for argument list

TARGET,CTA,GENLNGT

and which causes the printing in hexadecimal of (CTA) and on the same printed line of (GENLNGT) bytes starting at TARGET + (CTA). Develop PRNTCODE to accomplish the printing through invoking a FORTRAN program for the actual output and test it by inserting in ASSMBLR a few test sequences which set CTA and GENLNGT, and then invoke PRNTCODE to print accordingly. The FORTRAN program may be given as an argument the number of half words of code to be printed since (GENLNGT) will always be even.

4. Let OPCODATA be a linear data structure with eight-byte cells aligned to full-word boundaries. Each cell uses bytes 0–3 for a symbolic

representation of an operation code,† byte 5 for the corresponding numeric code, and bytes 6 and 7 for a two-letter instruction format type (RR, RS, or RX). Assume 32 cells will be adequate to provide the information on all instructions this assembler is to accommodate. Create a table lookup program named FNDOPCOD with argument list

MNEMOP,MATCH

which searches OPCODATA for a cell matching the contents of MNE-MOP in bytes 0–3 and deposits contents of bytes 4–7 of that cell in the four bytes beginning at MATCH. Consider OPCODATA to be local to the FNDOPCOD subprogram. Note that contents of this table are not dependent on the translation but are initial data for the assembler, so they should be set by Define Constant instructions during assembly of FNDOP-COD. One may test this program by a selection of sequences inserted in ASSMBLR. In each sequence, one sets MNEMOP to a particular symbolic operation code and uses PRNTCODE with MATCH as first argument, and cells containing integers 0 and 4 as second and third arguments, respectively, to print the result. Of course, the only complete test will be to try every symbolic operation code and verify its numeric operation code and instruction format type.

5.9.2 First-Scan Processing

5. The first scan of an assembler builds a symbol table, taking the symbol from the label field of an instruction in SOURCE and assigning an address to this label. This address is the current content of the current translation address (CTA), the address relative to target at which code generated from this instruction should begin. We have called the table SYMTAB and taken it to be a linear structure of 12-byte cells, bytes 0–7 containing the symbol and bytes 8–11 the address. Assume a pointer named TABINDX such that, when a symbol and its address are placed in the table, their cell begins at (TABINDX). Write a subprogram named TABNTRY with argument list

SYMBOL,ADDRESS,SYMTAB,TABINDX

which inserts the contents of SYMBOL in SYMTAB at the position given in TABINDX, places the contents of ADDRESS in the last four bytes of

---

† We will be ignoring any character in the symbolic operation code beyond column 13 (byte 12 in the string) but will speak of what is kept as the operation code. The only opcode affected will be USING. Any opcode with leftmost four characters USIN will be recognized as USING.

the same cell, and updates the value of TABINDX by adding 12. Of course, TABNTRY should be invoked only if the contents of SYMBOL are not blank and then only if there is room in the table (i.e., (TAB-INDX) < 4*(MAXLINZ)). The subprogram can be checked using data provided by temporary Data Constant instructions in ASSMBLR as symbols and addresses. Insertion of an instruction to set TABINDX to point to a cell in SYMTAB and invocation of TABNTRY with the label of a symbol constant as first argument and the label of an address constant as second argument will cause the symbol and address to be placed in the cell selected by TABINDX. Two or three such uses together with a table printout using PRNTAB should demonstrate the functioning of TABNTRY.

6. Let BLDTAB be a subprogram with argument list

SOURCE,MAXLINZ,SYMTAB,TABLNGT

which, on the basis of one scan of the instructions stored in SOURCE, builds a table of symbols and their assigned locations in SYMTAB. MAX-LINZ contains the number of lines permitted in the SOURCE table (which is also the number of cells permitted in SYMTAB). TABLNGT is computed as the number of bytes in the symbol table when the scan is completed.

BLDTAB sequences through the instructions in order as they appear in memory looking for nonblank symbols in the location field and entering these with corresponding (CTA) into SYMTAB. Several local variables are useful in this process as defined below:

Variable	Contents
LINECNT	Number of instructions already processed
LINEBGIN	Number of bytes beyond SOURCE at which current line begins
TABINDX	Number of bytes already in SYMTAB
CTA	Number of bytes of code generated in previous instructions
LOCSYM	Contents of bytes 0–7 of current instruction
MNEMOP	Contents of bytes 9–12 of current instruction
RANDFLD	Contents of bytes 15–39 of current instruction
GENLNGT	Byte length of code generated by current instruction
MATCH	Numeric opcode and instruction type as returned by FNDOPCOD

The steps in BLDTAB are as follows:

(a) Initialize LINECNT, LINEBGIN, TABINDX, and CTA to zero. Set MNEMOP from current instruction.

(b) Perform c–i while (MNEMOP) $\neq$ 'ENDb' and (LINECNT) < (MAXLINZ). Then go to j.

(c) Set LOCSYM and RANDFLD from current instruction.

(d) If (MNEMOP) = 'USIN', go to i.

(e) If (MNEMOP) ≠ 'DCbb', go to f. If (MNEMOP) = 'DCbb', then assume that either the type is X with implied length 4 or that zero occurrences of H, F, or D (to cause alignment to half-word, full-word, or double-word boundary, respectively) are called for by 0H, 0F, or 0D at the beginning of RANDFLD; set GENLNGT to 4 for type X; otherwise set GENLNGT to zero and align (CTA). Go to g.

(f) Align (CTA) to a half-word boundary and invoke FNDOPCOD with arguments MNEMOP, MATCH. On return, set GENLNGT to 2 if $(MATCH)_{2;3}$ = 'RR'; otherwise, set GENLNGT to 4.

(g) If (LOCSYM) ≠ 'bbbbbbbb' invoke TABNTRY with arguments LOCSYM, CTA, SYMTAB, TABINDX, remembering that the address of SYMTAB must be inserted in the argument list as available from the argument address of BLDTAB.

(h) Increment (CTA) by (GENLNGT).

(i) Increment (LINECNT) by 1. Increment (LINEBGIN) by 40. Set MNEMOP from the new instruction so selected. Go to b.

(j) TABLNGT ← (TABINDX). If (MNEMOP) ≠ 'ENDb' print diagnostic 'NO END CARD'. Return to calling program.

You are to construct BLDTAB and test it by invoking BLDTAB and then PRINTAB from within ASSMBLR.

7. To complete first-scan processing, we need an input program which will accept a source program as data to replace contents of the SOURCE data structure as initialized at assembly time. Construct an assembler program called RDSORCE with argument list

SOURCE,MAXLINZ

which is quite similar in function to SORCOUT of Problem 1. RDSORCE should invoke a FORTRAN subprogram named RD40CH once for each instruction card to be read. It will be necessary to compute in RDSORCE the address of the initial byte for storage of this instruction and place this address in the argument address list for RD40CH. Reading should end on detection of 'ENDb' in bytes 9–12 beyond the beginning of the current instruction cell or when the number of instructions which have been read is equal to (MAXLINZ), whichever comes first.

5.9.3   Second-Scan Processing

8. Translation of operand fields requires access to the symbol table created in the first scan to obtain the address assigned to a given symbolic lo-

cation name. Let SYMVAL denote a function subprogram with argument list

SYMBOL,SYMTAB,TABLNGT

which returns the address for a symbol provided as first argument if that symbol is in SYMTAB and otherwise returns zero. Create the SYMVAL subprogram using the search you find easiest to implement. SYMVAL can be tested by short sequences of code inserted into ASSMBLR, each of which

(1) assigns a symbol to LOCSYM,
(2) assigns a table length to TABLNGT,
(3) invokes the function,
(4) assigns the resultant value to a temporary location,
(5) prints the hexadecimal contents of the temporary location using PRNTCODE.

Tests should be included to demonstrate correct results for symbols in the table as well as for symbols not in the table.

9. Decimal numerals can occur in the operand field as register numbers or as address modifiers. We need to convert these to binary and then apply them as their use dictates. Having determined that a numeral begins at a position I bytes beyond the beginning of a string, it is reasonable to ask for a function subprogram GETBINT to return the binary value of that numeral and to adjust the value of the pointer to the address of the byte beyond it. Its argument list will be

RANDFLD,SCANPT

the second address carrying the initial position of the numeral as measured from RANDFLD. Design and test such a function, limiting its numerals to at most seven digits. This program can be tested using data provided in temporary Data Constants of type C (character) in ASSMBLR as samples of operand fields. These should contain decimal numerals of various lengths and at various positions so that successful application of GET-BINT to each will provide reasonable assurance of validity. The results may be assigned to a temporary storage location from which they are immediately printed using PRNTCODE.

10. Variable names occurring in the operand field must be extracted, and then extended to length eight with blanks if necessary (in table lookup a length of eight is assumed). A subprogram named GETSYM with argument list

RANDFLD,SCANPT,SYMBOL

is used for this purpose. SCANPT is the number of bytes beyond the beginning of RANDFLD at which the symbol should start. Its value is to be modified by execution of GETSYM to point to the first byte with contents unacceptable as a part of the symbol, and SYMBOL is to receive the symbol found (not to exceed eight characters). Testing can be done in a way similar to that suggested in Program 9, but of course printing should be in character mode.

11. Once it is determined that a given line of source code is to generate a machine instruction, it is necessary to pull together ingredients from a variety of sources to compute the instruction and its length. We shall name our subprogram to accomplish this ENCODE and propose the following argument list:

MNEMOP,SYMTAB,TABLNGT,RANDFLD,BASEVAL,
BASEREG,COMMAND,GENLNGT

We have seen in earlier problems that SYMTAB represents a symbol table of 12-byte cells, TABLNGT contains its length, MNEMOP holds the symbolic operation code, and RANDFLD holds the operand field for the current instruction. BASEVAL and BASEREG must have been determined from a USING instruction as the reference address from which displacements are computed and the number of the base register, respectively. The encoding obtained from these ingredients is to be justified left in a full-word cell named COMMAND and the length is to be stored in GENLNGT from which it can be used to increment the current translation address (CTA).

Within ENCODE, it will be convenient to utilize subprograms developed above and identified as FNDOPCOD, GETBINT, GETSYM, and SYMVAL. Aside from these, we will assume three subprograms named RAND2RX, RAND2RS, and RAND2RR which are intended to place in a four-byte cell named COMMAND (which already contains operation code and operand 1 coding in hexdigits 0–2) that part of the numeric instruction resulting from the second operand field. This must be done for RX, RS, and RR instructions, respectively. A flowchart for ENCODE appears in Figure 5.9.1 and one for RAND2RX in Figure 5.9.2. The remaining two are trivial. Note that we assume COMMAND is aligned to a full-word boundary. While it is not practical to have ENCODE fully operational until the subprograms it utilizes are available, it is possible to establish a great deal by using dummy subprograms for RAND2RX, RAND2RS, and RAND2RR. For example, a dummy for RAND2RX might just combine a constant—say $000BCFAE_{16}$—with COMMAND, ig-

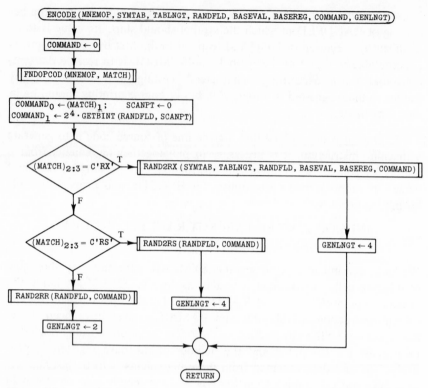

Figure 5.9.1   The object of this subprogram is to place in the (GENLNGT) bytes beginning at COMMAND the numeric instruction resulting from the current source line.

noring input to RAND2RX completely. This catenating of instruction segments will, with the current instruction set, require shifting, for in ordinary addition an opcode exceeding $7F_{16}$ would make COMMAND contents seem negative. Try to make ENCODE correct using three such dummies before programming their replacements.

12.   By far the most complex aspect of our assembler is the interpretation of the second operand field. Even with simplifying assumptions, we find it a challenge. The most complex instruction type we consider is RX. Here, we require a subprogram named RAND2RX with argument list

SYMTAB,TABLNGT,RANDFLD,BASEVAL,BASEREG,
COMMAND

The names in this list are explained in Program 11. The purpose here is primarily to calculate correct displacement for operand fields which may consist of a single symbol, a symbol modified by addition of a numeral (e.g. PLACE + 13), or either of these with an index register modifier (e.g., PLACE + 13(3)). Beyond this, we must insert the proper hex digits for index and base. A flowchart for this subprogram is shown in Figure 5.9.2. You should create the three subprograms used by ENCODE for interpreting operand 2 and test them out individually. When satisfied that they work, put them into use under control of ENCODE and test the package.

13. Taking into account all the possibilities in a Define Constant instruction would indeed be challenging, but by restricting types and options sufficiently we can make the problem manageable. To generate constant date, we propose a subprogram named GENCON which has argument list

RANDFLD,COMMAND,CTA,GENLNGT

The constant should be formed in the cell named COMMAND. To keep our problem simple, we require all data constants to be hexadecimal and one word in length so that GENLNGT is set to 4. To provide for alignment and labeling flexibility, we also permit zero occurrences of constants of type H (half word), F (full word), or D (double word). For these, we set GENLNGT to zero. Write a program to handle these limited types, remembering that each hexadecimal digit is read in character mode and must be converted. For example X'00A294C6' would have its quoted string converted to F0F0C1F2F9F4C3F6. Since the other types do not generate data, they require no conversion.

14. We may assume a simplified form of the USING instruction, allowing as first operand only "*" or a location name and for second operand only a numeral which is a register number. From the USING instruction, a reference address BASEVAL and a base register number BASEREG should be determined for use in encoding RX instructions. Create a subprogram with name ESTABASE (establish base) which has argument list

SYMTAB,TABLNGT,RANDFLD,CTA,BASEVAL,BASEREG

to set BASEVAL and BASEREG correctly.

15. The translation of one source line and its placement in the target field can be accomplished easily using the subprograms ESTABASE, GENCON, and ENCODE of previous problems. We call the subprogram to do this ONELINE2. The argument list we recommend is

SOURCE,LINECNT,SYMTAB,TABLNGT,TARGET,CTA,
STARTADR

All these symbols and their structures have been defined above. A flowchart for ONELINE2 is given in Figure 5.9.3.

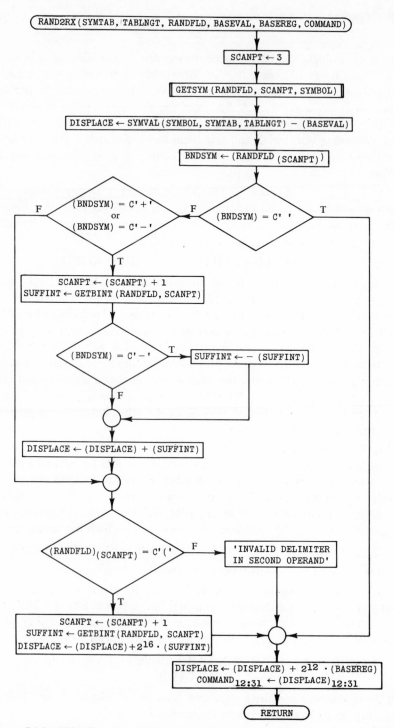

Figure 5.9.2 This diagram provides complete response to the second operand field of an RX instruction for our limited assembler.

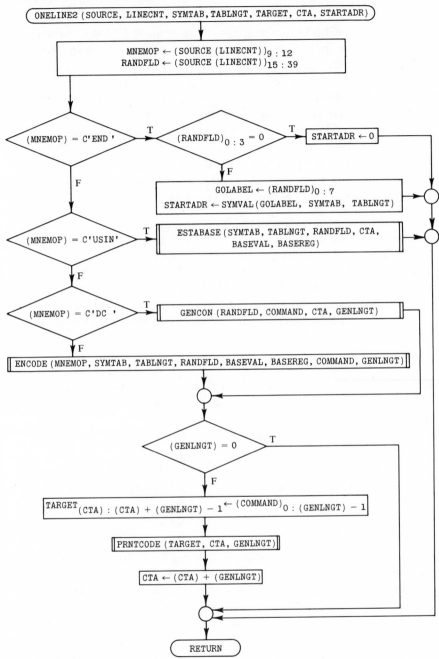

MNEMOP ← (SOURCE (LINECNT))$_{9:12}$
RANDFLD ← (SOURCE (LINECNT))$_{15:39}$

(MNEMOP) = C'END '

(RANDFLD)$_{0:3}$ = 0

STARTADR ← 0

GOLABEL ← (RANDFLD)$_{0:7}$
STARTADR ← SYMVAL(GOLABEL, SYMTAB, TABLNGT)

(MNEMOP) = C'USIN'

ESTABASE (SYMTAB, TABLNGT, RANDFLD, CTA, BASEVAL, BASEREG)

(MNEMOP) = C'DC '

GENCON (RANDFLD, COMMAND, CTA, GENLNGT)

ENCODE (MNEMOP, SYMTAB, TABLNGT, RANDFLD, BASEVAL, BASEREG, COMMAND, GENLNGT)

(GENLNGT) = 0

TARGET$_{(CTA):(CTA)+(GENLNGT)-1}$ ← (COMMAND)$_{0:(GENLNGT)-1}$

PRNTCODE (TARGET, CTA, GENLNGT)

CTA ← (CTA) + (GENLNGT)

RETURN

Figure 5.9.3 This translation of a single instruction is the heart of the assembly process and is built on availability of several key subprograms.

16. The TRNSLATE subprogram is analogous to BLDTAB in that its primary function is to control all the activities associated with one scan through the source language instructions up through and including the END card. It is easier because most of its activities have already been programmed in ONELINE2. One adjustment is necessary. An assembler listing should have the assembler instruction in source form printed close to the numeric code generated from it. This can be accomplished by printing the symbolic form of the instruction immediately and relying on ONELINE2 for printing its numeric translation.

The TRNSLATE subprogram should have for argument list

SOURCE,MAXLINZ,SYMTAB,TABLNGT,TARGET,STARTADR

TRNSLATE is most easily tested by having ASSMBLR successively invoke RDSORCE, SORCOUT, BLDTAB, PRINTAB, and TRNSLATE for this should constitute the "complete" assembler. Once it is working, a more usual printing can be obtained by adjusting PRNTCODE to print without spacing from within ONELINE2 and causing the symbolic form of the instruction to print at least 15 spaces from the left margin. This will give a more readable printout with source code and its translation on the same line.

PROBLEMS

1. Would either of the following two sequences of instructions be satisfactory substitutes for the prologue sequence shown under 9 in Section 5.1? If not, why?

```
(a) STM    14,12,12(13)    (b) STM    14,12,12(13)
    BALR   12,0                BALR   12,0
    USING  *,12                USING  *,12
    ST     13,SAVE+4           ST     13,8(10)
    LR     10,13               LA     13,SAVE
    LA     13,SAVE             LR     10,13
    ST     13,8(10)            ST     13,SAVE+4
```

2. In the main (assembler language) part of Program 5.2.1, the A-type address constants in the argument list must appear in the order corresponding to the order of the arguments in the FORTRAN SUBROUTINE statement. But in the main program, the constants themselves (with symbolic location names A, B, C, Q, R) can appear in any order or position in the program. Why?

3. Is it possible to use the Branch And Link instruction to enter a subroutine SINE with the instruction pair

```
                    EXTRN SINE
                    BAL    14,SINE
```

If so, what problems are involved? If not, why?

4. Each installation will have some of its own special macros used for instruction. We introduce here variations on two which were designed by T. H. Puckett[†] to simplify the prologue and epilogue aspects of subprogram calls. The first, named ENTER, has no parameters and yet will handle all the save area overhead and base establishment for a large class of simple programs. The second, named EXIT, provides a compatible return. Such macros should be understood before being used, but when their limitations are well known they are delightful companions. We must introduce a symbolic parameter &SYSNDX defined by the assembler, not by its appearance as an argument in the macro prototype. It represents a four-byte character-representation of a positive integer. The value of the integer is the number of macros which will have been expanded by the assembler in the current job when the current macrogeneration is complete. It will be used to form a unique name for a save area.

```
               MACRO
               ENTER
               USING *,15              TEMPORARY BASE
               STM   14,12,12(13)      SAVE REGISTERS
               B     SAVE&SYSNDX+72    JUMP OVER SAVE AREA
               DC    0F'0'             ALIGN CHARACTER
                                       STRING
               DC    C'SAVE&SYSNDX'    SAVE AREA ID
SAVE&SYSNDX    DC    18F'0'            SAVE AREA
               ST    13,SAVE&SYSNDX+4  LINK TO CALLING
                                       PROGRAM SAVE AREA
               LA    13,SAVE&SYSNDX    SAVE AREA POINTER
                                       AND BASE
               USING SAVE&SYSNDX,13    ESTABLISH 13 AS
                                       BASE
               DROP  15
               L     15,SAVE&SYSNDX+4
               ST    13,8(15)          GIVE SAVE AREA
                                       POINTER TO CALLER
               MEND
```

[†] Mexico State University, Computer Science Department, Las Cruces, New Mexico.

In a drastically reduced form, the EXIT macro has no parameters and can
be written

```
            MACRO
      &NAME EXIT
      &NAME L      13,4(13)          ADDRESS OF CALLER'S
                                     SAVE AREA
            LM     14,12,12(13)      RESTORE ALL REGS
                                     BUT 13
            BR     14                RETURN CONTROL
            MEND
```

This version of EXIT would be unacceptable to function subprograms
which return integer values by ordinary conventions, since it would destroy contents of register zero. One can get around this problem rather
easily. The EXIT macro does so little in the form just stated that it is no
problem to write its model out when saving register 0. Thus

```
      L    13,4(13)
      LM   14,15,12(13)
      LM   1,12,24(13)
      BR   14
```

will be suitable. Nevertheless, for those who wish to look up the RE-
TURN macro as provided by the Operating System and to read about
type attributes, conditional assembly, set symbols, and sequence symbols,
we recommend the enhanced version of EXIT given below.

```
            MACRO
      &NAM  EXIT   &R1,&R2,&T,&RC
            GBLC   &DR1,&DR2,&DT,&DRC
      &DR1  SETC   '14'              DEFAULT FIRST
                                     RESTORED REGISTER
      &DR2  SETC   '12'              DEFAULT LAST
                                     RESTORED REGISTER
      &DT   SETC   ' '               DEFAULT IS NOT TO
                                     FLAG SAVE AREA
      &DRC  SETC   '0'               DEFAULT RETURN
                                     CODE
            AIF    (T'&R1 EQ '0').A
      &DR1  SETC   '&R1'             REPLACE DEFAULT
                                     FIRST REGISTER
      .A    AIF    (T'&R2 EQ '0').B
```

```
&DR2 SETC    '&R2'                      REPLACE DEFAULT
                                        LAST REGISTER
.B   AIF     (T'&T EQ '0').C
&DT  SETC    '&T'                       SET TO FLAG SAVE
                                        AREA
.C   AIF     (T'&RC EQ '0').D
&DRC SETC    '&RC'                      REPLACE DEFAULT
                                        RETURN CODE
.D   ANOP
&NAM L       13,4(13)
     L       14,12(13)
     RETURN  (&DR1,&DR2),&DT,RC=&DRC
     MEND
```

Create your own copies of these macros and analyze their expansions in a
simple program to assure their validity.

5. This assignment is to create two relatively simple programs to be assembled and linked, but they need not be executed. One, called the *driver*,
has data available to be analyzed. The second is a subprogram called by
the driver to perform the analysis. As an exercise—not because it is good
practice—you are to pass no information as subprogram arguments. Instead, all communication is enabled by use of the external symbol dictionary under control of the relocation dictionary. The job to be done is to
evaluate a polynomial in X for which the value of X, the order of the polynomial, and the coefficients are all defined in the driver. During assembly, obtain printouts of the external symbol dictionary and of the relocation dictionary. Demonstrate with meticulous care the significance of each
line of the relocation dictionary and of the external symbol dictionary in
determining each data constant in each program. There should be included
examples of

(1) V-type address constants,
(2) A-type address constants resolved internally,
(3) A-type address constants which have a nonzero assembled value
and are resolved externally.

6. We have seen that it is possible to save copies of relocatable object
decks created on previous assemblies. These can be inserted in the input
deck as shown in Figure 5.4.1, thus saving the work of reassembling programs already checked out. This also results in a convenient shortening of
card decks to be handled. These ideas can be tested simply by creating a

driver in assembler language which invokes one FORTRAN program for input and another for output. Its computation need be no more complicated than adding two input numbers. Start with three programs all in source form. One at a time, replace source decks with objects decks so that there will be a second run with two source decks and one object deck, a third with one source deck and two object decks, and a final run with three object decks only. Document the results so that three months later the results can be easily repeated.

7. In Section 5.6, it was found that the SNAP macro could be used to print the contents of a data area not in one's own program area. This is a useful feature whenever data areas outside one's program are pertinent to execution. Save areas are such, as are the buffers to be examined in Section 6.5. To reinforce the significance of the pointers in words 2 and 3 of a save area, use the SNAP macro from within a program after a subprogram has been invoked. Print the save area provided to your program by calling program, the save area in your own program, and the save area in the last program called from your program without the SNAP SA option.

8. The SNAP macro can be invoked from another program than that which defines its Data Control Block. We can be sure we are able to use the macro effectively if we can establish communication among three separately compiled programs so as to establish the DCB in the first, and invoke the SNAP in the second to print a storage segment from the third. The responsibility to OPEN the SNAPDUMP data set before writing in it can be met most conveniently in that program in which execution starts. Write a set of three programs in which SNAP is used as described.

9. Consider the somewhat similar sequences in four columns below to determine which memory references will be properly made:

```
     BALR  12,0        BALR  12,0        BALR  12,0        BALR  12,0
     USING *,12        USING *,12        USING *,12        USING *,12
     L     10,A        L     10,A        L     10,A        L     10,A

       . . .             . . .             . . .             . . .
     BALR  12,0        BALR  12,0        BALR  10,0        BALR  10,0
     USING *,12        USING *,12        USING *,10        USING *,10
     L     9,B         L     9,B         L     9,B         L     9,B
       . . .           DROP  12            . . .             . . .
A DC       F'1'          . . .         A DC       F'1'   B DC       F'2'
B DC       F'2'   A DC       F'1'      B DC       F'2'      DROP 10
                  B DC       F'2'                        A DC       F'1'
```

10. If programs are properly segmented, there will seldom be one which occupies more than 4096 bytes. However, we do have provisions for longer segments which it is best to understand. To test the facilities without writing long programs, we may write a small program with an enormous data reservation followed by a few constants referred to near the beginning of the program. Write a program which establishes two bases differing by 4096, and show that, with appropriate reservations, some data can be referenced to one base and some to the other.

11. One may consider implementing macros for facilitating structured programming. Explicit control of looping by macros would be one step in this direction. In this exercise, define a macro named ITER and another macro named RETI which will serve as beginning and ending markers for a coding segment to be iterated under controls given as arguments in the former. The listing of controls is similar to that in the FORTRAN DO statement, but performance should be simpler. Here are the principal points:

1. The argument list for ITER should be made up of the label on the corresponding RETI, the number of the register holding the index, the name for the location of the comparand, and the name for the location of the increment.

2. Initialization of the index must precede entry into the ITER macros.

3. The iteration increment must be positive.

4. The ITER macro must have a label and that label must appear as the sole item in the operand field of the RETI macro.

5. Testing for completion is done before entry into the body of the iteration and precludes any iteration if the initial value of the index exceeds the comparand.

These conditions provide for some redundancy, permit very simple substitution-generated macros, and are consistent with the usual controls for structured programs. Write and test these macros.

Chapter 6

Character and Bit Manipulation

6.1 INTRODUCTION

The original stored-program computers were designed to be "number crunchers," whose purpose was to be able to predict the outcome of a physical event prior to its happening. One could expect predictions of earthquakes or weather to be such events, and indeed much effort has been devoted to such forecasts. But the prime backing for early computers was military, so it is to be expected that analysis of ballistic trajectories, atomic and nuclear explosions, atomic engines for naval vessels, and flight characteristics of aircraft were among the early uses.

Nevertheless, the prophets of machine applicability foresaw that a revolution in information handling would result from a proper understanding and evolution of computers. This vision was evident in the first commercially available computer, UNIVAC I, which had very substantial facilities for reading and writing alphabetic and special characters. Yet it has taken both a great amount of experience in applications and dramatic improvements in the instruction repertoire for nonnumeric processing to bring about the broad areas of successful applications realized by the

360/370 and its competitors. There are very few computer systems with such heavy emphasis on character-string facilities as the 360/370 systems. The problems which are dealt with in this chapter will be encountered on any general-purpose computer with compiler and assembler programs. However, they may be substantially more cumbersome to deal with if byte addressability is missing or special string-handling instructions are lacking. At this point, it will be valuable to distinguish the nature of the objects encountered in nonnumeric processing and some of the operations to be done on them.

Until now, we have dealt with representations (primarily of numbers) having standard lengths measured in bit positions. Numbers fit this scheme well, but people's names, addresses, educational records, and credit records do not. Computers are used to maintain personnel records, to set type for books, to search prose for keywords which indicate content, and to analyze the structure of poetry or music. They are used to translate programs from a formal language to another equivalent form, as evidenced in assemblers and compilers. In all these, the objects are strings of characters (defined and discussed in Chapter 1) with no standard length. The fundamental string operations are to

(1) *catenate* two strings (make one string of two so that the first character of one is the immediate successor of the last character of the other);

(2) *segment* a string into two (the inverse of catenation);

(3) *order* strings as words in a dictionary are ordered; this is also called *sorting*;

(4) *search* for the occurrence of a particular sequence of characters— which might be a word, a name, or a part number.

One can, of course, use a combination of these operations to edit text for printing. There are times when the ability to find the next character in a string which has a certain property—such as being alphabetic—is needed. We shall see evidence of all these capabilities in the 360/370 instruction set.

Hexadecimal strings are of importance in computing also, but they remain mostly hidden from the user's view. We think of the external representations of numbers as decimal, although for computer input the digits are recorded first in character form. The usual conversion from the character representation of individual digits to binary number, or from binary number to the character representation of digits, involves an intermediate form in which each has a four-bit hexadecimal representation. Instructions which facilitate conversions between the hexadecimal string and character string or between the hexadecimal string and binary number can be most useful. Some machines, including the 360 and 370, can actually use the hexadecimal string representations as arithmetic operands. While this facility may be highly useful to data processing applications, we defer it to Chapter 8 because it is really just a special arithmetic. Conversion, on the other hand, contains features of both arithmetic and string manipulation. Thus we treat it here.

Internal representations of character or hexadecimal strings determine binary strings which are the catenations of the binary representations of their individual elements. Some of the operations to be performed on character or hexadecimal strings actually are implemented as operations on equivalent binary strings. But beyond these, there are problems in which the information is best represented as binary strings and in which the algebra of logic (Boolean algebra) extended to strings provides the pertinent operations. Set membership is well represented by a binary string. For example, if 1 means "belonging" and 0 "not belonging," then a binary string of 100 bits will record the membership status of 100 persons with respect to the Democratic Party, each person having a unique place in the string. A similar string (with the same assignments of persons to place in the string) will give their status with respect to the Republican Party.

The Boolean operations AND, OR, and EXCLUSIVE OR are defined for 1-bit operands p and q as shown in Table 6.1.1. We can extend them to string operands easily. For any string S, let S(I) be its Ith element. Then for strings S1 and S2 of equal length, and $\mathcal{L}$ representing any logical operation, we define S1 $\mathcal{L}$ S2 to be a string S3 of the same length which has

$$S3(I) = S1(I) \mathcal{L} S2(I)$$

for each I which is the index of an element in S1 and S2.

Thus if D and R are strings giving membership in the Democratic and Republican parties, we can form the new strings

D AND R	to find persons who belong to both parties
D OR R	to find persons who belong to one or more parties, perhaps both
D EX OR R	to find persons who belong to one party but not both

It should be observed that AND, OR, and EX OR are being used as Boolean operators, and are not valid operation codes for the 360/370.

p q	p AND q	p OR q	p EX OR q
0 0	0	0	0
0 1	0	1	1
1 0	0	1	1
1 1	1	1	0

Table 6.1.1 The Boolean functions p AND q, p OR q, and p EX OR q are three of the sixteen Boolean functions of two variables.

6.2   SYMBOLISM FOR STRING HANDLING

It will be helpful to establish a uniform notation for specifying string elements and string segments. We would like the notation to apply both to information strings and to strings of memory positions. That which we adopt will be explicit and internally consistent. Since there are no standards in this area, the reader will probably have to adjust to other notation when using other references.

The elements of a string will be indexed by the nonnegative integers, the leftmost element having index zero. If an element of index n has a successor, its index is $n + 1$. If S is a string of length L and e_1 and e_2 are integer-valued expressions with $0 \leq e_1 \leq e_2 < L$, then $S(e_1 : e_2)$ is the segment of S beginning at element e_1 and ending at element e_2. We abbreviate $S(e : e)$ for $0 \leq e < L$ as $S(e)$. If either e_1 or e_2 is not an index within the string, then $S(e_1 : e_2)$ is undefined. If $0 \leq e_2 < e_1 < L$, we define $S(e_1 : e_2)$ to be empty.

We use the notation BYTES (A, $e_1 : e_2$) to denote the byte string beginning at @A + e_1 and ending at @A + e_2, where @A is the absolute address assigned to A, abbreviating BYTES (A, $e_1 : e_1$) as BYTES (A, e_1).

As in previous programs, there may be strings of information—we call them constant strings—which need to be given explicitly. Such a constant is conveniently defined with a type symbol followed by a string of elements (of that type) in quotes. Thus C'HOUSE', X'A46B2F3', and B'101110010' would qualify as strings. A string of information can also be represented by an identifier. Thus, if S = C'COMPUTER', then S(3:5) = C'PUT'. We shall expect that the identifier has a type (in this case it is *character*) and that all elements and segments of the string are of that type.

In defining instructions, it is of value to consider strings of memory elements which are designated in operand fields of string-oriented instructions. One byte in instructions of SS type will provide an explicit length for its operand strings, but string-oriented instructions of other types have their length implied in the operation code. When a register name constitutes an operand expression, we shall consider the contents of the entire register to be of concern and specify carefully what portion of the register is involved in the instruction.

6.3   CHARACTER STRING INSTRUCTION FORMATS

We have noted that a fundamental consideration in manipulating strings is their variability in length. There is no reasonable compromise for a standard length of a "string register." A solution to the problem is to let the two operand fields in the most versatile string-oriented instructions designate the beginning locations of sequences of bytes in memory, and to let the length of each designated string be specified by an instruction constant (immediate data in the instruction). Such instructions are said to be of SS (storage-to-storage) format. There are two versions of SS format: The first of these has a single length from 1 to 256 bytes which applies to both operands. The second, which pertains to conversion instructions and decimal arithmetic, provides two lengths, each of which is in the range 1–16 bytes. We now summarize all the formats which pertain to the string instructions of this section† (Table 6.3.1). Note that instruction constants specifying length must be increased by 1 to give the actual length in bytes.

Each string-oriented instruction will have two operand fields. Because the instructions are presented in isolation from other instructions, we have used the base-displacement form of memory reference. Yet, to define the instruction, it really is much more convenient to use single symbols for the strings of elements represented by the first and second operands, respectively. If the operand expression is a register, we will use a name like R1. If the operand expression is a storage reference (and hence in base-displacement form) we will use S1 or S2. While this may seem definitive, an example will help to understand actual practice. The STore Character instruction is of RX type. It moves only one byte, and therefore has an implied length of eight bits for its strings. The first operand name represents a register which has 32 bits. Only eight of these, the rightmost eight, are consulted in the execution. For the contents of the rightmost eight bits of register R1, we use the notation (R1 (24:31)). The second operand is a memory address of a single byte. In contrast with the RX instructions we have previously seen, this address need not be at a full-word boundary

Type	Assembler operand field	Instruction format						
		Byte 0	Byte 1		Bytes 2,3		Bytes 4,5	
RR	R1,R2	Op code	R1	R2	Empty		Empty	
RX	R1,D2(X2,B2)	Op code	R1	X2	B2	D2	Empty	
SI	D(B1),I2	Op code	I2		B1	D1	Empty	
SS1	D1(L,B1),D2(B2)	Op code	$L-1$		B1	D1	B2	D2
SS2	D1(L1,B1),D2(L2,B2)	Op code	$L1-1$	$L2-1$	B1	D1	B2	D2

Table 6.3.1 The last four formats are used for string-oriented instructions in the 360/370; there are RR-type string instructions only on 370 systems.

† There are two powerful RR-type string instructions, a move and a compare, which are special to 370 systems. These are discussed in Section 6.9.

(although it must be at a byte boundary), and the operand is truly only one byte. Therefore, S2 represents a single byte. The explanation of the effect of the instruction.

$$\text{STC R1,D2(X2,B2)} \quad \text{is} \quad \text{S2} \leftarrow (\text{R1(24:31)})$$

We could be even more specific by writing S2(0:7) ← (R1(24:31)) for the effect of the instruction.

6.3.1 Character Move Instructions

Segmenting and catenation of strings, as well as insertion of replacement characters, are accomplished by using one of the four character move instructions summarized in Table 6.3.2. The last of these, the storage to storage move, possesses great power and demands caution in its explanation and use. Our efforts will concentrate on this instruction. It is imperative to understanding the use of the MVC instruction that the transfer of characters is *one at a time,* in sequence from left to right, for, in the case that the string S1 begins within the string S2, elements of S2 may be replaced before they are copied. The second example makes an extreme use of this property to initialize an entire string of bytes to the same character.

Example 1. The MVC instruction furnishes a welcome alternative to initializing memory locations by means of Load and STore instructions. One instruction, for example, will initialize a half-word, full-word, or double-word without the need to disturb contents of any programmer-accessible register. As far as memory is concerned, the sequence

```
L   10,ONE
ST 10,COUNT
```

can be replaced by

```
MVC COUNT(4),ONE
```

We save one half-word of instruction space and avoid the use of a register for transfer.

Name	Type	Operation code	Length in bits	Effect
Insert Character	RX	IC	8	R1(24:31) ← (S2)
STore Character	RX	STC	8	S2 ← (R1(24:31))
MoVe Immediate	SI	MVI	8	S1 ← I2
MoVe Character	SS1	MVC	8L	S1(I) ← (S2( )) I = 0,1, . . .,8(L−1)

Table 6.3.2 These are the most generally useful character move instructions on 360/370 systems.

Example 2.   We can set all bytes in an 80-byte string beginning at a location named BUFFER to blanks with only two instructions:

Opcode	Operand field	Effect
MVI	BUFFER,C' '	Sets byte in location BUFFER with blank character provided as instruction constant
MVC	BUFFER+1(79),BUFFER	Propagates byte in location BUFFER into the following 79 bytes

While this example makes a very specialized use of the MVC instruction, it serves to demonstrate the need for caution in its use.

Example 3.   A string beginning at a location named STORY and consisting of 256 characters is to have the characters in STORY+74 through STORY+87 removed and the remaining segments joined as a revised version of the string. Vacated positions at the end should be filled with blanks.

Opcode	Operand field	Explanation
MVC	STORY+74(168),STORY+88	Joins tail segment to head segment
MVI	STORY+242,C' '	} Fills vacated bytes with blanks
MVC	STORY+243(13),STORY+242	

Such programming is clearly unrealistic, since it assumes that the positions in the string at which a deletion is to occur are known at assembly time. Therefore, we need to generalize this example.

There are two distinct problems which will be resolved in distinct ways: First, we should be able to specify as a computed quantity the position in the string at which surgery is to be done. Second, we should be able to use a computed length for the string to be moved. We handle these notions separately in Examples 4 and 5, and then return to a generalization of Example 3 in Example 6.

Example 4.   Assume that register 5 holds the length of a string (perhaps the result of computation) which is stored beginning at location STORY. A data string of length 17 beginning at PATCH is to be catenated onto the end of STORY to form a new version of STORY.

Lacking indexing facilities in SS instructions, we are forced to use an explicit base. We place it in register 6, in which case the following coding suffices:

Opcode	Operand field	Explanation
LA	6,STORY(5)	Address of first byte beyond current version of story
MVC	0(17,6),PATCH	Catenate 17-character patch onto story
LA	5,17(5)	Upd te length to that of revised story

In this example, the position of the surgery was just at the end of STORY. However the position for surgery is computed, it will be used as the contents of register 6 are used above.

The matter of a computed length is a more complex one. The length is actually a part of the instruction to be executed, and somehow it must be in the instruction when it is executed. As in Chapter 3, where instructions were modified in memory for lack of indexing facilities, we could store the computed length from a register by using the STore Character instruction. In that case, the instruction would need to be named and the storing would be into byte 1 of the instruction (byte 0 is the operation code). We shall illustrate that technique in Example 5, but we shall also illustrate the use of a new kind of control instruction (the EXecute instruction) which is ideally suited to our purposes.

6.3.2   The EXecute Instruction

This RX instruction uses its second operand address formed as D2(X2, B2) to locate an instruction skeleton and uses its register operand (which will be taken as zero if the register number is zero) as a modifier for this skeleton to synthesize an instruction. This computed instruction is to be executed as if it were in the place of the EXecute instruction (with suitable adjustments for length). Control then passes to the instruction following the EXecute instruction in the text unless the synthesized instruction indicates a branch. In the latter case, the branch is taken.

The resulting byte 1 of the instruction to be executed is the logical OR of bits 24–31 of the operand register of the EXecute instruction and bits 8–15 of the instruction skeleton. This means a bit in positions 8–15 of the synthesized instruction is zero only if the corresponding bits were zero in both the skeleton *and* in the register named as first operand in the EXecute instruction. One may look upon this application of the logical OR as a convenient way to form the sum of two numbers, one of which is zero. For the more general case, the bit-by-bit application of the OR operator in Table 6.1.1 is necessary.

The astute programmer will find again and again that the EXecute instruction is uniquely suitable for an intricate task. Without modification of memory or its register operand, it permits selection among a set of instructions and in the selected instruction, the use of a computed second byte which may designate length, mask, immediate value, or a register, depending on its format.

Example 5.   Given the strings of Example 4, catenate the string beginning at STORY onto the end of the string beginning at PATCH. In a sense this is the converse of Example 4, since the strings are now to be catenated in opposite order. A result is that the length of the string to be moved is not a data item, but must be computed and inserted into the MVC instruction.

Method 1

```
          S    5,ONE                L−1 for MVC instruction
          STC  5,MOVER+1            Modify MVC in place
     MOVER MVC PATCH+17(0),STORY    Execute MVC
          . . .
```

```
Data
area   ONE   DC   F'1'             Constant 1
```

Method 2

```
          S    5,ONE                L−1 for MVC instruction
          EX   5,MOVER              Modify and execute skeleton
          . . .
```

```
Data   MOVER MVC PATCH+17(0),STORY  Skeleton MVC
area   ONE   DC   F'1'              Constant 1
```

Although the results of these two program segments are the same, the modification of instructions in memory during execution as in Method 1 is hazardous. The EXecute instruction causes instruction modification in the processor rather than in memory (just as indexing and use of base registers do). One can expect Method 2 to prevail for this reason.

Example 6.   A string stored beginning at STORY and occupying 256 bytes is to have a segment of computed length L removed starting at offset M from STORY. The remaining segments are to be joined as a revised version of the string. Vacated positions at the end of the 256-byte string should be filled with blanks. Assume L is held in general register 5 and M in general register 6.

While this example seems simple, it requires several tests to avoid attempts to move empty strings, so the flowchart of Figure 6.3.1 is worthwhile. We use the notation BYTES (STORY,e_1:e_2) as defined in Section 6.2 to denote a string of storage elements beginning at e_1 bytes beyond STORY and continuing through e_2 bytes beyond STORY. An encoding follows the flowchart.

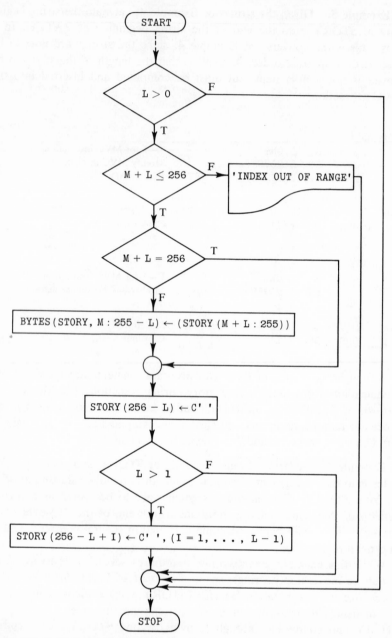

Figure 6.3.1 This flowchart illustrates the tests which must be made to suppress execution of the MVC instruction when using a computed length would be destructive.

Label	Opcode	Operand field	Explanation
	LTR	5,5	Test Length
	BNP	DONE	Exit if length ≤ 0
	LA	9,256	
	SR	9,6	$256 - M$
	SR	9,5	$256-(M+L)$ = length for tail
	BM	ERROR	Minus means invalid index
	S	9,ONE	Length-1 for tail
	BM	FILL	Minus means zero length for tail
	LA	7,STORY(6)	Beginning of new place for tail
	LA	8,0(5,7)	Beginning of tail
	EX	9,MOVER	
FILL	LA	8,STORY+256	
	SR	8,5	Address of first vacated position
	MVI	0(8),C' '	Blank into first vacated position
	S	5,TWO	$L-2$ to see if $L>1$
	BM	DONE	
	LA	7,1(8)	
	EX	5,MOVER	Fill with blanks
DONE	...		
ERROR	...		Invoke a FORTRAN subprogram with a diagnostic message
MOVER	MVC	0(0,7),0(8)	
ONE	DC	F'1'	
TWO	DC	F'2'	

Program 6.3.1. Encoding to accompany the flowchart in Figure 6.3.1.

The amount of testing in this example indicates there may be dire results when the MVC instruction is used with abandon. These matters are discussed in Subsection 6.3.3.

6.3.3 Comments on Character Moves

In the MVC instruction, we have a new and powerful way to move information about. Although it was primarily designed for moving character strings which do not usually conform to word boundaries, it is an excellent alternative to some routine programming as seen in Examples 1 and 2. There can be little question that it can conserve memory required for a program, and we have seen that it makes fewer demands on registers than would word-oriented instructions, none of which provide built-in loops. There remains a question of execution time consumed by alternate methods, and some comparisons will be made in the next chapter.

It should be clear from Example 6 that the MVC instruction was designed with a minimum of protection against the pathological case. Yet an MVC which gets an invalid length can be devastating to the memory con-

230 CHARACTER AND BIT MANIPULATION

tent to the right of the space allotted for its target string. We mention two ways this can happen:

1. A number used as a length causes information to be stored beyond the end of the target string.
2. A computed length for a string to be moved is zero or negative. A length of zero should signify the empty string but, since the instruction carries (length -1), the (length -1) will appear (in complement form) to be 255.

As a safeguard, we recommend that a computed length always be compared to zero and the move skipped if the length is zero. In like vein, the computed length should be tested against the maximum available length from the start of the target string. An error indication and abrupt termination of computation are probably appropriate in the case of an illogical length.

Finally, we caution that the hazards of the insertion of a computed length into the MVC instruction find their parallels in all other SS instructions. While some may not be so destructive of neighboring information, all will give erroneous results when lengths outside the limits inherent in the instruction are supplied.

6.4   THE COMPARE INSTRUCTIONS

In arithmetic computation, one is able to compare two quantities by testing the value of their difference for negative, zero, or positive:

$$A < B \quad \text{iff} \quad A - B < 0$$
$$A > B \quad \text{iff} \quad A - B > 0$$
$$A = B \quad \text{iff} \quad A - B = 0$$

There are Compare instructions for arithmetic quantities in the 360/370 repertoire and they can be a great convenience, because forming a difference in a register (as required above) destroys a quantity which must be restored if it is to be used later. We recommend the study of the Compare (C), Compare Register (CR), and Compare Half-word (CH) instructions for arithmetic use but are leaving it to the individual to experiment with them. They provide an excellent alternative to the testing of a difference which was used in previous chapters.

There is no such easy alternative available when strings are to be compared, because strings do not have bits distinguished as sign bits (see the discussion of strings in Section 1.5). Strings to be placed in order may not even be of the same length. It becomes necessary to define what is meant when one of two string operands is low or high. We must also define carefully what we mean by equality.

Every string of characters determines an equivalent binary string which is the catenation of the eight-bit representations of its characters. Similarly, a string of hexadecimal digits determines an equivalent binary string which is the catenation of the four-bit representations of its digits. Comparison of two strings is defined in terms of their binary equivalents.

A binary string comparison is applied over a length λ in bits which is determined from the instruction. For SS instructions λ is 8L, and for RR, RX, and SI instructions it is implied by the operation code. The comparison yields *equal* if the strings agree in all positions which are compared. If the strings agree in bit positions 0 through $I-1$ (left to right) but differ in the Ith position ($I < \lambda$), then the string with the Ith bit equal to zero is said to be *low* and the other is said to be *high*. We may define $<$ with respect to strings by the rule that, for strings Q_1 and Q_2,

$$Q_1 < Q_2 \text{ iff } Q_1 \text{ is low when compared to } Q_2$$
$$Q_1 > Q_2 \text{ iff } Q_1 \text{ is high when compared to } Q_2$$

Of course $Q_1 = Q_2$ iff the comparison yields equal. A comparison which treats all bits in like manner as described above is called *logical*. The use of the word logical is not meant to imply that this comparison is more logical than an arithmetic comparison, only that it is nonarithmetic in not involving a sign bit. There are four Compare Logical instructions, and these are listed in Table 6.4.1.

There are few pitfalls in using the first three Compare Logical instructions, but the last (CLC) has some of the same hazards as the MVC instruction. In particular, a calculated length which is zero or negative will cause a complement figure to be inserted for $L - 1$ in the instruction, and

Instruction format	Symbolic opcode	Numeric opcode	OP1	OP2	Bit string length
RR	CLR	15	(R1)	(R2)	32
RX	CL	55	(R1)	(S2)	32
SI	CLI	95	(S1)	(I2)	8
SS1	CLC	D5	(S1)	(S2)	8L

Table 6.4.1 The Compare Logical instructions can have both of their operand strings in registers (RR), or one string can be in a register and the other in memory (RX), or one string can be in memory and the other in the instruction itself (SI), or both strings can be in memory (SS). The only effect of these instructions is on the condition code; it is set to 0 if OP1 = OP2, 1 if OP1 $<$ OP2, or 2 if OP1 $>$ OP2.

will yield a completely invalid result. A calculated length exceeding the length of one of the strings being compared can also lead to invalid results. Thus tests like those shown in the flowchart in Figure 6.1.1 for character moves can be helpful for ensuring the validity of character-string comparisons also.

6.5 TEXTUAL RECORDS AND FILES

6.5.1 Units of Textual Information

In character-oriented instructions, we have dealt only with single characters and with sequences of characters called strings. When we begin to talk about the information to be processed, we find it convenient to introduce additional units of measure. Just as the author of prose speaks naturally of sentences which are sequences of words, paragraphs which are sequences of sentences, chapters which are sequences of paragraphs, and books which are sequences of chapters, the information handler seeks ways of talking about strings or collections of them which (for some reason having to do with their content) deserve to be treated as units. The words chosen are different from those of prose, but the spirit is the same. His units are usually taken to be *fields* (which are sequences of characters), *logical records* (which are sequences of fields), and *files* which are sequences of logical records). The modifier "logical" applied to records indicates there are other kinds of records in which the boundaries are determined in some "nonlogical" way; these are physical records.

The text of a book may be thought of as a single string, but the format of a book requires that certain breaks must be made in the string for convenience in recording. In addition to sentences and paragraphs, we distinguish lines on a page and pages in a book. Each is a unit of information called a *physical* unit because it is determined by physical properties of the recording medium rather than its content. Except for conventions that a paragraph begin on a new line and that each chapter begin at a page boundary, there is no obligation for content-determined units (usually called *logical* units of information) to conform to boundaries of physical units. Note that in this usage, "logical" means problem determined rather than machine determined.

In information processing, the designation of *physical record* is reserved for strings of information whose boundaries are set by characteristics of the recording medium. Examples are (1) the contents of a card, and (2) the contents of a printed line. There are others having to do with blocking information on magnetic tape or with the information available from one positioning of a reading mechanism for disk storage. Another physical unit of information, the *volume,* may be used to designate, for example, the contents of a magnetic tape, or the contents of a disk. Note that each of these would be expected to contain many logical records.

It may be convenient to plan a problem so that logical records or files conform to physical records or volumes, but that is not necessary. What is expected is that every logical unit be composed of an integral number of logical subunits; thus every logical record begins and ends on a field boundary, and every file begins and ends on a logical record boundary.

Lest one read too much meaning into the words "record" and "file" as used above, we remark that few bodies of information can be handled most effectively with only three units of information. Either one must have several levels of record or several levels of file, or both. Further, one person's file may be another person's record. One should always expect, however, that within any one system files are comprised of records rather than records of files.

Examples of Logical Organization of Files

1. The information on which payroll computations for hourly employees of a company is based might be considered a file. It would likely consist mainly of a sequence of logical records (in order on employee name), each providing all the information about one employee. Each of these records would have several fields which might have names such as NAME, ADDRESS, PAY RATE, NUMBER OF DEPENDENTS, and YR TO DATE PAY. One should also expect one or more records devoted to identifying the file. A record at the beginning of a file which provides the name of the file, the date the file was created, the number of records, and perhaps an index into the file is appropriately called a *label record.*

2. One could consider a computer program as a data file, each statement of the program constituting a record. In this connection, it is interesting to contrast FORTRAN with more recent procedure-oriented languages having statement delimiters, such as PL/1. If we take a statement in the language to be a logical record, then we find that every logical statement of FORTRAN begins and ends on a physical record boundary. Most statements require only one card and so the end of a physical record usually marks the end of a logical record. By contrast, statements in PL/1 end with a semicolon, and the next statement begins in the next source-language column, whether that is on the same card or the next. These log-

ical records are not required in any way to conform to physical record boundaries, but for reading convenience we may still find that the usual arrangement is one statement per card.

6.5.2 Buffering

We may look upon a program as a consumer of input data and a producer of output data. As such, it will be best served if the data it needs are always available when needed and if the output system which consumes its output is always ready to receive. But such arrangements are not trivial to make. The consumption of data by programs is usually quite irregular; a program may read a few cards and then compute for a long period before needing more input. Output is likely also to be irregular, perhaps occurring entirely at the end of a problem. Depending on the problem, it may be entirely predictable which items of input will be needed next so that they can be made ready (as in alphabetic updating of a personnel file), or it may be unpredictable (as when an interrogation by a police officer about a suspicious car requires prompt response). Once a request for certain data has been made, the total time required for mechanical positioning to begin readout is considerable (assuming it is electromechanical as are card readers, tape transports, magnetic drums, and magnetic disks). Even after that, the transfer of data requires very many instruction times, and for card readers or printers is very slow indeed. To halt all computation while requests for data are being serviced is too costly to tolerate if it can be avoided. Recording on a storage medium or printing results directly as they are generated brings about delays just as costly. Table 6.5.1 provides some typical startup times and data transfer times for a variety of storage media and gives two instruction execution times for comparison. A study of Table 6.5.1 will make clear the pressures to find ways of overlapping computation with input/output processes, for it is easy to see that applications which scan much information to do a small amount of computation, or which generate large volumes of output, can spend most of their time on these and only trivial amounts of computation. Such applications are called *I/O bound,* and in some installations they constitute the major load on the computer system. It was realized in the mid-1950s that processors were being used very inefficiently in I/O bound applications, and that led to machine modifications and programming techniques which helped restore a balance among the duty loads of peripheral devices and processors. The solutions have had a tendency to isolate the applications programmer more and more from direct communications with the outside world; often the programmer will not even specify intermediate storage explicitly. While we have no ready solution to the mysteries he faces as a result, we can profit from a review of the principles involved.

Normally Rotating Devices	Time (msec)			
	Average time to position heads	Average rotational delay	Transfer rate (Kilobytes/ sec)	Total capacity (bytes)
Movable read head IBM 2314/A Disk†	60	12.5	312.0	29.17×10^6
Head per track IBM 2303 Drum†	0	8.75	303.8	3.9×10^6

Normally Stationary Devices (Sequential Access)	Maximum time to physical record (msec)	(Kilobytes/sec)	Total capacity (bytes)
800 bits/in. tape at 75 in./sec	10	52.17 (4000 byte blocks)	20.2×10^6 (2400 ft)
80 column cards at 800 cards/min‡	500	1.067	

Instruction Execution Times	Time (msec)		
Symbolic operation code	360/30§	360/65G¶	370/145††
A	0.039	0.0015	0.002385
M	0.313	0.0049	0.020077

Table 6.5.1   Although times are shown for only a few specific devices, these data show that vast amounts of computation could take place during the retrieval of one word from auxiliary storage devices. This provides the incentive to bring in blocks of data at each access and to overlap computation with input or output operations.

† "Introduction to IBM System/360 Direct Access Storage Devices and Organization Methods," GC20–1649, p. 67.

‡ "IBM 2821 Control Unit Component Description," GA-24-3312, p. 29.

§ "IBM System/360 Model 30 Functional Characteristics," A24-3231, pp. 21–24.

¶ "IBM System/360 Model 65 Functional Characteristics," GA22-6884, pp. 3–36.

†† "IBM System/370 Model 145 Functional Characteristics," GA24-3557, pp. 42–45.

Principles Exploited to Balance Loads of Processor and Peripheral Devices

1. Where a device accepts data sequentially and its input rate is not well matched to the desired output rate, introduce a storage medium for gathering information at the input rate which can be transmitted at a later time at the appropriate output rate. As an example, record the output from a problem on magnetic tape and then feed the magnetic tape into a completely separate peripheral computer system for printing. In this case, the peripheral computer can be relatively inexpensive since it is dedicated to a single purpose. As another example, an input station to accept data from a telephone line will in all likelihood have a register for gathering incoming pulses to constitute the representation of a character or perhaps even a full word. Then when this register is filled, its entire contents will be transmitted at electronic transmission rates rather than mechanical reading or recording rates. Each of these constitutes an example of a *buffer,* an intermediate storage region to enable two devices to achieve a higher duty rate when their data rates are incompatible. Computers are full of hardware buffers, and systems programmers manage software buffers in almost every input/output program.

2. Where an expensive, versatile device such as a CPU is heavily used in routine ways for large proportions of its time, find ways to split off the routine usage to be handled another way. A prime application of this notion is to establish direct access paths between central memory and various storage devices. A data transfer on these paths, once initiated by the CPU, can continue between memory and the storage device without assistance from the central processor, thus enabling the processor to continue computation during data transfer. Whether these paths are called channels, ports, or buses, the fact is that special-purpose circuitry (amounting to a small computer) is dedicated to managing the data transfers on one of these paths between memory and from one to several I/O devices. Our schematics of a computer have indicated from the beginning a direct communication from I/O to memory, but historically this path included the CPU.

3. When one problem is I/O bound and another is *compute bound* (makes very slight demands on I/O compared to processor), a computing system should be able to overlap the two problems successfully, even though neither shows potential for improvement by itself. This concept is the motivation and basis for multiprogramming on large systems. Two or more jobs are in memory at one time. Computation is actually under con-

trol of a third program, the operating supervisor, which allots use of the processor to one program, then the other, alternating the processor assignment according to its estimate of their need. In particular, when one program is unable to proceed while awaiting completion of an I/O command, it yields the processor to the operating supervisor for reassignment. While most of these things go on behind the scenes so that they are transparent to the user, they place some interesting requirements on the machine and on the software. First, it must be possible for the supervisor to interrupt computation by a user when another user requires service, and on return to restore the environment so that the interrupted computation will be successfully completed. Second, even though there may be only one card reader or one printer, it should appear to each user that his is the only program using either so that users do not read each other's data nor intermingle print lines. The obvious answer here is to place a buffer between the user and each of his input/output units. The buffer between the card reader and user should have the capability of storing data arriving sequentially so that segments belonging to different jobs can be accessed independently through a set of pointers, one to the beginning of each job. Within a job, data are stored in sequence; but there are pointers (indexes) to job-starting points so that each user applies the pointer to his data and no other. Each user is then looking on his segment as his own private (simulated) card reader. The various users deposit output sequentially in separate storage areas. To each user, his storage area is a simulated printer. On delivery to the actual printer these are assigned some order and thus constitute a sequential file.

Without going any further into the role of an operating system in managing the sharing of a processor by two or more users, we see that a requirement for avoiding conflict between users is for the system to have complete control of the I/O devices. The user then communicates with simulated devices. Some I/O devices, such as magnetic tape transports or removable disk packs, can be assigned by the supervisor to one user only, each being available to only one job during the duration of that job. In that case, simulation is not necessary, but control of access is.

In this text, we will limit ourselves to demonstrating within the main memory of the computer some of the definitions and concepts which are essential to understand the I/O practices of a multiprogrammed system. We will take a look at buffering, at storage access methods, and at data moves as encountered in consolidating free storage cells for further use (affectionately called *garbage collection* by practitioners).

6.5.3   A Simple Analogy to Buffering

We consider time used by a central processor as a precious commodity, comparable in some sense to the time of a famous heart surgeon. The surgeon has a skill needed by many and, to do the most good, he finds it important to arrange his schedule so that he does only those things for which he is uniquely qualified, leaving routine tasks to subordinates. We assume that heart surgery can be segmented into three tasks which might be called (1) opening up, (2) heart repair, and (3) closing up. If the surgeon used computer vernacular these would appear as (1) input, (2) heart repair, and (3) output. Let us assume that each stage takes one hour. Then if there is only one operating room, it will take 9 hours for three heart repairs. But suppose our heart surgeon sees an unending caseload of heart problems and wants to be more productive. There is no hope until more space is available.

Now we assume his public service is rewarded by the addition of two more operating rooms. There is a variety of ways he could schedule their use, assuming enough subordinate help. We will take a look at two of them.

Schedule 1.   One supplementary *(buffer)* room is dedicated to opening up, the main room is dedicated to heart repair, and the other supplementary *(buffer)* room is dedicated to closing up. The patient progresses from room 1 to room 3, and we will assume the transport time from one room to the next is 20 min. A day's schedule would be as shown in Figure 6.5.1.

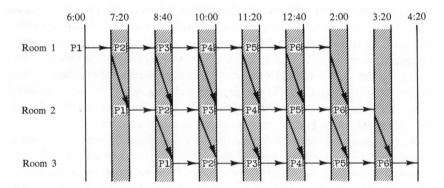

Figure 6.5.1 P*n* indicates presence of the *n*th patient in the room determined by its row for the time period given by column. Cross hatching indicates time devoted to moving the patient. In under eight hours (from 7:20 until 3:00) the heart surgeon can accomplish six heart repairs.

Schedule 2.   The doctor decides it is easier to have three identical operating rooms, so that a patient gets all his services in one room. The difference is that the doctor and his work crews rotate among rooms to perform their services. They can make the change in 10 min. Now each room is as much a buffer as the next. The buffers take turns being input, work, and output regions. This arrangement is diagrammed in Figure 6.5.2. The surgeon accomplishes seven heart repairs in the eight hours from 7:10 to 3:10. There is now spare time in two of the operating rooms for additional work.

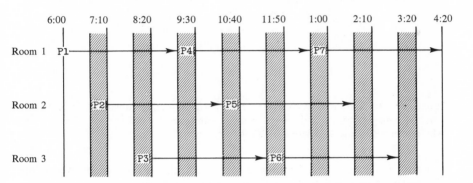

Figure 6.5.2   In this plan, a patient remains in the same room during the complete operation while surgical teams rotate among rooms.

The technique used here is known as *buffer swapping,* the notion being that the various functions rotate among the buffers as if they were on a circular path (see Figure 6.5.3) and functions pass from one to the next by rotating of the outer ring containing the various functions. Note that any kind of buffering seems to provide a great improvement, but more sophistication may give little added benefit.

While one might have worries about the survival of operating crews under the pressure of schedules we have devised, he need have no such worries about computers. They thrive on usage. But there is one special provision that would be necessary in a hospital, and this has its analog with computers. For some reason, a particular patient may provide special problems. A rigid schedule might keep the surgeon from finishing on time. Should he just stop where he is, or should he finish? Most of us would prefer to accept a little delay to be confident of completion. To assure it, we provide the surgeon an inquiry device and an initiating device. He can inquire of any input crew whether it is busy. If so, he waits for them to finish. Once he has started, he continues until finished, when he initiates

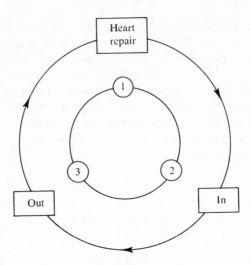

Figure 6.5.3 Nodes on the inner ring represent operating rooms, while nodes on the outer ring represent functions assigned to rooms. The inner ring stays fixed, while the outer ring rotates clockwise by 120° every hour.

output. Then he follows the same procedure at the next room. There remains the responsibility of the input crew to wait for the output crew to finish before moving in with the next patient. An inquiry device enabling the input crew to check on the output crew's status should complete the facilities. With such signaling devices and a faith in humanity that there will be no forgetting and no slowdowns, we can subscribe to the system.

6.5.4   Getting Down to Examples

The assembler planned in Chapter 4 made no mention of buffering. Yet it was concerned with information read from cards, and consequently there should be an opportunity to overlap card reading time with translation time. In that assembler, the assumption was made of a work area into which the instruction would be read. To introduce buffering without changing the program would require that one or more buffers distinct from this work area be reserved and that they be controlled so as to supply in proper sequence a new string of 80 characters (we have assumed that no instructions are continued from one card to the next) to the work area each time a card has been analyzed.

Buffer swapping would eliminate the moves of information to a work area, but it would require that the work area be movable. The user–programmer would become involved, perhaps only to the extent of accepting an address from buffering control for the beginning of the next logical record to be analyzed. His use of that address for getting information from the logical record would have to be done by indexing or by use of an explicit base. His programming is likely to be more numeric since fields will be referenced by their position relative to the beginning of the record rather than by symbolic names. Such programs are usually more difficult to read. There is a choice to be made, and that choice is both problem and programmer dependent.

We cannot obtain the benefits of buffering without the assistance of the operating supervisor, and this brings with it a need for vocabulary and concepts which we are just now developing. It seems reasonable to make certain first that we understand buffering even though there be time lost rather than gained in the way we implement it. The following sections will set the stage for the problems on buffering at the end of the chapter.

6.5.5 Providing for Buffer Pools

To gain acquaintance with concepts of buffering, we need to spend some effort on the analysis of data structures involved. We shall expect that within any program that refers to information available from an input/output device or from a supplemental storage device, there will be a collection of data about the way the information is stored and transmitted. This collection as provided in the 360/370 systems is called a Data Control Block (DCB). We shall provide for such a collection also, but it will be much less comprehensive. To avoid confusion, we shall call it BUFfer PARaMeters, or BUFPARM for short. Because we are taking input from the card reader and depositing output on the printer—and doing it through FORTRAN for simplicity—we may concentrate on the single issue before us, buffering. We start by discussing collections of buffers called *pools,* then management of buffers within pools, proceeding down the hierarchy to individual records.

The set of buffer parameters describes but does not constitute a set of buffers. Its buffers are contained in a buffer pool which is created by a process called *opening.* Opening may be thought of as establishing a communication "pipeline" between the program and a "data set" residing elsewhere and preparing for its use. In the case of opening an input pipeline, this includes "priming" the buffers with information from the data set. Such a communication link can be *closed* when no longer useful. When an output link is closed, the buffers are emptied so that no output will be lost, after which they are released for use by other BUFPARM's. When an input link is closed, there is no corresponding emptying of buffers. It is convenient to reserve one large segment of storage for holding the current buffer pools of a program. We call this segment POOLHALL.

Within this segment, we can expect to have a number of buffer pools, each associated with one BUFPARM. A *buffer pool* is a segment of storage largely devoted to buffers described in its associated BUFPARM but also containing some information about current status of buffer contents. One of our goals will be to make it easy to create and later to discard (free) a pool, for the POOLHALL will soon be filled with closed pools if we cannot return their storage segments for use by new pools that must be created. Pools must be variable in size, for the number of buffers in a pool and the length of buffers in the pool may vary from one pool to another. Our solution is to create a *list* of pools, a structure in which each pool carries a pointer to its *successor,* thus permitting pools to be scattered in storage yet easily found.

Even when POOLHALL is empty of pools, it has two important items of information at its beginning. These are:

(1) address of the far end of POOLHALL,

(2) POOLHALL + 8 (the least possible address for beginning of the next pool).

One might expect that the first pool would begin immediately after item 2, and the first pool established will begin there. But if that first pool is later closed, it is more convenient to leave a gap where it existed than to move existing pools into its place, in which case we will want a pointer to the beginning of the first open pool.

To insert the first pool into POOLHALL, we move the address of the end of POOLHALL to word zero of the first pool, place the address of the beginning of the first pool at POOLHALL and the address just beyond the end of the first pool, in its word one. We have shown the first pool placed so as to leave a gap of unused space between the initial two words of POOLHALL and its start. After pools have been opened and closed, that may be the case, but originally there should be no gap.

POOLHALL   End of POOLHALL

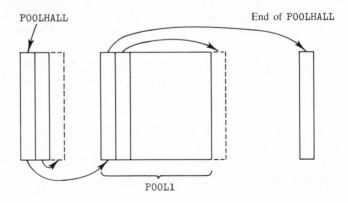

POOL1

Given a situation with several pools in POOLHALL and one more to be built, we determine its size and then use the pointers associated with the list of pools to find the first open space sufficiently large. Reserving space requires copying two pointers and creating one to point just beyond the new pool. Deleting a pool is equally easy. Making sure one does not overrun the extent of POOLHALL can be done by having a negative number mark the end of POOLHALL.

6.5.6 The Management of Buffer Pools

Once a place for a pool has been reserved, we must concern ourselves with its contents. Primarily, the pool will provide buffers, so we will concern ourselves first with understanding their management. That will tell us what other items of information to carry in the pool.

We assume a pool contains n buffers numbered $0, 1, \ldots, n - 1$.

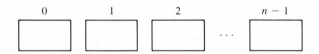

As soon as an input pool is created, information is read into its buffers in order starting from 0 until the buffers are filled or the data set is exhausted (we defer provisions for the latter until later). The object thereafter is to replenish the supply of information in the buffers as fast as it is used. It is helpful to think of one buffer as being in use and the others as constituting a queue to hold information for future processing. Four stages in use of a four-buffer pool are represented in Figure 6.5.4. Note from this sketch that the successor to buffer i is buffer $i + 1$ unless i is $n - 1$, in which case the successor is buffer 0. It is helpful to think of buffers as stationed around a ring in which case this succession comes naturally. To describe buffer status, we distinguish the pointers INUSE, QHEAD, and QTAIL. These do not actually point to a buffer but to the address of the intended buffer. We say one of these pointers *selects* a buffer if it points to the address of that buffer. Figure 6.5.5 indicates the indirect way we have chosen to designate current buffer function. When a buffer is initially set up or has just been exhausted by use, we place the character X'80' in the leftmost byte of its pointer. When it has been filled, we replace that character by X'00' except for putting a nonzero positive integer in this byte for the final bufferload (the value to be determined in the discussion of records below).

Initially, we set INUSE to select buffer 0, QHEAD to select the successor to buffer 0, and QTAIL to select buffer $n - 1$. In the usual case, these will select three distinct buffers. However, our explanation is in-

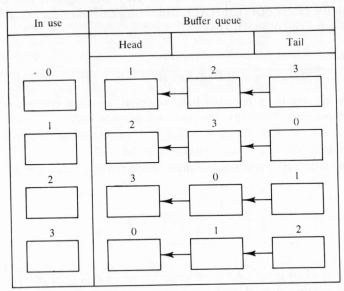

Figure 6.5.4 This sketch shows the cyclic use of buffers in a buffer pool.

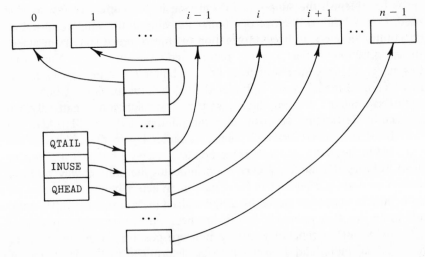

Figure 6.5.5 Three pointers serve in an indirect manner to show which buffer is in direct communication with the program and how the queue is formed.

tended to cover the case $n = 2$ (in which case QHEAD and QTAIL are equal) as well as $n = 1$ in which case all three pointers select buffer 0. To fill the pipeline as is needed to complete its opening if the pool is for input, we invoke a read subprogram which is to fill buffers starting with INUSE and continuing until all buffers are filled.

We now assume a situation after some computation such that the successor to INUSE needs to be selected. On input, this would mean information which follows in the pipeline is required. In output, this would mean information in the buffer selected by INUSE may now be transmitted and a new buffer readied for filling. These cases are quite similar, but we treat them separately for clarity. Reference to Figure 6.5.5 illustrates the adjustments.

Next Buffer (Input)

1. Place X'80' in the byte pointed to by INUSE to indicate that the associated buffer is ready for refill.
2. Move the pointer in INUSE to QTAIL.
3. Move the pointer in QHEAD to INUSE.
4. Adjust QHEAD to select the successor to the buffer it currently selects.
5. Initiate the filling of the buffer selected by QTAIL and mark the buffer when filled by X'00' in the leftmost byte of its pointer.
6. Return to computation.

Note that there is no guarantee that the buffer selected by INUSE will be filled by the time access to its information is attempted. Since a buffer should be full before it is accessed, the programmer must test and wait for completion if necessary.

Next Buffer (Output)

1. Place X'00' in the byte pointed to by INUSE to indicate that the associated buffer contents are ready to be transmitted.
2. Move the pointer in INUSE to QTAIL.
3. Move the pointer in QHEAD to INUSE.
4. Adjust QHEAD to select the successor to the buffer it currently selects.
5. Initiate emptying the buffer selected by QTAIL and mark an emptied buffer by placing X'80' in the leftmost byte of its address word.
6. Return to computation.

The new INUSE buffer must have been marked as emptied before filling it begins.

6.5.7   Structure within a Buffer

Ordinarily, buffers are large enough to hold the information in one physical record or block. These may contain several logical records. We have seen that logical records may continue across physical record boundaries, but we shall content ourselves with a somewhat simpler picture in which each buffer has the same fixed capacity, a fixed number of records of fixed length. Input card records and printline records are of this sort.

Ordinarily, the programmer is interested in processing one record, disposing of it, and then moving on to the next. When moving from one record to the next can be done within one buffer, none of the mechanism of pool and buffer control are involved. Instead a pointer to the top of one record is moved on to point to the top of the next. When advancing from the last record of one buffer to the first record of the next buffer is involved, then, even though it is implicit, the programmer by advancing to the next record is invoking the buffer control mechanism. The pool control mechanism is used only on opening and closing.

There is a special case which should be mentioned. We have assumed buffers of a given capacity, and we intend to fill them to capacity when there are sufficient records to do so. But on arriving at the end of a data set, we have no guarantee of being at the end of a buffer as well. The last buffer should not be empty, but it may have fewer records than its capacity. We propose that the leftmost byte of the address word for a buffer which has in it the last record of a file be set with the integer which is the number of records in that buffer. Since other buffers have this byte in their pointer word set to 0, this will distinguish the last buffer and also provide the information as to how many records are in it.

We have not reached the lowest level of structure within a buffer. In fact, there are fields, subfields, and individual characters to be considered. But we have developed sufficient structure for our purpose, which is to present some important concepts and to establish the base for some interesting problems concerning management of buffer pools.

6.6   OPERATIONS OF LOGIC WITH BIT STRINGS

6.6.1   Instructions for Logic

The adjective "logical" has too many shades of meaning in computer terminology to be useful in separating out those instructions implementing the operations of Boolean algebra and of propositional calculus. We have seen "logical" used as a modifier in character-oriented instructions. It also appears in the names (Add Logical and Subtract Logical) of arithmetic instructions modified in their response to carry into and out of the sign position. Our interest here is to explore just those instructions which perform the AND, OR, and EXCLUSIVE OR mentioned in Section 6.1. For each of these operations, there are four instructions, the only differences being the way in which operands are obtained. The four types and their operand fields in base-displacement form are given in Table 6.6.1.

Type	Assembler operand field	Length in bits	Instruction format			
			Byte 0	Byte 1	Bytes 2,3	Bytes 4,5
RR	R1,R2	32	Opcode	R1 R2	Empty	Empty
RX	R1,D2(X2,B2)	32	Opcode	R1 X2	B2 D2	Empty
SI	D1(B1),I2	8	Opcode	I2	B1 D1	Empty
SS	D1(L,B1),D2(B2)	8L	Opcode	L–1	B1 D1	B2 D2

Table 6.6.1   There are four instruction types and formats for instructions which perform the operations AND, OR, and EXCLUSIVE OR.

Now, as with character strings, we use S1 (S2) to signify a first (second) operand field designating a storage location. The instructions themselves can be described in the compact Table 6.6.2.

Instruction name	Type	Opcode	Effect
AND register	RR	NR	R1 ← (R1) AND (R2)
OR register	RR	OR	R1 ← (R1) OR (R2)
EXCLUSIVE OR register	RR	XR	R1 ← (R1) EX OR (R2)
AND	RX	N	R1 ← (R1) AND (S2)
OR	RX	O	R1 ← (R1) OR (S2)
EXCLUSIVE OR	RX	X	R1 ← (R1) EX OR (S2)
AND immediate	SI	NI	S1 ← (S1) AND I2
OR immediate	SI	OI	S1 ← (S1) OR I2
EXCLUSIVE OR immediate	SI	XI	S1 ← (S1) EX OR I2
AND string	SS	NC†	S1 ← (S1) AND (S2)
OR string	SS	OC†	S1 ← (S1) OR (S2)
EXCLUSIVE OR string	SS	XC†	S1 ← (S1) EX OR (S2)

Table 6.6.2   The operation codes and the effects of execution for the various AND, OR, and EXCLUSIVE OR instructions are shown. In each case, the condition code is set to zero if each bit of the result is zero, and is set to one otherwise.

† The C in this mnemonic operand code is clearly a carryover from that in the MoVe Character instruction. It can serve as a reminder that the length parameter in the instruction is an integral number of bytes.

While there are exciting applications of these operations of logic in various problem areas, we have chosen as examples some of the powerful uses in programming.†

Example 1.   A constant mask used as an operand can provide a convenient way to modify selected bits in a string. As an example, we consider a one-byte mask and apply it as a second operand to first operands in various ways to display the following simple rules:

An AND with 0 sets a bit position to 0.
An OR with 1 sets a bit position to 1.
An EX OR with 1 changes 0 to 1 and 1 to 0.

First operand	Opcode	Second operand	Result
10111001_2	NI	00001111_2	00001001
10111001_2	OI	00001111_2	10111111
10111001_2	XI	00001111_2	10110110

These properties are valuable in setting switches in a program, in initializing variables, and also in applications where the "logical negation" or complementation of a string is needed.

Example 2.   It may seem almost magic until analyzed that the interchange of two storage operands or of two register operands can be accomplished by three successive applications of the EXCLUSIVE OR. For the simplest case let us consider the matter with one-bit operands p and q. All possible cases can be analyzed in four lines:

p q	$p' = p$ EX OR q	$q' = q$ EX OR p'	$p'' = p'$ EX OR q'
0 0	0	0	0
0 1	1	0	1
1 0	1	1	0
1 1	0	1	1

Note that if $p = (P)$ and $q = (Q)$

$P \leftarrow p$ EX OR q (replaces p by p EX OR q)
$Q \leftarrow q$ EX OR p (replaces q by the original p)
$P \leftarrow p$ EX OR q (replaces p by the original q)

and the interchange is accomplished. This analysis applies to each bit position when the operands are bit strings.

Example 3.   For any logical variable p, p EX OR p is zero. This provides a convenient way to set any byte string of storage to zeros. If the

† Most of these are in the manual "IBM System/360 Principles of Operation," Order Number GA22-6821. Examples are collected in programming shops. A paper by R. H. Williams in *Data Processing*, August, 1967, includes several.

length of the string does not exceed 256 bytes, this can be done with one XC instruction. As the instruction is executed, the condition code is set to 00 if the result in each bit is zero, and to 01 if the result is not zero in some bit. Testing for a zero string without resetting can be accomplished with the OR instruction. We illustrate for an eight-bit string:

A	Sets to zeros		Tests for zeros	
	A EX OR A	CC	A OR A	CC
10100111	00000000	00	10100111	01
00000000	00000000	00	00000000	00

Example 4.   A rotary shift feeds bits shifted off one end of a register into vacated positions at the other end of the same register. One can obtain a rotary left shift by n places of the contents of the odd-numbered register of an even–odd pair by clearing the even-numbered register, performing a Shift Left Double Logical by n places, and then using the OR of the two registers as a result.

XR   2, 2   Clears register 2
SLDL   2, n Shifts n bits into register 2, filling the n vacated positions
         with zeros at the right of register 3
OR   3, 2   Puts n bits from register 2 into register 3

The programmer who is given one example of this sort can find many related ones.

Example 5.   If the components of an instruction are not all available at once (as in the assembly process) it is convenient to start with a target string of the proper length consisting entirely of zeros. One then positions components in strings of the same length which have zeros except in the bits reserved for the component. These can be inserted into the target string by successive uses of the OR instructions:

58A3CDEF = (58000000)OR(00A00000)OR(00030000)OR
           (0000C000)OR (00000DEF)

This notion is used at execution time by the EXecute instruction to insert bits as desired from its register operand (no effect if register 0 is named) into positions 8–15 of an instruction designated by its storage operand. It permits insertion in each of bits 8–15, but also permits leaving some of these bits undisturbed as might be desirable in an SS instruction with two four-bit lengths (e.g., the PACK and UNPacK instructions). Bit positions in the register operand corresponding to the portion of the instruction to remain unchanged would be zero.

6.6.2   An Application of Logic Instructions

One often suspects that if he knew the right friend to call, and if each friend called another friend, he could in a short sequence of calls get a message through to any designated person. The problem is to find the shortest path between two people, if there is one. We idealize the situation by assuming that if A is a friend of B, then B is a friend of A (the relation is symmetric), and that, given a name, a person knows whether that person is or is not a friend. Suppose that the population to be considered is reasonably small and that by some means we obtain an ordered list of names of all persons in that population. We give a copy of this list to each person and ask him to place a one beside the name of each friend and a zero beside nonfriends. To be definite, we define each person to be his own friend (the relation is reflexive). We collect the lists and hope to determine a shortest path from them. Surely all the information is there.

Suppose we need a shortest path from person A to person B; let these names also stand for their friend strings. If A has a 1 in the B position of his string, then there is a path of length 1 from A to B (because of the symmetry assumed, there would also be a 1 in the A position of B). If not, consider another person C, whom A and B each know; then a path A to C to B is as good as will be found. All such possibilities can be detected by forming A AND B and detecting the 1's in the resulting string. If it is a string of zeros, then we must look for paths of length three.

Suppose that for each person we consider a sequence of strings denoted by a suffix n attached to the string name. For person X, Xn has a 1 in the bit for person Y if there is a path of length n from X to Y. Note that $X1 = X$ and that $X2$ has its bit for person Y equal to 1 if X AND Y is not a zero string and zero if it is a zero string. This is exactly a condition remembered in the condition code after an AND instruction.

The same sort of string building carries us to the conditions for longer paths. Suppose Xn is known; then if the string Xn AND $Y1$ is nonzero, there is some person n units distant from X and 1 unit distant from Y, therefore yielding a path of length $n + 1$ from X to Y.

We have seen that simple use of logical instructions will build the ingredients of a string Xn, if in fact we can put these bits together to form a new bit string. We have isolated an interesting bit-manipulation problem: How does one catenate a bit to an existing bit string when the least unit for the move instruction is the byte? We use this example as an analogy to the more general theory of nondirected graphs, and as a source of several exercises at the end of this chapter.

6.7 BACKGROUND OF CONVERSION METHODS

When a card punched with a sign followed by decimal digits, say −5029, is read in character mode, the internal representations of these characters will be deposited in a string of bytes in an input area. For this example, the EBCDIC representation given in hexadecimal would be 60F5F0F2F9. The job to be done as indicated in Problem 15 of Chapter 3 is to separate out binary representations of the individual decimal digits, then to evaluate in binary the sum $(((5 \cdot 10) + 0) \cdot 10 + 2) \cdot 10 + 9$, and finally to apply the sign represented by 60. These manipulations can be accomplished using only the shift and arithmetic instructions, but conversion is so frequently required that the 360/370 systems have instructions to make this process (and the inverse from binary to character) simpler and faster. The choice of instructions for accomplishing conversion is strongly affected by another feature of the 360/370 systems called *decimal arithmetic*. We digress for a moment to explain why there should be decimal arithmetic when binary is already available, and to specify the way operands of decimal arithmetic instructions are represented.

The arithmetic involved in most commercial applications is a very small part of the problem. In the process of converting numbers to binary, and then the results back to character representation of decimal answers, one might be doing far more arithmetic than is required in binary as part of the original problem. One alternative is to have instructions which perform arithmetic on decimal representations of operands. Even though these instructions are relatively slow in execution, they may save overall computing time since they eliminate the need to convert from decimal to binary and also from binary to decimal. They have an added advantage of rounding as a person would round in manual computation with decimal numbers.

The 360/370 internal decimal representation of a number (called *packed decimal*) is a string of hexadecimal representations of its digits followed by a hexadecimal representation of its sign. Note that a decimal digit is just the rightmost hex digit of the internal character representation of the digit, as shown in Table 6.7.1. The hexadecimal representations of + and − are partly historical. In commercial applications, it is a column-conserving custom to record the sign of a number by a punch over

Decimal integer	0	1	2	3	4	5	6	7	8	9
Hexadecimal integer	F0	F1	F2	F3	F4	F5	F6	F7	F8	F9

Table 6.7.1 The EBCDIC representation of decimal integers.

its rightmost digit. A punch in the top (12) row indicates positive. A punch in the next lower (11) row indicates negative. A punch in either row 11 or row 12 is called an overpunch, and the absence of an overpunch indicates a positive sign. One finds by reference to the EBCDIC table that the rightmost digit will read as a nondigit (a letter unless the digit is zero) if there is an overpunch and as a digit if there is not. A letter in A, . . . , I will signify positive, a letter in J, . . . , R will signify negative. The *zone* portion of this character (its leftmost hexadecimal digit) will then be C (the first hex digit of the internal representations of the letters A, . . . , I) or F (the first hex digit of the characters with no overpunch) for positive signs, and D (the first hex digit of the internal representations of the letters J, . . . , R) for negative. For the 360/370 packed-decimal notation, this coding has been extended so that every hex digit will represent either a decimal digit or a sign. The extension is that A, C, E, and F represent positive (it spells FACE), while B and D represent negative. Listed in Table 6.7.2 are some decimal number representations which illustrate the packed decimal format of the 360/370.

Since decimal arithmetic will require conversion from character representation to packed decimal (and something similar must be done to convert from character to binary), it is natural that character to binary conversion is accomplished in two stages: first comes the conversion from character to packed decimal, and then packed decimal to binary follows.

6.7.1 Conversions between Character and Packed-Decimal Representations

There are two instructions dedicated to these conversions, and in function (but not detail) one is the inverse of the other. They are called PACK and UNPK (UNPacK), each being of SS2 type; they are our first examples in which two lengths are to be provided. Thus the operand fields in base-displacement form are

$$D1(L1, B1), D2(L2, B2)$$

External	Hexadecimal	
	Character	Packed decimal
54$\overline{7}$	F5F4D7	547D
$+$		
803	F8F0C3	803C
607	F6F0F7	607F

Table 6.7.2 Examples of character and packed-decimal representation of integers.

where L1 and L2 are each numbers of bytes in the storage strings. As with the move instructions, the second operand field determines the source string (to be converted) and the first operand field determines the location of the result. The character string representation used in these instructions is that in which the sign is carried as the left half of the rightmost digit representation. Thus a character string of $2n - 1$ bytes should yield a packed-decimal representation of $2n - 1$ digits and a sign digit, occupying n bytes in total. A character string of $2n$ bytes will require places for $2n$ digits and a sign, thus requiring a length in bytes of $n + 1$, the leftmost digit being zero. There is no checking in PACK to confirm that characters being converted really represent decimal digits nor that the zone of the rightmost character is a valid sign in packed decimal. Similarly, the UNPK instruction does no checking to ensure that a valid packed-decimal representation is being converted. These instructions can therefore be accurately described as "bit rearrangers". Both PACK and UNPK work from right to left in their operand strings. When operand storage strings overlap, there is a chance that the result string will destroy some of its input before use.

If the first operand is longer than required for the second operand, the result (whether character or packed decimal) is filled on the left with occurrences of the digit zero. If it is not adequate for holding the complete conversion, there is truncation on the left. We limit our examples to non-overlapping operand strings in which space is provided for the entire result. The reference manual will guide those who are not happy to practice such conservatism.

With the bit rearrangements as complex as they are, the sequence of examples in Table 6.7.3 seems to be the most reasonable explanation of PACK and UNPK.

Symbolic opcode	Operand field	Operand 1	Operand 2
PACK	D1(3,B1),D2(4,B2)	04708C	F4F7F0C8
PACK	D1(3,B1),D2(3,B2)	00862F	F8F6F2C5
PACK	D1(2,B1),D2(4,B2)	625C	F8F6F2C5
UNPK	D1(5,B1),D2(3,B2)	F5F6F7F0C5	56705C
UNPK	D1(3,B1),D2(3,B2)	F9F3D8	02938D
UNPK	D1(4,B1),D2(2,B2)	F0F6F2F4	624F

Table 6.7.3 As usual with SS-type instructions, the length(s) specified in the operand field is (are) the actual number of bytes, whereas the assembler subtracts one to obtain the number inserted in the instruction.

6.7.2   Conversions between Packed Decimal and Binary

By contrast with the string-to-string conversions between character and packed-decimal notation, one of our operands is now a full-word binary number. It is therefore reasonable to expect that the two instructions ConVert to Binary (CVB) and ConVert to Decimal (CVD) are in RX format, and that the storage operand will in each case designate the packed decimal operand. The RX format makes no provision for its length to be given explicitly. Instead, the instruction assumes the packed-decimal operand occupies a double word which, in contrast to the packed-decimal strings in PACK and UNPK instructions, must begin on a double-word boundary. Each representation is taken to be an integer, the decimal operand being the digits of the absolute value with sign, the binary operand being in two's complement form. In the CVB instruction, either a digit position of the packed decimal number which does not hold a valid digit, or a sign position which does not hold a valid sign, causes program interruption.

Since the largest integer representable in a general register is $2^{31}-1$ and the least is -2^{31}, the packed-decimal operand may be too large in amplitude to convert properly to binary. This condition is detected as a failure in executing a divide and the program is interrupted. By appropriate planning and testing, the programmer should be able to forestall such an overflow rather than attempt to recover from it.

The ConVert instructions (CVB and CVD) are unlikely to have extensive use except in conjunction with PACK and UNPK instructions, for if one is planning to compute in binary, he is unlikely to compute in decimal from the same quantities. It is to be expected that a ConVert to Binary instruction is immediately preceded by a PACK instruction, and a ConVert to Decimal instruction is immediately followed by an UNPacK instruction. That is a convenient assumption to make in giving examples. Since the packed-decimal intermediate form is used at once as an operand to the next instruction it is expedient to take it in the second instruction from the place it was put by the first. Restrictions on the ConVert instructions therefore dictate that the length be 8 and that the strings be aligned on a double-word boundary.

Examples.   We assume that numbers to be converted from binary to character representation are stored in register 4, that a double-word PACKDEC receives the intermediate packed-decimal representation, and that conversion of character mode is from PACKDEC into CHARDEC. Then the only parameters free for us to choose are the length of CHARDEC and the number to be converted. The three representations are given for several choices of parameters to the following instruction sequence:

```
CVD   4,PACKDEC
UNPK  CHARDEC(L1),PACKDEC(8)
```

$L1_{10}$	$REG4_{16}$	$PACKDEC_{16}$	$CHARDEC_{16}$
4	00000019	00000000 0000025C	F0F0F2C5
2	FFFFFFA8	00000000 0000098D	F9D8
4	00008000	00000000 0032768C	F2F7F6C8
10	7FFFFFFF	00000214 7483647C	F2F1F4F7 F4F8F3F6 F4C7
10	80000000	00000214 7483648D	F2F1F4F7 F4F8F3F6 F4D8

6.7.3   Limitations of the Conversion Instructions

It may be disappointing, but we come to realize in working with computers that no instruction will be versatile enough to fit all situations. Clearly this is true of the ConVert instructions, for if a computed integer N exceeds $2^{31}-1$, we cannot convert it directly into packed decimal with one use of the CVD instruction. What we can do is to resolve N by division into the form

$$N = Q \cdot 10^9 + R \qquad (0 \leq R < 10^9)$$

Then $R < 2^{31}-1$ and can be converted to packed decimal using the CVD instruction. We suppose that Q also is less than $2^{31}-1$, in which case it can be converted in the same way. But now a catenation of two packed-decimal representations is in order. This catenation is accomplished using the MoVe Character and the MoVe with Offset instructions. The unpacking into character representation is most effectively done after the packed-decimal representation is complete. Should one encounter a binary integer so large that 16 characters will not suffice to represent it in decimal, then additional "cutting and pasting" will be required in conversion to characters. In every case, one finds that precision beyond that built into instructions is possible, but demands extreme care. Examples of the same kind of adjustment to techniques when number representations exceed the capacity of the instruction can be found in conversion to binary.

It should also be noted that the ConVert instructions assume integers as operands. What about fractions? Let f represent a positive proper binary fraction, and suppose we want a five-decimal rounded equivalent. We make use of the identity

$$f + 5/10^6 = [(10^6 f) + 5]/10^6$$

We want to calculate the integer that is $10^6 f + 5$, convert it to packed decimal, discard its rightmost digit, and understand that the packed-decimal form now has five decimal places. The integer $10^6 f + 5$ is obtained by multiplying f by 10^6, shifting off the fractional part of the double-word product, and adding 101_2 into the result. The binary equivalent of a proper decimal fraction, $d_1 \ldots d_p$, comes from converting the integer $10^p \cdot (.d_1 \ldots d_p)$ to a binary integer and then dividing the result by the binary representation of 10^p.

The programmer who has followed and applied these somewhat intricate techniques for reducing a conversion to one or more uses of the 360/370 ConVert instructions will prefer to conceive his own attack for the next such problem rather than look in this text or any other for a similar case.

6.8   THE TRANSLATE AND TRANSLATE AND TEST INSTRUCTIONS

The 360/370 systems contain many instructions which are intricate to use but can be unusually rewarding in execution time savings. We have ignored several of these, including Branch on CounT, Branch on indeX Low or Equal, and Branch on indeX High, which compress two or three simpler instructions into one. Eventually, any good programmer will learn when and how to use them. But those instructions which incorporate their own looping control, such as MoVe Character, Compare Logical Character, and the bit string logic instructions (OC, NC, XC) enhance certain processes by an order of magnitude and offer a far greater payoff for the situations to which they apply. The ones we will consider carefully are called TRanslate and TRanslate and Test. Two others which are recommended but are too intricate to include until Chapter 8 are EDit and EDit and MarK.

There are also some instructions with built-in looping which are special to the 370 system. We consider two of these in Section 6.9. Their explanation will be enhanced by building on TRanslate and Test which is explained in this section.

6.8.1   The TRanslate Instruction

Any assignment of internal binary codes to characters determines an ordering of these characters which also determines the ordering achieved in a sorting or collating process using the Compare Logical instructions. This same assignment has much to do with the ease with which one may test a character for membership in a particular subset—e.g., is it a digit or is it an arithmetic operator? These assertions may suggest that it is desirable to be able to translate from one internal representation to another.

Other machines, or other installations of the same machine, may use different character coding from that which we are using. EBCDIC is widely used on IBM machines, but there is another internal representation known as USASCII (USA Standard Code for Information Interchange) which, although only proposed and not accepted as a standard, is widely used. Further, keypunches with other character sets, cards coded in a special way, and special paper-tape or magnetic-tape codings can all lead to a character-by-character translation requirement. The TRanslate instruction handles such translation with great speed and convenience.

While our interest in translating may be spurred by the correspondence between printable characters and their internal representations, we are truly concerned here only with replacement of one eight-bit integer (an internal character) by another, each occurrence of a particular integer having the same replacement. The easiest way to specify the replacement of n by r_n for all n in $0 \leq n \leq 255$ is to supply a string of hexadecimal representations of r_n in order on n. This string may rightfully be called the *translation table*. For example, if the translation table begins

$$0 \quad 1 \quad 2 \quad 3 \quad 4$$
$$C6C5C3C4C1$$

and the source string to be translated consists of the four bytes

$$00040201$$

then the translation would be the four-byte string

$$C6C1C3C5$$

which in EBCDIC represents FACE.

The TRanslate instruction makes reference to two strings of bytes and conforms to SS1 type, the symbolic form being

$$\text{TR} \quad \text{D1(L,B1),D2(B2)}$$

The input string to be translated is of length L, where $1 \leq L \leq 256$, and begins at D1 + (B1). The output string replaces the input (source) string one byte at a time. The translation table is a string of length 256 beginning at D2 + (B2).

The TRanslate instruction presents the same opportunity for destruction of program or data as was found in the MoVe Character instruction. A length (L − 1) which extends the translated output string beyond the space reserved for it can wipe out program or data, or possibly a portion of the translation table. A computed length of zero, when decremented by one to provide the length parameter in the instruction, will cause 256 bytes to be translated and must be guarded against. A computed length might also exceed expectations and therefore should usually be tested against the available length. These considerations will apply as well to the TRanslate and Test instruction, which is a far more versatile and challenging instruction than TRanslate.

6.8.2 The TRanslate and Test Instruction

This instruction builds on the TRanslate instruction, which should be thoroughly understood before TRT is contemplated. Its symbolic form is

$$\text{TRT} \quad \text{D1(L,B1),D2(B2)}$$

This instruction does not translate anything directly, but rather scans a source string for characters of key importance and provides in the table a code which determines the response to that character. Thus for the TRT instruction we call the 256-byte table to which the second operand field points the *response table*. As an example in getting acquainted with the instruction, we can think of scanning a source language program to find delimiters such as parentheses and commas, and responding differently to left paren, right paren, and comma, which might have response codes 4, 8, and 16, respectively. All other characters would have zero for a response code for this simple example. There must be a nonambiguous way to associate characters with the desired response code, and this is done by assigning one byte of the response table to each possible character code and putting the response code for a character into its byte of the table. Since the normal mode of the 360/370 systems is to use EBCDIC for the representation of characters, the usual ordering is the same as that of the EBCDIC characters. This is given in Table 6.8.1, where the order is obtained by traversing columns from top to bottom starting with column 0 and moving from left to right.

Execution of TRT amounts to a scan starting at the leftmost byte of the source string (pointed to by the first operand field) and continuing to the right, one byte at a time until a nonzero code is encountered or the source string is exhausted. The scan terminates when either of these conditions is encountered. Its effect is to be found distributed among register 1, register 2, and the condition code bits.

During the left-to-right scan of the input string, if the contents of the scanned byte have zero response code, the only action is to test for the end of the string. If the scanned byte is the rightmost byte of the string, then the condition code is set to zero, register 1 and register 2 are not changed, and the instruction terminates. In this case, we say the string was

Zeroth hexadecimal digit

	0	1	2	3	4	5	6	7	8	9	A	B	C	D	E	F
0					†	&	-									0
1							/		a	j			A	J		1
2									b	k	s		B	K	S	2
3									c	l	t		C	L	T	3
4									d	m	u		D	M	U	4
5									e	n	v		E	N	V	5
6									f	o	w		F	O	W	6
7									g	p	x		G	P	X	7
8									h	q	y		H	Q	Y	8
9									i	r	z		I	R	Z	9
A					¢	!		:								
B					.	$	,	#								
C					<	*	%	@								
D					(	)	_	'								
E					+	;	>	=								
F					|	¬	?	"								

(a) First Hexadecimal digit

	0	1	2	3	4	5	6	7
0								
1								
2								
3								
4								
5								
6								
7								
8								
9								
A								
B							16	
C								
D					4	8		
E								
F								

(b) First hexadecimal digit

Table 6.8.1 (a) The response table for the TRT instruction has 256 entries. Assuming EBCDIC is used, the EBCDIC listing provides placement of codes in the response table; for example, the response code for the character '9' would be the 250th entry in the response table because in EBCDIC 9 is preceded by 15 columns of 16 elements and 9 digits in its column.

(b) For the case where the response code for left paren is 4, for right paren is 8, and for comma is 16, the nonzero entries in the response table are shown.

† Although many internal character representations cause no printing, only 40_{16} explicitly represents the blank character.

exhausted. If the scanned byte is not the rightmost byte of the string and the response code is zero, then the only effect is to advance the scan to the next byte. If the scanned byte contents have a nonzero response code, then the address of the scanned byte is inserted as the rightmost 24 bits of register 1, the response code is inserted as the rightmost eight bits of register 2, and the condition code is set to a nonzero value. The condition code value is 1 if the scanned byte is not at string end and is 2 if the scanned byte is at string end. A nonzero response code causes termination.

These effects are not difficult to understand, but they are not necessarily what one wants to use. There are two conditions under which register 1 will remain unchanged by one application of the instruction:

(1) the leftmost character has nonzero response code, or
(2) every character has zero response code.

There are times when one would prefer that register 1 contain the scan pointer and be incremented whenever a zero is detected, so that it points beyond the rightmost element if all elements have zero response code. However, this is not the case.

One must be careful in using the contents of register 2. Its contents are unchanged and therefore may be meaningless if all characters in the input string had zero response code. Further, if register 2 has nonzero bits in positions 0–23, these will never be changed by execution of the instruction. If one is using the response code as an address increment (see the example of this section), then it is desirable to initialize register 2 to zero before starting the scan (a complete scan may involve several applications of the TRT instruction). To be able to judge solely from examination of register 2 whether a use of the TRT instruction has exhausted the input string, we need to have taken care to set register 2 to zero before each use of the TRT instruction. If register 2 is zero on termination, we know the last use exhausted the string; if it is nonzero we initiate another application. If this practice is used, there will be times when the last element of the input string will terminate the instruction, placing a nonzero response code in register 2. Since exhaustion is not indicated, the TRT will be applied once more, this time with zero length.

It is possible to consider a complex instruction to be a wired-in subprogram. We find this a helpful way to proceed, for it permits sensible incorporation of the use of the instruction in a flowchart without its degenerating to specifying steps in terms of machine instructions. The flowchart of Figure 6.8.1 defines such a subprogram. The following glossary defines the variables in that flowchart, each signifying an address:

Variable	Contents
SCANORG	Address of the initial byte to be examined
L	Length of the string to be scanned
LSTAR	(L)−1
TABLE	Beginning address of a string of one-byte integers in which the byte displaced by j from TABLE contains the response code to be returned when a character with internal character code j is scanned
TERMCODE	Code whose value at termination is:
	0 if all elements in SCANORG to SCANORG+(LSTAR) have zero for a response code
	1 if the scan terminates with a nonzero response code before the last element of the string to be scanned is reached
	2 if the scan terminates with a nonzero response code on the last element of the string to be scanned
BREAKPT	Unchanged by the subprogram if (TERMCODE)=0 at termination; otherwise, the address of the leftmost element in the scanned string with a nonzero response code
RESPCODE	Unchanged by the subprogram if (TERMCODE)=0 at termination; otherwise, the two-digit hexadecimal number at (BREAKPT)
QUITFLAG	A local switch

In the machine implementation, input items are:

SCANORG	The effective address of the first operand
TABLE	A byte string of length 256 beginning at the effective address of the second operand
LSTAR	Byte one of the TRT instruction; it is derived from L in the first operand field

The output items are:

BREAKPT	Register $1_{8:31}$
RESPCODE	Register $2_{24:31}$
TERMCODE	$PSW_{34:35}$ (the condition code)

Example.   It is desired to analyze the frequency of occurrence of members of the following sets in a string named TEXT.

Set 0 = {0, 1, . . ., 9}
Set 1 = {A, E, I, O, U}
Set 2 = {+, −, *, /}

We will plan a program which will count the members of each of these three sets in TEXT by use of the TRT instruction. One of the exercises at the end of this chapter proposes using the TRanslate instruction in an easier solution to this problem.

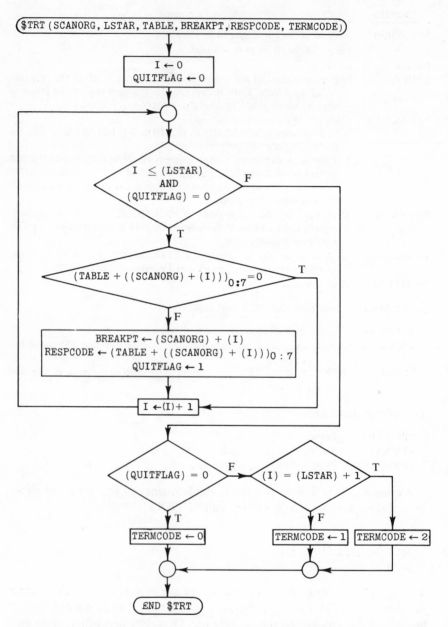

Figure 6.8.1 A flowchart for a subprogram named $TRT which accomplishes the same computation as one use of the TRT instruction. The dummy argument list is SCANORG,LSTAR,TABLE,BREAKPT,RESPCODE,TERMCODE.

Solution.   Establish an array of counters, COUNT(I) (I = 0, 1, 2), each initially zero, where COUNT(I) will accumulate the number of elements in set I. Scanning of TEXT will be from left to right, and is interrupted each time a member of one of the designated sets is detected. On each interruption, one and only one of the counts will be incremented. Scanning will be resumed, after each interruption and incrementing of a count, until the scan pointer reaches the last element of TEXT for which the address is held in SCANEND. We utilize the subprogram $TRT to facilitate scanning. Our flowchart is then a control for repeated use of the TRT instruction. In it, we denote by ACT(RESPCODE) a one-argument subprogram which provides the fitting action to be taken on termination of the TRT instruction, depending on the value of the response code. That action will be provided subsequently.

Let J be an internal character code. If J represents a member of the Ith set for I = 0, 1, 2, then the byte at TABLE + J contains binary 4I + 4. If J is not in one of the named sets, let the byte at TABLE + J contain binary zero. Then

```
L   10,COUNT-4(2)
LA  10,1(10)
ST  10,COUNT-4(2)
```

will accomplish the counting in ACT(RESPCODE).

A more versatile way to use the response code is by means of a *jump table,* for then each response can have its own flavor. The jump table is an array of jumps to distinct program segments, each providing its own unique response. Then the index in register 2 is used to select the correct jump.

```
BAL  14,JMPTAB-4(2)
                .
                .
                .
JMPTAB  B    RESP0
        B    RESP1
        B    RESP2
```

In this case, each response can be a segment of arbitrary length which could return via register 14 to the next line; in some cases it is helpful to branch to a special place such as an error routine.

In Program 6.8.1, we have an implementation of SETCOUNT as diagrammed in Figure 6.8.2. For instructional purposes, it uses a jump table to select among responses. Each of the subroutines invoked by SETCOUNT is implemented as in-line code.

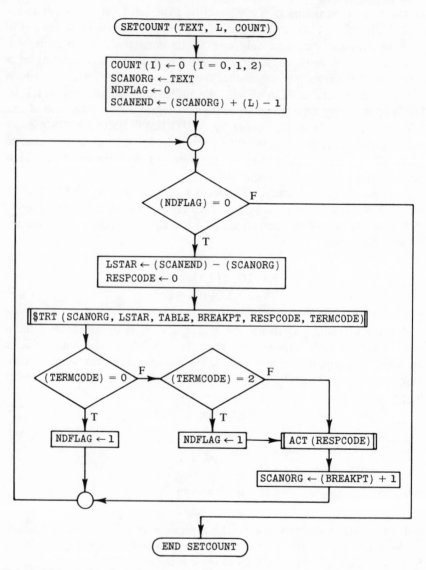

Figure 6.8.2   A flowchart for counting the occurrences of set members in a string of length L beginning at TEXT.

```
STMT           SOURCE STATEMENT

   1 SETCOUNT CSECT
   2          STM   14,12,12(13)
   3          BALR  12,0
   4          USING *,12
   5          LA    10,SAVE
   6          ST    13,4(10)
   7          ST    10,8(13)
   8          LR    13,10
   9          SR    11,11
  10          LM    1,3,0(1)        ARGUMENTS ARE TEXT,L,COUNT
  11          LA    10,8
  12 ZROCOUNT ST    11,0(10,3)⎤
  13          S     10,FOUR   ⎬    SETS THREE COUNTS TO ZERO
  14          BNL   ZROCOUNT  ⎦
  15          MVI   NDFLAG,X'00'
  16          L     4,0(2)          L
  17          S     4,ONE           L-1
  18          LA    5,0(1,4)        SCANEND
  19 ONEUSE   CLI   NDFLAG,X'00'
  20          BNE   OUT
  21          LR    4,5
  22          SR    2,2             RESPCODE←0
  23          SR    4,1             LSTAR←SCANEND – SCANORG
  24          EX    4,SCAN
  25          BZ    OFFND
  26          BM    ACTION
  27          MVI   NDFLAG,X'01'
  28 ACTION   LA    10,1
  29          BAL   14,JMPTAB-4(2)
  30          LA    1,1(1)          SCANORG←BREAKPT + 1
  31          B     ONEUSE
  32 OFFND    MVI   NDFLAG,X'01'
  33          B     ONEUSE
  34 JMPTAB   B     RESP0
  35          B     RESP1
  36          B     RESP2
  37 RESP0    A     10,0(3)         INCREMENT COUNT(0)
  38          ST    10,0(3)
  39          BR    14
```

Program 6.8.1   Using the TRT instruction and a response table (which was constructed with twenty DC statements), a string named TEXT in an associated driver program is scanned for characters belonging to the sets {0,1,2,. . . ,9}, {A,E,I,O,U}, {+,−,*,/}. The jump table beginning at statement number 34 and ending with statement number 36 is an elementary example of a selection among alternatives by means of a jump to an address determined by the response code, a technique which requires no comparisons to be made to implement the selection. Program is continued on next page.

```
STMT          SOURCE STATEMENT

40 RESP1     A     10,4(3)          INCREMENT COUNT(1)
41           ST    10,4(3)
42           BR    14
43 RESP2     A     10,8(3)          INCREMENT COUNT(2)
44           ST    10,8(3)
45           BR    14
46 SCAN      TRT   0(0,1),TABLE
47 OUT       L     13,SAVE+4
48           LM    14,12,12(13)
49           BR    14
50 TABLE     DC    78X'00'
51           DC    X'0C'            +
52           DC    13X'00'
53           DC    X'0C'            *
54           DC    3X'00'
55           DC    X'0C'            -
56           DC    X'0C'            /
57           DC    95X'00'
58           DC    X'08'            A
59           DC    3X'00'
60           DC    X'08'            E
61           DC    3X'00'
62           DC    X'08'            I
63           DC    12X'00'
64           DC    X'08'            O
65           DC    13X'00'
66           DC    X'08'            U
67           DC    11X'00'
68           DC    10X'04'          0 THRU 9
69           DC    6X'00'
70 SAVE      DC    18F'0'
71 ONE       DC    F'1'
72 FOUR      DC    F'4'
73 NDFLAG    DC    C'?'
74           END
```

Program 6.8.1   *(continued)*

6.9   THE MOVE CHARACTER LONG AND COMPARE LOGICAL CHARACTER LONG INSTRUCTIONS OF THE IBM 370

In storage management activities, comparing and moving character strings is very important. However, the limitation of the MVC and CLC instructions to a maximum operand length of 256 bytes is restrictive and cumbersome. To get away from it, one needs an instruction which finds its length parameter outside the instruction; the choice made in the MVCL and CLCL instructions is to use the rightmost 24 bits of a register named in the instruction to provide length (not length decremented by one). This permits lengths up to 2^{24-1}, but it leads to another complication: one cannot initiate a gigantic character-string operation and preclude an interruption by the supervisor until the operation is ended. Rather, the supervisor must be able to save enough information at an interruption to resume the operation afterwards so that the interruption has no influence on the end result of the operation. Starting over is not the answer, since the number of tries to get to completion without interruption could be very large. What would seem appropriate would be to save in a register the address of the leftmost byte not yet responded to (one such register for each string) and to resume (after interruption) at these addresses with a corresponding reduction in length. From here it is only a short step to settle on four registers for these long-operand instructions so that each operand string has a register for a starting address and one for a length.

The considerations above, and the even–odd pairing of registers in the 360/370, make it natural to use RR format for the long-operand character-string instructions, so we have the anomaly of storage-to-storage instructions being given in register-to-register format. Table 6.9.1 defines the setting of registers required to begin execution. That table and the subsequent flowcharts use some extensions of the notational conveniences introduced in previous sections. We give them first.

Let n be an integer expression. Then $R@(n)$ is the general register numbered n, and $B@(n)$ is the byte which has n for address. Thus, if R1 is a register number, then $R@(R1)$ denotes the register, and if $R1 \neq 15$, $R@(R1 + 1)$ denotes the successor register.

Note that if the index n is stored in a word of memory and if it is to be referred to by naming its location, then this symbolism results in nested parentheses. For example, if the word is labeled INDEX, then we use

Register segment	Symbolic name	Contents prior to execution
$R@(R1)_{8:31}$	A1	Beginning address for first operand
$R@(R1+1)_{8:31}$	L1	Length of first operand
$R@(R2)_{8:31}$	A2	Beginning address for second operand
$R@(R2+1)_{0:7}$	PAD	Padding character (discussed next)
$R@(R2+1)_{8:31}$	L2	Length of second operand
$PSW_{34:35}$	CC	Condition code; it has no influence

Table 6.9.1 The controls for execution of the CLCL and MVCL character-string instructions are held in two even–odd pairs of general registers. R1 and R2 must be even numbers. $R@(R1)_{0:7}$, $R@(R2)_{0:7}$, and $PSW_{34:35}$ have no influence on execution, but the condition code does receive significant results.

(INDEX) to denote n, and either $B@(n)$ or $B@((INDEX))$ to denote the byte with address n. In the latter denotation, the outer set of parentheses delimits the argument of $B@$, while the inner set signifies "contents of." For any string S of length L, $S_{m:n}$ (also written $S(m:n)$) will be defined (if $0 \leq m \leq n \leq L - 1$) to be the string beginning m positions beyond the leftmost element of S and ending n positions beyond. We also take $S(m:n)$ to be empty if $m > n$ and $S(m)$ to mean $S(m:m)$.

The padding character PAD mentioned in Table 6.9.1 is part of a convenient shorthand for extending a string contained in storage to a length as required for an instruction operand. In the comparison command CLCL, the operand strings need to be equal in length, and, if they are not equal, the shorter is extended by occurrences of the padding character until its length equals that of the longer string. Thus, the longer string determines the maximum number of comparisons to be made. For the move command MVCL, however, only the first operand string is ever extended by occurrences of the padding character. After the second operand string is moved to the locations of the first string, then, if $(L1) > (L2)$, the $(L1) - (L2)$ remaining low-order bytes (those with higher addresses) of the first operand string are filled with repetitions of the padding character.

In explaining the maintenance of register contents in the next section, we find it important to distinguish (1) the information in the string of bytes determined by the beginning address of an operand together with the length of that operand from (2) the possibly longer string formed from it by extension with the padding character. The former will be called the *stored portion* of the operand string. That portion of the string which is formed from occurrences of the padding character we call the *generated portion* of the operand string. By *operand string* without qualifiers, we mean the catenation of the stored portion and generated portion. Either of these may be an empty string.

6.9.1 The Maintenance of Register Contents during Execution

The instructions we are describing have their own looping facilities, once through the loop accomplishing the moving or comparing at one character position in the string. In analyzing the controls for such looping, it will almost always be best to choose one observation point in the loop portion of the flowchart and observe control parameters from that viewpoint on each traversal. The following discussion assumes the observations are taken when a test to determine whether looping should continue has just been made, and the result is that another character position in each string is still to be processed.

On any traversal in the execution of the CLCL or MVCL instruction, if neither (L1) = 0 nor (L2) = 0, then the address in A1 points to a byte in the stored portion of operand string 1, and the address in A2 points to a byte in the stored portion of operand string 2. During execution, L1 contains the length of the remainder of the stored portion of the first operand string beginning at (A1), and L2 contains the length of the stored portion of the second operand string beginning at (A2). Thus, the four registers containing addresses and lengths reflect precisely the progress that has been made in the comparing or moving of characters.

With the address and length information available for both strings, an interruption due to an I/O condition or an external event is not fatal; after the interruption is cleared, execution can continue from precisely the point at which the interruption occurred.

The operand string lengths are never decremented below zero, and so a flowchart for the register-maintenance algorithm STEP uses two tests. The actual register-maintenance algorithm used in the computer may differ in some details, as illustrated in the problems at the end of the chapter. But the flowchart shown in Figure 6.9.1 is adequate for both the CLCL and MVCL instructions.

6.9.2   The Effect of the CLCL Instruction

If the string operands of the CLCL instruction are identical, then its only effect is that the condition code is set to zero. But a much more important capability is that if the strings are not identical, then the address register corresponding to the longer operand string contains (on termination) a pointer to locate the leftmost position at which the strings do not agree. In this case the condition code will hold the result of the comparison. The CLCL subprogram in Figure 6.9.2 specifies an algorithm which will provide these characteristics. It passes lightly over a side effect which could be important, namely, that the leftmost bytes of the two registers named in the instruction are set to zero.

6.9.3   The Effect of the MVCL Instruction

The effect of MVCL is easier to define than that of MVC, for, in the case that an element of the source string (second operand string) would be replaced before qualifying as the element to be copied (called *destructive overlap*), moving characters is inhibited. Execution then only clears byte 0 of each register operand and sets the condition code to 3.

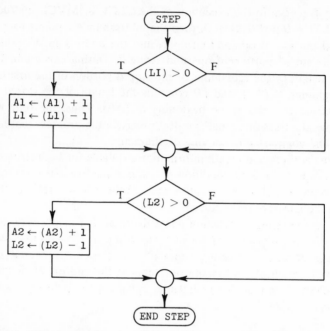

Figure 6.9.1 We picture that the STEP subprogram which updates storage string addresses and lengths is invoked on each traversal of the loop in a string comparison or move instruction except possibly the last. The termination criteria for the instructions are separate from STEP, as shown in the instruction flowcharts in Figures 6.9.2 and 6.9.3.

When there is not destructive overlap, the primary result is a straight-forward copying of the source string extended where its length (L2) is less than (L1) by occurrences of the padding character. Register pairs named in the instruction are left appropriately set for a continuation. For example, if (L2) > (L1) prior to execution, then after execution the address in A2 points to the beginning of the uncopied portion and (L2) will have been reduced to the length of the uncopied portion. In that case, one would look for another space in which to copy the remainder. Another possibility is that one is catenating several disjoint items (short strings) into one long string beginning at A1 (as in packing storage which has un-used segments). For each new item to be attached, A2 must be set by the program. If for each item, L1 is set to the length of the short string and L2 is set to the total available remaining space for the catenated string, then after the item is attached, L2 holds the available length remaining.

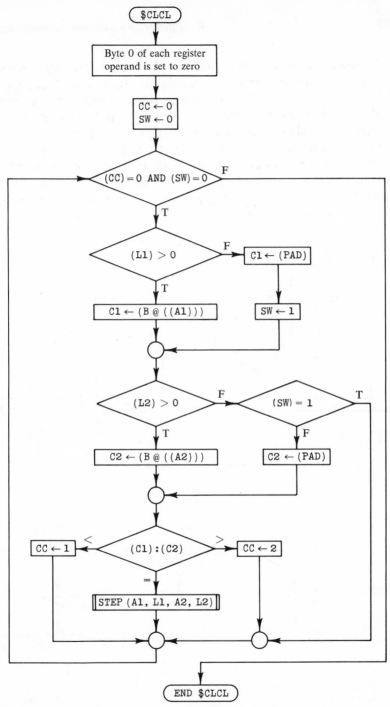

Figure 6.9.2 The invocation $CLCL(A1,L1,A2,L2,PAD,CC), when its arguments are assigned to partial registers as in Table 6.9.1, will accomplish the same as the CLCL instruction.

271

The condition code is always set by MVCL execution. While we may choose to ignore any distinction among the 0, 1, and 2 settings for (L1) = (L2), (L1) < (L2), and (L1) > (L2), respectively, we cannot safely avoid testing for condition code equal to 3 to detect whether or not the move was inhibited because conditions for destructive overlap were satisfied. The flowchart of Figure 6.9.3 represents an algorithm which is equivalent in execution to the MVCL instruction. As with the CLCL instruction, there is the side effect that the leftmost bytes of the two registers named in the instruction are set to zero even when destructive overlap inhibits the entire execution.

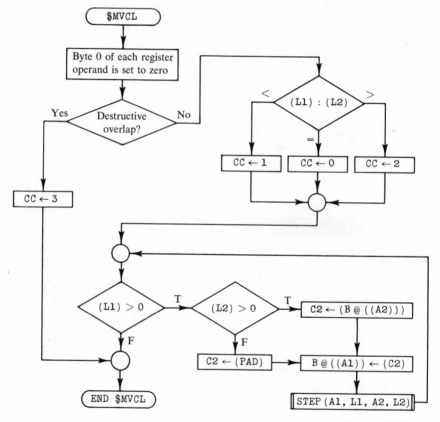

Figure 6.9.3 The invocation $MVCL (A1,L1,A2,L2,PAD,CC), when its variables are assigned to partial registers as in Table 6.9.1, will accomplish the same as the MVCL instruction.

PROBLEMS

1. If A = 10010111 and B = 01000110, find bit strings representing A AND B, A OR B, and A EX OR B.

2. Given the character string

STR = C'THERE ARE OBSTACLES AT EVERY TURN'

determine what is represented by the following:

STR(23:26) _____ STR(4:−2)   _____
STR(3:3)   _____ STR(32:24) _____
STR(15:13) _____ STR(1:5)   _____
STR(5)   _____ STR(37:36) _____

3. Given that the character string

C'THERE ARE THREE TEASPOONS IN A TABLESPOON'

is in storage beginning at a location named RULE1, what is denoted by

BYTES(RULE1, 0)
(BYTES(RULE1, 0))
BYTES(RULE1, 16:18)
(BYTES(RULE1, 16:18))
BYTES(RULE1, 42:44)
BYTES(RULE1, 4:2)

4. Write an instruction sequence to place the contents of four consecutive bytes (not necessarily on a word boundary) in a register.

5. Assume the famous quotation of Churchill made in May of 1940:

'I HAVE NOTHING TO OFFER BUT BLOOD, TOIL,
TEARS AND SWEAT'

is stored as a string beginning at a location named WINSTON. Use the move instructions to form from this sentence the "equivalent FORTRAN statement"

OFFER = BLOOD + TOIL + TEARS + SWEAT

6. It is possible to write subprograms with a variable number of arguments. The IBM FORTRAN IV convention for the 360/370 systems to mark the last address in an argument address list is to place the character X'80' in the leftmost byte of its location. Write a subprogram to sum the variables named in its actual argument list and a main program which will test it for number of arguments equal to 1, 3, and 5. For a calling program in assembler language, consider the instructions

```
DC  0F'0'
DC  X'80'
DC  AL3(LASTARG)
```

to establish the last word in the address list.

7. If the calling program in the previous exercise had been written in FORTRAN, no special arrangements for marking the end of the argument address list would have been needed. Is it reasonable to conclude that the last argument address will be so marked in every invocation of a subprogram from FORTRAN? Check this by making a snapshot of the argument address list from within a FORTRAN calling program. Do so and annotate the printout as a convenient means for stating and justifying your conclusions.

8. If a MoVe Character instruction is to be executed under control of an EXecute, its second byte (byte number one) should be zero. This suggests that, in symbolic form, the length should be given as one. Assemble an MVC instruction with length zero and with length one, and determine whether there is a difference. This can be done easily without execution. In the same program, execute an MVC under control of an EXecute instruction with −1 in the operand register and immediately SNAP the area into which the move was made. Was a 256-character string moved? What might lead a programmer to invoke an EXecute of an MVC instruction with such a length parameter?

9. Hexadecimal input is natural for BAREBONZ, but what the machine gets is character representations of the hexadecimal digits. Write an assembler program called LOADBRBZ and an input FORTRAN subprogram which provides it with twelve-character strings of characters from the first twelve columns of BAREBONZ input. The assembler program should convert these to hexadecimal instructions properly placed in a reserved area named PROGRAM so that they could be executed. Do not execute, but rather state how to do so and comment on the hazards to the system.

10. For BAREBONZ II, half-word instructions are permitted as well as full-word instructions. This means that full-word instructions may begin on half-word boundaries and complicates somewhat the placement of code in the string beginning at PROGRAM. Write and test a program named LDBRBZ2 which accomplishes everything specified in Problem 9 and allows for half-word instructions as well.

11. In assembler notation, a string constant is enclosed in apostrophes. If the string constant contains an apostrophe, its representation in assembler language is a succession of two apostrophes. The internal representation of a string will have no enclosing apostrophes and will have each succession of two apostrophes within the external string replaced by one apostrophe. Suppose that the operand field of a DC instruction is stored as a string beginning at OPFIELD, that the length of that string is stored in RANDLNGT, and the C' are its leftmost two characters. Write instructions to deposit its length in a word named BINLNGT and the internal representation of the string at BIN. Are there any conditions such that the operand field would be recognizeable as invalid?

12. Blanks may be inserted arbitrarily in FORTRAN statements for readability. These statements are easier to translate into machine language after all blanks have been removed. Removing blanks can be done by building a new string one character at a time from the characters of the source string in which nonblanks are included but blanks are omitted. Write a subprogram named DEBLANK to remove the blanks from a string and demonstrate its validity.

13. While labels in 360/370 assembler language are limited to at most eight characters, labels in PL/1 may have as many as 31. A symbol table which reserves 31 bytes for each symbol is wasteful. Instead, one may have all symbols of the table catenated into one long string and use an array of half-word pointers to mark the beginnings of the table entries. If the last pointer is to the byte just beyond the last label, then length is available as a difference of successive pointers. Write a subprogram which accepts a label and its length as input and searches the table for that label. If the label is found, it signals an error. If it is not found, the label is added to the table with appropriate adjustments in such table characteristics as length, number of entries, and final pointer.

14. To make statements conform more closely to mathematical notation, it is convenient to assign meaning to symbols in a way different from FORTRAN. As examples, it might be preferred to punch

$$A < -B = C$$

and mechanically translate this to

$$A = B.EQ.C$$

The replacement process could be ambiguous, because one must decide whether to rewrite

$$A < -B < -2$$

as

$$A = B = 2 \quad \text{(multiple assignment)}$$

or as

$$A = B.LT. -2$$

Develop a subprogram for replacement as follows:

Operator	Substitution	
$< -$	$=$	
$< =$	.LE.	
$< X$	.LT.X	(where X is not $-$ or $=$)
$X =$	X.EQ.	(where X is not $<$ or $>$)
$> =$	.GE.	
$> X$	.GT.X	(where X is not $=$)
$\neg =$	.NE.	
$\neg X$	.NOT.X	(where X is not $=$)

15. For compactness, a FORTRAN program has been converted to one long string. Statements are separated by semicolons; labeled statements have a colon between statement number and the statement it labels. Unlabeled statements begin with a colon. To prepare this program for compilation, convert the string into a sequence of FORTRAN card images:

	Columns	1–5	Statement number or blank
		6	Blank except on continuation cards
		7–72	Source field
		73–80	Label field

16. Library space is sufficiently limited that a decision is made to condense all FORTRAN programs into strings as described in the previous problem. Write a program to do this for a single FORTRAN program.

17. Suppose there is a portion of memory reserved for the closed subprograms used in conjunction with a main program. A table is maintained which contains the names of those subprograms currently in memory and for each such name a pointer to its beginning and a length. If a subprogram is no longer needed, its name and entries are removed from the table. If a new one is needed and there is space after the last entry, it is placed there. If there is not room, current holdings are consolidated toward the low address end in hopes of making room. After consolidation, the needed subprogram may fit into allotted space. If it fits, it is placed there; if it does not, then the programmer must be warned to intervene. Write a program to allocate and reallocate storage in this fashion, keeping the assignment table current throughout.

18. Suppose an input string is a statement from a higher-level language such as PL/1. A blank in such a string serves no grammatical function unless

(1) it separates two nonblanks, each of which is a letter or digit, or

(2) it is part of a string constant delimited by apostrophes (single quotes).

Since a single quote can itself be part of a string constant, a single quote inside the string constant is represented by two single quotes in succession. Write a subprogram named COMPRESS which has as first argument the name of the location of the leftmost byte of the string and as second argument its length. Execution is

(1) to move characters of the input string as far to the left as possible while deleting only unnecessary blanks, and

(2) to replace the input length by that of the compressed string. For simplicity, assume the string to be of length ≤ 256.

19. Suppose a segment of storage containing 2^{12} bytes is to be established as POOLHALL. Devise a subprogram which will (1) accept the address of the name of a BUFPARM and the length of its pool in bytes as its arguments, and (2) create a pool of that length in POOLHALL according to the plan in Section 6.5.5. Assume that the name has at most eight characters and is to be stored starting eight bytes beyond the beginning of its pool. Name the subprogram ADDPOOL. Checkout of ADDPOOL will be simplified if POOLHALL can be initialized as if it already had a list of pools with gaps separating some of them.

20. This problem builds on the previous one. It is to create a subprogram named KILLPOOL which will accept the address of the name of a BUFPARM and delete its pool from POOLHALL, adjusting pointers so that other pools in POOLHALL remain properly available. Now, use ADDPOOL and KILLPOOL to process the following sequence of POOL management actions as a reasonable test of its correctness:

Action	Pool name	Length in bytes
ADD	POOL1	100
ADD	POOL2	160
ADD	POOL3	320
KILL	POOL1	
ADD	POOL4	220
ADD	POOL5	300
KILL	POOL4	
ADD	POOL6	400
ADD	POOL7	210

21. Within a pool, there is a need for a number of items of information as can be seen from Figure 6.5.5. In a sense, the most important item is the address of BUFPARM, for the data it contains determine pool dimensions. The layout below is somewhat generous in duplicating data from BUFPARM. Let the contents of a pool be:

Leftmost byte	Parameter
0	Pointer to next buffer away from origin of POOLHALL
4	Pointer to first word beyond this pool
8	Name of BUFPARM
16	Address of BUFPARM
20	Records per buffer (computed in program)
24	QTAIL
28	INUSE
32	QHEAD
36	Buffer length in bytes
40	Number of buffers (stored in NB)
44	Logical record length
48	Pool length
$52 + 4i$	Address of buffer i, where $0 \leq i < n$
$52 + 4n + (i*\text{bufferlength})$	Beginning of buffer i, where $0 \leq i < n$
$52 + 4n + (n*\text{bufferlength}) - 1$	End of pool

One aspect of opening a communication link between a program and a data set is to establish such a pool from information contained in BUFPARM. This of course requires a definition of BUFPARM. Let it be as follows:

Leftmost byte	Parameter
0	Pool name
8	Buffer length
12	Number of buffers
16	Logical record length
20	Pool address

With these conventions, write a program to establish a pool and insert proper pointers in BUFPARM and in the pool.

22. In considering only the management of buffers and not the records within, it is appropriate to work with one record per buffer. The natural example to consider is that of reading cards and printing from their contents. The FORTRAN subroutines providing input and output will need to receive as an argument the address of the particular buffer which is to receive or transmit, since each buffer in the pool gets its turn. Set up a program which uses buffer pools on input and output for the trivial task of printing cards. It can copy directly from the INUSE buffer of the input pool to the INUSE buffer of the output pool. If it does, the program will provide a trivial example of what is called *locate mode* in the 360/370 software systems.

23. Figure 6.5.5 has been made overly complicated for the simple buffering mentioned to this point in order that it would be readily modifiable to fit the buffer swapping concept. Assume a file of information which is to be read, made current by *updating* certain items which have changed, and then written out as a revised file. There is an analogy with freight cars which are taken off-line to be unloaded and reloaded, at which time they once again are traded for an empty car into an outgoing train. To enable buffer swapping, we add one more buffer to the sketch and call it the *working buffer*. Initially, the working buffer is an area within the user program. When information is ready to be used, the address of the working buffer is interchanged with that of the inuse buffer (the inuse buffer is taken off-line). When the working buffer information has been updated and is ready for output, the working buffer address is swapped into the output pool. Revise the sketch of Figure 6.5.5 to allow for buffer swapping and revise the Next Buffer procedures for input and output accordingly.

24. In a workable system, opening a data set pipeline for a data set which already has an equivalent one should be a do-nothing operation. But opening a data set pipeline for output when it is currently opened for input should evoke diagnostics and terminate computation. Devise a plan for checking the validity of an open or close command before executing it and for including additional information in BUFPARM or pools to accommodate your plan.

25. We saw in Problem 6 that an address constant location may have its leftmost byte nonzero. The same is true of the address placed in the first operand register by a Branch After Linking instruction. There are occasions when one wants to compare address portions of two registers rather than the entire register. Assuming the leftmost eight bits need not be saved, write an instruction sequence to assure that only the addresses are compared.

26. Given that the components of an RX instruction are stored in separate words as full-word binary integers justified to the right, in cells named

OPCODE,RAND1REG,INDXREG,BASEREG,DISP

write an instruction sequence to form the numeric instruction they represent.

27. Given a single precision, floating-point number stored in a floating-point register, construct in that same register a representation for its absolute value. Consider the same construction when the number is stored in a general register. How could the number be negated in each case?

28. A bit string begins at bit 0 of the cell named FLAGS and has length 2048 bits. Let n be the index of a position in the string which is to receive

1 or 0 according as register 10 is 1 or 0. One approach is to calculate byte displacement from FLAGS by shifting n right by three. The rightmost three bits of n determine position within the byte and can be used to calculate an amount of shift or to select a mask. Determine a sequence of instructions which will accomplish the insertion for any n such that $0 \leq n < 2048$.

29. If one systematically computes the elements of a bit string from left to right, then he can deposit one character of new information in a bit string at one time and thus avoid some complexities of bit handling. Suppose the leftmost i bits of the character being formed are rightmost in a register which is elsewhere 0; then a logical left shift by one is followed by addition of 1 if and only if the condition code is nonzero. This advances by 1 the forming of one byte of a result string as required in "An Application of Log Instructions" in Section 6.6. Write such an instruction sequence and test it by manual examples.

30. As discussed in "An Application of Logic Instructions" in Section 6.6, write a program which will generate the strings of zeros and ones giving a record of all paths of length n between persons. Start with $n = 1$ and continue until a path connecting any two people (given beforehand) is found. Test your program with the strings

	A	B	C	D
A	1	0	1	0
B	0	1	0	1
C	1	0	1	0
D	0	1	1	1

Find the length of the shortest path between A and B and of the shortest between B and C.

31. Having found the length of the shortest path between two people A and B, as in Problem 30, we may ask ourselves what other persons are on paths of that length between those same people. If we have saved the strings generated on the way to finding a path of length n, we can check all persons at unit distance from B to find some which are at distance $n - 1$ from A. These persons are all on paths of length n from A to B. Any of these persons, say P_1, will suffice if all we want is one path of length n. We now seek paths of length $n - 1$ from that person to A and do so by seeking persons at unit distance from P_1 and distance $n - 2$ from A. We keep one, calling him P_2, and continue. Use the printed results from Problem 30 to make this determination by hand. If you were developing a machine program for this purpose, would it be necessary to keep all the strings in fast memory at one time? If not, suggest an order of processing to conserve memory.

32. One is confronted with conversion the instant the input and output facilities of FORTRAN are given up. Sometimes there is good reason for making the sacrifice, for these facilities require much memory and time. We can prepare for giving up the FORTRAN input and output facilities by using FORTRAN only to read 80-character strings from cards and to print 120-character strings. Then it is a simple matter to substitute macros for FORTRAN subprograms. Suppose nonnegative integers are punched in columns 1–8 of a sequence of cards, with the units position in column 8. Write an assembler language program to find their sum using binary arithmetic, and convert the result to character representation for printing. Use a FORTRAN subprogram for reading the cards and printing the result as discussed above. The number of cards is not to be specified by the program. The FORTRAN READ statement can be written

$$\text{READ(5,M,END=N) CARD}$$

in which M is the number of the corresponding format statement and N is the number of the FORTRAN statement to be executed next when the data cards are exhausted. Declare CARD to be an array of 20 full words —INTEGER CARD(20)—so that the entire card will be read in. Will blanks be read as zeros in all positions?

33. Signs of integers can be provided by a punch over the units position on the card (11 for negative, blank or 12 for positive). It should also be possible to type a unary + or − to the left of the leading digit. Extend the program in the previous problem to permit either representation with the punched + or − on the left overriding the sign above the units position in case of inconsistent data.

34. We have seen the floating-point representation of a number in Chapter 2. Assume a positive X with representation

$$X = f \cdot 16^e \qquad \text{where} \quad \tfrac{1}{16} \leq f < 1$$

Then to prepare for conversion to base 10 we should multiply a power of 10, say 10^{-p}, times this number to get a floating-point result

$$q = 10^{-p}(f \cdot 16^e) \qquad \text{where} \quad \tfrac{1}{10} \leq q < 1$$

in which case $X = q \cdot 10^{+p}$. It is important to note that the normalized machine representation of this q has exponent 0. We shall assume this adjustment has been done, so that our job is to convert the mantissa of q. This fraction can be isolated by placing q in the general registers (in a double register if X is double precision) and performing an arithmetic left shift by 7. This problem begins with a binary floating-point representation of a number q in the range $\frac{1}{10} \leq q < 1$ and requires a subprogram to convert the fraction to decimal, rounding to six places. Demonstrate its functioning on several examples by supplying E- and D-type data constants of acceptable magnitude and converting their mantissas back to decimal with your subprogram.

35. Construct the same response table as was done in Program 6.8.1 but using fewer instructions. State advantages and disadvantages of each method.

36. What features should be included in the driver program associated with Program 6.8.1?

37. In Program 6.8.1, we used the TRT instruction in searching for set members. An alternate attack on this problem uses the TRanslate instruction to replace the internal code of each character by 0 if it is not in any of these sets, by 4 if in set 0, by 8 if in set 1, and by 12 if in set 2. Note that the table for the TRanslate instruction is the same as the table previously used for TRT. It is now a simple matter to scan the resultant string in either direction and use the byte as an index to select which counter is to be incremented. Write a program to do this.

38. The TRanslate instruction can be used to decrease the size of a jump table in some instances of string analysis. Such a replacement would not be fruitful if there were a distinct response for each character. But suppose there are fewer responses, say 12: A use of the TRanslate instruction with length 1 can make available a response code which will select among 12 branch instructions. Storage required is 256 bytes for the TRanslate instruction's table and 48 for the jump table, a total of 304 bytes compared with 1024 bytes if the character selected its branch directly. Write a program of this sort for examining the first letter of a symbolic operation code and finding the address in the opcode table of those entries which begin with that letter.

39. An alternative to the method in Problem 38 is to use the TRanslate instruction to map the letters into internal character codes $00-19_{16}$ and all others into some other, say FF. Then we can translate one character at a time. A result of FF means an invalid opcode. A result in 00–19 can be used to select the starting address of its letter. Implement this method of facilitating table-lookup.

40. The TRanslate and Test instruction can be used to compress the blanks out of a FORTRAN statement. One TRT starting at a nonblank should isolate a segment to be included in the compressed string. Note that a statement containing no blanks will require only one use of the TRT instruction to scan the entire FORTRAN statement, but of course one still must determine that the remainder of the source language field is blank. Write the TRT version of the COMPRESS function (see Problem 18) and demonstrate its use.

41. Write a loop of instructions which will accomplish the moving of strings of enormous length by repeated use of the MoVe Character instruction. Try to do this in such a way that register use is like that in the MVCL instruction. In particular, the program should deal with length rather than (length − 1) and have no complications with computed lengths.

42. The CLCL instruction has a distinct advantage over CLC, for it yields a pointer to the leftmost disagreement between operand strings. It also has a capability for extending strings with a fill character. Try to find a reasonable way to accomplish the equivalent of CLCL but for strings no longer than 256 bytes, using 360 system instructions only.

43. As an extension of Problem 42, extend the effectiveness of the sequence developed there by a loop to advance through all segments of 256 bytes in which the operand strings are identical to reach a situation in which the solution of Problem 42 applies.

44. In discussing the effect of the MVCL instruction in the latter part of Section 6.9, an example of catenating several short, disjoint strings into one long string (packing storage) was given. What is the disadvantage of associating both A1 and L1 with the long string and A2 and L2 with the short strings?

45. Using the results of Problems 41 and 43, we are in a position to use the MVCL and CLCL instructions even if our computer does not have them in its instruction set. Assume there is an 8K segment of directly addressable memory throughout which programs have been deposited. The problem is to consolidate them into the lower end (smaller addresses) of the space, leaving a large single segment of memory available at the top. Current assignments are given in a table symbolized as follows:

Eight-character name	Beginning address	Ending address
A	A_B	A_E
B	B_B	B_E
C	C_B	C_E

Since it is easy to cut a string and insert an entry, given the MVCL instruction, we assume that the names in the table are ordered lexicographically although their addresses may not be in numerical order. Write a program to consolidate memory and update the table.

46.   Given a segment named ROSCOE, and a table as shown in Problem 45, search the table for the unused memory segment of minimum address nearest the bottom of memory which is long enough to accommodate ROSCOE. If there is one, insert the entry for ROSCOE into the table and move ROSCOE into place. If there is no suitable unused segment, apply the tactics of the previous exercise and then test whether ROSCOE will fit.

47.   Suppose parts of a program are being overwritten during execution and it is not clear when this is done nor how this is caused. A desperation measure is to make a copy of the program as it is loaded into core, and then at strategic times during execution compare the program as it is to the way it was when loaded. Once a discrepancy is found, save enough information to tell how far advanced execution was and where the discrepancies are. Develop a plan for this method of finding trouble.

Chapter 7

Instruction Execution Times and Factors Affecting Them

7.1 INTRODUCTION

There is hardly an instruction sequence that cannot be replaced by another which accomplishes results just as appropriate, though perhaps not identical. Even when the instruction set is severely limited, we find alternative methods from which to select. For example, suppose it is desired to multiply an integer in register 11 by five. We might consider three possibilities:

```
1. LR   10,11        2. M 10,=F'5'        3. LR  10,11
   SLA 11,2                                   AR 11,11
   AR   11,10                                 AR 11,11
                                              AR 11,10
```

The choice may be inconsequential. On the other hand, if the number is so large that overflow is possible, or if we desire to preserve the original in register 10, then the second possibility looks poor. But what about execution time—is there a difference? What about storage requirements? In this case data storage is about the same for each sequence, since the constant 5 used in the second sequence is probably useful elsewhere, but the sequences take 4, 2, and 4 half words, respectively, for program statements and that can be important.

The string-oriented instructions of the previous chapter offer opportunities galore to do things in alternate ways. We noted some of these in character move instructions. We know that there is a choice between binary and decimal arithmetic (also floating point, discussed in Chapter 8), since instructions are available for each. With respect to bit strings, we might weigh the advantages of register-shift instructions (which are at bit level) versus the operations of logic for bit manipulation.

As in all complex situations, there is no easy answer, but at least we can build a foundation for choice by assembling some pertinent information. What we need most is comparative instruction times. On early computers, these times were readily available, but recent trends in computer construction have made the information more difficult to supply and more complex to apply. As a consequence, instruction timing has often been neglected.

The IBM 360/370 systems represent a broad class of actual computers which may differ widely in computing power but have a common architecture (organization) detailing such things as instruction set, register set, word size, addressing scheme, internal character representation, data channels, and interrupt facilities. One may claim that it is improper to consider the 370 to have the same architecture as the 360, for one can construct programs which will run on every model of the 370 and will not run on any model of the 360. But the total effort of describing two such similar organizations is minimized by considering the IBM 370 organization to be that which we attribute to both machines (and identified as IBM 360/370 organization) with a few special features which pertain mainly to hardware reliability and the operating system. Until now, the only programming mentioned in this text which would be modified on the 370 is that pertaining to character-string moves and comparisons. The MoVe Character Long and Compare Logical Character Long instructions which were treated in some detail in Section 6.9 are distinct improvements over their 360 counterparts.

Two computers may be identical in organization and yet differ vastly in speed of computation; this is true of implementations of the IBM 360/370 organization. There are several different models of the central processor with this architecture. Not only do they vary in overall processing power, but ratios of instruction times will vary from one model to another. For example, lower-speed models may have no special registers in the central processor, but instead substitute reserved words in memory; in this case, some of the speed advantage of RR instructions over RX instructions is lost. Some models may have serial data transfer where others use parallel transfer. The fastest models have a very high-speed buffer in which currently applicable program segments and data areas may be held, thus gaining a factor of as much as 10 in speed by replacing main memory access time with buffer access time.

Speed comparisons between different machines (in contrast to comparisons between distinct ways of programming a task on the same machine) become increasingly difficult as various means are introduced to overlap steps we have previously considered sequential. These include overlapping memory accesses by interleaving memory banks, buffering memory accesses, decoding instructions while their predecessors are being executed, and taking advantage of every possible special case in instruction execution (such as zero digits in a multiplier). With unlike implementations, it may be necessary to compare execution times for typical programs rather than for individual instructions in order to obtain a valid estimate of computing power. This is especially appropriate in the sense that the relative frequency of use of different instructions varies from one application to another, and this frequency may not be known to the evaluator.

Within the 360/370 systems there are several major results of such contrasts as we have mentioned among machines:

1. The organization is usually documented for the 360 system with add-ons for the 370 system.

2. With some exceptions, software is also documented for 360 systems with add-ons for 370 system software.

3. Model-dependent data are documented separately (and are less widely distributed).

4. Timing comparisons of instruction sequences must be made with a particular model, and for different models may yield contradictory results.

In spite of these complications, we consider it important to make some comparisons of time consumed by alternate instruction sequences for a particular model, at the same time gaining some impression of "absolute" computing power. Times which we obtain should be roughly verifiable by experiment on a computer, a subject we cannot now explore but worthy of investigation. However, when a computer is shared by several active programs, the time kept by the operating system as one's use of the central processor will include some which permits input and output to be interlaced with computation. Again, large systems may have one directly addressable memory of highest speed, and another which is much larger and slower. Clearly, one must know in which of these his program and data reside during execution in order to obtain valid comparisons, and even then he may not be able to eliminate a variability among sums of as much as 20%.

General Observations about Instruction Times

It is easy to succumb to the notion that computers are so fast that it makes no difference how a program is written; one can also fall prey to the game of writing a program with so much emphasis on speed of computation that the program is unintelligible, unmodifiable, and perhaps very difficult to use. We hope to establish a middle ground so as to recognize particular situations in which attention to timing is valuable, as well as others where it is a minor consideration. Some actual times will provide a helpful background.

We can look to the peripherals of a computer for examples of high-speed electromechanical devices. A good card reader may read 800 cards/min; a line printer may print 1200 lines/min. Considering the mechanical element, these times of 0.075 sec per card read and 0.050 sec per line printed are spectacular. When, as in these examples, measured times become a small fraction of the unit of measure, it is convenient to introduce a smaller time unit. The millisecond (msec), equal to 1/1000 sec, is appropriate to high-speed electromechanical devices. The card read and line print times given above are then stated as 75 and 50 msec.

Devices which are purely electronic obsolete even the millisecond as a unit of time. Instruction execution times for run-of-the-mill computers require that a still smaller unit, the microsecond (μsec), equal to 10^{-6} sec, be introduced. We will see that individual instruction times are quite conveniently expressed in units of microseconds, and that larger machines execute some of their instructions in well under 1 μsec. The fact is that still another unit, the nanosecond (nsec), equal to 10^{-9} sec, is getting wide usage. One finds that register access time on the IBM 360 model 85 and on the IBM 370 model 168 is 80 nsec, for example. Recalling that the speed of light is approximately $3 \cdot 10^8$ m/sec, we find that light should travel only 0.3 meters in one nanosecond. Truly, there is blazing speed in electronic computers.

Expensive as machines may be, a programmer cannot justify striving to improve program performance by timing considerations on individual instructions except in highly repetitive portions of the program. This justifies a widely accepted practice of using higher-level languages in developing a program, and then using machine-level programming to improve the most frequently executed segments. Even though there may appear to be some spectacular gains in certain instances from replacement of selected segments in this way, these gains may be more than offset by the difficulty of adapting the program to other machines the complications of debugging, and the inflexibility of the completed program with respect to modification. Burroughs pioneered the development of general-purpose computer systems with hardware designed for the direct use of higher-level languages. In fact, the B5000 announced in 1960, and its successors, the B6700 and B7700, have *no* machine-level facilities available to the user. All systems software, including the operating system, are written in an extension to ALGOL 60. Clearly, the role of assembler language in future systems may be less significant than in the 360/370 systems. For the time being, there is no better language in which to explore hardware concepts as they influence computation speed. That is our current objective.

We preface all considerations of timing by the caution that instruction execution time is a proper concern only in the innermost loops of programs which are costly in execution time. But we can demonstrate that there are such programs. Among these, we cite assemblers, compilers, operating supervisors, natural language translators, and programs in artificial intelligence (theorem proving and chess playing are examples), in simulation of ecological systems, in weather forecasting, and in many other scientific and engineering problems. Execution time becomes important in another way in applying a medium-capacity computer system to monitoring a real-time process when computation must be sandwiched in between servicing of demanding sensing devices.

7.2   COMPUTER CHARACTERISTICS INFLUENCING
INSTRUCTION TIMES

There are some fundamental constants of a computer which are reflected in instruction execution times. Their values will help one to understand the variations in execution times from one instruction to another on a given machine model, and from one machine model to another for a given instruction. Since a part of the art of getting high-speed computation from a given hardware configuration is to overlap nominally sequential portions of the execution of an instruction or of sequential instructions, we cannot expect the few characteristics we name in Table 7.2.1 to determine execution times; but they will help understanding.

	IBM 360 models		IBM 370 models	
	30	85	135	155
CPU machine cycle	1	0.08	0.165	0.115
Register access time	8	0.08	NA	NA
Main memory cycle	2	1.04	0.275:1.43	NA
Bytes per memory access	1	16	2:4	16
Second indexing time	6	0	0.44:3.46	0.115
Memory buffer access time		0.08		0.600

Table 7.2.1 These times, given in microseconds, provide some selected computer characteristics influencing execution times for four models of the IBM 360/370 systems. (NA: No information available through normal IBM channels.)

In Table 7.2.1, we assume the first three items are self-explanatory. When the number of bytes per memory reference is less than four, it indicates that a word-oriented instruction will require multiple accesses to obtain a full-word operand from memory or to deposit one there. Getting 16 bytes in one reference, as in the models 85 and 155, may be helpful in obtaining several instructions at a time, or in loading a buffer store, but for four-byte operands may save nothing in data movement. The fifth line of the table assumes that the use of a register other than 0 for an index or base constitutes a first indexing; if an indexable instruction names both index and base registers other than zero, we have a second indexing. Instruction times we consider will include one indexing but not a second.

Larger machines of the 360/370 systems have extremely high-speed memory buffers into which currently used portions of memory are automatically copied. These buffers are transparent to the programmer, because they cannot be referenced for either access or storage from a user-level program. The last line of Table 7.2.1 pertains to these buffers. Both instruction access and data movement times can be enhanced by a factor of three or four by such buffers. Their time savings will be program dependent, as can be seen by considering a program in which every other instruction is a jump. Having available a sequence of instructions in the buffer will be an advantage only if several instructions consecutive in memory are executed in sequence.

Times we will give for instruction execution assume that instructions and data reside in the storage which would minimize execution time (in the storage buffer if there is one). In some installations, user programs and data reside in a byte-addressable mass memory which is slower. For relations between instruction sequences on the same machine, this may not be important, but for valid comparisons between machine models, one must adjust for such practices (which are not characteristics of the computer, but of how it is used).

It would be a very complex assignment to try to establish and use a consistent practice for computing effective instruction times. Execution time can depend in intricate ways on the operands for an instruction. Every table of times makes some statistical assumptions about the operand digits, and the assumptions can differ from one manual to the next. So when we accept execution times from manuals for various models, we must remember that only large percentage differences are significant. Simplification of tables of execution times must be done with the assumptions clearly stated, or misunderstanding will result.

For use in evaluating elapsed times for particular sequences of instructions, and as an instance of technological advancement, we show in Appendix F the execution times for the model 158 replacement for the 155. But aside from being able to apply these times to an existing sequence of instructions, we need to develop intuition for constructing efficient sequences based on comparative times. One approach to this is to construct several tables, each designed to look at execution times from a different viewpoint. No one of them is definitive or complete, but as an introduction they can prompt some conclusions. Each table described below serves to contrast properties of four models of the 360/370 systems. Their functions are as follows:

Table 7.2.2   To display the variation of execution times for word-oriented instructions with the complexity of the operation. For this reason, we select register operand instructions to eliminate memory access time where possible.

Table 7.2.3   To show the effect of memory access requirements on instruction execution times.

Table 7.2.4   To determine where shift operations may be effective.

Table 7.2.5   To display the execution times of some of the SS instructions in the expectation that they may not only far surpass the word-oriented instructions in character string processing but may even compete favorably in some aspects of word-oriented computation.

We can conclude the following about instructions which use only register operands:

1. In the sense that using the most straightforward instruction is desirable for reasons of clarity, it is not a bad approximation to consider all operations except those in multiply, divide, and convert instructions to be of equal speed.

	IBM 360		IBM 370	
	30	85	135	155
LA	25	0.16	2.021	0.499
NR	30	0.08	2.090	0.844
LR	22	0.08	1.375	0.384
LTR	28	0.08	2.063	0.384
CR	26	0.08	2.200	0.384
AR	29	0.08	2.503	0.499
MR	304	0.78	23.815	3.489:9.469
DR	550	1.96	40.212	9.354
LER	23	0.08	3.740	0.844
LTER	25	0.08	4.290	0.729
CER	55	0.32	13.039	2.523
AER	65	0.38	13.559	2.255
MER	310	1.15	32.072	6.778
DER	390	1.64	49.225	8.952
LDR	39	0.08	5.225	0.844
LTDR	42	0.08	6.050	0.959
CDR	87	0.24	14.828	2.476
ADR	105	0.30	16.077	2.230
MDR	1050	1.87	49.397	15.219
DDR	2180	2.65	77.935	23.269
CVB	118:382	0.40:1.20	25.2:70.1	8.47:12.15
CVD	61:381	0.64:1.92	12.5:170.9	8.47:12.15

Table 7.2.2 Here we display execution times (in microseconds) for instructions of varying complexity, eliminating memory access time as a factor by permitting only register operands. Three kinds of arithmetic are represented—integer, single-word floating point, and double-word floating point. Floating-point arithmetic is discussed in detail in Chapter 8. For now, we are concerned only with comparing its execution times to those of integer arithmetic.

2. Using several (five to ten) instructions of a simpler type to avoid a multiplication or a division is worth consideration. Division is especially costly so that its replacement by one multiplication, if possible, may be worthwhile.

3. Logic instructions (such as NR) are usually a little more costly than integer arithmetic, but if one logic instruction can replace any two other instructions it is appropriate.

4. The floating-point multiply and divide with one-word operands (MER and DER) are nearly as fast and sometimes faster than their binary integer parallels (MR and DR). Even floating point with long operands appears to be tolerable when one considers that only a small proportion of instructions in a problem are actually directly associated with the arithmetic of the problem, most of them being overhead. Note that the model 85

is designed for efficient use of long floating-point operands, and on some operations it requires less time for long than for short operands. The merits of floating-point arithmetic will be considered in Chapter 8.

5. Slow as it may seem, one ConVert instruction replaces a whole sequence of multiplications or divisions, and hence its use saves program space as well as time when binary arithmetic is used.

6. One can estimate from the table that word-oriented instructions of the model 85 are typically 300 times as fast as those of the model 30. In Table 7.2.5, we find much less dramatic ratios of speeds for character-string instructions. Such contrasts make programming techniques for economy of execution dependent on machine model.

7. Execution time comparisons such as in Table 7.2.2 will tell little about the architectural contrasts between 360 and 370 models, for every instruction of the 360 is also an instruction of the 370. The contrast is really in a few instructions and in addressing features (virtual memory) which the 370 has and the 360 does not have.

With respect to instructions requiring a memory access as opposed to instructions using only register operands one can see in Table 7.2.3 that

	IBM 360		IBM 370	
	30	85	135	155
NR	30	0.08	2.090	0.844
N	40	0.16	3.671	1.223
LR	22	0.08	1.375	0.384
L	32	0.16	2.956	0.648
CR	26	0.08	2.200	0.384
C	39	0.16	3.781	0.763
AR	29	0.08	2.503	0.499
A	39	0.16	4.084	0.993
MR	304	0.78	23.815	3.489:9.469
M	313	0.78	25.396	4.098:10.078
LER	23	0.08	3.740	0.844
LE	33	0.16	4.056	0.993
CER	55	0.32	13.039	2.523
CE	65	0.32	13.081	3.017
AER	65	0.38	13.559	2.255
AE	75	0.38	13.601	2.749
MER	310	1.15	32.072	6.778
ME	320	1.15	32.113	7.387

Table 7.2.3   This sampling of instructions shows that a one-word memory access usually increases execution time over that for the same operation with no memory access by approximately the time required for a one-word access to memory (to memory buffer store if there is one). Long executions on high-speed models may hide this effect.

the completely serial machine tends to be more predictable than those incorporating parallelism. Note that on the model 30 a memory reference consistently costs 10 μsec. On the simpler instructions of the model 85, a memory reference requires an additional buffer access and therefore more time. However, its more complex instructions suffer no penalty in time for a memory access. The 135 and 155 models are both intermediate between these extremes. The times recorded for them show just the opposite effect, namely the slower machine has been able to mask the time for memory access on complex instructions while the faster has not.

Given any machine model in which memory accesses are costly in execution time, one can consider using programming techniques to minimize their number. Some suggested ways to do this are:

1. Save an intermediate result in a register rather than in memory if it will be an operand shortly.

2. Use the Load Address instruction to provide constants from within the instruction (see Section 4.6.4 for a discussion of constants) rather than from storage. This works for nonnegative integers less than 4096.

3. Since getting an item via an explicit base may require loading that base from memory each time it is needed, consider holding the item in a register or storing it in a working storage accessed with implicit base.

4. If m items or more are to be stored from registers in consecutive locations ($2 \leq m \leq 15$), the STore Multiple instruction will usually do it faster than successive stores of individual words and may merit arrangement of data storage accordingly.

Shifting in the general registers was the only means in early machines for rearranging bit strings. It had an additional use there as a high-speed

	IBM 360		IBM 370	
	30	85	135	155
SLA	62:93	0.12	6.339:35.874	1.495:5.635
SRA	62:72	0.12	6.339:23.527	1.380:3.795
SLL	58:68	0.12	5.651:25.424	1.035:4.945
SRL	58:68	0.12	5.651:23.804	1.035:3.220
SLDA	104:145	0.12	7.274:41.099	1.725:8.28
SRDA	104:124	0.12	7.274:28.092	1.725:6.21
SLDL	98:118	0.12	6.586:30.649	1.380:5.635
SRDL	98:118	0.12	6.586:28.369	1.380:3.565

Tables 7.2.4 This table gives bounds on times, in microseconds, for the eight shift instructions, since actual times fluctuate strongly on most models with the bits in the binary representation of the amount of shift.

device for multiplying or dividing by a power of two. Now we have alternative instructions for bit string modification, the logic instructions, and we are in a position to evaluate the advantages of shifting over multiplication. Unfortunately, the time required for a shift is highly dependent on the amount of shift and the complex time formulas are not very helpful. To glean something from them without undue detail, we have recorded in Table 7.2.4 for each type of shift its minimum and maximum execution times.

While individual cases would have to be timed with precise attention to the amount of shift involved, we have enough information in this table to formulate some general principles about shift instructions:

1. Shifting will hardly ever compete with the logic operations for bit string rearrangement since the shifting instructions are likely to be more time consuming and less powerful.

2. Shifting will multiply a number in a general register by a power of two more rapidly than the Multiply instruction in three models, and almost always on the 135. There will be special cases where the advantage is trivial or even reversed.

3. Shifting by 32 places is a poor choice as a replacement for the Load Register instruction in moving information.

4. Because of its specialized use in positioning a dividend for integer division we observe that the times for an arithmetic shift right of 32 positions is 104 for the model 30, 0.12 for the model 85, 12.2 for the model 135, and 3.68 or 3.91 for the 155. The alternative of a multiplication by one is not at all competitive on the first three models, but on the 155 it is almost as good.

5. Maximum times for arithmetic left shifts are consistently longer than for the corresponding right shifts. Also, arithmetic shifts take longer than logical shifts. One can appreciate why these observations are reasonable by considering that arithmetic left shifts must detect any nonzero bit shifted off the left end while arithmetic right shifts only need to fill vacated positions with the sign bit. Of course logical shift instructions do neither of these.

The most powerful and time-consuming instructions are the memory-to-memory (SS-type) instructions. Each of these instructions is powerful enough to require a considerable sequence of other instructions to be equivalent; but the SS-type instructions are efficient enough so that the actual replacement would not often be profitable. Table 7.2.5 shows the execution times of some of these powerful instructions.

	IBM 360		IBM 370	
	30	85	135	155
CLC	$43 + 5K$	$0.51 + 0.08K + 0.05N$	$6.353 + 1.568K$	$1.886 + 0.167K + 0.5(N/8)$
MVC	$40 + 4N$	$0.77 + 0.033N$	$5.541 + 0.990N$	$1.979 + 0.265N + 0.834(N/8)$
PACK	$41 + 3(N_1 + N_2)$	$0.85 + 0.17N$	$6.889 + 5.638N_1$	$2.430 + 0.259N_1 + 0.073N_2$
UNPK	$41 + 3(N_1 + N_2)$	$0.95 + 0.08N$	$9.694 + 3.108N_1$	$2.580 + 0.219N_1 + 0.073N_2$
TR	$41 + 7N$	$0.79 + 0.25N$	$4.606 + 4.318N$	$2.480 + 0.647N + 0.505(N/8)$
TRT	$51 + 8K$	$0.89 + 0.24K + 0.07N$	$6.971 + 4.07K$	$2.370 + 0.690K + 0.505(N/8)$
NC	$43 + 5N$	$0.816 + 0.104N$	$10.189 + 2.448N$	$1.900 + 0.306N + 0.505\,(N/8)$
CLCL			$33.6 + 2.365K + \cdots$	$(N_1/256)3.8 + 0.402K + \cdots$
MVCL			$34.30 + 0.990K + \cdots$	$(N_1/256)8.66 + 0.325N + \cdots$

Table 7.2.5. This table shows the execution times in microseconds of some of the memory-to-memory instructions of different models in the 360/370 systems. N_1, number of bytes in first operand; N_2, number of bytes in second operand; K, total number of bytes of the first operand which are processed; N, total number of bytes of the first operand for instructions with a single field length; the terms $N/8$ and $N_1/256$ must be rounded to the next higher integer.

We find from the string operations shown in Table 7.2.5 that each one has an initial overhead in getting started but that the cost in time per byte decreases rapidly with the number of bytes in the strings being processed. Even the starting overhead takes little more time than a Load, STore sequence so that other considerations (no use of general registers and clarity of purpose) may make string moves preferable to word-oriented moves.

Table 7.2.5 shows the model 30 to be within a factor of 50 of the model 85 in speed for most string operations. Since we found the ratio of arithmetic speed of the model 85 to that of the model 30 to be about 300, we should expect string operations to have a special emphasis in model 30 programming. The 370 models 135 and 155 are more difficult to compare. While the 155 advantage for startup in string operations is not dramatic, its character rate from then on is excellent by comparison. Operations with long strings will tend to display the model 155 to advantage. These comparisons show that programming patterns must be adjusted from one machine model to another to get the best results.

The special 370 instructions CLCL and MVCL (Table 7.2.5) are much more expensive in startup as well as in time per byte than CLC and MVC, respectively. The more powerful instructions are probably more economical to use where their features are utilized, but where the simpler instructions suffice they should still be used both for execution time savings and to minimize unnecessary traffic through the registers.

7.3 SOME ALTERNATIVE SEQUENCES OF INSTRUCTIONS

This section consists of four examples. The purposes of the examples are to compare the merits of alternate instruction sequences to accomplish the same task (allowing for minor variations in effects on auxiliary registers and in exception responses) and also to compare speeds of various machine models. The third example is limited to comparing machine execution times on a particular sequence but does provide some insight into the merits of macros, while the fourth example displays the overhead in looping versus straight-line coding.

Execution time is only one aspect of the cost to develop and use a sequence of instructions. Enlightened programming will take into account "overall costs" including debugging, validation, documentation, and perhaps other costs of a less quantitative nature. One of the costs which is difficult to quantify is the intricate use of instructions. When a large number of persons are likely to examine an instruction sequence (as in a text example or in a widely distributed or continually reworked program) one should place a high premium on readability and be willing to sacrifice execution time to gain it.

Example 1. Multiplication by a decimal digit.

We will examine the merits of the three alternate ways of multiplying by 5 given in Section 7.1.

		360		370	
		30	85	135	155
1.	LR 10,11	22	0.08	1.375	0.384
	SLA 11,2	62	0.12	8.869	1.955
	AR 11,10	29	0.08	2.503	0.499
		113	0.28	12.747	2.838
2.	M 10,=F'5'	313	0.78	25.396	5.018
3.	LR 10,11	22	0.08	1.375	0.384
	AR 11,11	29	0.08	2.503	0.499
	AR 11,11	29	0.08	2.503	0.499
	AR 11,10	29	0.08	2.503	0.499
		109	0.32	8.884	1.881

Note that, on the model 85, the fastest method is the first and, on the other machines listed, it is the third. The most readable, however, is the second method. For initial program debugging, and for programs in which the execution time of the operation is not so crucial, the second method is preferable.

Example 2.   Initialization of memory.

We will initialize a word at location B with the constant in location A using two methods.

		360		370	
		30	85	135	155
1. L	10,A	32	0.16	2.956	0.533
ST	10,B	32	0.32	3.231	0.460
		64	0.48	6.187	0.993
2. MVC B(4),A		56	0.87	9.501	3.873

The primary conclusion to be drawn from this example is that, even though the MoVe Character instruction is not at its best (compared to word-oriented instructions) in moving short strings which conform to word boundaries, it does remarkably well. Its other advantages of requiring no general register involvement, of being easily understood, and of requiring fewer bytes for program, justify its selection in many cases. In fact, since initialization is not ordinarily a part of the innermost iteration, we find it difficult to imagine a program being executed enough times that a saving of a few microseconds on each initialization can make up for the programmer effort incurred in avoiding the MoVe Character instruction. We recommend a standard practice of using the MoVe Character instruction for all similar initialization.

Example 3.   The overhead of closed subprograms.

One choice a programmer faces is that of creating a closed subprogram for a simple task versus repeating a coding pattern in several places (or writing a macro which will repeat it automatically). Although there are intermediate possibilities, we assume a standardized sequence for saving register contents. The overhead instructions are:

```
LA      1,ARGLIST        ⎫
L       15,=V(SUBR)      ⎬   In the calling program
BALR    14,15            ⎭
STM     14,12,12(13)     ⎫
BALR    12,0             ⎪
USING   *,12             ⎪
LA      11,SAVE          ⎬   Prologue in called program
ST      13,4(11)         ⎪
ST      11,8(13)         ⎪
LR      13,11            ⎭
L       13,SAVE+4        ⎫
LM      14,12,12(13)     ⎬   Epilogue in the called program
BR      14               ⎭
```

Of course, any use of parameters would require additional overhead instructions to transmit them. The execution times for this sequence are
given in the following table for the 360/30 and the 370/155.

	360/30	370/155
LA 1,ARGLIST	25.00	0.384
L 15,=V(SUBR)	32.00	0.533
BALR 14,15	24.00	0.959
STM 14,12,12(13)	257.00	28.479
BALR 12,0	19.00	0.729
LA 11,SAVE	25.00	0.384
ST 13,4(11)	32.00	0.460
ST 11,8(13)	32.00	1.960
LR 13,11	22.00	0.384
L 13,SAVE+4	32.00	0.533
LM 14,12,12(13)	256.00	17.313
BR 14	14.00	0.729
	770.00	52.847

These computations suggest that macros, which have no such linkage
overhead during execution, will be favored in inner loops over closed
subprograms, for in any program large enough to make execution time
critical a loss of 25 to 50 storage-to-register addition times is bound to be
important.

Example 4.   The effective time for an addition of integers.

In Program 4.3.1 we have a simple example of a loop which sums the
elements of an array. By incrementing before testing and using a nonde-

structive compare instruction for testing, we arrive at the four-instruction sequence which will perform the sum in a loop†:

```
LOOP A   10,GRADES(1)
     LA  1,4(1)
     C   1,TESTVAL
     BNH LOOP
```

For a many-element array, other instructions in that program are of little import. The computation time is essentially the product of the number of elements in the array and the time for one traversal of the loop. We time it as follows:

	360/30	370/155
LOOP A 10,GRADES(1)	45	0.993
LA 1,4(1)	25	0.384
C 1,TESTVAL	39	0.648
BNH LOOP	22	0.878
	131	2.903

These times are a fair measure of the arithmetic addition time on each machine, for there is no meaningful way to avoid the incrementing, testing, and branching required for a sequence of additions. Of course, a loop may control the execution of several arithmetic operations on each traversal and in this way achieve better effective times.

7.4 SUMMARY

A casual introduction to estimating execution time such as we have given can do little more than establish grounds for some working principles. Even so, we find it important that a programmer know whether he is wringing his hands over pennies or dollars, and in what direction to explore for time savings if they really are essential. Conclusions we feel it appropriate to set forth for consideration are:

1. Sacrifice clarity or expend memory to save execution time only on innermost loops of oft-repeated programs.

---

† The overhead in a structured version of this sequence would be higher since two branching instructions would be required. There are composite instructions which can lower our estimates somewhat, so we have chosen to estimate low here by testing at the end.

2. Sacrifice execution time for clarity or to save memory willingly except in innermost loops.

3. Consider string-oriented instructions for data movement to deemphasize register use without excessive cost.

4. Consider macros as highly advantageous over closed subprograms if the job to be done is small.

5. Consider straight-line coding to avoid looping if it does not make a program too inflexible.

The examples of this chapter should provide adequate guidance for the programmer to investigate the merits of his own special shortcuts. Some may be suggested by the exercises in this chapter. There will be excellent opportunities to use the techniques in Chapter 8, for there we introduce specialized arithmetic instructions (decimal for accountants and hexadecimal floating point for engineers and scientists). Each kind of arithmetic could either be accomplished by subprogram or circumvented by elaborate analysis, so it becomes of interest to know the cost of the approach chosen.

In general, we have been able to abstract some principles of programming to save execution time which should be broadly applicable. We caution that the use of intricate details of instructions for this purpose may be valuable but much less transferable to another situation than the machine-independent aspects of programming.

PROBLEMS

Except for Problems 9, 10, 13, and 14, a machine model should be assigned on which to make execution time comparisons.

1. Attempt to write an instruction using each operation code in the set

L,LH,SR,LA,SLL,SRL,SLA,SRA

to set register 10 to zero. Compare the merits with respect to execution time, clarity, and side effects or incompleteness.

2. Integer counters can often be stored in memory in half-word cells rather than full-word cells, thereby saving storage. Evaluate the merits of using half-word cells as counters in saving time. Do you see any opportunity for confusion in parameter passing?

3. It is possible to add the contents of two registers using an Add Register or a Load Address instruction. State conditions for each under which it is the appropriate choice. Consider time consumed, space occupied, side effects, and special capabilities.

4.   Consider summing the elements of an array using one pass through a loop for each term added. The most economical way to retrieve the element is by use of an index register to modify an appropriate Add instruction in the processor just prior to execution. What losses are incurred if an index register is not available and the instruction is modified in memory as in Chapter 3? Can you devise a better way to proceed when there is no register free to hold an index? If so, evaluate it.

5.   To calculate AB + CD requires temporary storage of a computed result. Calculate the least time required if you are free with register usage and compare it to the time using as few registers as possible.

6.   In comparing various alternatives for looping control, we may ignore time for entering and exiting the loop and count only the time required for an iteration through the loop which is not the first or last. Compare execution times for the following three loops on that basis:

(a)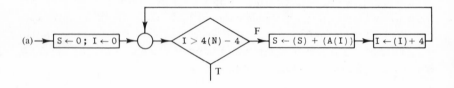

(b)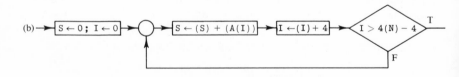

(c)

In this comparison, assume I, S, and $4N - 4$ are held in registers. There is a way (not strictly consistent with (c)) for avoiding an unconditional branch after incrementing. Can you find it?

7. The MoVe Character instruction could be replaced with a programmed loop using the Insert Character and STore Character instructions. One should be able to determine an expression.

$$T_0 + NT_1$$

for the time to move a string of length N. In this expression, T_0 represents time special to getting started or terminating while T_1 represents time in the loop for moving a character not first or last. Compare the result to the formula given for the MVC instruction.

8. Some powerful composite instructions for loop control are available on the 360/370. Two of these are:

> BXLE Branch on indeX Low or Equal
> BXH   Branch on indeX High

With sufficient care and the right situation, one can accomplish incrementing, testing, and branching all in one instruction and in the order given. Consider Branch on indeX High. We should hope that branching occurs when the loop is to be continued and fails at termination, for this avoids an extra branch. Then BXH requires a negative increment. Similarly, BXLE requires a positive increment. If the index is to be used in progressing through an array, BXH will do so from high index to low. We explain an application of BXLE for which the index should progress from low to higher value.

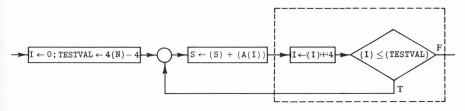

The portion of this diagram encased in dotted lines is accomplished by the BXLE instruction.

The BXLE instruction is of RS type with symbolic operand field

$$R1,R3,D2(B2)$$

Use of registers is as follows:

Quantity	Its Register
Index of the loop	R1
Increment for the index	R3
Comparand (test value for index)	$\begin{cases} \text{R3 if R3 is odd} \\ \text{R3} + 1 \text{ if R3 is even} \end{cases}$

In this example, we assign the index I to register 3, the increment to register 4, and the comparand to register 5. If summing is done in register 10, the loop can be written as

$$\text{LOOP} \quad \text{A} \quad 10,\text{A}(3)$$
$$\text{BXLE} \quad 3,4,\text{LOOP}$$

Calculate the savings in time for each execution of the loop accomplished by use of the BXLE instruction, omitting from consideration the cost of freeing three registers for use in its control. Times in microseconds for the BXLE instruction on the models compared in this chapter are:

	360/30	360/85	370/135	370/155
No branch	51	0.48	5.321	1.108
Branch	52	0.42	4.881	1.453

9. It is a saving in register space and perhaps in preparation for use of the BXLE instruction to use the increment as the comparand. This would suggest an index starting at a negative initial value and incremented toward zero. Such an adjustment in the index calls for a corresponding adjustment to the displacement in the instructions being modified by the index. We might consider, for example, the instruction sequence

$$\text{LOOP} \quad \text{A} \quad 10,\text{A+N}(3)$$
$$\text{BXLE} \quad 3,5,\text{LOOP}$$

where it is understood that the index is initialized to value $-N$ prior to entry into the loop and that the increment is now in register 5. Comment on the usefulness of this application.

10. Analyze ways to utilize the BXH instruction as was suggested for BXLE in Problems 8 and 9, and draw conclusions as to conditions under which these instructions should be used and conditions under which they are not advantageous.

11. The simplest instruction designed to incorporate the three aspects of looping commonly known as incrementing, testing, and branching is named Branch on CounT. It is based on the concept of starting with a positive index and decrementing toward zero. The first operand names the index register, and the destination of the branch is given by the second operand field. There is an RX version (BCT) and there is also an RR version (BCTR). The decrement is always one. Since address increments between consecutive memory half words and full words are 2 and 4, respectively, this instruction is limited in looping control to those cases in which one is processing character strings or where the index is required only to count and not to modify half-word or full-word memory references. Determine whether or not BCT or BCTR is a useful instruction in simulating the MVC instruction as in Problem 7 and demonstrate.

12. Decrementing a register by one is frequently necessary and cannot be done with the Load Address instruction unless -1 is stored in a register. However, BCTR R1, 0 will decrement register R1 with no side effects. Discuss the pros and cons of each method. Could a macro be used to improve the mnemonics?

13. If you had the power to modify machine logic, would you consider it worthwhile to introduce a set of instructions BD1, BD2, BD4, BD8 of which BD1 would be identical to BCT and the others would use the digit in their mnemonics as decrement? If so, would you also find as much justification for BI1, BI2, BI4, BI8 where I stands for increment? These instructions would increment an index through negative values until the index reached zero.

14. There is a saying "garbage in, garbage out" which is a familiar way of asserting that invalid input cannot provide valid answers. We may also observe among our peers the faith that "if a computer prints it, it must be correct." Discuss what programming practices these observations suggest and make qualitative arguments about the feasibility of these practices with regard to cost in execution time and with respect to investment in programming time.

15. Consider a two-dimensional array of full-word cells named SEAT in which there are M rows numbered 1, 2, ..., M and N columns numbered 1, 2, ..., N. If the elements are stored by columns (as in FORTRAN), then SEAT(I,J) refers to a cell which begins $4[(J-1)*M+I-1]$ bytes beyond the initial address. For computational ease, one would write this expression as $4[J*M+I-(M+1)]$ and precalculate the constant $M + 1$. Multiplication by 4 amounts to a shift of 2. Compare the time required for obtaining an element from the array, given its row and column indices, to that for retrieving a full-word item which is a simple variable (identified completely by its name). Tell how to use such information to improve execution time in the following tasks:

(1)   initializing an array to zero;
(2)   making elements of array A equal to those of B, assuming each array is the same size;
(3)   calculation of $((A(I, J) + 4) \cdot A(I, J) + 3) \cdot A(I, J) + 2$.

Which of these are likely to be most usable and why?

16.   In the assembler project in Chapter 5, we proposed keeping the instruction type in a table in character form, that is as internal code (EBCDIC) for RR, RS, or RX. Suppose the problem is enlarged to include types SS and SI as well. To select the appropriate subprogram for a given operation code will require several comparisons. As an alternative, we could have coded types numerically and used the type code as an index in a BAL instruction whose destination was a jump table. Compare these alternatives with respect to time and space requirements.

17.   One can determine whether or not an integer is even in a variety of ways. Devise two methods, one relying on shifts and one relying on instructions of logic, and compare the methods for efficiency and clarity.

Chapter 8

Specialized Arithmetic

8.1 INTRODUCTION

For many years, there was a dichotomy of machines—a machine was either scientific in orientation or it was for data processing. Engineers and scientists, it seemed, could not possibly share a computer with accountants, partly because they placed different requirements on equipment and partly because scheduling of computer use by engineers and scientists was intolerable to accountants, and scheduling by accountants was intolerable to engineers and scientists. It will help us to review these contrasts.

The economies of binary arithmetic have consistently been prized in scientific computation and a headache to the accountant. Fixed word length is most convenient for the number representations of engineers and scientists, while the strings of characters with which accountants have to deal refuse to conform to any fixed lengths. Engineers tend to consider each day like any other, short problems in the regular working day and long problems at night. Accountants work by the week, the month, the quarter, and the year. Their peak uses of machines at the end of the quarter or year must in their minds override any other use. How can it be that today engineers and accountants do share the same computer in most institutions? How have they been brought together? We see four forces:

1. There is much more in common between the needs of engineers and accountants than was first realized.

2. There are tremendous economies to be obtained by investing one's available money in one powerful system. Management has forced togetherness.

3. Modern systems, which allow several problems to be resident in the computer and in execution at one time, permit scheduling practices which are conducive to sharing.

4. Machines have been given a general organization suitable for any application, together with special features for data processing and special features for scientific computation.

It is these special features to which this chapter is devoted: decimal arithmetic for accountants and floating-point arithmetic for scientists. It is unlikely that either will use the other's prize package, but with these special features each can consider the machine as having been designed with his needs in mind.

8.2   DECIMAL ARITHMETIC

8.2.1   Addition, Subtraction, and Comparison

In Section 6.7, we developed a justification for decimal arithmetic operations in computers. The primary goal was to avoid the expense of conversions to and from binary which constituted far more arithmetic than needed to be done in the application. Another goal was to avoid the discrepancies between machine computation and manual verification resulting from the differences in rounding when fractions have to be chopped† in length to fit machine word size. Decimal arithmetic is an answer to these problems. With it come some complications which we may as well anticipate:

1. For every operand, the programmer must maintain his positioning of the decimal point and his estimate of result size so as to align operands

† Chopping, truncation, and rounding are discussed in Appendix G.

properly for addition or subtraction, to insert the decimal point properly in printed results, and to assure adequate storage capacity for each result.

2. The programmer must be aware of the packing of two decimal digits or one decimal digit and sign into one byte of storage and the complications this may bring when operand lengths are specified in bytes. Multiplication by shifting, for example, is not trivial.

3. Decimal arithmetic is extremely slow relative to binary, and extensive use of it should be made only after careful consideration.

All decimal arithmetic instructions are of SS2 type so that the assembler operand format is

$$D1(L1,B1),D2(L2,B2)$$

where each operand has its own length in bytes. In the operand expression, L1 and L2 provide these lengths, which must be integers between 1 and 16 inclusive. In the machine instruction, the lengths are represented by a pair of hex digits occupying byte 1 of the instruction; the leftmost hex digit of this byte has value $L1 - 1$ while the rightmost has value $L2 - 1$.

Each decimal number is represented by a string of hexadecimal digits in which the rightmost represents the sign and the others are the decimal digits of the absolute value. Each representation occupies an integral number of bytes, and therefore has an odd number of decimal digits to represent the decimal number. The limits on length for the entire representation are 1–16 bytes (1–31 decimal digits) inclusive. Any of A, C, E, or F in the sign position indicates positive, while B or D indicates negative. Even though zero has a hexadecimal sign (which is normally plus) the condition code will be set to zero (not 2) when an instruction which sets it has a zero result.

The result of a decimal arithmetic instruction is calculated one byte at a time from right to left. As soon as a byte of the result is calculated, it is stored (again from right to left) in the first operand string. If the result string has length less than L1, it is padded on the left with occurrences of zero (two per byte) to length L1. After the rightmost L1 bytes of the result are stored, any that remain to be stored are lost.

While overlap of operand fields is possible, and generally will be as anticipated when processing proceeds from right to left, it seems unjustified to clutter our first uses of decimal instructions with such details. Instead, we assume nonoverlapping operand fields unless we specifically state otherwise. Next we study specific decimal instructions.

Add Packed and Subtract Packed (with Operation Codes AP and SP)

Alignment of decimal points in the two operands is assumed. As necessary, the shorter operand is extended on the left by occurrences of zero. Standard decimal addition (subtraction) is then performed to produce a result and a corresponding setting of the condition code (0, 1, or 2, according to whether the result is zero, negative, or positive). The sign digit is C if this result is nonnegative and D if negative. After these settings, the rightmost L1 bytes of the result are stored in the first operand string. Overflow will be detected and the condition code reset to 3 if nonzero digits on the left are lost in this step. Thus, it is possible that all decimal digits stored are zero while the sign digit is D. The instruction execution is interrupted if a digit or sign representation in either operand is invalid.

Examples of addition and subtraction:

L1	Operand 1	L2	Operand 2	Opcode	Result	CC
2	413A	3	00068C	AP	481C	2
2	537A	2	819B	AP	282D	1
2	537A	2	819B	SP	356C	3
2	000A	3	51000B	AP	000D	3
2	500A	2	500A	SP	000C	0

Zero and Add Packed (ZAP, of Course!)

This instruction is equivalent to an addition in which the first operand has been set to zero. Thus, it serves only as a move which sets the condition code, may chop or pad with zeros on the left, and may be used to assure that zero has a positive sign.

Examples:

L1	L2	Operand 2	Opcode	Result	CC
2	2	000B	ZAP	000C	0
1	2	314A	ZAP	4C	3
3	2	314A	ZAP	00314C	2
1	2	050B	ZAP	0D	3

Compare Packed (CP)

The concept of algebraic comparison is no different for packed decimal than for binary. But since sign representations are not unique in packed decimal and zero may have a negative sign, the Compare Packed instruction is most easily explained as setting the condition code exactly as it would be set by a Subtract Packed decimal instruction with the same operand fields. It differs from the SP instruction in that the operands are left untouched and there is no possibility of overflow.

8.2.2 Special Considerations for Multiplication and Division

The design of the arithmetic unit for binary arithmetic included provisions for extended results of multiplication and division. In multiplication, the result register had to have as many digit positions as multiplier and multiplicand together. Division required saving an approximation to the quotient and also a remainder which could be used to extend the accuracy of the quotient if that were necessary. Decimal arithmetic has no processor registers visible to the programmer, so we find special attention must be given to providing a first operand string which will be adequate for the first operand as well as for saving the product in multiplication and the quotient and remainder in division.

In multiplication, it is required that operand 1 have as many leading zeros as there are sign and digit positions in the multiplier (operand 2). This provides enough space to save the entire product in the location of the first operand. In division, the quotient with sign occupies the leftmost L1 − L2 bytes of the string designated by operand 1, and the remainder occupies the rightmost L2 bytes of that string.

Multiplication and division also provide the possibility of getting negative zero for a result since the sign of the product in multiplication and of the quotient in division will be negative if one operand has positive and one has negative sign, even if the product or quotient is zero. Negative zero will result as a remainder if the dividend has negative sign and the remainder is zero, since the sign of the remainder is taken to be that of the dividend.

These instructions will be explained as operations with integers so that the decimal point is always understood to be between the rightmost digit and the sign. In practice, however, the programmer may prefer to keep track of the decimal position for each result according to the well-worn rules:

1. The number of decimals (digits to the right of the decimal point) in a product is the sum of the number of decimals in the multiplier and in the multiplicand.

2. The number of decimals to which a quotient is computed is the

number of decimals in the dividend less the number of decimals in the
divisor. Additional precision is accomplished through use of the remainder.

We shall illustrate both multiplication and division in the examples
which follow.

Multiply Packed (MP)

The product of first and second operands is stored in the first operand
string. The multiplier is limited to at most fifteen decimal digits. Since
$L1 \leq 16$ bytes, the product field is limited to at most 31 digits. To ensure
that there is room for the product, it is required that $2 \cdot L2$ leading digits
of the first operand be zero. Hence the multiplicand has $2 \cdot L1 - 2 \cdot L2 - 1$
positions. A Zero and Add Positive instruction provides a convenient way
to move the multiplicand into a first operand string adequate to hold the
product. The sign of the result is determined from those of the operands
without reference to magnitude of the answer. Thus negative zero is a
possible result. The condition code is unchanged by multiplication.

Examples of multiplication:

L1	Operand 1	L2	Operand 2	Result
3	00007A	2	345B	02415D
3	00003B	2	345B	01035C
3	00001B	2	000C	00000D
3	00000B	2	000C	00000D
3	00023A	2	000C	Overflow

In the last multiplication, even though the second operand is zero, the instruction will not be executed and the program will be terminated because
the first operand has only one byte of significant zeros, whereas the second
operand is two bytes long.

Divide Packed (DP)

Operand 1 is the dividend and operand 2 the divisor. The quotient and
remainder are packed into the first operand string with the remainder occupying the rightmost L2 bytes. Thus, the quotient representation must fit
into $L1 - L2$ bytes. It follows that $L1$ is determined by the programmer
to provide for the largest quotient magnitude contemplated.

When the divisor is placed with its leftmost digit (possibly zero) aligned
with the second dividend digit from the left (possibly zero) its magnitude

so shifted must exceed that of the dividend or overflow will occur.† The condition code remains unchanged by division.

Examples of division:

L1	Operand 1	L2	Operand 2	Result
3	00649C	2	123C	5C|034C
4	0000625B	2	025C	025D|000D
4	0000001B	2	007C	000D|001D
4	0002048B	1	2B	01024C|0D
4	0512000B	2	512C	Overflow

The last example of division will not be executed, since there is insufficient space for the quotient representation in the two bytes (L1 − L2) allotted for it.

8.2.3   Alignment of the Decimal Point

It would be difficult to get more basic than the computation of interest on a loan. A savings account which stood at $1024.57 at the beginning of a quarterly interest period where the interest is 8% per year is multiplied by 1.02 at the end of the quarterly period. Decimal arithmetic saves all digits of the result, yielding $1045.0614. But to store this amount as the new balance in the same string that held the previous balance, we need to chop off the rightmost two digits by a "right shift". This is just one example of a need which permeates decimal arithmetic for alignment of decimal points in operands.

This alignment can be done with multiplication or division by the appropriate power of 10. That we consider shifting with nonarithmetic instructions as a worthy alternative to shifting by arithmetic is explained only in terms of instruction execution times. What we call a shift in decimal arithmetic is not so much a shift of digits in memory as a change in length together with movement of the sign hexdigit. For example, a left

---

† In division by subtractions and shifts, we expect the rightmost position of the divisor for subtraction to have its units position aligned with that of the dividend. There are $2(L1 - L2) - 1$ digit positions in the quotient, so the leftmost position of the divisor in which a subtraction is permissible without overflow places the divisor that far from the sign position of the dividend. Its leftmost digit is $2 \cdot L2 - 2$ positions farther to the left, altogether $2 \cdot L1 - 3$ positions from the sign, while that of the dividend is $2 \cdot L1 - 1$ positions away, this verifying that no subtractions should be possible when the leftmost digit of the divisor is only one position to the right of that for the dividend.

shift by an even number ($2m$) of places can leave all decimal digits exactly where they are, move the sign hexdigit m bytes to the right, and insert $2m$ decimal zeros in between. Since rightmost digits are aligned on addition, the extension by $2m$ zero digits on the right makes a representation appear to have been multiplied by 10^{2m}. Of course, a left shift of this sort requires that there be unused bytes of storage on the right into which a representation can expand.

A right shift by an even number of places which is less than the number of digits in the number to be shifted will leave the left extreme untouched and will move the sign hexdigit to the left. Since the representation is shortened, no additional bytes are required. For example, a right shift by 2 of 19357C yields 193C.

Since we have in the logical AND a way to replace selected bits in a string by zeros, we should expect that only the moving of the sign hexdigit into the right half of a byte without disturbing the left half will be a concern. That too could be accomplished with bit string logic, for to combine the left half of byte A with the right half of byte B can be accomplished with an OR if we have first zeroed the right half of byte A and the left half of byte B. The reference manuals choose to take advantage of two specialized MOVE instructions in these shifts. These are MoVe Numerics and MoVe Zones. Since they do offer a slight advantage over bit string logic in this application and can be useful elsewhere, we introduce them here.

The MoVe Numerics (MVN) and MoVe Zones (MVZ) Instructions†

These instructions are really specialized move instructions of format SS1 that happen to be useful in decimal arithmetic. Thus, the format of the symbolic operand field is

$$D1(L,B1),D2(B2)$$

As would be expected of move instructions, they perform no validity checking and proceed from left to right in the operand strings, storing the result of processing one byte position before moving to the next. It is easiest to define each of them in terms of the standard MoVe Character instruction which we introduced in Section 6.3.

---

† For EBCDIC representation, the alphabet is divided into three zones which are A–I, J–R, and S–Z. The left half-byte selects the zone (and so is called the *zone* hexdigit). The right half-byte is the binary representation of the decimal digit in the Hollerith punched card representation of the character (and hence is called the *numeric* hexdigit).

We may define the MVN (MVZ) instruction to be an MVC with the same operand field but in which the left (right) hexdigit of each byte of operand 1 is protected from change so that only the right (left) hexdigit of an operand 1 byte can be modified.

Example.   Suppose that the operand 1 information string in hexadecimal is 95A6B7C8 and the operand 2 information string is F1E2D354. Then the result string after MVN is 91A2B3C4 and after MVZ is F5E6D758.

Chopping a Representation on the Right by an Even Number of Places

One instruction to move the sign digit into the right half of a byte n positions to the left of the byte which now holds it is all that is needed to chop $2n$ digits from the right of a representation. The number's address is of course that of the leftmost byte of the representation, and that of the byte holding the sign is displaced from it by $L - 1$ while the byte to which the sign is moved is displaced from it by $L - 1 - n$. More precisely, if the name of a decimal representation is DECNUM and its length is L, then to chop $2n$ digits from its right, where $n < L$, we use the single instruction

$$\text{MVN DECNUM+}(L-1)-n(1)\text{,DECNUM+L}-1$$

Note that further reference to DECNUM must specify a length of $L - n$ rather than L.

Extending a Representation on the Right by an Even Number of Places

Extending a representation on the right by n bytes requires that the n bytes just beyond the sign byte be free for reassignment. In that case, we set these n bytes to zero, move the sign n places to the right, and then replace the original sign digit by zero. We assume a constant string of zeros of at least n bytes beginning at ZERO. A sequence to do these three things for a representation of length L at DECNUM follows:

```
MVC  DECNUM+L(n),ZERO
MVN  DECNUM+(L-1)+n(1),DECNUM+L-1
NI   DECNUM+(L-1),240
```

MoVe with Offset (MVO)

Because two decimal digits are represented in one byte, a shift by an odd number of places will move every decimal digit in the lower half of a byte to an upper half and vice versa. The sign digit is the exception, for it is in the lower half of a byte before and after. There is a special instruction to adjust to byte boundaries in this way. It is called MoVe with Offset.

The second operand byte string contains those decimal digits of the unshifted number which are to appear in the shifted representation. The first operand byte string contributes only its sign hexdigit to the representation. The result is as if the nonsign digits of operand 1 were all set to zero, the bit string for operand 2 were shifted left by four bits, and then the logical OR of these two operands were the result.

In this instruction, we should expect overlapping operand strings since the sign and the digits of the result are taken from different operands, but these operands each come from the same decimal representation. The way we use the instruction ensures that bytes in the first operand are not destroyed before use.

Shifting an Odd Number of Places

If DECNUM is a decimal representation of length L and a right shift by $2m - 1$ places is required, then

```
MVO   DECNUM(L),DECNUM(L-m)
```

will accomplish the necessary chopping. Note that the length for operand 1 naturally begins with the byte at DECNUM and must include the sign byte as its last. The result now begins at DECNUM + $m - 1$.

A left shift by $2m - 1$ places will be accomplished as a left shift by $2m$ places followed by a right shift of one place. Thus, we now have all the puzzle pieces available. The sequence will be

```
MVC   DECNUM+L(m),ZERO
MVN   DECNUM+(L-1)+m(1),DECNUM+L-1
NI    DECNUM+(L-1),240
MVO   DECNUM(L),DECNUM(L-1)
```

8.2.4 Rounding of Decimal Results

If a result X is to be represented in decimal with p digits to the right of the decimal, we would like to use the closest such approximation we can get. Limiting ourselves for the moment to nonnegative numbers, we find the closest such number $\leq X$ by chopping off all digits past the pth. Call it X_{LE}. If we add one in the pth decimal place to X_{LE}, we get a number X_{GR} such that $X < X_{GR}$. Thus, we know

$$X_{LE} \leq X < X_{GR}, \qquad X_{GR} = X_{LE} + 1/10^p$$

Either X_{LE} or X_{GR} will always be within $5/10^{p+1}$ of X. If

$$X + 5/10^{p+1} = X_{\text{GR}},$$

then the approximations are equidistant and the choice is arbitrary. If

$$X + 5/10^{p+1} < X_{\text{GR}},$$

then X_{LE} is the closer. If

$$X + 5/10^{p+1} > X_{\text{GR}},$$

then X_{GR} is the closer. This tells us that adding $5/10^{p+1}$ and chopping to p digits gives the approximation we are after. It is convenient to denote it as X_{RD} (X rounded).

If X can be either negative or positive, this rounding procedure must be refined. A quantity of magnitude $5/10^{p+1}$ is to be subtracted from X if X is negative and added to X if X is positive. Either adjustment can be applied successfully in case X is zero. We may use the sign function defined in Section 3.3.2 in specifying this operation; namely, we calculate $X + \text{sign}(X) \cdot 5/10^{p+1}$ and chop the result to p decimals.

8.2.5   The EDit Instruction

An attempt to print a number directly as it would be from use of the UNPK instruction would be disappointing. We are used to seeing leading zeros replaced by blanks; on checks, we may expect another replacement, perhaps the asterisk. We expect a decimal point to be inserted between the integer and fractional parts, and if the integer portion exceeds 999, we expect one or more commas to mark off triples of digits to the left of the decimal point. And we would be disillusioned to see a letter in the rightmost digit position as would be printed from a byte with C or D in its left half representing a sign. In fact, we are accustomed to printing a sign indicator only if the number is negative. The EDit instruction is designed to cope with all these concerns. It is reasonably complex and we propose to present its concepts in easy stages.

We consider a string of bytes known as a *pattern,* which is supposed to describe how printing is to be done. Except for the fill character introduced in Exercise 2 of this section, the pattern is to have exactly as many bytes as are reserved for the print field. Suppose that we begin by distinguishing only two kinds of characters in the pattern. One type is called a *digit selector* and the other a *message character.* Message characters may be printable characters (such as a comma or period), which are usually inserted between digits, or may be sign indicator or label, which would likely precede or follow the digits. There should be precisely one digit selector in the pattern for each digit in the packed decimal number.

The action of editing causes each digit selector to be replaced by its corresponding digit from the packed representation. Message characters are not to be modified in the pattern. The result of execution is the pattern as modified by these replacements. These provisions give the power to insert commas, periods, and letters in the representation. In the following, we use the letters DS to represent the digit select character (its internal representation in hexadecimal is 20) and message characters represent themselves.

Example:

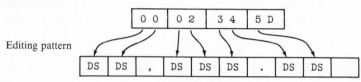

Packed decimal number

Editing pattern

Editing with this pattern should replace the pattern with the character string

$$0\ 0\ ,\ 0\ 2\ 3\ .\ 4\ 5$$

Note that our interpretation is incomplete. What we would like is a way to respond to the sign digit in the packed-decimal number. We could have a sign selector which inserts " − " into its place if the sign is B or D and blank if it is not. A set of increasingly detailed programming exercises will be used to illustrate the EDit instruction.

Exercise 1. Implement an editing program which works as in the preceding example, with the added condition that the hexdigits in the packed representation control advancement of a "pattern pointer" through the pattern from left to right. If a hexdigit is less than or equal to 9, the pattern pointer advances to the next digit selector and the digit replaces that selector. Intervening message characters are undisturbed. If the hexdigit is greater than or equal to A, the pattern pointer advances to the next pattern character, which must not be a digit selector; the message character is undisturbed for a negative sign and is replaced by a blank (we consider other replacements in Exercise 3) for a positive sign. The editing is terminated when the entire hex string has been scanned.

In the example preceding Exercise 1, we would have preferred not to print zeros or commas until the first nonzero digit on the left is encountered. It is usual to call the leftmost nonzero digit the *first significant digit*. We could build into our plans an on–off indicator (flag) which is set to the off position prior to the beginning of a left-to-right scan and is turned on when the leftmost nonzero digit is detected. Once on, this indicator (SIG) stays on until the sign digit is encountered. Then it is turned off if the sign digit is one of F, A, C, E, and is left on if the sign digit is B or D. The pattern pointer is advanced just as in Exercise 1. With SIG off, each pattern position reached by the pointer is replaced by a *fill character,* which for Exercise 2 will be a blank. Note that, as in Exercise 1, the hex digit value controls advancement of the pattern pointer, and in fact its influence on the significance indicator is realized before the pattern pointer is advanced.

Exercise 2.   Modify the edit program of Exercise 1 to include a significance indicator which functions in the manner just described.

We have used the blank character to replace the digit selector and message character in the process of editing. But especially in such cases as check writing, it is better to print a special fill character in all positions of the print field where blanks might have been placed; this printing is to forestall illegal changing of amounts. All that is needed is to specify the character to be used for this purpose. It is given as the leftmost character of the pattern. Thus, our pattern can no longer begin with a digit selector as in Exercise 1. We repeat the printing from Exercise 1 with "*" for fill character and with a significance indicator functioning.

Packed-decimal number

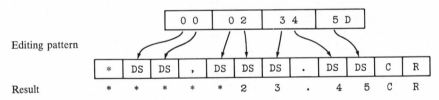

Had the sign digit been C, the result would have been

$$* \quad * \quad * \quad * \quad * \quad 2 \quad 3 \quad . \quad 4 \quad 5 \quad * \quad *$$

One can picture the need for editing several results into one line of printing using a longer pattern. In that case, we need another control character in the pattern which signifies the termination of a field by turning off the significance indicator (if the number just finished was negative, it will still be on). This character is called the *field separator* and has hexadecimal code 22. It is always replaced by the fill character after serving its function. Also, one can see opportunity for checking that a sign digit occurs only in the right half of a byte. These features are easily added to the edit program.

Exercise 3. Extend the edit program of Exercise 2 to permit a field separator which turns off the significance indicator. Also include a check to insure that a sign digit occurring in the left half of a byte is detected as erroneous. Provide for an arbitrary fill character.

There is one facility clearly needed which we have not provided. One does not always want to replace all digits to the left of the first significant digit—as defined above—by the fill character. We may want to print a decimal point and all digits to its right, even if the digits are all zero. For example, the column on the left seems more appropriate than that on the right:

$$1\ 2\ 3\ .\ 4\ 7\ 5 \qquad 1\ 2\ 3\ .\ 4\ 7\ 5$$
$$.\ 0\ 0\ 3 \qquad\qquad\qquad 3$$
$$.\ 1\ 2\ 1 \qquad\qquad 1\ 2\ 1$$
$$.\ 0\ 0\ 0$$

With the features just described, we need only introduce one more pattern character which is called the *significance starter.* Its hex code is 21 and its only function is to turn on the significance indicator if it is not already on. Once it has turned on that indicator, it is replaced by digit or fill character exactly as if it were a digit selector.

Exercise 4. The edit program of Exercise 3 with significance starter added should be equivalent to the EDit instruction of the 360/370 except that it may have different length limitations. Implement the significance starter and try your program against the EDit instruction, which is of type SS1 with operand field of the form

$$D1(L,B1),D2(B2)$$

The length parameter in operand 1 applies to the pattern string, which is operand 1. The second operand is the packed decimal source string.

Since the pattern used in an EDit instruction is modified by execution, it will have to be initialized prior to each use (preferable to refreshing it after each use).

8.3 FLOATING-POINT ARITHMETIC

8.3.1 The Concept of Significant Figures

One has only to measure a distance with a variety of measuring tapes, each marked off in its own units, to realize that the number of units equal to that distance is completely dependent on the unit. That distance which measures 1359.72 m is also 1.35972 km and 135972 cm. Even though these numbers vary by powers of ten in magnitude, there is something in common among them. The number of meters carries only two digits to the right of the decimal point, a fact which is normally interpreted to mean that the precise measurement would lie somewhere between 1359.715 and 1359.725 m. That is, the measurement is good to within 0.005 m = 5 mm. Exactly the same conclusion (that the error does not exceed 5 mm) can be drawn from the measurements in kilometers and in centimeters. Had the measurement been good only to the nearest meter, it would have been misleading to give the distance as 1359.72 m. When the same measurement is given in centimeters, we are obliged to write it as 1360×10^2 cm, showing the number to be correct to the nearest 100 cm.

Although the measurements of a distance can result in numbers differing widely in size (depending on the unit chosen), the number of significant digits† is the same in all, assuming equally precise measuring instruments. Clearly, the number of significant digits is an indication of precision, while the size of the number is not. With such an understanding, it behooves us to avoid loss of precision by the casual representation of data. If one sees the number 1, should it be considered to be an integer and therefore equal to 1.000 . . . ? What about 1., 1.0, 1.00 . . . ? The usual practice is to assume that integers as counting numbers are precise, and that there is nothing to be gained by assuming fewer significant digits than one computer word will hold, even when the number (integer or real) appears in a real expression. Hence, each of the numbers above would be extended by zeros on the right and then represented as accurately as possible in one word. But beware, for the PL/1 language is not so kind. It will store quite different fractions for .1 and .1000.

8.3.2 Preserving Significance through Calculation

Significance, like virginity, is easy to lose and impossible to regain. If we multiply a number with six significant digits by a number with two, the result has only two significant digits. If we take the difference of two numbers of six significant digits each, the result can have as many as six or as few as zero significant digits! These dismal notions are demonstrated in Figure 8.3.1.

Rather than try to estimate the significance of results through a long sequence of computations, the programmer finds it much more convenient to

† We will define the number of significant digits as the index of the rightmost digit after starting from one at the leftmost nonzero digit and counting to the right.

$$
\begin{array}{ll}
594876 \times 50 \quad = 29\ 743800 & \\
 \times 50.5 = 30\ 041238 & \text{Only two digits can be trusted} \\
 \times 49.5 = 29\ 446362 & \\
81.9483\text{--}81.9483 \quad = 0 & \text{Zero significant digits} \\
81.9483\text{--}0.000002 = 81.948298 & \text{Round to six significant digits}
\end{array}
$$

Figure 8.3.1. These examples of the preservation of significance through arithmetic demonstrate the ease with which significant figures may be lost.

use number representations which will preserve all the significance that can be saved (within machine and time limitations) in each arithmetic operation. Thus it is left to the theoretician or to numerical experiment to determine the validity of computed results. This is the foundation for floating-point computation. Although we shall not dwell further on the matter, we caution that some of the finest applied mathematics has to do with formulating a computation so that errors which develop through rounding or approximation die away and become less significant as computation progresses. Computing without such a mathematical basis can lead to computations in which such errors are actually amplified. The floating-point arithmetic on which programmers depend is at best a crutch, and, until significance is assured in some other way, we should look on all results with suspicion.

8.3.3 Floating-Point Representation

We assume a positive base (radix) b for floating-point representations and take X to be a nonzero, real number. We define e (the exponent) and m (the mantissa) by the conditions

$$
\begin{array}{ll}
1/b \leq |m| < 1 & \text{for normalized representations} \\
0 < |m| < 1/b & \text{for unnormalized representations} \\
X = b^{e} \cdot m &
\end{array}
$$

Clearly, we need only start with a representation of X with base b and determine e as a number of shifts of the radix point to the left to convert X to m (if $|X| > 1$) and as the negative of the number of shifts to the right to convert X to m if $|X| < 1/b$. Every nonzero number has such a representation. All integers (but not all fractions) have a mantissa which terminates after q places and can be represented as a fraction with denominator b^{q}, whereas a nonterminating fraction cannot be so represented. Thus $1/5$ has a nonterminating binary or hexadecimal representation, and $1/3$ will have a nonterminating representation for base 2, 10, or 16.

If the base is implicit—as it is in every machine representation—then the pair (e, m) determines a floating-point representation, so that the problem is reduced to packing this representation into a cell. Beyond the necessity to round or chop m, there is the fact that both e and m are signed numbers, yet a word (as used thus far) has only one sign position.

The usual practice is to store the sign of the mantissa in the sign position of the cell (usually a single or double word) used for the representation, and store an approximation to $|m|$ in the rightmost positions of the cell. Between these, there is space for an integer to represent the exponent. The leftmost bit of the exponent field provides the sign for the exponent through the practice of adding to the exponent a positive amount called the *bias*,† and storing that biased integer to represent the exponent. It will help to be specific, so we give characteristics of the 360/370 floating-point number representation now:

1. The base for 360/370 floating-point representation of nonzero numbers is 16.

2. Bit 0 represents the sign of the mantissa (0 for $+$, 1 for $-$).

3. Bits 1–7 represents the exponent, the bias being $64_{10} = 1000000_2$.

4. Bits 8–31 represent the absolute value of the mantissa in one-word floating-point representations.

5. Bits 8–63 represent the absolute value of the mantissa in two-word floating-point representations.

6. All bits are zero for the representation of zero.

These properties are shown in Figure 8.3.2.

Some limitations on 360/370 floating-point representation are worth noting. They are

$$0 \le |m| \le (1 - 16^{-6}) \quad \text{in one-word representation}$$
$$0 \le |m| \le (1 - 16^{-14}) \quad \text{in two-word representation}$$
$$-64 \le e \le 63$$

Thus if $X = b^e \cdot m$, where $-64 \le e \le 63$ or if $X = 0$, then X is within the domain for floating-point representation. Since b is 16, this means $-16^{63} < X < 16^{63}$. The magnitude of these bounds seems beyond comprehension, but it is still easy to write numbers outside these bounds, $\pm 16^{100}$ being examples.

---

† The choice of applying a bias to the exponent is rooted in a desire to use the same comparison logic for floating-point numbers as for integers. The position of the biased exponent between sign and mantissa is also dictated by this restriction. The last exercise at the end of the chapter bears on these matters.

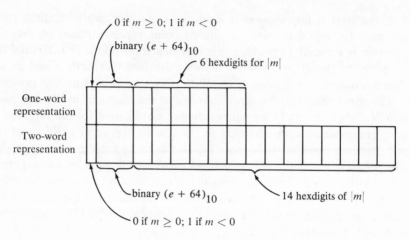

Figure 8.3.2 The 360/370 floating-point representation for nonzero numbers uses a base of 16 and dedicates bit 0 of the cell to the sign of the mantissa; the exponent biased by 64_{10} is in bits 1–7. The remaining hexdigits represent the absolute value of the mantissa. The representation of zero is special and is zero in every bit position.

8.3.4 Significant Figures in 360/370 Floating Point

There is no rounding when the 360/370 tailors a floating-point number to fit into a cell. Therefore, the largest error in absolute value of the mantissa is 16^{-6} in one-word floating point and 16^{-14} in two-word floating point. It helps comprehension for those whose experience is almost entirely rounded decimal to determine the number of digits in a rounded decimal representation of about the same accuracy. We assume q positions in the mantissa. Then we seek approximate solutions to

$$10^{-q_1}/2 = 16^{-6} \quad \text{and} \quad 10^{-q_2}/2 = 16^{-14}$$

These yield

$$10^{q_1} = 2^{23} \quad \text{and} \quad 10^{q_2} = 2^{55}$$

Therefore

$$q_1 = 23 \log_{10} 2 \quad \text{and} \quad q_2 = 55 \log_{10} 2$$

From $\log_{10} 2 \cong 0.3$, we get

$$q_1 \cong 6.9 \quad \text{and} \quad q_2 \cong 16.5$$

Our conclusion is that the one-word floating-point representation of the 360/370 is almost as precise as seven-digit rounded-decimal floating-point representation, while two-word floating point is better than 16-digit rounded-decimal floating point.

8.3.5 Calculation in Floating-Point Representation

There is a process called *normalization* which permeates all arithmetic with floating-point operands. It is based on the observation that

$$X = b^e(m) \quad \text{implies also} \quad X = b^{e+p}(b^{-p} \cdot m)$$

for any integer p. For example, if

$$X = 16^5(0.1\text{AF})$$

then also

$$X = 16^3(1\text{A.F}) = 16^7(0.001\text{AF})$$

While we will choose to work with normalized floating-point representations (those with $1/b \le |m| < 1$), the arithmetic operations will force us into unnormalized representations during their execution; thus, we will need to normalize at the end of many computations. With this explanation we consider arithmetic. Let the operands be

$$X1 = b^{e_1}(m_1) \quad \text{and} \quad X2 = b^{e_2}(m_2)$$

Addition and Subtraction

Define $e = \max(e_1, e_2)$. Then

$$X1 \pm X2 = b^e \cdot [b^{e_1-e} \cdot m_1 \pm b^{e_2-e} \cdot m_2]$$

One of $e_1 - e$ and $e_2 - e$ is zero and the other is zero or negative. If one is negative, shift the point in its mantissa, adjusting its power of b accordingly until the power of b is zero, so that the numbers can be combined. The resultant number may need to be renormalized.

Example 1. Let

$$X1 = 16^3 \cdot 0.\text{E95F} \quad \text{and} \quad X2 = 16^1(0.3\text{A2})$$
$$X1 + X2 = 16^3(0.\text{E95F} + 16^{-2} \cdot 0.3\text{A2}) = 16^3(0.\text{E95F} + 0.003\text{A2})$$
$$X1 + X2 = 16^3(0.\text{E9992})$$

Example 2:

$$X1 = 16^{-2}(0.1004) \quad \text{and} \quad X2 = 16^{-3}(0.\text{FFD})$$
$$X1 - X2 = 16^{-2}(0.1004 - 16^{-1} \cdot 0.\text{FFD}) = 16^{-2}(0.1004 - 0.0\text{FFD})$$
$$= 16^{-2}(0.0007) = 16^{-5}(0.700)$$

Multiplication

$$X1 \cdot X2 = b^{e_1+e_2} \cdot (m_1 \cdot m_2)$$

Example:

$$X1 = 16^{-7}(0.3AF) \quad \text{and} \quad X2 = 16^4(0.412)$$
$$X1 \cdot X2 = 16^{-3}(0.3AF \cdot 0.412) = 16^{-3}(0.0EFE4E) = 16^{-4}(0.EFE4E)$$

Division

$$X1/X2 = b^{e_1 - e_2}(m_1/m_2)$$

Example:

$$X1 = 16^4(0.3) \quad \text{and} \quad X2 = 16^{-1}(0.1)$$
$$X1/X2 = 16^5(3.0) = 16^6(0.3)$$

8.3.6   Implementation of Floating-Point Arithmetic

The use of floating-point arithmetic is so widespread that registers and instructions devoted to floating-point arithmetic are standard features on large computers and available at extra cost on most smaller computers. These facilities, unmentioned until now, make floating-point computation easy to understand and use.

The 360/370 system has four 64-bit registers for floating-point computation numbered 0, 2, 4, and 6. Although those numbers also identify general registers, there should be no confusion, since every operand register reference (not base or index) in a floating-point instruction is interpreted as a floating-point register reference, and all other register references are to the general registers. Each floating-point instruction has in its symbolic operation code either an E, signifying one-word floating point, or a D (double), signifying two-word floating point.

Each floating-point instruction except the Halve instructions (HER or HDR) is the counterpart of a fixed-point instruction of type RR or RX which we have already seen. Floating-point instructions of type RX have symbolic operation code formed from that of the counterpart by a suffix of E for one-word floating point and D for two-word floating point as shown in Table 8.3.1. Those of type RR have this letter inserted just before the R which terminates the operation code.

The hexadecimal operation codes are systematically formed also. Hexdigit 1 of the code is just the same as for the fixed-point counterpart, while hexdigit 0 is 7 and 6 for RX instructions with one- and two-word operands, respectively, and 3 and 2 for RR instructions with one- and two-word operands, respectively. These notions are illustrated in Table 8.3.1.

	RX TYPE			RR TYPE			
Fixed	One-word float	Two-word float	Fixed	One-word float	Two-word float	Sets
sym hex	sym hex	sym hex	sym hex	sym hex	sym hex	CC
L 58	LE 78	LD 68	LR 18	LER 38	LDR 28	NO
C 59	CE 79	CD 69	CR 19	CER 39	CDR 29	YES
A 5A	AE 7A	AD 6A	AR 1A	AER 3A	ADR 2A	YES
S 5B	SE 7B	SD 6B	SR 1B	SER 3B	SDR 2B	YĚS
M 5C	ME 7C	MD 6C	MR 1C	MER 3C	MDR 2C	NO
D 5D	DE 7D	DD 6D	DR 1D	DER 3D	DDR 2D	NO

Table 8.3.1   The systematic naming and numbering of operations for various operand types promotes recall.

The remaining instructions for normalized floating point have fewer variations. These are given adjacent to their fixed-point counterparts in Table 8.3.2.

Fixed point			One-word float		Two-word float		Sets
sym hex		Type	sym hex		sym hex		CC
LPR 10		RR	LPER 30		LPDR 20		YES
LNR 11		RR	LNER 31		LNDR 21		YES
LTR 12		RR	LTER 32		LTDR 22		YES
LCR 13		RR	LCER 33		LCDR 23		YES
none		RR	HER 34		HDR 24		NO
ST 50		RX	STE 70		STD 60		NO

Table 8.3.2   This table completes the naming and operation codes for normalized floating-point instructions.

Summarizing, we can make the following observations about floating-point instructions:

1. The first operand field must always provide the number of a 64-bit floating-point register (0, 2, 4, or 6). If the instruction specifies one-word (two-word) operands, then bits 0–31 (0–63) of this register provide the first operand and receive the 32- or 64-bit result. Bits 32–63 of that register are not read for a one-word instruction and are modified only in case of a multiply instruction.

2. The second operand field of an RR instruction must provide the number of a 64-bit floating-point register (0, 2, 4, or 6). If the instruction specifies one-word (two-word) operands, then bits 0–31 (0–63) of this register provide the second operand.

3. The second operand field of an RX instruction with one- or two-word operands must provide an address on a full-word or double-word boundary, respectively, and the full word or double word with that address provides the second operand. Note that registers named in the second operand field of a floating-point RX instruction are general registers, not floating-point registers.

4. The execution of each floating-point instruction can now be inferred from that of its fixed-point counterpart. The Halve instructions have no fixed-point counterparts. Each of them causes division by two.

8.3.7 An Example Using Floating-Point Arithmetic

We will devise a function subprogram named SQUART, which for a nonnegative full-word floating-point argument A returns a positive square root.

A straightforward procedure for estimating a square root is to create

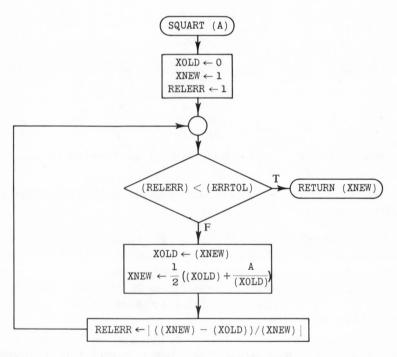

Figure 8.3.3 This flowchart specifies a simple iterative process for computing the square root of a positive argument.

a sequence of approximations $X_0, X_1, X_2, \ldots$ starting from an initial value of $X_0 = 1\dagger$ in which

$$X_{n+1} = (X_n + A/X_n)/2 \qquad \text{if} \qquad n > 1$$

When $| X_{n+1} - X_n/X_{n+1} |$ is less than a prescribed error tolerance, X_{n+1} will be a suitable approximation. In one-word floating point the chopping error places practical limits on error tolerance at about 10^{-6}. These considerations are implemented in the flowchart of Figure 8.3.3. Program 8.3.1 is an implementation of this flowchart.

STMT		SOURCE STATEMENT		
1	SQUART	CSECT		
2		STM	14,12,12(13)	
3		BALR	12,0	
4		USING	*,12	
5		LA	10,SAVE	
6		ST	13,4(10)	
7		ST	10,8(13)	
8		LR	13,10	
9		L	1,0(1)	
10		LE	0,=E'1'	XNEW ←1
11		LER	4,0	RELERR ←1
12	LOOP	CE	4,ERRTOL	
13		BL	OUT	BRANCH IF < ERRTOL
14		LER	4,0	XOLD← XNEW
15		LE	0,0(1)	ARG OF SQUART
16		DER	0,4	ARG / X
17		AER	0,4	X+ ARG / X
18		HER	0,0	XNEW ← (X+ARG/X)/2
19		SER	4,0	XOLD–XNEW
20		DER	4,0	(XOLD–XNEW)/XNEW
21		LPER	4,4	ABSOLUTE VALUE OF REL ERROR
22		B	LOOP	
23	OUT	L	13,SAVE+4	
24		LM	14,12,12(13)	
25		BR	14	
26	ERRTOL	DC	E'1E–6'	
27	SAVE	DC	18F'0'	
28		END		
29			E'1'	

Program 8.3.1 An assembler language implementation of a square root function subprogram, this short sequence illustrates the use of several floating-point instructions.

$\dagger$ A much better choice for X_0 can be easily formed by manipulation of the floating-point representation. It is discussed in Problem 26 at the end of this chapter.

PROBLEMS

1.   There are two types of Data Constants associated with decimal arithmetic. They are identified by P (for packed decimal) and Z (for zoned decimal). Constants acceptable for these types are signed or unsigned decimal numbers without scaling or exponent modifiers. They may not exceed 16 digits. A decimal point may appear in the constant for readability, but it has no effect on internal representations. Some valid examples of DC instructions satisfying these criteria are:

Opcode	Operand field	Internal representation
DC	Z'123'	F1F2C3
DC	P'123'	123C
DC	Z'+574.1'	F5F7F4C1
DC	P'+574.1'	05741C
DC	Z'−2196'	F2F1F9D6
DC	P'−2196'	02196D
DC	ZL5'−13'	F0F0F0F1D3
DC	PL5'−13'	000000013D

The last of these has a length parameter inserted between the type code and the quoted string which specifies the number of bytes in the internal representation. Note that the effect is that which would have resulted from extending the constant on the left by zeros until it would occupy the specified number of bytes. This facility is of some importance to decimal arithmetic since one will often need extra positions on the left to accommodate the arithmetic operations on packed decimal operands.

Check your understanding of these data types and of PACK, UNPK, CP, and CLC by creating and executing a short program with data constants of type P and Z for each of three decimal numbers, converting each representation to the other internally by use of PACK or UNPK, and comparing the result to the alternate input form for equality. Obtain output by SNAP or FORTRAN, and annotate the output by hand for easy understanding.

2.   Each of two numbers is stored in two-byte packed decimal format in cells named A and B, respectively. Each is an integer of three or fewer digits, but their sum S can be a four-digit integer. Write an instruction sequence for forming the sum correctly.

3.   A savings account is maintained to three-decimal accuracy to permit accurate accrual of interest. Deposits to the account are submitted with two-decimal accuracy. Assuming that deposits and accounts are each limited to be less than $1,000,000, write a sequence which will handle deposits which leave the account under $1,000,000 and will suppress deposits which will send the account over the limit, printing a diagnostic instead. Do not round.

4. Interest is computed quarterly at the rate 0.0175 per quarter on savings accounts which are at each transaction rounded to the nearest tenth of a cent. For the annual statement, results are rounded to the nearest cent. Write an instruction sequence which rounds correctly at an interest accrual and another which rounds correctly at an annual printing. Demonstrate this with proper choice of test numbers.

5. Retirement pay is calculated at 1.5% of the average salary over the last seven years of employment for every year employed. Thus if the average salary were $10,000 and years of service were 13, the pay would be

$$13(0.015)(\$10,000) = \$1950$$

Write a program to sum the salaries for the last seven years, divide the sum by 7, multiply by 0.015, and then by the number of years of service. Carry extra accuracy throughout the computation, and round at the end to the nearest dollar.

6. On federal income tax, one calculates deductible medical expenses as the excess over 3% of adjusted gross of (nonpharmaceutical items + excess of pharmaceutical items over 1% of adjusted gross). Write a program to calculate deductible medical expense to the nearest dollar when all items submitted are to the nearest cent.

7. Decimal integers are stored in ten consecutive four-byte locations. They are to be printed with the following characteristics:

  (a) No leading zeros will print—they will be replaced by blanks. The integer zero will print only blanks.

  (b) Commas are to be used as delimiters between triples of printed digits counting from the right.

  (c) Negative integers will have the letters CR (for credit) printed immediately to their right.

Devise a pattern to edit these numbers for printing.

8. Write a program to test the pattern obtained from Problem 7 and develop test data to demonstrate its functioning. Print the results, placing on one line the hexadecimal representation and the edited result. Be sure to look for special cases.

9. Dollar amounts, some positive and some negative, are to be printed from three-byte cells which have two digits to the right of the point (dollars and cents). Devise a pattern to edit and print these amounts, suppressing leading zeros to the left of the decimal point but not to the right. The EDMK variation on ED provides controls for positioning the $ sign.

10. State how many significant digits are in each of the following numbers:

$$\text{(a)} \quad 3.14159 \quad \text{(b)} \quad .00396 \quad \text{(c)} \quad (2340)10^4$$
$$\text{(d)} \quad 5720.0 \quad \text{(e)} \quad 0.02030$$

11. Write each of the following numbers as a power of 16 multiplied by a decimal fraction f for which $1/16 \le |f| < 1$ as a preliminary to conversion.

$$\text{(a)} \quad 8 \quad \text{(b)} \quad .0032 \quad \text{(c)} \quad 24 \quad \text{(d)} \quad \tfrac{1}{25}$$

12. Give normalized internal floating-point represenations for

$$.01101_2 \quad (.101_2)2^{-6} \quad 11.11_2 \quad -11.11_2 \quad (.0011_2)2^3$$

13. Numbers A and B have internal floating-point representations

$$\text{BFA40000} \quad \text{and} \quad \text{401B0000}$$

Determine external floating-point representations for A and B and internal representations for

$$\text{(a)} \quad A + B \quad \text{and} \quad \text{(b)} \quad A * B$$

14. There are two types of normalized floating-point data constants, E for one-word representations and D for double-word representations. They have implied lengths of 4 and 8 bytes respectively. There is the possibility of explicit length (as for the decimal constants of Problem 1) but it is of little purpose. In the absence of an explicitly given length, E and D types are justified to full-word and double-word boundaries respectively. The string which provides a decimal representation of a floating-point number may begin with + or − or be unsigned (positive understood). It may have only an integer part (decimal point understood), or it may have a fractional part in which case a point is necessary. It may be modified by a scale-factor (a power of 10) which is specified by a suffix consisting of an E followed by a signed or unsigned integer. The resultant value must convert to a hexadecimal number representable in a cell of designated size. Clearly, significant digits beyond the seventh will have little influence in one-word floating point as will those beyond the sixteenth in double-word floating point. Since for an X to be representable in binary floating point, it is necessary that $16^{-65} \le |X| < 16^{63}$, we conclude that a decimal number outside an interval with lower bound approximately 10^{-78} and upper bound approximately 10^{75} is inappropriate. A comma-separated list of numbers of the same type may be included in the quoted string of one operand field. Assemble data constants which demonstrate a variety of representations for a few given numbers and check for consistency of internal representation. Include in your assembly the following DC operand fields:

E' +25.7, −25.7',E'257E−1,.257E+02',E'.123456,.1234567'
E'.12345678,.123456789',E'17,1.7E1',E'17E0,17.E−0'
D'.17E+2',D'.12345678',D'.123456789',D'.123456789123456789'

15. Write a program to determine the value of n for which $n! \leq 10^{40} < (n + 1)!$.

16. Write a subprogram to calculate double-precision reciprocals and return by function reference.

17. We have concentrated on the normalized floating-point representation of numbers, and yet there are some occasions in which unnormalized results are natural. One of these is in the conversion of a floating-point result to fixed point. Unnormalized floating-point is like that which we call normalized up to the last step of shifting off leading hexadecimal zeros in the mantissa. That left shift with corresponding adjustment of the exponent representation is not done in unnormalized floating-point arithmetic. The unnormalized instructions for single precision are distinguished by a U in the symbolic operation code while the double-precision versions are distinguished by a W. These replace the E and D components, respectively, of the normalized floating-point symbolic operations. Use a computer program to evaluate.

$$(5.000000 − 4.999999) + .12345678E−5$$

in normalized floating point and in unnormalized floating point. Explain the differences, if any, by annotating the printed output.

18. The unnormalized addition introduced in Problem 17 can be used to convert from floating-point to binary integer representation. A subprogram to perform this conversion is the goal of this exercise. Since the intent is to store the result as a full-word integer, the conversion must be limited to numbers X such that $−2^{31} \leq X < 2^{31}$. For such X, we desire the representation to be in unnormalized double-precision form with exponent 14. To see this, note that the normalized form has its radix point 14 places to the left of that for an integer with zero exponent. When this is accomplished, we intend to discard the exponent and keep the signed mantissa as stored in the right half of the double-word representation. Having assured ourselves that X is within the proper limits, we apply an unnormalized floating-point addition to add to it an unnormalized floating-point number which has hexadecimal representation

$$4E00000100000000$$

Note that if $X \geq 0$, the 1 in the rightmost bit of the left half will not affect the result in the right half. On the other hand, if $X < 0$, the complement representation of X will be formed in the right half. To save the one-word result, we must copy the double-word answer into memory, after which we can limit our attention to the right half of the answer.

19. The best use of instructions requires a precise knowledge of the logical steps in their execution. We have assumed in a previous exercise that AW does not normalize its operands before adding. We will have reason to know for the square root program whether or not floating-point divide normalizes its operands before division. Choose constants as operands and perform floating-point instructions with them sufficient to tell for each of AE, AU, ME, MU, DE, and DU whether or not prenormalization takes place.

20. In the performance of instructions, one ordinarily does not expect to disturb the contents of registers not explicitly holding an operand or a portion of the result. An exception to this is the single-precision floating-point multiply instruction, for it can be expected to modify the entire 64-bit register which holds its multiplicand and receives its result in the leftmost 32 bits. Determine by experiment or by reading whether it would be valid to accumulate single-precision products in a double-precision register using as an addend the full floating-point register holding the multiplication result. Report your findings and how you got them.

21. We have mentioned that a function subprogram of FORTRAN receives its result back via register 0. Considering that there are now two registers numbered 0, it becomes clear that the calling program must be informed by its typing of function names where it will go to get its result. Summarize these by filling in the following table:

Result type	Where available	How typed	
		In subprogram	In calling program
Integer			
Short real			
Long real			

22. There are conventions to be followed in saving contents of the general registers so that the calling program will receive them intact. Are there any for the floating-point registers? Take a reading on these registers before and after calling a FORTRAN function subprogram to see whether or not they are preserved. Would you expect that the system would need to preserve them in alternating among programs in a multiprogrammed environment? Explain.

23. To convert a number I stored as an integer to floating-point representation requires care to avoid loss of significance. We propose to form a double-word floating-point representation in an even–odd general register pair. In one register we will form the biased exponent and sign, and in the other the mantissa. The conversion begins with loading I into the even register. We next place its absolute value in the odd register using the LPR instruction. Next, clear the even register except for the sign bit with an AND instruction; then OR into bits 0–7 of the even register the biased representation of 14 (which is 4E). This adjusts for the fact that the floating-point representation assumes that the mantissa is a fraction having 14 hexdigits when it is really an integer. The resulting two words provide an unnormalized floating-point representation of I. It can be normalized by storing the register pair in memory on a double-word boundary (with the exponent word on the left) and then using it as an operand in a double-word floating-point addition with zero as the other operand. Write and test such a program. Can you normalize differently?

24. Write an instruction sequence to form a number which is the power of 16 greater than or equal to the floating-point number X.

25. Write instructions to evaluate the polynomial

$$A_0X^n + A_1X^{n-1} + \cdots + A_nX^0$$

where all coefficients and X itself are floating-point numbers. The preferred way is to initialize R_0 to A_0 and then calculate R_n by the recursion

$$R_i = (R_{i-1})X + A_i \quad (i = 1, 2, \ldots, n).$$

26. The square root subprogram given as Program 8.3.1 takes many repetitions of its basic loop if its initial guess is poor. That will surely be the case for large numbers, for example in finding the square root of 10^{40}. One can obtain a very reasonable guess to the square root of a normalized floating-point number by halving its exponent. For example,

$$\sqrt{16^{38}f} = 16^{19}\sqrt{f} \quad (\tfrac{1}{16} \le f < 1)$$

and as long as f is the mantissa of a normalized number, $\tfrac{1}{4} \le \sqrt{f} < 1$ ($f = \tfrac{1}{16}$ is the worst case). An easily programmed approximation is attained by noting that $64 + e/2 = 1/2(128 + e)$. Assuming that $64 + e$ is the exponent representation, we want to add 1 in bit position 1 in such a way that a carry into the zero sign position is permitted. The appropriate instruction is Add Logical. A logical right shift by one will then give a floating-point representation (perhaps unnormalized) with the desired exponent. Its mantissa is somewhat unpredictable but must satisfy $\frac{1}{32} \leq m < 1$ so that it makes a reasonable initial approximation. It is important to the use of this approximation that operands of a normalized floating-point divide are normalized prior to division. Modify Program 8.3.1 to count and print repetitions of its loop and test it over a wide range of arguments. Then modify its initial guess as above and test it. Evaluate your findings.

27.   If computation is done in binary floating point, then, for convenience, there must eventually be a conversion to decimal floating point for printing. Given

$$X = (16^e)f \quad \text{where} \quad \tfrac{1}{16} \leq f < 1$$

we must determine p and q such that

$$X = (10^p)q \quad \text{where} \quad \tfrac{1}{10} \leq q < 1$$

It follows that

$$(10^{-p})X = q \quad \text{where} \quad \tfrac{1}{10} \leq q < 1$$

If p can be found, so that multiplication by 10^{-p} is possible, then conversion of q is relatively straightforward. We can get a good estimate of p from e:

$$\tfrac{1}{10} \leq (10^{-p})X < 1$$

yields

$$-1 \leq -p + \log_{10} f + e \log_{10} 16 < 0 \quad \text{and}$$
$$p - 1 \leq \log_{10} f + 4e \log_{10} 2 < p$$

Now $\log_{10} f < 0$, so we have

$$p - 1 \leq 4e \log_{10} 2 \quad \text{and} \quad p \leq 1 + 4e(.302)$$

We calculate $p_0 = $ (largest integer $\leq 1 + 1.298e$) and q_0 $(10^{-p_0})X$. If $q_0 < \tfrac{1}{10}$, then we decrease p_0 by 1 and multiply q_0 by 10. If $q_0 \geq \tfrac{1}{10}$, then p is the current value of p_0. Write a program to perform this conversion and test it.

28.   Convert the square root subroutine of Section 8.3.7 to double precision, and write a driver program to test it. Make certain that the answers you get are precise to 15 digits by squaring the result and printing it.

Extended Binary-Coded Decimal Interchange Code (EBCDIC)†

The 256-position Table A.1, outlined by the heavy black lines, shows the graphic characters and control character representations for EBCDIC. The bit-position numbers, bit patterns, hexadecimal representations and card hole patterns for these and other possible EBCDIC characters are also shown.

To find the card hole patterns for most characters, partition the 256-position table into four blocks as follows:

Block 1: Zone punches at top of table; digit punches at left

Block 2: Zone punches at bottom of table; digit punches at left

Block 3: Zone punches at top of table; digit punches at right

Block 4: Zone punches at bottom of table; digit punches at right

† The material in this appendix is reprinted by permission from "IBM System/360: Principles of Operation," IBM System Products Division, Poughkeepsie, New York. © 1966 by International Business Machines Corporation.

Table A.1 Extended binary-coded decimal interchange code (EBCDIC).

Row/column key (left side): Bit Positions 4,5,6,7 · Second Hexadecimal Digit · Digit Punches
Top key: Bit Positions 0,1 · Bit Positions 2,3 · First Hexadecimal Digit · Zone Punches · Digit Punches

Bit Positions 4,5,6,7	Second Hex	Digit Punches	0 (00 00)	1 (00 01)	2 (00 10)	3 (00 11)	4 (01 00)	5 (01 01)	6 (01 10)	7 (01 11)	8 (10 00)	9 (10 01)	A (10 10)	B (10 11)	C (11 00)	D (11 01)	E (11 10)	F (11 11)
0000	0	8-1	NUL ①	DLE ②	DS ③	④	SP ⑤	& ⑥	- ⑦	⑧					⑨	⑩	⑪	0 ⑫
0001	1	1	SOH	DC1	SOS				/ ⑬		a	j			A	J	⑭	1
0010	2	2	STX	DC2	FS	SYN					b	k	s		B	K	S	2
0011	3	3	ETX	TM							c	l	t		C	L	T	3
0100	4	4	PF	RES	BYP	PN					d	m	u		D	M	U	4
0101	5	5	HT	NL	LF	RS					e	n	v		E	N	V	5
0110	6	6	LC	BS	ETB	UC					f	o	w		F	O	W	6
0111	7	7	DEL	IL	ESC	EOT					g	p	x		G	P	X	7
1000	8	8		CAN							h	q	y		H	Q	Y	8
1001	9	8-1		EM							i	r	z		I	R	Z	9
1010	A	8-2	SMM	CC	SM		¢	!		:								
1011	B	8-3	VT	CU1	CU2	CU3	.	$	, ⑮	#								

Zone Punches:

Card Hole Patterns

① 12-0-9-8-1
② 12-11-9-8-1
③ 11-0-9-8-1
④ 12-11-0-9-8-1
⑤ No Punches
⑥ 12
⑦ 11
⑧ 12-11-0
⑨ 12-0
⑩ 11-0
⑪ 0-8-2
⑫ 0
⑬ 0-1
⑭ 11-0-9-1
⑮ 12-11

Control Character Representations

ACK	Acknowledge	EOT	End of Transmission
BEL	Bell	ESC	Escape
BS	Backspace	ETB	End of Transmission Block
BYP	Bypass	ETX	End of Text
CAN	Cancel	FF	Form Feed
CC	Cursor Control	FS	Field Separator
CR	Carriage Return	HT	Horizontal Tab
CU1	Customer Use 1	IFS	Interchange File Separator
CU2	Customer Use 2	IGS	Interchange Group Separator
CU3	Customer Use 3	IL	Idle
DC1	Device Control 1	IRS	Interchange Record Separator
DC2	Device Control 2	IUS	Interchange Unit Separator
DC4	Device Control 4	LC	Lower Case
DEL	Delete	LF	Line Feed
DLE	Data Link Escape	NAK	Negative Acknowledge
DS	Digit Select	NL	New Line
EM	End of Medium	NUL	Null
ENQ	Enquiry		

PF	Punch Off
PN	Punch On
RES	Restore
RS	Reader Stop
SI	Shift In
SM	Set Mode
SMM	Start of Manual Message
SO	Shift Out
SOH	Start of Heading
SOS	Start of Significance
SP	Space
STX	Start of Text
SUB	Substitute
SYN	Synchronous Idle
TM	Tape Mark
UC	Upper Case
VT	Vertical Tab

Special Graphic Characters

¢	Cent Sign	-	Minus Sign, Hyphen
.	Period, Decimal Point	/	Slash
<	Less-than Sign	,	Comma
(	Left Parenthesis	%	Percent
+	Plus Sign	_	Underscore
|	Logical OR	>	Greater-than Sign
&	Ampersand	?	Question Mark
!	Exclamation Point	:	Colon
$	Dollar Sign	#	Number Sign
*	Asterisk	@	At Sign
)	Right Parenthesis	'	Prime, Apostrophe
;	Semicolon	=	Equal Sign
¬	Logical NOT	"	Quotation Mark

1100	C	8-4	FF	IFS	ENQ	DC4	<	*	%	@
1101	D	8-5	CR	IGS	ACK	NAK	(	)	|	'
1110	E	8-6	SO	IRS		SUB	+	;	∧	=
1111	F	8-7	SI	IUS	BEL		-	⌐	?	"

Fifteen positions in the table are exceptions to the above arrangement. These positions are indicated by small numbers in the upper right corners of their boxes in the table. The card hole patterns for these positions are given at the bottom of the table. Bit-position numbers, bit patterns, and hexadecimal representations for these positions are found in the usual manner.

Following are some examples of the use of the EBCDIC chart:

| | | | | Hole pattern | |
| | | | | Zone | Digit |
Character	Type	Bit positions 01 23 4567	Hex	punches	punches
PF	Control Character	00 00 0100	04	12–9	4
%	Special Graphic	01 10 1100	6C	0	8–4
R	Upper Case	11 01 1001	D9	11	9
a	Lower Case	10 00 0001	81	12–0	1
	Control Character, function not yet assigned	00 11 0000	30	12–11–0–9	8–1

Appendix B

List of Instructions by Set and Feature for the IBM 360/370 Systems[†]

STANDARD INSTRUCTION SET

Name	Mnemonic	Type[‡]	Code
Add	AR	RR C	1A
Add	A	RX C	5A
Add Half-Word	AH	RX C	4A
Add Logical	ALR	RR C	1E
Add Logical	AL	RX C	5E

[†] These lists of instructions are reprinted with permission from "IBM System/360: Principles of Operation" and "IBM System/370: Principles of Operation," IBM System Products Division, Poughkeepsie, New York. © 1966 and 1970 by International Business Machines Corporation.

[‡] A C in the "Type" column indicates that the instruction may change the condition code, and an L indicates that a new condition code is loaded.

Name	Mnemonic	Type‡	Code
AND	NR	RR C	14
AND	N	RX C	54
AND	NI	SI C	94
AND	NC	SS C	D4
Branch and Link	BALR	RR	05
Branch and Link	BAL	RX	45
Branch on Condition	BCR	RR	07
Branch on Condition	BC	RX	47
Branch on Count	BCTR	RR	06
Branch on Count	BCT	RX	46
Branch on Index High	BXH	RS	86
Branch on Index Low or Equal	BXLE	RS	87
Compare	CR	RR C	19
Compare	C	RX C	59
Compare Half-Word	CH	RX C	49
Compare Logical	CLR	RR C	15
Compare Logical	CL	RX C	55
Compare Logical	CLC	SS C	D5
Compare Logical	CLI	SI C	95
Convert to Binary	CVB	RX	4F
Convert to Decimal	CVD	RX	4E
Diagnose		SI	83
Divide	DR	RR	1D
Divide	D	RX	5D
Exclusive OR	XR	RR C	17
Exclusive OR	X	RX C	57
Exclusive OR	XI	SI C	97
Exclusive OR	XC	SS C	D7
Execute	EX	RX	44
Halt I/O	HIO	SI C	9E
Insert Character	IC	RX	43
Load	LR	RR	18
Load	L	RX	58
Load Address	LA	RX	41
Load and Test	LTR	RR C	12
Load Complement	LCR	RR C	13
Load Half-Word	LH	RX	48
Load Multiple	LM	RS	98
Load Negative	LNR	RR C	11
Load Positive	LPR	RR C	10
Load PSW	LPSW	SI L	82

Name	Mnemonic	Type‡	Code
Move	MVI	SI	92
Move	MVC	SS	D2
Move Numerics	MVN	SS	D1
Move with Offset	MVO	SS	F1
Move Zones	MVZ	SS	D3
Multiply	MR	RR	1C
Multiply	M	RX	5C
Multiply Half-Word	MH	RX	4C
OR	OR	RR C	16
OR	O	RX C	56
OR	OI	SI C	96
OR	OC	SS C	D6
Pack	PACK	SS	F2
Set Program Mask	SPM	RR L	04
Set System Mask	SSM	SI	80
Shift Left Double	SLDA	RS C	8F
Shift Left Single	SLA	RS C	8B
Shift Left Double Logical	SLDL	RS	8D
Shift Left Single Logical	SLL	RS	89
Shift Right Double	SRDA	RS C	8E
Shift Right Single	SRA	RS C	8A
Shift Right Double Logical	SRDL	RS	8C
Shift Right Single Logical	SRL	RS	88
Start I/O	SIO	SI C	9C
Store	ST	RX	50
Store Character	STC	RX	42
Store Half-Word	STH	RX	40
Store Multiple	STM	RS	90
Subtract	SR	RR C	1B
Subtract	S	RX C	5B
Subtract Half-Word	SH	RX C	4B
Subtract Logical	SLR	RR C	1F
Subtract Logical	SL	RX C	5F
Supervisor Call	SVC	RR	0A
Test and Set	TS	SI C	93
Test Channel	TCH	SI C	9F
Test I/O	TIO	SI C	9D
Test under Mask	TM	SI C	91
Translate	TR	SS	DC
Translate and Test	TRT	SS C	DD
Unpack	UNPK	SS	F3

FLOATING-POINT FEATURE INSTRUCTIONS

Name	Mnemonic	Type‡	Code
Add Normalized (Long)	ADR	RR C	2A
Add Normalized (Long)	AD	RX C	6A
Add Normalized (Short)	AER	RR C	3A
Add Normalized (Short)	AE	RX C	7A
Add Unnormalized (Long)	AWR	RR C	2E
Add Unnormalized (Long)	AW	RX C	6E
Add Unnormalized (Short)	AUR	RR C	3E
Add Unnormalized (Short)	AU	RX C	7E
Compare (Long)	CDR	RR C	29
Compare (Long)	CD	RX C	69
Compare (Short)	CER	RR C	39
Compare (Short)	CE	RX C	79
Divide (Long)	DDR	RR	2D
Divide (Long)	DD	RX	6D
Divide (Short)	DER	RR	3D
Divide (Short)	DE	RX	7D
Halve (Long)	HDR	RR	24
Halve (Short)	HER	RR	34
Load and Test (Long)	LTDR	RR C	22
Load and Test (Short)	LTER	RR C	32
Load Complement (Long)	LCDR	RR C	23
Load Complement (Short)	LCER	RR C	33
Load (Long)	LDR	RR	28
Load (Long)	LD	RX	68
Load Negative (Long)	LNDR	RR C	21
Load Negative (Short)	LNER	RR C	31
Load Positive (Long)	LPDR	RR C	20
Load Positive (Short)	LPER	RR C	30
Load (Short)	LER	RR	38
Load (Short)	LE	RX	78
Multiply (Long)	MDR	RR	2C
Multiply (Long)	MD	RX	6C
Multiply (Short)	MER	RR	3C
Multiply (Short)	ME	RX	7C
Store (Long)	STD	RX	60
Store (Short)	STE	RX	70
Subtract Normalized (Long)	SDR	RR C	2B
Subtract Normalized (Long)	SD	RX C	6B
Subtract Normalized (Short)	SER	RR C	3B
Subtract Normalized (Short)	SE	RX C	7B

Name	Mnemonic	Type‡	Code
Subtract Unnormalized (Long)	SWR	RR C	2F
Subtract Unnormalized (Long)	SW	RX C	6F
Subtract Unnormalized (Short)	SUR	RR C	3F
Subtract Unnormalized (Short)	SU	RX C	7F

DECIMAL FEATURE INSTRUCTIONS

Name	Mnemonic	Type‡	Code
Add (Packed) Decimal	AP	SS C	FA
Compare (Packed) Decimal	CP	SS C	F9
Divide (Packed) Decimal	DP	SS	FD
Edit	ED	SS C	DE
Edit and Mark	EDMK	SS C	DF
Multiply (Packed) Decimal	MP	SS	FC
Subtract (Packed) Decimal	SP	SS C	FB
Zero and Add (Packed)	ZAP	SS C	F8

Commercial Instruction Set

The commercial instruction set includes the instructions of both the standard instruction set and the decimal feature.

Protection Feature Instructions

Name	Mnemonic	Type‡	Code
Insert Storage Key	ISK	RR	09
Set Storage Key	SSK	RR	08

Scientific Instruction Set

The scientific instruction set includes the instructions of both the standard instruction set and the floating-point feature.

Universal Instruction Set

When the instructions associated with storage protection are added to the commercial and scientific features, a universal instruction set is obtained.

Direct Control Feature Instructions

Name	Mnemonic	Type‡	Code
Read Direct	RDD	SI	85
Write Direct	WRD	SI	84

ADDITIONAL INSTRUCTIONS, 370 SYSTEM ONLY

The IBM 370 system has available the entire instruction set of the 360 system, and the fourteen additional instructions listed below.

Name	Mnemonic	Type‡		Code
Compare Logical Characters under Mask	CLM	RS	C	BD
Compare Logical Long	CLCL	RR	C	0F
Insert Characters under Mask	ICM	RS	C	BF
Load Control	LCTL	RS		B7
Monitor Call	MC	SI		AF
Move (Character) Long	MVCL	RR	C	0E
Set Clock	SCK	SI	C	B204
Shift and Round (Packed) Decimal	SRP	SS	C	F0
Start I/O Fast Release	SIOF	SI	C	9C
Store Channel ID	STIDC	SI	C	B203
Store Characters under Mask	STCM	RS		BE
Store Clock	STCK	SI	C	B205
Store CPU ID	STIDP	SI		B202
Store Control	STCTL	RS		B6

Appendix C

Description of BAREBONZ Instructions

The machine language instructions for the BAREBONZ machine were listed and defined in precise terms in Tables 3.3.1 and 3.6.1. Here, we provide a convenient summary with a word description of each instruction. Of the three types of instructions in Table C.1—RR, RX, and RS—only the RX instructions can be indexed. This is accomplished at the instruction level by choosing an index register and inserting its hexadecimal number into hexdigit 3 (the fourth position from the left) of the instruction.

For the set of instructions in Table C.1, the three instruction formats are:

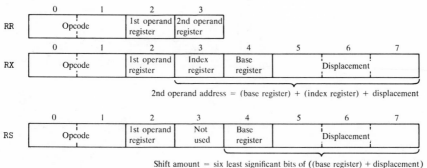

Table C.1 Summary of BAREBONZ Instructions

	Operation mnemonic	Type, cond. code	Operation code	First operand	Action	Second operand	Defined in table
Data copying	L	RX	58	Register	loaded with word from	Memory address	3.3.1
	LR	RR	18	Register	loaded with word from	Register	3.6.1
	LA	RX	41	Register	loaded with	Memory address	3.3.1
	ST	RX	50	Register	contents stored in	Memory address	3.3.1
	STH	RX	40	Register	contents (right half) stored in	Memory address	3.3.1
One-operand arithmetic	LTR	RR,CC	12	Register	loaded with word from	Register	3.6.1
	LCR	RR,CC	13	Register	loaded with complement of word from	Register	3.6.1
	LPR	RR,CC	10	Register	loaded with magnitude of word from	Register	3.6.1
	LNR	RR,CC	11	Register	loaded with negated magnitude of word from	Register	3.6.1
Two-operand arithmetic	A	RX,CC	5A	Register	contents have added to them word from	Memory address	3.3.1
	AR	RR,CC	1A	Register	contents have added to them word from	Register	3.6.1
	S	RX,CC	5B	Register	contents have subtracted from them word from	Memory address	3.3.1

SR	RR,CC	1B	Register contents have subtracted from them word from	Register	3.6.1
M	RX	5C	Even-odd pair of registers receives product of odd register and contents of	Memory address	3.3.1
D	RX	5D	Even register receives remainder and odd register receives quotient of even-odd pair of registers divided by contents of	Memory address	3.3.1
Branching					
BAL	RX	45	Register receives address of next instruction and branching occurs to	Memory address	3.3.1
BALR	RR	05	Register receives address of next instruction and branching occurs to address in	Register	3.6.1
BC	RX	47	Mask determines branch conditions to	Register	3.3.1
BCR	RR	07	Mask determines branch conditions to address in	Memory address	3.6.1
Shifting					
SRDL	RS	8C	Even-odd pair of registers shifted right by	Shift amount	3.3.1
SLDL	RS	8D	Even-odd pair of registers shifted left by	Shift amount	3.3.1
SRDA	RS,CC	8E	Even-odd pair of registers shifted right and sign bit propagated right by	Shift amount	3.3.1
SLDA	RS,CC	8F	Even-odd pair of registers shifted left (sign bit preserved) by	Shift amount	3.3.1

There are some precautions to be observed in using these instructions, and some of the pitfalls are:

1. In multiplication, one of the numbers must have been previously loaded into the odd register numbered one higher than the even register which is the first operand.

2. In the integer division assumed in BAREBONZ, if the dividend fits in one register it must have been previously loaded into the odd register numbered one higher than the even register which is the first operand. Then it is very important to be sure the contents of the even register are zero. If the dividend is the result of multiplication, it need not be changed in any way before division occurs.

3. The double arithmetic shifts preserve the sign bit (leftmost bit in the pair of registers). For SLDA, overflow occurs if a bit unequal to the sign bit is shifted out of the even register. For SRDA, the sign bit is copied into positions vacated by shifting right, and there is no possibility for overflow. Since, in BAREBONZ, one has only double-shift instructions to accomplish single-shift functions, it is important to realize that the condition code after a double-arithmetic shift reflects the double-register result.

Appendix D

Analysis of a System Dump

There are occasions when a computer system can detect that the computation it is being asked to perform cannot be meaningful; examples are division by zero or an illegal operation code. At such times, the only reasonable action is to terminate the computation. Since this termination is initiated by the system rather than by the programmer, the termination is called *abnormal* (ABEND for abnormal ending in 360/370 jargon).

If there seems to be no printout at all, the first guess must be that the control cards are unacceptable. One should then examine the account card, EXEC card, and DD cards. Since these are all examined by the system before any action is taken on the program, it may well be that the offending card occurs far down in the input deck beyond a perfectly good program which is not given a chance. The moral is to examine control cards all the way through the deck, not just the first few.

If there is any printing, then at its top there should be an indication that the job was successfully completed or that it was abnormally ended. Here, we are concerned with the latter case, in fact with the case that the ABEND was system initiated.

Almost any job is a sequence of steps controlled by different processing programs (examples are an assembler, FORTRAN compiler, linker, and loader). For each job step completed. a *return code* will be printed.† If 0000 is printed, then no errors were detected in execution of that step. If it is nonzero, there was at least a hint of trouble; the higher the code the more severe the warning and the less likely that subsequent job steps can be executed. These return codes are found among the control card printouts and may provide the clue that is needed, even if there is no other printing. On the operating system with which the authors are familiar this return code is labeled COND CODE. The return codes may be tested by successive steps of the job and be used to suppress execution where it cannot be successful. Interpretations for the various severity levels are listed in the publication *IBM System/360 Operating System: Messages and Codes* and in the publications associated with each processing program.

A systems program such as an assembler, compiler, linker, or loader will detect errors in the program it is processing and transmit diagnostic messages to appear in the printout. Since the systems program being executed is a thoroughly tested one, it should not commit errors which would require a diagnostic by the operating system. Suspected errors in the user's program will result in the printing of a nonzero return code at step completion (the more severe the error the higher the code), but they do not necessarily cause processing to terminate. We know, for example, that it is most useful for an assembler to attempt translation of all instructions so as to detect as many errors as possible in one assembly, even if the first instruction is incorrect.

By contrast, in a program not yet debugged, the system may detect trouble and have to provide its own messages. These are called *completion codes,* and they are printed only when an ABEND occurs; then the completion code is found in the job control portion of the printout. If the ABEND was user initiated, then the completion code will be one assigned by the user in an ABEND macro, and the user must interpret it. If it was system initiated, then the user should look up its explanation in the manual entitled *IBM System/360 Operating System: Messages and Codes,* which should be available at the computer facility. There is a table of some common completion codes at the end of this appendix.

Until a user's program gets into execution, a programmer must try to progress on information obtained from return codes and system diagnos-

---

† It is the contents of register 15 interpreted as an integer which are printed. A user program often sets no return code in register 15; but upon return from each job step, the last information left in register 15 is interpreted as the return code.

tics. When termination occurs in execution of a user's program, the user has more control but a much less reliable program than the system programs to work with. If execution terminates without any printing initiated within the user's program, the programmer may be almost helpless to detect the cause, even with a completion code. There are two ways to proceed. One is to install small snapshots along the computation path to help estimate what progress had been made by the time an **ABEND** occurred. Alternatively, one can provide a data set to the system for recording the information which might be pertinent for trouble-shooting. If that is done, a dump of all information likely to be pertinent is recorded by the system in that data set. Since it is extremely difficult to eliminate any information about the computation from being of possible use, the resulting "system dump" can be massive. Fortunately, it doesn't occur unless specifically requested. The situation under which one gets a system dump to analyze is therefore likely to be a run following one in which there was an abnormal termination and in which the user-initiated output gives no indication of the cause. It may even be that there was no program output at all. In that situation, insertion of a control card which is either

or
$$//\text{GO.SYSUDUMP DD SYSOUT} = \text{A}$$
$$//\text{GO.SYSABEND DD SYSOUT} = \text{A}$$

will cause a dump to be recorded on the printer. **SYSUDUMP** collects less information than **SYSABEND** and for that reason is usually better to use. For this appendix, we assume that the user has a system dump requested by his program and that the goal is to get some useful information from it.

There is a vast amount of information in a system dump, and much of it is intelligible only to the systems programmer. For the casual assembler language user, it is adequate to operate on some simplifying assumptions and pinpoint only the data essential to applying them. These are:

1. The cause of the difficulty was probably with the user's program.

2. The most likely cause of trouble is in execution of the last one or two instructions attempted.

3. Since current control and some recent intermediate operands are in the registers, attempting to understand the contents of each register is likely to help.

4. If the PSW points into system programs, then the key concern is how control got there. Then the most helpful information will be in the areas where register contents were saved in program linkage.

5. To be able to avoid another such dump and at the same time make progress, one should try to initiate one's own snapshot (e.g., **SNAP** or

FORTRAN) before the system has a chance but far enough along to display the cause of the ABEND.

To the man adrift on a raft, the most important item of information may be to know where he is. As programmers, we know the location at the time of the ABEND from the instruction pointer in the rightmost three bytes of the PSW; it will show near the top of a dump as:

PSW   at   ENTRY TO ABEND----------hhhhhh

where the six h's stand for the hexdigits in the instruction pointer. But absolute location in memory is not nearly so helpful as position within the program where execution went awry. For that, we need to find where our program begins in memory. In the dump, we should expect to find pairs in the form

NM cccccccc EPA hhhhhh   or   NM cccccccc USE/EP hhhhhh

standing for program name (eight characters) and entry point address (six hexdigits). Among these, we choose the one with the name of our program. The corresponding address, labeled EPA or USE/EP, is the hexdigit representation of the beginning of our program. It is worth noting that the name can be one assigned by the system (GO is a favorite) even though the programmer has provided control section names. Figure D.1 shows segments from two dumps with the entry point address marked. In the first case, the heading under which to look is PRB (program request block). In the second case, it is CDE (contents directory entry). These correspond to two distinct versions of operating system.

USING THE ENTRY POINT ADDRESS

Subtracting the entry point address from the instruction pointer obtained from the PSW gives a location with respect to the relocatable assembly at which to look. Hopefully, it is in the program. Excution may have failed on the instruction immediately before this address, and that possibility should be thoroughly explored. On larger versions of 360/370 systems, many instructions are being decoded simultaneously and the error can be any of several instructions preceding this address. On the other hand, there may have been a branch which would have replaced the IAC contents. In that case, PSW contents may be of little use. A branch outside the program area can only be the result of branching to register contents, so it may be important now to examine register contents or to follow the save area chain as discussed a little later.

```
SEGMENT TABLE ORIGIN REGISTER  0101D580

TCB  00CA8R   RB   000AFC50   PIE    00000000   CMP   900C1000   TIOT  000AF790   DFB   000AD698   PIF    00000000   TPN  00000000
              MSS  0000C888   PK/FLG 20810008   JLR   00000000   LLS   00000000   FLG   000002E1   TMF    00000000   JST  0000CA88
              FSA  0A0AF740   TCB    0000CCF8   NTC   00000000   PIB   E0007768   FCB   00000000   TCB    00000000   OTC  00000000
              LTC  00000000   IQE    00000000   LPXFL E1050000   XTCB  00000000   USER  00000000   RFSV   00000000   RFSV 00000000
              STAF 00000000   TCT    00000000   MDIDS 00000000   NDSP  00000000   RESV  00000000   USER   00000000   JSCB 87012F24
              RFSV 00000000   RFSV   00000000   BITS  00000000   FXTI  00000000   GQE   000AFFD0   RESV   00000000   DAR  00000000
              EXT2 00000000   PCR    0000C868                     ARB   000AFFD0
              GTF  00000000   ST/RCM 000C1000
       EXT2


ACTIVE RBS                              SZ/STAB 2005D0C0   USE/EP 00090000                PSW  072N0000 00000000         WT/LNK 0000CA88
PRB   0AFE60   NM GO                    NOTE/LDAD 00090000   MDLNTH 00000057         Q 000000
               CDR

SVRB  0AFD00   NM SVC-601C   SZ/STAR 00140062   USE/EP 001FB000   PSW 040C0000 COIFB1DE   Q 00C273   WT/LNK 000AFF60
               RG 0-7   F000006C   000AF680   40090FF   00090112   000AF740   000AFC68   000AF448   00000058
               RG 8-15  000AF620   000AF388   000AFBA0   40090002   40090002   00090030   0009011C   00000000

SVRB  0AFC50   NM SVC-A05A   SZ/STAB 0014N062   USE/EP 001FB000   PSW 070C0000 CO19F05E   Q 00C273   WT/LNK 000AFD00
               RG 0-7   00000048   000AFD60   401FR002   000002E8   0000CA88   000AFD00   00090290   00090540
               RG 8-15  000AF658   00090402   0000CBA6   00000000   0000CA88   00090290   801FB17E   50005DC2

              Segment of dump from 370/135 with OS-MFT format

LOAD LIST
      NE 00021FF0   RSP-CDE 02021A70   NE 00021FF8   RSP-CDE 0102DA28   NE 00022000   RSP-CDE 0102D9F8
      NE 00022008   RSP-CDE 0102D828   NE 00022010   RSP-CDE 0102DAE8   NE 00022510   RSP-CDE 0102DA28
      NE 00024308   RSP-CDE 0102D9F8   NE 00024C58   RSP-CDE 0102D828   NE 00000000   RSP-CDE 0102DAE8

CDE
   024C60   ATR1 08   NCDE 000000   ROC-RB 00022A40   NM GO        USE 01   EPA 0D6158   ATR2 20   XL/MJ 029230
   021A70   ATR1 30   NCDE 024C60   ROC-RB 00000000   NM IGC0A05A  USE 02   EPA 0F4858   ATR2 28   XL/MJ 021FE0
   02DA28   ATR1 80   NCDE 02DA58   ROC-RB 00000000   NM IGG019CF  USE 02   EPA 23D120   ATR2 20   XL/MJ 02DA18
   02D9F8   ATR1 80   NCDE 02DA28   ROC-RB 00000000   NM IGG019CL  USE 02   EPA 23E800   ATR2 20   XL/MJ 02D9E8
   02D828   ATR1 80   NCDE 02D858   ROC-RB 00000000   NM IGG019BA  USE 02   EPA 23D640   ATR2 20   XL/MJ 02D818
   02DAE8   ATR1 80   NCDE 02D828   ROC-RB 00000000   NM IGG019BB  USE 02   EPA 23D818   ATR2 20   XL/MJ 02DAD8

   XL                       LN                 ADR                   LN                ADR              LN            ADR

   029230   SZ 00000010   NO 00000001   80005EA8   00D6158
```

Segments of dump from 360/65 with OS-MVT format

Figure D.1 To find the entry point to one's program amid the masses of numbers in an ABEND dump, one looks under the heading PRB (under systems with PCP or with MFT) or CDE (under systems with MVT).

USING REGISTER CONTENTS

We have seen that the general registers are the center of computational activity. Even though the computation has gone awry, it may well be that the registers still retain useful information. Almost any dump, whether initiated by the system or by the programmer, will print the contents of registers at the time the dump is initiated as shown in Figure D.2. We favor printing just the hexadecimal number of the register with its contents, but, in some dumps, acronyms for some of the linkage registers are used. In the case of system-initiated ABEND, register 15 may still contain the entry point address for the routine which was in execution; register 14 may still contain a return address which is meaningful; register 13 may point to a save area which is in the program; and the base register may be as set within the user program. If any of these is true, the register value may help to determine where execution was when disaster struck.

```
REGS AT ENTRY TO ABEND

FLTR 0-6     0000000000177000      0000000100000000      0000000000000000      0000000000000000

REGS 0-7     00000030   800004D2   0013D2A0   0013D818   0013D688   0013D81C   00000003   00000018
REGS 8-15    0013D408   00000190   00000060   40404000   4023E93A   0013D8A4   6013DD2A   00000000
```

Figure D.2 Contents of the general registers at the time of an abnormal ending may provide valuable pointers as well as indicators of progress through loops.

Clues as to the cause of termination may also be found in the contents of other registers. One may look in these registers for initial values, argument addresses, argument values, or for counters, the last of which may indicate progress through a loop. The inability to be specific about how to proceed gives weight to the principle that one should segment his programs and, in each computer run, include only one which has not been tested. This strategy localizes the search for instructions which caused registers to be as they are.

USE OF SAVE AREA PRINTOUTS

The elaborate chaining of save areas described in Chapter 5 is particularly advantageous in the analysis of a system dump. The pointer in the third word of the save area of a calling program is just the address of the save area of the program it calls. Starting from the save area it provided, the operating system can therefore find and print every active save area. This chain should enable the programmer to determine what user program was last in control when the ABEND occurred.

JOB JOBN5355   STEP GO   TIME 130927   DATE 74198

COMPLETION CODE   SYSTEM = OC9

PSW AT ENTRY TO ABEND FFC5000D 800D6D88 | ABEND was initiated with this setting of IAC |

```
TCB  01F130   RBP  0000C878   PIE   00000000   DEB  0001E5BC   TIO 0001E618   CMP  800C9000   TRN 00000000
              MSS  02024E18   PK-FLG CO850400   FLG  00007F78   LLS 00021C70   JLB  00022468   JPQ 00021A70
              FSA  010F5768   TCB   00021B78   TME  00000000   JST 0001F130   NTC  00000000   OTC 00263A8
              LTC  00000000   IQE   00000000   ECB  00021B14   STA 20000000   D-PQE 00029BE8   SQS 0001E448
              NSTAE 00000000  TCT   00000000   USER 00000000   DAR 00000000   RESV  00000000   JSCB 87027D8
```

ACTIVE RBS

```
PRB  022A40   RESV 00000000   APSW 80006D88   WC-SZ-STAB 00040082   FL-CDE 00024C60   PSW FFC5000D 800D6D88
              Q/TTR 00000000  WT-LNK 0001F130
```

```
SVRB 00C908   TAB-LN 00780220  APSW  F9F0F1C3   WC-SZ-STAB 00120002   TQN 00000000   PSW 00040033 5000A3FA
              Q/TTR  00006B1D   WT-LNK 00022A40
              RG 0-7  00000030  00006E60   00006290   00006808   00006680C   00000003   00000018
              RG 8-15 000063F8  00000190   00000060   4040400000  4023E93A   6006D2A   00000000
              EXTSA  0000218E   8F0F56D8   00000000   00000000   FF030000   0000C984   E2E8E2C9
                     C5C1F0F1   C9C5C130   C1C2C5D5   C4F93C90
```

```
SVRB 00C878   TAB-LN 001803C8  APSW  F1F0F5C1   WC-SZ-STAB 00120002   TQN 00000000   PSW FF04000C 400F4FA6
              Q/TTR  00006805   WT-LNK 0000C908
              RG 0-7  00105BB0  0000C968   8000A312   0008B370   0001F130   0000C908   0000C908
              RG 8-15 0001F130  4000A25A   0001F130   8F0F56D8   0001E6AC   0000C98C   00000000
              EXTSA  E2E8E2C9   C5C1F0F1   00000000   00036080   50016A0A   0008B370   0000C878
                     C6F24040   00190500   022B001A   05007852
```

LOAD LIST

```
NE 00021FF0   RSP-CDE 02021A70   NE 00021FF8   RSP-CDE 0102DA28   NE 00022000   RSP-CDE 0102D9F8
NE 00022008   RSP-CDE 0102DB28   NE 00022010   RSP-CDE 0102DAE8   NE 00022510   RSP-CDE 0102DA28
NE 000243D8   RSP-CDE 0102D9F8   NE 00024C58   RSP-CDE 0102DB28   NE 00000000               RSP-CDE 0102DAE8
```

Figure D.3 Continued on following page.

357

Contents directory entry

System name for user's job

Entry point address for user's job

Entry points for subprograms in save area chain at time of ABEND

```
CDE
     024C60  ATR1 08  NCDE 000000  ROC-RB 0022A40   NM GO        EPA 0D6158  USE 01  ATR2 20  XL/MJ 029230
     021A70  ATR1 30  NCDE 024C60  ROC-RB 00000000  NM IGCOA05A  EPA 0F4858  USE 01  ATR2 28  XL/MJ 021FE0
     02DA28  ATR1 B0  NCDE 02DA58  ROC-RB 00000000  NM IGG019CF  EPA 23D120  USE 02  ATR2 20  XL/MJ 02DA18
     02D9F8  ATR1 B0  NCDE 02DA28  ROC-RB 00000000  NM IGG019CL  EPA 23E800  USE 02  ATR2 20  XL/MJ 02D9E8
     02DB28  ATR1 B0  NCDE 02DB58  ROC-RB 00000000  NM IGG019BA  EPA 23D640  USE 02  ATR2 20  XL/MJ 02DB18
     02DAE8  ATR1 B0  NCDE 02DB28  ROC-RB 00000000  NM IGG019BB  EPA 23D818  USE 02  ATR2 20  XL/MJ 02DAD8

                                                LN            ADR      LN            ADR       LN    ADR

XL   029230  SZ 00000001  NO 00000010                        80005EA8          00D6158

                        Intervening data omitted


SAVE AREA TRACE
GO   WAS ENTERED VIA LINK      AT EP ASSMBLR
SA   0F5768  WD1 00000000  HSA 00000000  LSA 000D6174  RET 0000EC34  EPA 010D6158  R0  FD000008
             R1  000F57F8  R2  00021AB0  R3  5C021B18  R4  00026200  R5  000263A8  R6  0001E6C0
             R7  00027630  R8  00021AF0  R9  00000000  R10 00021B18  R11 00000000  R12 4023E93A

GO   WAS ENTERED VIA CALL      AT EP BLDTAB
SA   0D6174  WD1 00000000  HSA 000F5768  LSA 000D68A4  RET 400D61E0  EPA 000D6888  R0  00000030
             R1  000D6818  R2  00021AB0  R3  5C021B18  R4  00026200  R5  000263A8  R6  0001E6C0
             R7  00027630  R8  00021AF0  R9  00000000  R10 00021B18  R11 00000000  R12 4023E93A

GO   WAS ENTERED VIA CALL      AT EP TABNTRY
SA   0D68A4  WD1 00000000  HSA 000D6174  LSA 000D6914  RET FF0D6D2A  EPA 000D68F8  R0  00000030
             R1  000D6E60  R2  000D6290  R3  00000000  R4  000D6678  R5  000D680C  R6  00000003
             R7  00000018  R8  000D63F8  R9  00000000  R10 D9E70000  R11 00000004  R12 4023E93A

SA   0D6914  WD1 00000000  HSA 00000000  LSA 000D6BA4  RET 00000000  EPA 00000000  R0  00000000
             R1  00000000  R2  00000000  R3  00000000  R4  00000000  R5  00000000  R6  00000000
             R7  00000000  R8  00000000  R9  00000000  R10 00000000  R11 00000000  R12 00000000

                        Intervening data omitted
```

```
FLTR 0-6    00000000177000   000000010000000   00000000000000

REGS 0-7    00000030   000D6E60   00000D6290   000D6808      00006678   00000003   00000018
REGS 8-15   000D63F8   00000190   00000060   40404000        4023E93A   600D602A   00000000
                                                             000D680C   00000003
                                                             000D6BA4   600D602A
LOAD MODULE  GO
```

[box] Return from BLDTAB

[box] Save area in ASSMBLR for BLDTAB;
compare with 2nd item in save area trace

```
0D6140  D4C2D3D9 90EC000C 47F0F064 E2C1E5C5  F0F0F0F1 00000000 47F0F00C 07C1E2E2  *K>J      K R OK      OO ASS*
0D6160  400D61E0 000D6888 00000030 000D6818  00021AB0 5C021B18 00026200 000263A8  *MBLR     OO SAVE0001     .U*
0D6180  0001E6C0 00027630 00021AF0 00000000  00021818 00000000 4023E93A 50D0F020  * /  ,H   O*              Y*
0D61A0  41D0F01C 58F0D004 50DF0008 45100060  8FD06238 0A134110 D6A458F0 D68C05EF  * O   O  &  O   -   Z & O  *
0D61C0  45100084 00130000 D2C90309 D6E840E6  C1E240C8 C5D9C52C 0A244110 D6B458F0  * D     KILROY WAS HERE  OU OO *  04 0*
0D61E0  D6C005EF 45100DAC 00180000 C8C540C6  D6E4D5C4 40D5D6C2 D6C4E840 C8D6D4C5  *O      HE FOUND NOBODY HOME*
0D6200  0A2458DF 000458ED D00C98EC D00C92FF  D00C41F0 0000007E 00000000 00000000  *Q        K      O*
0D6220  00000000 00000000 00480000 00000001  00004000 00000001 04000000 54000000  *a     04K O   Q*
0D6240  007C0020 0001F0B4 92230640 00230818  07000001 00000372 28022828 00F57301  *J    J .  Q  TESTR   M*
0D6260  01230120 00230120 0000007D 00000001  E3C5E2E3 D9404040 40D44040 40404040  *A      10,PUMPKIN    HORSE*
0D6280  40404040 40404040 40404040 40404040  40404040 C8D6D9E2 C5404040 40404040  *     DC  X'E2C5D4C1D7C8D6D0*
0D62A0  40C14040 40404040 F06BD7E4 D4D7D2C9  D5404040 40404040 F8C4F6C4 40404040  *     LACE     BALR  14,15*
0D62C0  F9704040 40404040 D3C1C3C5 40404040  D94040F1 F46BF1F5 40404040 40404040  *9'                    USIN*
0D62E0  40404040 40404040 40C4C340 40404040  40404040 F5C4F6C4 40404040 40404040  *,12                   SHEEP*
0D6300  40404040 40404040 40404040 40404040  40404040 40E4E2C9 D5404040 40404040  *ST     12,DESSERT+13(11)*
0D6320  68F1F240 40404040 40404040 40404040  40404040 E2C8C5C5 D7404040 40404040  *PEARL  DC   OH*0'*
0D6340  40EE2340 40404040 F26BC4C5 E2E2C5D9  E34EF1F3 4DF1F150 40404040 40404040  *      OPAL   DC   OF'0'*
0D6360  D7C5C1D9 D3404040 40C4C340 40404040  40C4C340 40404040 C670F07D 40404040  *D'0'          ONYX   DC*   O*
0D6380  40404040 40404040 D6D7C1D3 40404040  40404040 C3D6E640 40404040 40404040  *S      5,LETTUCE    COW*
0D63A0  40404040 40404040 40404040 40404040  D6D5E8E7 40404040 40404040 40404040  *              END*
0D63C0  C470F07D 40404040 40404040 40404040  40404040 40404040 40404040 40404040
0D63E0  40E24040 40404040 68D3C5E3 E3E4C3C5  40404040 40404040 40404040 40404040
0D6400  40404040 40C5D5C4 40404040 40404040  40404040 40404040 40404040 40404040
0D6420  40404040 40404040 40404040 40404040  40404040 40404040 40404040 40404040
0D6440  D7404040 0000000E D7C5C1D9 D3404040  40404040 D6D7C1D3 40404040 00000014  *P     HORSE   LACE   TESTR *

LINES 0D6460-0D6640 SAME AS ABOVE

0D6660  40404040 40404040 40404040 40404040  40404040 E3C5E2E3 D9404040 40404040  *P     HORSE   LACE   TESTR *
0D6680  0000000D C8D6D9E2 C5404040 00000004  D3C1C3C5 40404040 E2C8C5C5 E2C8C5C5  *      PEARL   OPAL   SHEE*
0D66A0  D7404040 0000000E D7C5C1D9 D3404040  00000012 D6D7C1D3 D6D7C1D3 00000014  *P     PEARL   OPAL*
```

Following data omitted

Figure D.3 Distributed through the masses of numbers in a system dump are a few relatively straightforward items of information of use to the beginning programmer. These have been annotated for convenience.

Save area printouts can also be a substantial help in the analysis of linkage between calling and called programs. Even competent programmers will occasionally use an address instead of a value (or vice versa) in other than routine problems. Nothing is so convincing of one's mistakes as seeing them displayed in the save area printout. Note that registers holding pointers, such as register 1, point to the address lists which permit checking of argument values as they were left in memory. An example of a system dump in Figure D.3 shows three save areas from a simple program.

GETTING AWAY FROM THE SYSTEM DUMP

If one has succeeded in locating the portion of program causing the system dump, a correction is often evident. Once that is done, execution should continue farther. If the cause of the system dump is not found, the programmer will almost surely have to provide some sort of execution trace such as small snapshots placed along the computation path to localize the trouble area. If a correction is made, one must decide whether to let things go to the next ABEND, or to try to control the output. There are practitioners from each school. We feel that it is not enough to get the program to run to a certain point without stopping; one must also try to determine that, up to that point, reasonable answers are being generated. We can do this and let execution run farther too by inserting a snapshot at about the point in execution where the ABEND occurred so as to display registers and storage where key values are held.

In Chapter 4 we used the SNAP macro for displaying the PSW, contents of the general registers, and selected portions of memory within one's own program. As described in the manual entitled *IBM System/360 Operating System: Supervisor and Data Management Macro Instructions* it is more versatile, and can also be used to display the contents of save areas and portions of memory not in one's program.

If one takes pains to save registers 0 and 1 before invoking SNAP (in case their contents have further use) and to restore them afterward, execution can continue after the SNAP. Some of these features are mentioned in Chapter 5. Clearly, a snapshot in a tight loop can have a devastating effect on the paper supply and should be guarded against by controls on lines printed as well as by thoughtful programming. When an ABEND occurs, one should expect to verify correctness of results through the snapshot and then grope as before for the cause of the next ABEND. The novice may detect a rather pessimistic tone here, for we assume there is always one more abnormal ending ahead. We can only say that that assumption is false only once per program and true most of the time in the debugging stage.

There is another ridiculously simple but nevertheless effective way to mark progress through a user's program. It relies on the WTL (write to log) macro which is not effective with PCP or MFT. With MVT operating systems, it writes the character string appearing enclosed in quotes in its operand field in the control card portion of the printout. If each WTL card has its own distinct message, a scattering of these through the program can be extremely effective in localizing the search for program faults without being expensive in machine time. The key consideration is that two messages appear in the same order in the printout as that in which they were transmitted during execution. Figure D.4 displays the log and job control portion of a run in which two uses of the WTL macro were made. An overlay on this sheet shows the portion of the program containing the macro invocations. Return codes and a completion code for the last step are marked. Beware: even WTL destroys some registers.

SELECTED COMPLETION CODE EXPLANATIONS †

0CX   *Explanation:* A program interruption occurred during execution of any instruction other than those listed under completion codes 0F1 and 0F2. When the interruption occurred, the program had not specified a routine to handle this type of program interruption.

The last digit of this completion code is a hexadecimal number that indicates the cause of the program interruption:

Last digit	Program interruption cause
0	*Imprecise or multiple-imprecise program interruption:* on the Model 91 or the Model 195, a program exception (or series of program exceptions) was detected during execution of an instruction that cannot be precisely identified by the instruction address in the current program status word (PSW). (The instruction-length code is 0.)
1	*Operation exception:* an operation code is not assigned or the assigned operation is not available on the particular model. (The operation is suppressed. The instruction-length code is 1, 2, or 3.)

---

† These completion codes are reprinted with permission from "IBM System/360 Operating System: Messages and Codes," and "IBM System/360 Operating System: Programmer's Guide to Debugging," IBM System Products Division, Poughkeepsie, New York. © 1967 by International Business Machines Corporation.

H A S P   S Y S T E M   L O G

```
N 13 11 28      JOB 367 -- JOBN6162 -- BEGINNING EXEC - INIT 2 - CLASS *
L*13 18 11      JOB 367 KILROY WAS HERE
L*13 18 12      JOB 367 HE FOUND NOBODY HOME
$*13 18 22      JOB 367 ESTIMATED LINES EXCEEDED
 *13 18 44      JOB 367 IEF450I JOBN6162.GO           ABEND SOC9      TIME=13.18.44
N 13 18 50      JOB 367 END EXECUTION.        STMT   SOURCE STATEMENT
```

The appearance of 'KILROY WAS HERE' in the system log shows that execution proceeded through statement 60, and the appearance of 'HE FOUND NOBODY HOME' shows that execution proceeded through statement 71.	36 ASSMBLR CSECT
	37 PRINT NOGEN
	38 ENTER
	51 OPEN (SNAPPER,OUTPUT)
	57 LA 1,=A(SOURCE,MAXLINZ,SYMTAB,TABLNGT)
	58 L 15,=V(BLDTAB)
	59 BALR 14,15
	60 WTL 'KILROY WAS HERE'
	68 LA 1,=A(SYMTAB,TABLNGT)
	69 L 15,=V(PRINTAB)
	70 BALR 14,15
	71 WTL 'HE FOUND NOBODY HOME'
	            D 10,ZERO
	            EXIT

```
//JOBN6162 JOB MSGLEVEL=(2,0),MSGCLASS=A,
//*
//**OPART,3COPY
//**MCSTOO1D,075-28-3665-0,STARK
// EXEC ASMGC
//SYSIN       DD *              GENERATED STATEMENT
```
| Job step 1 | IEF142I - STEP WAS EXECUTED - COND CODE 0000 |
```
             NMSO11I STEP ASM     EXECUTION TIME =    016.19 SEC.
             NMSO13I STEP ASM     REGION = 0128K   MAX CORE USED = 0128K
// EXEC ASMGC
//SYSIN       DD *              GENERATED STATEMENT
```
| Job step 2 | IEF142I - STEP WAS EXECUTED - COND CODE 0000 |
```
             NMSO11I STEP ASM     EXECUTION TIME =    003.74 SEC.
             NMSO13I STEP ASM     REGION = 0128K   MAX CORE USED = 0128K
// EXEC ASMGC
//SYSIN       DD *              GENERATED STATEMENT
```
| Job step 3 | IEF142I - STEP WAS EXECUTED - COND CODE 0000 |
```
             NMSO11I STEP ASM     EXECUTION TIME =    003.80 SEC.
             NMSO13I STEP ASM     REGION = 0128K   MAX CORE USED = 0128K
// EXEC ASMGC
```

> There is one return code (labeled COND CODE) generated for each job step completed.

```
//SYSIN       DD *              GENERATED STATEMENT
             IEF142I - STEP WAS EXECUTED - COND CODE 0000
```
| Job step 4 | NMSO11I STEP ASM   EXECUTION TIME =   004.30 SEC. |
```
             NMSO13I STEP ASM     REGION = 0128K   MAX CORE USED = 0128K
// EXEC ASMGC
//SYSIN       DD *              GENERATED STATEMENT
             IEF142I - STEP WAS EXECUTED - COND CODE 0000
```
| Job step 5 | NMSO11I STEP ASM   EXECUTION TIME =   005.34 SEC. |
```
             NMSO13I STEP ASM     REGION = 0128K   MAX CORE USED = 0128K
// EXEC FORTGCLG
//SYSIN       DD *              GENERATED STATEMENT
             IEF142I - STEP WAS EXECUTED - COND CODE 0000
```
| Job step 6 | NMSO11I STEP FORT   EXECUTION TIME =   000.75 SEC. |
```
             NMSO13I STEP FORT    REGION = 0128K   MAX CORE USED = 0082K
             IEF142I - STEP WAS EXECUTED - COND CODE 0000
```
| Job step 7 | NMSO11I STEP LKED   EXECUTION TIME =   001.10 SEC. |
```
             NMSO13I STEP LKED    REGION = 0128K   MAX CORE USED = 0096K
//GO.SNAPDUMP DD SYSOUT=A
//GO.SYSUDUMP DD SYSOUT=A
```
> Division by 0 caused an ABEND with a completion code of 0C9.

```
             COMPLETION CODE - SYSTEM=0C9  USER=0000
```
| Job step 8 returns a completion code rather than a return code because execution of the composite program was not successful. | IEF242I ALLOC. FOR JOBN6162 GO   AT ABEND
IEF237I 236   ALLOCATED TO PGM=*.DD
IEF237I 236   ALLOCATED TO STEPLIB
IEF237I 50E   ALLOCATED TO FT06F001
IEF237I 40D   ALLOCATED TO FT07F001
IEF237I 63E   ALLOCATED TO SNAPDUMP
IEF237I 53E   ALLOCATED TO SYSUDUMP
IEF285I   SYS74180.T210306.RV000.JOBN6162.GOSET   PASSED
IEF285I   VOL SER NOS= NMSU03.
IEF285I   SYS74180.T210306.RV000.JOBN6162.GOSET   DELETED
IEF285I   VOL SER NOS= NMSU03.
NMSO11I STEP GO   EXECUTION TIME =   004.30 SEC.
NMSO13I STEP GO   REGION = 0128K   MAX CORE USED = 0044K
NMSO12I TOT. JOBN6162 EXECUTION TIME =   039.52 SEC.
NMSO16I TIME OF DAY = 13.18.47 |

Figure D.4 Return codes on completed steps and a completion code for the interrupted step are key items in error diagnosis. Progress of computation through the user program is shown by invocations of the WTL macro.

Last digit	Program interruption cause

2   *Privileged-operation exception:* a privileged operation is encountered in the problem state.
(The operation is suppressed. The instruction-length code is 1 or 2.)

3   *Execute exception:* the subject instruction of EXECUTE is another EXECUTE.
(The operation is suppressed. The instruction-length code is 2.)

4   *Protection exception:* the key of an instruction half word or an operand in storage does not match the protection key in the PSW.
(The operation is suppressed on a store violation, except in the case of STORE MULTIPLE, READ DIRECT, TEST AND SET, and variable-length operations, which are terminated. Except for EXECUTE, which is suppressed, the operation is terminated on a fetch violation. The instruction-length code is 0, 2, or 3.)

5   *Addressing exception:* an address specifies any part of data, an instruction, or a control word outside the available storage for the particular installation.
(In most cases, the operation is terminated for an invalid data address. Data in storage remain unchanged, except when designated by valid addresses. In a few cases, an invalid data address causes the instruction to be suppressed—AND (NI), EXCLUSIVE OR (XI), OR (OI), MOVE (MVI), CONVERT TO DECIMAL, DIAGNOSE, EXECUTE, and certain store operations (ST, STC, STH, STD, and STE). The operation is suppressed for an invalid instruction address.
The instruction-length code normally is 1, 2, or 3; but may be 0 in the case of a data address.)

6   *Specification exception:* one of the following occurred:

• A data, instruction, or control-word address does not specify an integral boundary for the unit of information.

• The R_1 field of an instruction specifies an odd register address for a pair of general registers that contains a 64-bit operand.

• A floating-point register address other than 0, 2, 4, or 6 is specified.

Last digit	Program interruption cause

• The multiplier or divisor in decimal arithmetic exceeds 15 digits and sign.

• The first operand field is shorter than or equal to the second operand field in decimal multiplication or division.

• The block address specified in SET STORAGE KEY or INSERT STORAGE KEY has the four low-order bits not all zero.

• A PSW with a nonzero protection key is encountered when protection is not installed.

(The operation is suppressed. The instruction-length code is 1, 2, or 3.)

7   *Data exception:* one of the following occurred:

• The sign or digit codes of operands in decimal arithmetic or editing operations or in CONVERT TO BINARY are incorrect.

• Fields in decimal arithmetic overlap incorrectly.

• The decimal multiplicand has too many high-order significant digits.

(The operation is terminated. The instruction-length code is 2 or 3.)

8   *Fixed-point-overflow exception:* a high-order carry occurs or high-order significant bits are lost in fixed-point add, subtract, shift, or sign-control operations.

(The operation is completed by ignoring the information placed outside the register. The interruption may be masked by PSW bit 36. The instruction-length code is 1 or 2.)

9   *Fixed-point-divide exception:* a quotient exceeds the register size in fixed-point division, including divison by zero, or the result of CONVERT TO BINARY exceeds 31 bits.

(Division is suppressed. Conversion is completed by ignoring the information placed outside the register. The instruction-length code is 1 or 2.)

A   *Decimal-overflow exception:* the destination field is too small to contain the result field in a decimal operation.

(The operation is completed by ignoring the overflow information. The interruption may be masked by PSW bit 37. The instruction-length code is 3.)

B   *Decimal-divide exception:* a quotient exceeds the specified data field size.

Last digit	Program interruption cause

(The operation is suppressed. The instruction-length code is 3.)

C *Exponent-overflow exception:* the result characteristic in floating-point addition, subtraction, multiplication, or division exceeds 127 and the result fraction is not zero.
(The operation is completed. The fraction is normalized, and the sign and fraction of the result remain correct. The result characteristic is made 128 smaller than the correct characteristic. The instruction-length code is 1 or 2.)

D *Exponent-underflow exception:* the result characteristic in floating-point addition, subtraction, multiplication, halving, or division is less than zero and the result fraction is not zero.
(The operation is completed. The setting of the exponent–underflow mask (PSW bit 38) affects the results of the operation. When the mask bit is zero, the sign, characteristic, and fraction are set to zero, making the result a true zero. When the mask bit is one, the fraction is normalized, the characteristic is made 128 larger than the correct characteristic, and the sign and fraction remain correct. The instruction-length code is 1 or 2.)

E *Significance exception:* the result of a floating-point addition or subtraction has an all-zero fraction.
(The operation is completed. The interruption may be masked by PSW bit 39. The manner in which this operation is completed is determined by the mask bit. The instruction-length code is 1 or 2.)

F *Floating-point-divide exception:* division by a floating-point number with zero fraction is attempted.
(The operation is suppressed. The instruction-length code is 1 or 2.)

If bit 15 of the old program PSW (PSW at entry to ABEND) is on, the problem program had control when the interruption occurred. The correct register contents are reflected under the heading "REGS AT ENTRY TO ABEND" in an ABEND/SNAP dump. In a stand-alone dump, register contents can be found in the register save area for ABEND's SVRB.

122 *Explanation:* The operator canceled the job and requested a dump.

124 *Explanation:* The error was detected during execution of a WTL macro instruction.

The control program found one of the following:

• The buffer that should contain the message text from the macro instruction's operand did not contain any text; that is, the text length was less than five characters.

• The address in register 1 was not a multiple of 4.

Programmer Response: Correct the macro instruction to specify at least five characters of text. If the macro instruction was correct, check for program errors that could have incorrectly modified the macroexpansion of register 1. After making corrections, execute the job step again.

213 *Explanation:* The error occurred during execution of an OPEN macro instruction for a data set on a direct-access device. Possibilities are:

1. A data set control block (DSCB) could not be found on the direct access device.

2. An uncorrectable input-output error occurred in reading or writing a data set control block.

Register 4 contains the address of a combined work and control block area. This address plus X'64' is the address of the data set name in the JFCBDSNM field of the job file control block (JFCB).

222 *Explanation:* The operator canceled the job without requesting a dump. The cancelation was probably the result of a wait state or loop.

2F3 *Explanation:* In systems with MFT or MVT, the job was being executed when system failure occurred. A system restart was performed; a system job queue entry for the job existed at the time of failure.

Programmer Response: If results of the job are unsatisfactory, resubmit the job or job steps, as desired.

322 *Explanation:* Execution of a job step, cataloged procedure, or cataloged procedure step took longer than the time specified in:

• The TIME parameter of the EXEC statement;

• The standard time limit specified in the cataloged procedure for the SYSIN reader, if the TIME parameter was not specified by the EXEC statement.

System Action: The system abnormally terminated the job step, procedure, or procedure step.

Programmer Response: Check for program errors, such as endless loops, that would cause the job step, procedure, or procedure step to take too long. Correct any such errors. If no errors are found, specify longer time in the TIME parameter. Then execute the job again.

Appendix E

FORTRAN Input and Output Subprograms

For the material in Chapters 5, 6, and 8 it is convenient to be able to call on the input/output facilities of a higher-level language such as FORTRAN. For these purposes, the actual knowledge of FORTRAN required of the student is extremely small, and the simple examples given in Programs E.1–E.5 should suffice. The techniques of Chapter 5 can be used for linking with FORTRAN. If more complex FORTRAN subprograms are needed, they can easily be written with the aid of one of the many references available.

```
      SUBROUTINE WR40CH(LINE)
      INTEGER LINE(10)
      WRITE(6,1) LINE
    1 FORMAT(' ',30A4)
      RETURN
      END
```

Program E.1 This FORTRAN subroutine will print a line of 40 characters starting at location LINE. It can be changed to print $4m$ characters by replacing the numeral 10 with the value of m in the INTEGER statement. For example, INTEGER LINE(20) would print contents of a complete card of 80 characters.

```
      SUBROUTINE WRVBLN (LINE,N)
      INTEGER LINE(30),I,N
      WRITE(6,1) (LINE(I),I = 1,N)
    1 FORMAT (' ',30A4)
      RETURN
      END
```

Program E.2   This FORTRAN subroutine will print a line of 4N characters starting at location LINE where N $\leq$ 30.

```
      SUBROUTINE CHRHEX(SYMBOL,WORD)
      INTEGER SYMBOL(2),WORD(5)
      WRITE(6,1) SYMBOL,WORD
    1 FORMAT(' ',2A4,4X,5Z8)
      RETURN
      END
```

Program E.3   This FORTRAN subroutine will print a string of eight characters starting at the location SYMBOL and, to its right, a string of 40 hexadecimal digits from the locations starting at WORD. To change the number of words in the character string to m, one replaces the 2 in the INTEGER and FORMAT statements by the value of m. A similar replacement of 5's by a numeral n would cause n words of hexadecimal information to be printed. From the FORMAT statement, a rule is that $4m + 4 + 8n$ must not exceed the number of positions in one printline.

```
      SUBROUTINE RDVBLN(CARD,N)
      INTEGER CARD(20),I,N
      READ(5,1) (CARD(I),I = 1,N)
    1 FORMAT(20A4)
      RETURN
      END
```

Program E.4   This FORTRAN subroutine reads the entire contents of an 80-column card punched in character mode and deposits the resulting character string in memory starting at the location named CARD.

```
      SUBROUTINE CHRINT(NAME,AGE)
      INTEGER NAME(5),AGE(7)
      READ(5,1) NAME,AGE
    1 FORMAT(5A4,5X,7I4)
      RETURN
      END
```

Program E.5   This FORTRAN subroutine reads the leftmost 20 columns of a card into a string of 20 bytes starting at NAME, skips five columns, and then reads seven integers from columns 26–30, 31–35, . . . , 56–60. It can be adjusted to other layouts as described for Program E.3.

Instruction Times for System/370 Model 158†

These timing formulas show, in microseconds, the approximate time required to execute instructions in the System/370 Model 158. Because channel response time varies widely with the type of I/O device used, the times for the I/O instructions are not included. No CPU degradation due to channel interference is assumed.

These formulas are subject to change due to subsequent engineering change activity.

TIMING ASSUMPTIONS

The following assumptions were used in developing the instruction timing formulas:

† The material in this appendix was reprinted by permission from the manual entitled "IBM System/370 Model 158 Functional Characteristics," IBM Systems Products Division, Poughkeepsie, New York. © 1972 by International Business Machines Corporation.

369

General

1. No delay occurs during instruction execution because of conflicts caused by I/O or other asynchronous operation.

2. No program interruptions occur during the execution of the instruction (including overflow, underflow, and significance).

3. The instruction fetch time is overlapped with the execution of the previous instruction if the instruction buffer is not empty.

4. All operands and instructions are in the buffer storage 90% of the time and in the backing storage 10% of the time, unless otherwise assumed.

5. All data fetches are on appropriate boundaries; that is, the operands are on integral multiples of operand length. No boundary alignment is required. If boundary alignment should be required, the instruction times will be significantly longer.

6. The interval timer adds an additional 795 μsec to the instruction times every 1 sec of elapsed time.

7. The CPU timer adds an additional 4.5 μsec to the instruction times every 1 sec of elapsed time.

8. Each instruction time is increased by its share (which varies with the instruction type) of the time required to fill the instruction buffering registers if they should become drained during instruction processing.

9. The times do not include the local execution mode of the OS/DOS compatibility feature.

10. The instruction times do not include additional translation time for relocate mode. Translations are contained in the translation look aside buffer (TLB) 100% of the time.

The time in microseconds that is added to the CPU select time when translation is not in the TLB is shown in the table below:

		Segment not in latch	
	Segment in latch	Segment in buffer	Segment in backing storage
Page in buffer storage	0.690	1.150	1.725
Page in backing storage	1.265	1.725	2.300

11. All RX-type instructions are 0.115 μsec faster if either the base or the index register is zero.

12. In a test and set (TS) operation, the bit tested is a 1 in 50% of the cases.

13. Rounding occurs after a rounding operation 50% of the time.

SS-Format Instructions

1. Operand 1 and operand 2 are both in the buffer 75% of the time. Operand 1 or 2 is in the buffer 20% of the time. Both operand 1 and operand 2 are not in the buffer 5% of the time.

2. The operands of the VFL operations do not overlap.

3. For the move character long (MVCL) instruction, 50% of the data fetches and all of the data stores are to main storage.

4. For the pack (PACK) instruction, the length of operand 2 is two times the length of operand 1. The length does not include the sign byte.

5. For the unpack (UNPK) instruction, the length of operand 1 is two times the length of operand 2. The length does not include the sign byte.

6. For decimal add (AP), subtract (SP), and zero and add (ZAP) operations, the length of operand 1 is greater than or equal to the length of operand 2. No recomplementation occurs for the AP and SP operations.

7. The multiply decimal and divide decimal instructions are data dependent and the calculated instruction times will vary by a significccant amount for different data combinations.

8. In edit (ED) and edit and mark (EDMK) operations, 75% of the pattern bytes are digit-select.

Floating-Point Instructions

1. All floating-point numbers are already in normalized form.

2. All floating-point instruction times are data dependent; they depend on the number of hexadecimal digits that are preshifted due to exponent difference and postshifted for normalization and fraction overflow, as well as the number of times that recomplementation of a result occurs, and any sign difference. The times are given to one decimal point for these instructions to show that the time is data dependent and will vary by a significant amount. The times given include the following weighted averages for the listed variables (recomplementation is not included):

Add and Subtract Instructions

Time (μsec)	Operation
0.23	Preshift of long operands
0.16	Preshift of short operands
1.35	Preshift of extended operands
0.27	Postshift of normalized long operands
0.24	Postshift of normalized short operands
0.55	Postshift of extended operands
0.06	Sign difference

Compare Instructions

Time (μsec)	Operation
0.23	Preshift of long operands
0.16	Preshift of short operands
0.12	Sign comparison

Multiply and Divide Instructions

Time (μsec)	Operation
0.07	Postshift of multiply long operands
0.12	Postshift of multiply short operands
0.12	Postshift of multiply extended operands
0.23	Postshift of divide long operands
0.06	Postshift of divide short operands

3. The times required for preshifts and postshifts are:

Add and Subtract Instructions

Time (μsec)	Operation
0.230	Each preshift of long or short operands
1.150	First preshift of extended operands
0.805	Subsequent preshifts of extended operands
1.035	First postnormalization of long operands
0.690	Each subsequent postshift of long operands
0.920	First postnormalization of short operands
0.805	Each subsequent postshift of short operands
0.345	Fraction overflow for long or short operands
1.265	First postnormalization of extended operands
0.920	Subsequent postshifts of extended operands
1.495	Fraction overflow for extended operands

Compare Instructions

Time (μsec)	Operation
0.230	Each preshift of long or short operands

Multiply and Divide Instructions

Time (μsec)	Operation
0.345	Each postshift of multiply long operands
0.575	Each postshift of multiply short operands
0.575	Each postshift of extended operands
0.460	Each postshift of divide long operands
0.115	Each postshift of divide short operands

Multiprocessing

1. All the timing assumptions for non-MP models apply as well for the MP models.

2. In UP mode, non-MP-model instruction times apply when each CPU is assigned its main storage.

For statements 3 through 6, assume that all main storage is on-line and that both CPUs are running.

3. In UP mode, when one CPU is assigned only the main storage of the other CPU, storage instruction times can increase as much as 0.230 μsec per storage reference.

4. In UP mode, when one CPU is assigned only one-half its main storage, storage instruction times increase as much as 0.400 μsec per storage reference.

5. In UP mode, when one CPU is assigned all its main storage and one-half the main storage of the other CPU, storage instruction times increase as much as 0.315 μsec per storage reference.

6. In MP mode, when both CPUs are assigned all the available main storage, storage instruction times increase as much as 0.515 μsec per storage reference. Main storage result-storing instructions increase as much as 0.790 μsec per reference. Also, the ISK, SSK, and RRB times can increase as much as 1.495 μsec.

LEGEND FOR TIMING FORMULAS

B		Number of bytes processed. The terms B/8 and B/256 must be rounded to the next whole number.	DL		Number of decimal digit positions to be shifted left.
			DR		Number of decimal digit positions to be shifted right.
BT	1	If the branch is taken.			
	0	Otherwise.	DW		Number of double-words processed, not rounded.
CC	1	If an unsuccessful branch is caused only by the branch-to register being zero.	DW1		Number of double-words in operand 1, not rounded.
	0	Otherwise.	DW2		Number of double-words in operand 2, not rounded.
CM	0	If the fields compare.	E		Time for the subject instruction, which is executed by the 'execute' instruction. The instruction time is decremented by 0.115 μsec if no modification of the instruction is required.
	1	Otherwise.			
C1	1	If operand 1 crosses a double-word boundary.			
	0	Otherwise.			

EC   1 For EC mode.
      0 Otherwise.

F0   1 If the fraction is zero.
      0 Otherwise.

I   1 If program interrupt is taken.
      0 Otherwise.

I2   Contents of the I2 field expressed
      as a decimal number 0–15.

M   1 If the mask is not all zeros.
      0 Otherwise.

MB   Number of I-bits in the mask.

N   Total number of bytes in operand 1
      for instructions with a single
      length field. The terms N/4, N/8
      and N/16 must be rounded to
      the next whole number.

NRD   1 If no rounding is required.
      0 Otherwise.

N0   Number of high-order hex zeros
      in operand 1.

N1   Total number of bytes in the first
      operand (destination). The terms
      N1/2, N1/4 and N1/8 must be
      rounded to the next whole
      number.

N2   Total number of bytes in the second
      operand (source). The terms
      N2/4 and N2/8 must be rounded
      to the next whole number.

N3   −1 If only one byte is to be proc-
           essed.
       0 Otherwise.

N8   1 If left shift is required.
      1 If N1 is equal to or greater than
         two times the shift amount.
      1 If N1 + 1 is equal to or greater
         than two times the shift
         amount and the I3 field is not
         equal to zero.
      0 Otherwise.

N16   1 If N1 is equal to 2 or 16.
      0 Otherwise.

N21   0   If N2 is greater than N1.
      0.75 If N1 is equal to N2.
      1   Otherwise.

PNM   1 If postnormalization is required.
      0 Otherwise.

P1   0 If operand 1 is positive.
      1 Otherwise.

P2   0 If operand 2 is positive.
      1 Otherwise.

P3   1 If the signs of operand 1 and 2
         are different.
      0 Otherwise.

QWB   Number of quad-word boundaries
      crossed.

R   Number of registers to be loaded
      or stored.
      The term R/4 must be rounded to
      the next whole number.

R0   0 If operand 2 points to an
         address on a double-word
         boundary.
      0 If an odd number of registers is
         to be loaded or stored.
      1 Otherwise.

R1   0 If an even number of registers
         is to be loaded or stored.
      1 Otherwise.

R2   0 If the number of registers to be
         loaded or stored is greater
         than 2.
      1 Otherwise.

S   1 If no 4-bit shifts are taken.
      0 Otherwise.

S0   0 If no 1-bit shifts are taken.
      1 Otherwise.

S1		Number of 1-bit shifts remaining after completion of the 4-bit shifts.	S6	1	If two 1-bit shifts are taken.
				0	Otherwise.
S3	1	If more than eight 4-bit shifts are to be taken.	S7	1	If two or more 4-bit shifts are taken.
	0	Otherwise.		0	Otherwise.
S5	1	If shift is greater than three.	S9	1	If three 1-bit shifts are taken.
	0	Otherwise.		0	Otherwise.

SYSTEM/370 MODEL 158 INSTRUCTION TIMINGS

Instruction	Instruction format	Op code	Mnemonic	Time (μsec)
Add	RR	1A	AR	00.495
Add	RX	5A	A	00.933
Add Decimal	SS	FA	AP	$02.315+00.115(N1)+00.430(N1/4)$ $+00.430(N2/4) + 00.660 (C1)$
Add Halfword	RX	4A	AH	$01.163 + 00.230 (P2)$
Add Logical	RR	1E	ALR	00.380
Add Logical	RX	5E	AL	00.703
Add Normalized (Extended)	RR	36	AXR	05.0
Add Normalized (Long)	RR	2A	ADR	02.2
Add Normalized (Long)	RX	6A	AD	02.5
Add Normalized (Short)	RR	3A	AER	02.0
Add Normalized (Short)	RX	7A	AE	02.4
Add Unnormalized (Long)	RR	2E	AWR	02.0
Add Unnormalized (Long)	RX	6E	AW	02.2
Add Unnormalized (Short)	RR	3E	AUR	01.8
Add Unnormalized (Short)	RX	7E	AU	02.1
AND	RR	14	NR	00.840
AND	RX	54	N	01.163
AND (Immediate)	SI	94	NI	00.829
AND (Characters)	SS	D4	NC	$00.406+00.115(N)+00.702(N/4)$ $+00.593(N/8)$

Instruction	Instruction format	Op code	Mnemonic	Time (μsec)
Branch and Link	RR	05	BALR	00.725 + 00.288(BT)
Branch and Link	RX	45	BAL	01.163
Branch on Condition	RR	07	BCR	00.380+00.288(BT)+00.345(CC)
Branch on Condition	RX	47	BC	00.530+00.288(BT)
Branch on Count	RR	06	BCTR	00.380+00.403(BT)
Branch on Count	RX	46	BCT	00.645+00.288(BT)
Branch on Index High	RS	86	BXH	00.875+00.518(BT)
Branch on Index Low or Equal	RS	87	BXLE	00.990+00.403(BT)
Compare	RR	19	CR	00.380
Compare	RX	59	C	00.703
Compare and Swap	RS	BA	CS	01.163+00.115(CM)
Compare Decimal	SS	F9	CP CP CP	02.315+00.115(B)+00.430(N1/4) +00.345(C1) + 00.430(N2/4) +01.610(1-N21)-00.920(P3)(1-N21)
Compare Double and Swap	RS	BB	CDS	01.393+00.403(CM)
Compare Halfword	RX	49	CH	00.933+00.230(P2)
Compare Logical	RR	15	CLR	00.380
Compare Logical	RX	55	CL	00.703
Compare Logical	SI	95	CLI	00.588
Compare Logical	SS	D5	CLC	00.785+00.115(B) +00.702(DW) +00.914(B/8)
Compare Logical Long	RR	0F	CLCL	00.725+00.368(B) +00.529(B/8) +04.037(B/256)
Compare Logical Characters Under Mask	RS	BD	CLM	00.703+01.035(M)+00.115(MB)
Compare (Long)	RR	29	CDR	02.3
Compare (Long)	RX	69	CD	02.5
Compare (Short)	RR	39	CER	02.1
Compare (Short)	RX	79	CE	02.4
Convert to Binary	RX	4F	CVB	02.198

Instruction	Instruction format	Op code	Mnemonic	Time (μsec)
Convert to Decimal	RX	4E	CVD	02.370
Divide	RR	1D	DR	09.350
Divide	RX	5D	D	09.903
Divide Decimal	SS	FD	DP	06.535+02.875(N1)−03.450(N1/4) −04.600(N2)+02.875(N2)(N1−N2)
Divide (Long)	RR	2D	DDR	23.2
Divide (Long)	RX	6D	DD	23.3
Divide (Short)	RR	3D	DER	08.6
Divide (Short)	RX	7D	DE	08.9
Edit	SS	DE	ED	01.130+01.668(N)+02.128(DW) −01.323(C1)
Edit and Mark	SS	DF	EDMK	01.130+01.668(N)+02.128(DW) −01.323(C1)
Exclusive OR	RR	17	XR	00.840
Exclusive OR	RX	57	X	01.163
Exclusive OR (Immediate)	SI	97	XI	00.829
Exclusive OR	SS	D7	XC	00.406+00.115(N)+00.702(N/4) +00.593(N/8)
Execute	RX	44	EX	01.623 + E
Halt Device	SI	9E01	HDV	Indeterminate
Halt I/O	SI	9E00	HIO	Indeterminate
Halve (Long)	RR	24	HDR	01.070 + 00.690(PNM)
Halve (Short)	RR	34	HER	00.840 + 00.575(PNM)
Insert Character	RX	43	IC	00.818
Insert Characters Under Mask	RS	BF	ICM	00.703+01.035(M) +00.115(MB)
Insert Program Key	SI	B20B	IPK	01.565
Insert Storage Key	RR	09	ISK	01.185
Load	RR	18	LR	00.380
Load	RX	58	L	00.588

Instruction	Instruction format	Op code	Mnemonic	Time (μsec)
Load Address	RX	41	LA	00.530
Load and Test	RR	12	LTR	00.380
Load and Test (Long)	RR	22	LTDR	00.610
Load and Test (Short)	RR	32	LTER	00.610
Load Complement	RR	13	LCR	00.495
Load Complement (Long)	RR	23	LCDR	00.840+00.115(F0)
Load Complement (Short)	RR	33	LCER	00.840+00.115(F0)
Load Control	RS	B7	LCTL	11.915+00.483(R) −01.955(R2) +00.345(EC)
Load (Long)	RR	28	LDR	00.495
Load (Long)	RX	68	LD	00.703
Load Halfword	RX	48	LH	00.933+00.230(P2)
Load Multiple	RS	98	LM	01.070+00.207(R)+00.023(R1) +00.115(R0)
Load Negative	RR	11	LNR	00.380
Load Negative (Long)	RR	21	LNDR	00.610+00.115(F0)
Load Negative (Short)	RR	31	LNER	00.610+00.115(F0)
Load Positive	RR	10	LPR	00.380+00.115(P2)
Load Positive (Long)	RR	20	LPDR	00.610+00.115(F0)
Load Positive (Short)	RR	30	LPER	00.610+00.115(F0)
Load PSW	SI	82	LPSW	03.072
Load Real Address	RS	B1	LRA	05.590
Load Rounded (Extended to Long)	RR	25	LRDR	01.415 − 00.230(NRD)
Load Rounded (Long to Short)	RR	35	LRER	01.185 − 00.345(NRD)
Load (Short)	RR	38	LER	00.380
Load (Short)	RX	78	LE	00.703
Monitor Call	SI	AF	MC	01.113+00.115(I2)+07.830(I) +02.576(EC)
Move (Immediate)	SI	92	MVI	00.530

Instruction	Instruction format	Op code	Mnemonic	Time (μsec)
Move (Characters) 16 Bytes or Less	SS	D2	MVC	Formula is dependent on length: 00.784+00.115(N)+00.702(N/4) +00.092(DW)
More than 16 Bytes				01.797+01.271(N/8)−00.805(N/16)
Move Long	RR	0E	MVCL	01.070+00.633(B/8) +00.547(N2/8) +04.439(B/256)
Move Numerics	SS	D1	MVN	00.406+00.115(N)+00.702(N/4) +00.593(N/8)
Move with Offset	SS	F1	MVO	00.923+00.196(N1)+00.782(N1/4) +00.403(C1)+00.115(N3)
Move Zones	SS	D3	MVZ	00.406+00.115(N)+00.702(N/4) +00.593(N/8)
Multiply	RR	1C	MR	01.645
Multiply	RX	5C	M	01.991
Multiply (Extended)	RR	26	MXR	19.0
Multiply Decimal	SS	FC	MP	−01.030+04.600(N1)−03.330(N1/4) +02.875(DW1)−01.150(NC)
Multiply Halfword	RX	4C	MH	01.416
Multiply (Long)	RR	2C	MDR	03.2
Multiply (Long)	RX	6C	MD	03.9
Multiply (Long to Extended)	RR	27	MXDR	08.7
Multiply (Long to Extended)	RX	67	MXD	09.9
Multiply (Short)	RR	3C	MER	01.8
Multiply (Short)	RX	7C	ME	02.1
OR	RR	16	OR	00.840
OR	RX	56	O	01.163
OR (Immediate)	SI	96	OI	00.829
OR (Characters)	SS	D6	OC	00.406+00.115(N)+00.702(N/4) +00.593(N/8)
Pack	SS	F2	PACK	01.585 + 00.230(N1/2) −00.012(DW1−C1)
Purge TLB	SI	B20D	PTLB	09.155
Read Direct	SI	85	RDD	Indeterminate

Instruction	Instruction format	Op code	Mnemonic	Time (μsec)
Reset Reference Bit	SI	B213	RRB	02.485
Set Clock	SI	B204	SCK	01.462
Set Clock Comparator	SI	B206	SCKC	04.498
Set CPU Timer	SI	B208	SPT	05.245
Set Prefix	S	B210	SPX	188.0
Set Program Mask	RR	04	SPM	00.610
Set PSW Key From Address	SI	B20A	SPKA	01.680
Set Storage Key	RR	08	SSK	01.530
Set System Mask	SI	80	SSM	01.416+00.805(EC)
Shift and Round Decimal	SS	F0	SRP	05.541+00.230(N)+01.018(N/4) +00.190(N/8) + 00.432(C1) −00.564(N8) + 00.104(N16) +00.863(DL) + 00.805(DR)
Shift Left Double	RS	8F	SLDA	02.945+00.230(P1)+00.805(S3)
Shift Left Double Logical	RS	8D	SLDL	01.105+00.230(S1)
Shift Left Single	RS	8B	SLA	01.795+00.115(S)−00.115(S0) +00.115(S5)+00.805(S3)
Shift Left Single Logical	RS	89	SLL	00.875−00.230(S)+00.115(S7) +00.115(S9)+00.115(S)(S9) +00.115(S)(S6)
Shift Right Double	RS	8E	SRDA	01.450+00.230(S1)+00.230(P1)
Shift Right Double Logical	RS	8C	SRDL	01.105+00.230(S1)
Shift Right Single	RS	8A	SRA	00.875+00.115(S1)
Shift Right Single Logical	RS	88	SRL	00.875−00.230(S) +00.115(S7) +00.115(S9)+00.115(S)(S9)
Signal Processor (See Note)	RS	AE	SIGP	Indeterminate
Start I/O	SI	9C00	SIO	Indeterminate
Start I/O Fast Release	SI	9C01	SIOF	Indeterminate
Store	RX	50	ST	00.645
Store Channel ID	SI	B203	STIDC	04.210
Store Character	RX	42	STC	00.760
Store Characters Under Mask	RS	BE	STCM	01.680

Instruction	Instruction format	Op code	Mnemonic	Time (μsec)
Store CPU Address	S	B212	STAP	02.370
Store CPU ID	SI	B202	STIDP	01.565
Store CPU Timer	SI	B209	STPT	02.025
Store Clock	SI	B205	STCK	02.428
Store Clock Comparator	SI	B207	STCKC	01.220
Store Control	RS	B6	STCTL	02.140+00.403(R) − 00.058(R1) +00.575(R/4)
Store Halfword	RX	40	STH	00.875
Store (Long)	RX	60	STD	00.875
Store Multiple	RS	90	STM	02.370+00.115(R)+00.920(QWB)
Store Prefix	S	B211	STPX	02.485
Store (Short)	RX	70	STE	00.875
Store Then AND System Mask	SI	AC	STNSM	02.255 + 00.920(EC)
Store Then OR System Mask	SI	AD	STOSM	02.255 + 00.920(EC)
Subtract	RR	1B	SR	00.495
Subtract	RX	5B	S	00.933
Subtract Decimal	SS	FB	SP	02.315+00.115(N1)+00.430(N1/4) +00.430(N2/4)+00.660(C1)
Subtract Halfword	RX	4B	SH	01.163+00.230(P2)
Subtract Logical	RR	1F	SLR	00.380
Subtract Logical	RX	5F	SL	00.703
Subtract Normalized (Extended)	RR	37	SXR	05.0
Subtract Normalized (Long)	RR	2B	SDR	02.2
Subtract Normalized (Long)	RX	6B	SD	02.5
Subtract Normalized (Short)	RR	3B	SER	02.0
Subtract Normalized (Short)	RX	7B	SE	02.4
Subtract Unnormalized (Long)	RR	2F	SWR	02.0
Subtract Unnormalized (Long)	RX	6F	SW	02.2
Subtract Unnormalized (Short)	RR	3F	SUR	01.8
Subtract Unnormalized (Short)	RX	7F	SU	02.1
Supervisor Call	RR	0A	SVC	05.107 + 02.415(EC)

Instruction	Instruction format	Op code	Mnemonic	Time (μsec)
Test and Set	SI	93	TS	01.565
Test Channel	SI	9F	TCH	Indeterminate
Test I/O	SI	9D	TIO	Indeterminate
Test Under Mask	SI	91	TM	00.703
Translate	SS	DC	TR	02.980+00.662(N)+01.725(DW)
Translate and Test	SS	DD	TRT	01.200 + 01.110(B)
Unpack	SS	F3	UNPK	01.613+00.202(N2/4)−00.028(C1)
Write Direct	SI	84	WRD	Indeterminate
Zero and Add	SS	F8	ZAP	02.315+00.115(N1)+00.430(N1/4) +00.430(N2/4)+00.660(C1)

Note: For the signal processor (SIGP) instruction, the condition code (CC) is set to 3 when:

1. The addressed CPU is not configured to the sending CPU (as when the system is in UP mode).

2. The addressed CPU has an address other than 0000 or 0001.

3. A malfunction occurs that prohibits the addressed CPU from responding.

4. Certain CE functions (such as single cycle or ROS stop) prohibit the addressed CPU from responding.

In items 1 and 2, the response time to set the condition code to 3 is in the microsecond range. In items 3 and 4, the response time to set the condition code to 3 is approximately 35 sec.

The response time for most SIGP instructions is in the microsecond range, with the following exceptions:

Restart: While the response to the SIGP instruction is in the microsecond range, the CPU appears busy (CC = 2) to later SIGP instructions until the SVP goes to the program frame. This action may take several seconds.

Resets: The response to the SIGP instruction depends on the SVP frame. If the SVP is in the manual frame, the response is in the millisecond range. If the SVP is in the program frame, the response time is approximately 1.5 sec.

Appendix G

Chopping, Rounding, and Truncation Error

Much of mathematics is based on the concept that representations of numbers and of functions are exact. This is a great convenience, for it permits the use of equality. Where exact representations are impossible, approximations are necessary and the tolerance in the approximation becomes a necessary consideration.

Integers which are within machine capacity can be represented exactly; even very large integers will qualify if one distributes the representation over several words. But except for fractions which are exactly equal to $m/2^p$ for some p, the binary representation of fractions will be nonterminating. Any rational number (quotient of integers) can be represented by a number pair, say (m, n), which signifies m/n, but computation with such number pairs is exhausting and still will not avoid the necessity to approximate irrational numbers such as $\sqrt{2}$.

In practical computation, we must face the limitations of the computer which force us to approximate nonterminating fractions or fractions with length greater than a computer representation by fractions terminating with length to conform to the sizes of operand registers and storage cells. We distinguish two ways to make this approximation. One is called *chopping,* and the other is called *rounding.* After we have defined these carefully, we will distinguish another form of approximation called truncation. All these words are essential to the vocabulary of a computer scientist, and his understanding of them should be precise.

Chopping.   If the exact representation of the fractional part of a nonnegative number to base b is

$$f = .q_1q_2\cdots q_n\cdots$$

then chopping to m places yields

$$f_l = .q_1q_2\cdots q_m$$

as an approximation to f. We denote this as $f_l = \text{chop}_m(\text{f})$; clearly, $f_l \leq f$.

Rounding.   If the exact representation of the fractional part of a nonnegative number to base b is

$$f = .q_1q_2\cdots q_n$$

then rounding to m places is intended to select as a result that one of $f_l = .q_1q_2 \ldots q_m$ and $f_h = .q_1q_2 \ldots q_m + b^{-m}$ which is the closer to f. These approximations differ only by 1 in the last place. It may be that f_l and f_h differ from f by the same amount, in which case either approximation is appropriate.

Examples of rounding and chopping for base 10:

Exact number	Chopped to 2 places	Rounded to 2 places
0.176	0.17	0.18
0.003	0.00	0.00
0.155	0.15	0.15 or 0.16

Implementation of rounding.   If in the examples just above we had added 0.005 to each exact number, we would have gotten 0.181, 0.008, and 0.160. Chopping these numbers to two digits would have given a correctly rounded result. This notion can be formulated more generally, and we begin by using a graphical illustration.

If f is greater than or equal to f_l and less than $f_l + b^{-m}/2$, then the appropriate approximation is f_l. It will be of this size if and only if adding $b^{-m}/2$ to f yields a result less than f_h.

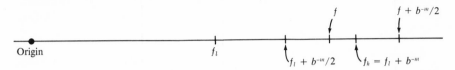

If f is greater than $f_l + b^{-m}/2$ and less than f_h, then the appropriate approximation is f_h. But f will be of this size if and only if adding $b^{-m}/2$ to f yields a result greater than f_h.

If f is actually equal to $f_l + b^{-m}/2$, then f_l and f_h are equally close to f, and the choice must be made on another criterion. Often that criterion is ease of implementation. Sometimes an attempt to choose f_l and f_h with equal frequency is made. Built-in rounding is chosen to be simple and reproducible and is likely to be very close to chop $(f + b^{-m}/2)$.

Explanation of rounding for negative numbers can be reduced to the above case by insistence that $\text{round}(-x) = -\text{round}(x)$.

To round nonnegative $f = .q_1q_2 \ldots q_n$ to m places, form

$$f' = f + b^{-m}/2$$

and then chop f' to m places. Thus we have defined for nonnegative f

$$\text{round}_m(f) = \text{chop}_m(f + b^{-m}/2)$$

Truncation.   Truncation is the replacement of one function by another, usually for the purpose of simplifying analysis or computation. We illustrate before defining the concept of truncation error. Suppose that g is a function for which estimates are needed in the interval from x_0 to x_2. It may be good enough for computation to approximate g as a straight line through $(x_0, g(x_0))$ and $(x_1, g(x_1))$ in the interval (x_0, x_1), and as a straight line through $(x_1, g(x_1))$ and $(x_2, g(x_2))$ in the interval (x_1, x_2). Let h represent that function made up of two straight-line segments as shown in Figure G.1. It is convenient when making such an approximation to write

$$g = h + e$$

where, for our purposes, we have decided that e is small enough over the interval (x_0, x_2) to be neglected. The error incurred in replacing e by 0 so that g is represented by h is an example of what we define just below as truncation error. There is truncation error in using tables to evaluate func-

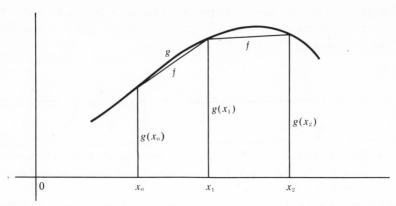

Figure G.1 The broken-line segment h may be looked upon as defining an approximation to g over the interval $x_0 \leq x \leq x_2$. The difference, $g - h$, would be the truncation error in this approximation.

tions such as logarithm, sine, and exponential. Chopping is a special case of truncation in which the item being approximated is a numeral.

Truncation error (single-variable functions). Let $g = h + e$, where g, h, and e are functions of a single variable x. Then the error incurred in replacing g by h is called *truncation error*. Ordinarily, this replacement substitutes a simple, finite process to compute h for an elaborate (perhaps infinite) process for computing g. It is justified only if answers obtained in so doing are meaningful.

Rounding is always helpful, but its importance grows as the base in number representation becomes larger. For this reason, and also because of the human custom of rounding when performing hand calculations in decimal, we devoted a great deal of space in Section 8.2 to rounding for decimal arithmetic. There are some complications with incorporating rounding into the arithmetic instructions. Extended-precision arithmetic (in which one devotes more words to storing a result than can be utilized in an operand of a machine instruction for arithmetic) requires deferring rounding until the full result is formed. Thus, any machine must have arithmetic without rounding. A possible solution is to have arithmetic performed unrounded and to have a separate rounding instruction to be applied just before chopping takes place. That is a solution provided in the 370 System with its shift and round decimal instruction (mnemonic SRP).

Index

A

A (Accumulator) register, 6, 7, 99
A-type address constant, 176, 184
ABEND (ABnormal ENDing), 351, 354, 360
Abnormal ending (ABEND), 351
Absolute address, 141, 179
Absolute expression, 141
Absolute-value operator, 67
ACC (ACCumulator) register, 99
Access time, 290
Access width, 290
Accumulator (A or ACC) register, 6, 7, 99
ACM (Association for Computing Machinery), 186
Action, 125
Add instructions
    complete table, 341
    A, 65, 72
    AD, 327
    ADR, 327

AE, 327
AER, 327
AP, 310
AR, 97
Addition
    floating-point, 325
    integer, 72
    packed decimal, 308, 310
Address
    absolute, 141
    BAREBONZ, 57, 59
    computation, 94, 189
    conventions for 360/370, 84
    effective, 94, 142
    exceptions, 363
    modification, 94
    as a parameter, 89
    relative (* as ''self''), 143, 158, 170
Address constants (A-type and V-type), 176, 184
Addressable constants, 148

387

ALGOL, 31, 289
Algorithm, 41–42, 124, 128
Alignment
  addresses, 114–115
  decimal point, 313
  forced, 98, 114–115
  instructions, 98
Alphanumeric symbols, 27
Alternative instruction sequences, 297
AMQ (double register formed by coupling ACC and MQ), 99
AND instructions
  complete table, 341
  N, 247
  NC, 247
  NI, 247
  NR, 247
Approximation, 385
Architecture, 30, 286
Argument address list, 168
Arguments, *see* Parameters
Arithmetic, *see also* Addition, Chopping, Conversion, Division, Exponent, Halve instruction, Multiplication, Rounding, Shifting, Subtraction, Truncation, Two's complement
  binary, 49–50
  decimal, 308–314
  economy of binary representation, 49
  floating point, 325–326
  by hand, computation, 47–49
Arrays, (appear implicitly following discussions)
  argument address list, 168–169
  assembler building project, 200–212
  DC pseudoinstructions, 115
  string oriented instructionsl 222, 250
  symbol tables, 117–118, 203
ASCII (USASCII), 27, 257
ASMGC catalogued procedure, 182, 193
ASMGCLG catalogued procedure, 183
ASMGD catalogued procedure, 182, 193
ASMGLG catalogued procedure, 181
Assembler (translator), 108, 140, 175, 200
  one scan (one pass), 146–148
  two scan (two pass), 117–124
Assembly, 68, *see also* Translation (assembly)
Assignment operator, 66
ASSMBLR (driver program of assembler project), 201
Asterisk, *
  comment card, 112

instruction's own location (relative address), 143
  multiplication, 143
Automation, 4
AXXICOMP, 14
AXXION, 5

B

Baker, F. T., 125, 128
BAREBONZ
  components of machine model, 57
  instruction set, 64, 347
BAREBONZ II, 56, 93
Base address, 56, 61, 84, 85, 112, 158
Base of number representations, 38
Base registers, 84, 112, 193
Batched compilation (appears implicitly in discussion of deck assembly), 180
BCD (Binary-Coded Decimal), 25
Bias in floating-point exponent, 323
Binary arithmetic, 19, 47–50, 72
Binary-Coded Decimal (BCD), 25
Binary constants, 114
Binary point, 44
Bit (binary digit), 25, 59, 84
Bit manipulation, 221, 246–250
Bit-string selector, 64
Black box, 22
BLKSIZE parameter, 136
Boolean operations, 221, 246–250, *see also* AND instructions, EX OR instructions, OR instructions
Boundary alignment
  of constants, 114, 153
  forcing, 114–115
Branch instructions, 14, 63
  complete table, 341
  BAL, 86, 87, 133
  BALR, 97, 133
  BC, 78
  BCT, 305
  BCTR, 305
  BXH, 303, 304
  BXLE, 303, 304
  extended mnemonics, 154
Buffers, 234–246, 290
  at end of file, 246
  management of, 243
  pool of, 241
  structure of, 246
  swapping of, 239

BUFPARM parameters, 241

Bug (flaw in program leading to invalid results), 124, 361–366, *see also* Error

Burroughs Corporation, 29, 30, 289

Byte content (character) manipulation, 219–246, 251–272

Bytes, 25, 59

C

C (base register), 61

Call (invoking) of subprogram, 86, 167, 299

Called program, 86, 167, 299

Calling program, 86, 167, 299

Canonical positional representation, 37

Card hole representation of characters, 26, 337

Catalogued procedure, 180, 182, 193

Catenate (string operation), 220, 224–230

CC (Condition Code), 77

CDE (Contents Directory Entry), 354

Cell (data structure element), 200

Central Processing Unit (CPU), 58, 60

CESD (Composite External Symbol Dictionary), 183

Channel, 57

Character move instructions
  complete table, 341
  IC, 224
  MVC, 224
  MVCL, 266
  MVI, 224
  MVN, 314
  MVO, 315
  MVZ, 314
  STC, 224

Character representation, 24–26, 259, 337

Character set, 2, 25, 26, 259, 337

Character string processing, 224–231

Character strings (long), 266

Character to binary conversion, 252

Character to packed decimal conversion, 252

Checkout, 124, 190, 351

Checkout, 124, 190–193, 351

Chopping, 315, 321–324, 383

CIR (Current Instruction Register), 61, 132

Circular (rotary) shift, 249

CLCL (Compare Logical Character Long instruction), 266–272

Clearing a string (use of EX OR), 248

Clerical errors, 129

CLOSE (a macro to close a file), 241

Closed subprogram, 195

Coin analogy, 35

Command, *see* Instructions

Comment, 112

Compare instructions
  complete table, 341
  C, 293
  CD, 327
  CDR, 327
  CE, 327
  CER, 327
  CL, 231
  CLC, 231
  CLCL, 266
  CLI, 231
  CLR, 231
  CP, 310
  CR, 292, 293

Complement arithmetic, 19, 46

Complement representation of numbers, 45–47

Completion codes, 352

Complications of decimal arithmetic, 308–309

Composite External Symbol Dictionary (CESD), 183

Compute bound, 236

Computer, 2, 10, 19, 29–31, 57

Computerization, 5, 20

Concatenate (catenate), 220, 224–230

COND CODE (job step return code), 352

Condition Code (CC), 77

Conditional branch (BC instruction), 14, 21, 77–78

Constants
  address, 176, 184
  addressable, 149
  binary, 114, 151
  character, 114, 151
  decimal, 330
  floating-point, 332
  full-word integer, 72, 114, 151
  half-word integer, 114, 151
  hexadecimal, 114, 151
  immediate, 148
  instruction, 149
  literal, 150
  packed, 330
  problem, 151
  self-defining, 148
  zoned decimal, 330

Contents Directory Entry (CDE), 354

Contents operator, 64

Continuation card, 138

Control, 13, 58, 61
Control cards, 70, 180, 182, 193, 353
Control concept, 13–17
Control instructions, 75
Control panels, 8
Control path, 86
Control SECTion (CSECT), 177
Control section pointer, 185
Conversion, 40–42, 80–84
  binary to decimal, 40
  binary to hexadecimal, 47
  binary to packed decimal, 254
  character to packed decimal, 252
  decimal to binary, 40
  floating-point binary to floating-point deci-
    mal, 336
  hexadecimal to binary, 47
  hexadecimal to decimal, 254
  integer to floating-point, 335
  packed decimal to binary, 254
  packed decimal to character, 252
Conversion background (character to decimal),
    251–252
Conversion extensions, 255
Conversion instructions
  complete table, 341
  CVB, 254
  CVD, 254
  PACK, 252
  UNPK, 252
Conversion to canonical representation, 39
Correctness, 19, 128
CPU (Central Processing Unit, or processor),
    58, 60
CSECT (Control SECTion), 177
CTA (Current Translation Address), 117
Current Instruction Register (CIR), 61, 132
Cycle, instruction execution, 58, 62
Cycle, machine, 290

                              D

Dahl, O. J., 125
Data (input), 2, 57, 129, 367
Data constants, 151–152, *see also* Constants,
    DC
Data Control block (DCB), 135–137, 191, 241
Data set, 241
Data structure, 200
DC (Define Constant), 70
  address, 176, 274

decimal, 330
floating-point, 332
full-word integer, 72, 114, 151
integer constants, string constants, 113–116,
    149–153
DDNAME (parameter in DCB), 136
Debug (checkout), 124, 190, 351
Decimal arithmetic, 43, 251, 308–309
Decimal instructions
  complete table, 341
  AP, 310
  CP, 310
  DV, 312
  MP, 312
  SP, 310
Decimal rounding, 316, 386
Decimal scaling, 308, 311, 313–316
Decimal shifting, 313–316
DECK (an option of the EXEC card), 193
Deck assembly, 70, 193, 353
Define Constant, 147–153, 330, 332, *see also*
    DC
Define storage (DS), 158, *see also* DC
Delete (buffer pool), 277
Destructive overlap, 269
Development cycle of programs, 124
Diagnostics, 361–366
Digit, 38
Digit punch, 26
Digit selector, 317–320
Digital computers, 2
Digital representation, 2, 23–27
Dijkstra, E. W., 125, 128
Disk storage, 29
Displacement, 84, 141–145
Distributed function computer, 31
Divide overflow, 74, 312, 323
Division
  hexadecimal, 49
  by zero, 74
Division instructions
  complete table, 341
  D, 65, 74
  DD, 327
  DDR, 327
  DE, 327
  DER, 327
  DP, 312
  DR, 292
Domain of an operation, 21
Do-nothing program, 71

Double word, 59, 60, 81, 99, 326–328
Driver (main) program, 177, 181
DROP (base register pseudoinstruction), 195
DSORG (parameter in DCB), 136
Dump, 68, 131, 191, 351
Duplication factor, 115
Dynamic storage allocation, 31

E

EBCDIC (Extended Binary-Coded Decimal Interchange Code), 27, 252, 337
Eckert, J. Presper, 19
Economy of binary arithmetic, 49
Economy of binary for storage, 49
Edit instructions
  complete table, 341
  ED, 317
  EDMK, 332
EDVAC (Electronic Discrete VAriable Calculator), 19
Effective address, 84, 142
Elapsed instruction execution times, 291
Elimination of leading zeros, 317
ENCODE (translation to machine language), 122
END pseudoinstruction, 116
ENTER macro, 213
Entry Point Address (EPA or USE/EP), 354
ENTRY pseudoinstruction, 178
Entry symbols, 184
EPA (Entry Point Address), 354
ER (External Reference), 183, 185
  examples, 187–188
Error
  chopping, 316–317, 384
  messages and codes, 361–366
  programming, 124, 128
  rounding, 316–317, 384
  truncation, 386
ESD (External Symbol Dictionary), 176, 179, 183–186
  examples, 187, 188
Evolution of computers, 5–19
EX OR (exclusive or) instructions, 221, 247
Exception, 131, 361–366
EXEC control card, 181–182, 193
EXecute instruction (EX), 226
Execution cycle, 58, 62
Execution times of instructions, 285
Exit from loop

first example, 76–79
  use of condition code, 77, 78
EXIT macro, 214
Exit register, BAREBONZ, 61
Explicit length
  of addressable constants, 153
  of character strings, 223–232, 256–272
Exponent, floating-point numbers, 50, 322–324, 333–336
Extended conversions (binary and decimal), 255
Extended mnemonics, branch instructions, 154
External Reference (ER), 183, 185
  examples, 187, 188
External representation of information, 25
External Symbol Dictionary (ESD), 176
  examples, 187, 188
EXTRN pseudoinstruction, 177
  examples, 187, 188

F

Fenn, George S., 20
Field separator character, 319
Fields, character string, 232
Files of logical records, 232
Fill character, 319
First operand of instruction, 110
Fixed-point constants, 114
Fleck, Glen, 20
Floating-point arithmetic, 320–329
  instructions, 326–329, *see also* Add, Compare, Divide, Load, Multiply, Subtract instructions
  table of normalized instructions, 327
Floating-point constants, 332
Floating-point conventions of the 360/370, 323
Floating-point representation, 50, 322
Flowcharts, 19
  basic symbols for structured flowcharts, 126
  structured, 125–128
Format of assembler language statement
  card-column conventions, 112
  definitions of fields, 109–111
Format of BAREBONZ input, 67
Formats of instructions
  BAREBONZ, 61
  RR, 96–97, 223, 247
  RS, 60, 61, 64, 65, 167
  RX, 60, 61, 64, 65, 223, 247
  SI, 223, 247

SS, 223, 247
FORTGLG catalogued procedure, 181, 182
FORTRAN I/O subprograms, 174, 367
FORTRAN linkage, 171–175
Fractions, binary representation of, 42
Free a buffer pool, 242

G

Garbage collection, 237
General purpose computer, 2
General registers, 96, 133
Generated portion of character string, 268
Goldstine, H. H., 19
Grosch, H. R. J., 20

H

Half word
    alignment of instructions, 98, 117, 158
    complete table of instructions, 341
    instructions, 96, 223, 231, 247, 266, 292,
        293, 297, 326–327, *see also* Instruction
        types, RR
    memory address, 59
Halve instructions, 326
    complete table, 341
    HDR, 326, 344
    HER, 326, 344
Hazards of CLC and MVC instructions, 229–
    231
Hewlett–Packard computer, 29, 31
Hexadecimal (base 16 representation of num-
    bers)
Hexadecimal
    dump, 68, 131, 191, 351
    integer arithmetic, 47
    number representation, 26, 47
    snapshot, 131, 134, 191
High (string comparison), 231
Hoare, C. A. R., 125
Hollerith, Herman, 26
Host machine for BAREBONZ, 56

I

"I trust everybody" philosophy, 87–88, 90–92
"I trust nobody" philosophy, 87–89
IAC (Instruction Address Counter), 61–62, 65,
    70, 86, 97
IAS (Institute for Advanced Study), 57

IBM (International Business Machines Corpora-
    tion), 26
IEEE (The Institute of Electrical and Electron-
    ics Engineers, Inc.), 31
ILC (Instruction Length Code), 132
ILLIAC IV computer, 30
Immediate constants, 148
Immediate operands, 64, 110
Immediate values, 141
Implied length of constants, 151
Index registers, 55, 94
Indexable instruction, 94, *see also* Instruction
    types, RX
Indexing in the control unit, 94
Infinite loop, 22
Initialization, 78, 159, 201, 298
Input data, 2, 57, 129, 367
Institute for Advanced Study (IAS), 57
Instruction Address Counter (IAC), 61–62, 65,
    70, 86, 97
Instruction constants, 141, 148–149
Instruction execution times, 285–300
Instruction modification, 15, 91, 94, 226–229
Instruction types
    complete instruction list, 341
    RR (Register-to-Register), 96, 223, 247,
        267, 285, 292, 296, 327
    RS (Register-to-Storage), 64, 65, 83, 167,
        294, 303
    RX (Register-and-indeXed-storage), 64, 65,
        94, 223, 224, 247, 292, 326, 327
    SI (Storage-Immediate), 223–231, 247, 248
    SS (Storage-to-Storage), 223–231, 247, 252–
        266, 296, 309, 314, 320
Instructions
    BAREBONZ, 64, 93–99, 347–350
    macroinstructions, 108, 134–139, 195–199,
        213–215, 217
    pseudoinstructions, 70, 108, 112–117, 151,
        193–195, 330, 332
    symbolic machine instructions, 69, 108–111
Integer arithmetic, 72–75
Interchange of operands, 248
Internal character set, 25
    ASCII (USASCII), 27, 257
    BCD, 26
    EBCDIC, 27, 252, 337
    ISO, 27
    USASCII (ASCII), 27, 257
Invalid operand expressions, 143
Invariant expression with respect to relocation,

141
Invoking subprograms, 86, 165
I/O bound applications, 234–237
ISO (International Standards Organization)
 Code, 27

J

Jump table, 263

K

Keyword parameters for macros, 134–138, 191

L

Label Definition (LD), 184
Label record, 233
LD (Label Definition), 184
LD ID (Label Definition IDentification), 184
Linear data structure, 200
Linkage conventions, 86, 166–175
LinKage EDitor program (LKED), 181, 183
Linkage of program sequences, 87
Linking of object modules, 175
Linking with FORTRAN, 171
List of pools, 242
Literal constant, 150
Literals (self-defining constants), 148
LKED (Linkage EDitor), 182, 183
Load instructions
 complete table, 341
 explanation, 65, 97
Load module, 183
Loader program, 181
Locate mode in buffer management, 278
Location field, 67, 110, 112
Logical comparisons of strings, 231, 266
Logical instructions
 discussion, 246–250
 complete table of N, O, X, and type var-
  iants, 247
Logical records, 232
Logical units, 232
Long character strings, 266
Looping
 by indexing, 94–96
 by instruction modification, 15–19, 75–80
Low (string comparison), 231
LRECL (maximum length for logical records),
 136

M

Macroinstructions (macro for short), 108
 defining a macro, 195–199
 ENTER and EXIT, 213–215
 ITER, 217
 precautions, 138–139
 use of SNAP, 134–138, 191–192
Management of buffers, 243
Mantissa, 50, 322–325
Mask, 77–78
Mauchly, John W., 19
Mechanization, 4
Memory, 19, 57, 59, 241, 287, *see also* Stor-
 age
Memory access, 287, 290–293
MEND (Macro END), 197
Message character (in EDit instruction), 317
Minicomputers, 31, 55
Mnemonic, 68, 153–154
Model
 in macro definition, 197
 of computer, 55
Move instructions
 complete table, 341
 MVC, 146, 224
 MVCL, 266
 MVI, 224
 MVN, 314
 MVO, 315
 MVZ, 314
MQ (Multiplier-Quotient) register, 7, 99
Multiplication, 48, 73, 311, 325
Multiplication instructions
 complete table, 341
 M, 73
 MD, 327
 MDR, 327
 ME, 327
 MER, 327
 MP, 312
 MR, 292
Multiplier, 73, 99
Multiplier-Quotient (MQ) register, 7, 99
Multiprogramming, 236, 308

N

Negative integers, 45
Negative zero, 45
NM (program name in dump), 354

Normalization of floating-point operands, 325
Notation for string designation, 64–66, 267
Number representation
    binary integer, 44–47
    decimal digit, 23, 38
    floating point, 50, 322–324
    fraction, 40–43
    hexadecimal, 26, 47
    one's complement, 46
    packed decimal, 251–253
    two's complement, 46

O

Object code (on assembler listing), 123
Object language, 107
Object modules, 175–177
Objects (as operands), 20–21
Octal representation of numbers, 47
Offset (Mo Ve with Offset instruction), 315
One-pass (one-scan) assemblers, 146–148
One's complement representation of binary
    numbers, 46
One-scan assemblers, 146–148
OPEN macro, 137, 192
Open subprograms, 195
Opening a buffer pool, 241
Operand
    expressions, 140–146
    fields, 110–112, 145
    formats, 110–112, 145
    strings, MVCL and CLCL instructions, 268
Operating room analogy to buffering, 238–240
Operation mnemonic of symbolic instructions,
    110
Operations on objects in a set, 21
Operators
    absolute value, | |, 67
    assignment, ←, 66
    bit-string selector, i:j, 64
    Boolean AND, OR, EXCLUSIVE OR,
        221, 247–250
    contents, ( ), 64
    sign ( ), 67
OR instructions, 247
Organization (computer architecture), 29–32,
    57–63, 94, 98, 286–288
Output, 2, 58
    assembler listing, 123, 124
    BAREBONZ, 69
    FORTRAN, 174, 367–368

snapshot, 130–134, 191–192, 353, 360
    system dump, 131, 351, 353–360
Overflow
    decimal arithmetic, 310, 313
    floating-point arithmetic (exponent), 323
    integer arithmetic, 48, 72, 74
Overhead of instructions for closed subpro-
    grams, 298
Overlap of operand storage strings, 229–231,
    253, 269, 309

P

PACK instruction, 252, 254
Packed-decimal arithmetic, 308–313
Packed-decimal conversion, 252–256
Packed-decimal representation, 251
Padding, 45, 267–268
Pan balance (number conversion analogy), 40
Pan balance weighing algorithm, 41
Paper approach to computer design, 8
Parallel computation, 30
Parallel processing, 30
Parameters, 88, see also Argument address list
    addresses as, 89–92
    job step, 181, 193
    keyword, 134–138, 191–192
    values as, 88–89
PARM (provides parameters), 181, 193
Pass (scan) of an assembler, 117–124, 146–147,
    203–212
Pattern (for the EDit instruction), 317–320
Pattern pointer, 318
Physical record, 232
Physical unit, 232
Pitfalls, see also Complications of decimal ar-
    ithmetic, Hazards of CLC and MVC in-
    structions, Precautions
    character string compare, 231–232
    character string moves, 227–229
    clerical errors, 129
    in decimal arithmetic, 308–309
    in TRanslate and Test, 260
    use of macros, 138–139
PL/1 language, 233, 276
Pointer
    buffer, 243–245
    buffer record, 246
    control section, 185
    instruction, 13, 354
    pattern, 318

position, 185–188
relocation, 183, 185–188
save area, 167
Polachek, Harry, 20
POOLHALL (storage reserved for buffer pools), 241–243
Position pointer, 185
Positional notation, 36–38
Positive zero, 45
PRB (Program Request Block), 354
Precautions, 138–139, *see also* Complications of decimal arithmetic, Pitfalls
Precision, 321, 324, 383–386
Presser, L., 186
Primitive operations, 21
Print, 24–27, 57–58
Printable character set, 25, 259
Problem constants, 151–153
Procedure, 21–22, 86, 165–175, 192, 201, *see also* Algorithm, Program, Subprogram
Processing, computer, 20
Processor (CPU), 28–32, 58, 60
Program, 22, 86, 165–175, 192, 201, *see also* Subprogram
Program development cycle, 124–125
Program fetch, 181
Program Request Block (PRB), 354
Program Status Word (PSW), 132–133, 169, 353–354
Programmer-initiated snapshot, 131, 134, 191, 360
Prototype of a macro instruction, 197
PS (file organization option), 136
Pseudoinstructions, 69, 108, 112–117, 151–153, 193–195, 330, 332
Pseudoprimitive operations, 22
PSW (Program Status Word), 132–133, 169, 353–354
Puckett, T. H., 213
PUT macro, 136

Q

Quotient, 74, 311–313, 326, *see also* Division instructions

R

R (relocation) pointer, 185–188
Radix, 38, 43, *see also* Base of number representations

Range of an operation, 21
Reader (input device), 57
RECFM (in DCB macro), 136
Register-and indeXed-storage (RX) instructions, 60–61, 64–65, 94–95, *see also* Instruction types
Register approach to computer design, 8
Register content (in MVCL and CLCL), 267–268
Register content save area, 166, *see also* Save area
Register-to-Register (RR) instructions, 96, *see also* Instruction types
Register-to-Storage (RS) instructions, 60–61, 64–65, *see also* Instruction types
Relocatable expression, 140–144
Relocation, 140–144, 176–179
Relocation Dictionary (RLD), 175, 183–189
Relocation invariant, 141
Relocation pointer, 183, 185–188
Representation of characters, 25–27
  BCD table, 26
  EBCDIC table, 259, 337–340
  USASCII (ASCII), 27, 257
Representation of numbers, 43
  binary integer, 44–47
  decimal digit, 23, 38
  fraction, 40–43
  hexadecimal floating-point, 50–51
  one's complement, 46
  packed decimal, 251–253
  two's complement, 46
Response table, 258–259
Return address, 63, 86, 169, 172
Return code, 352, 362
RLD (ReLocation Dictionary), 175, 183–189
Rotary (circular) shift, 249
Rounding, 316–317, 383–385
RR instructions, *see* Instruction types
RS instructions, *see* Instruction types
RX instructions, *see* Instruction types

S

Save area, 87–89, 91–93, 134, 166–175
SAVE macro, 139
Saving registers, 87–89, 91–93, 134, 166–175
Scaling, 50, 80–82, *see also* Decimal shifting, Floating-point representation
Scan of symbolic program, 117–124, 146–147, 203, 205

SD (Section Definition), 184
Search for substring in character string, 220
Second operand of instruction, 110
Section Definition (SD), 184
Segment (applied to strings), 220
Segment of memory, 133–134
Segmentation of programs, 165, 175, 177
Segmented programs, 190–193
Selective snapshot, 130–134, 191–192
Selector of substring, 64
Self-defining constants, 148
Shift and Round Packed (SRP instruction), 386
Shift instructions,
    complete table, 341
    SLA, 294
    SLDA, 65, 294
    SLDL, 65, 294
    SLL, 294
    SRA, 294
    SRDA, 65, 294
    SRDL, 65, 294
    SRL, 294
    SRP, 386
Shift rotary, 249
Shifted decimal number, 152
Shifting
    binary, 80–83
    decimal, 313–316
Sign
    binary integer, 45
    decimal input from card, 251–252
    decimal output, 318
    floating-point, 323
    packed decimal, 252, 309
Sign functionl 67, 74
Significance, 321–322
    first significant digit, 318, 321
Significance starter, 320
Significant figures, 318–321, 324
Simulated I/O devices, 237
SNAP macro, 134–139, 191–192, 353, 360
SNAPDUMP file, 136, 191–192
Snapshot of storage segments, 130–134, 191,
    353, 360
Social implications of computers, 2–4
Sort key, 27
Sorting character strings, 220
Source language, 107
Specification error (exception), 98, 363
Speed (instruction execution), 285–306
Stack (hardware in processor), 30

Statement, 118, see also Instructions
STEP (ingredient of CLCL and MVCL), 269
Stop (execution of a program), 71
STORAGE (keyword of SNAP macro), 137,
    191
Storage, 59, see also Memory
Storage-Immediate (SI) instructions, 223–231,
    see also Instruction types
Storage-to-Storage (SS) instructions, 223–231,
    see also Instruction types
STore instructions
    complete table, 341
    ST, 65
    STC, 224
    STD, 327
    STE, 327
    STH, 90
    STM, 167–168
Stored portion of operand string, 268
Stored program, 14–15, 19, 56
Stored program computer, 14–15, 19, 56
Straight-line coding, 17, 78, 301
Strings, 24, 220–284
Structure within a buffer, 246
Structured program, 125–128, 199, 217
Subprogram linkage, 55–56, 85–92, 166, 171–
    175
Subprogram, 85–92, 165–175, 192, 201
Substitution-generated macros, 196–199, 213–
    215
Subtract instructions
    complete table, 341
    S, 65, 72–73
    SD, 327
    SDR, 327
    SE, 327
    SER, 327
    SP, 310
    SR, 97
Subtraction
    floating-point, 325
    integer, 72
    packed decimal, 308–310
Suffix modifier, 144–146
Supervisor, 71, 165, 360
Swapping
    of buffers, 239, 240
    of program segments, 29
Symbol table, 117–118, 203
Symbolic location, 68, 110
Symbolic machine instructions, 68, 108

Symbolic name, 68, 109
Symbolic parameter, 197, 213
Syntax, 129
SYSABEND, 353
SYSOUT, 193, 353
SYSPUNCH, 182, 193
System dump, 131, 351, 353–360
System-initiated snapshot, 131, 353
System, operating, 352, 360
SYSUDUMP, 353

T

Taub, A. W., 57
Termination, 71, 351
Time units, 288
Times (instruction execution), 285
Trailer, 197
TRanslate and Test instruction (TRT), 256, 258–265
TRanslate instruction (TR), 256–258
Translation (assembly), 68, 107, 117–124
Translation table, 257
TRT (TRanslate and Test instruction), 256, 258–265
Truncation, 383, 385–386
Truncation error, 386
Two's complement arithmetic, 19, 46
Type code (in defining constants), 114, 149, 176, 330, 332
Type code of instructions, *see* Formats of instructions

U

Unconditional branch, 77
Units for timing, 288
UNPacK instruction, 252–254
Updating items in a file, 279

USASCII (USA Standard Code for Information Interchange), 27, 257
USE/EP (USEr Entry Point address), 354
USING pseudoinstruction, 110, 112–113, 142, 158, 170, 193–195

V

V-type address constants, 176–179
Variable-length argument address list, 176
VBA (record format), 136
Venn diagram of operands, 143
Virginity (in every discussion there are some undefined concepts), 321
Virtual machine, 22
Virtual memory, 29
Volume as a unit of information, 233
von Neumann, John, 19, 20, 46, 56, 57, 68

W

Weighing algorithm, conversion, 41
White, J. R., 186
Word length, 43
Word, 44, 59
Working buffer, 279
Write, *see* Output, Print, Dump, Snapshot
WRITE (FORTRAN statement), 367–368
WRITE macro, 136
Writer (output device), 57

Z

Zero and Add Packed instruction (ZAP), 310
Zeroing a string, 248
Zone (portion of character), 252
Zone punch, 26, 252
Zones (MoVe Zones instruction), 314